The United States and the Ends of Empire

New Approaches to International History
Series Editor: Thomas W. Zeiler, Professor of American Diplomatic History, University of Colorado Boulder, USA

Series Editorial Board:
Anthony Adamthwaite, University of California at Berkeley (USA)
Kathleen Burk, University College London (UK)
Louis Clerc, University of Turku (Finland)
Petra Goedde, Temple University (USA)
Francine McKenzie, University of Western Ontario (Canada)
Lien-Hang Nguyen, University of Kentucky (USA)
Jason Parker, Texas A&M University (USA)
Glenda Sluga, University of Sydney (Australia)

New Approaches to International History covers international history during the modern period and across the globe. The series incorporates new developments in the field, such as the cultural turn and transnationalism, as well as the classical high politics of state-centric policymaking and diplomatic relations. Written with upper-level undergraduate and postgraduate students in mind, texts in the series provide an accessible overview of international diplomatic and transnational issues, events and actors.

Published:
Militarization and the American Century, David Fitzgerald
American-Iranian Dialogues, ed. Matthew K. Shannon
America's Road to Empire, Piero Gleijeses
The International LGBT Rights Movement, Laura Belmonte
Global War, Global Catastrophe, Maartje Abbenhuis and Ismee Tames
Globalizing the U.S. Presidency, ed. Cyrus Schayegh
Public Opinion and Twentieth-Century Diplomacy, Daniel Hucker
Europe's Cold War Relations, ed. Federico Romero, Kiran Klaus Patel, and Ulrich Krotz
Canada and the World since 1867, Asa McKercher
Scandinavia and the Great Powers in the First World War, Michael Jonas
The First Age of Industrial Globalization, Maartje Abbenhuis and Gordon Morrell
Reconstructing the Postwar World, Francine McKenzie
Activism across Borders since 1870, Daniel Laqua
Leftist Internationalisms, ed. Mathieu Fulla and Michele Di Donato

American Sport in International History, Daniel DuBois
Climate Change and International History, Ruth Morgan
The Fear of Chinese Power, Jeffrey Crean
An International History of US Immigration, Benjamin Montoya
From World War to Cold War, Andrew N. Buchanan
Beyond the Nixon Shocks, Thomas W. Zeiler

Forthcoming:
China and the United States since 1949, Elizabeth Ingleson

Series Editor Preface

New Approaches to International History takes the entire world as its stage for exploring the history of diplomacy, broadly conceived theoretically and thematically, and writ large across the span of the globe, during the modern period. This series goes beyond the single goal of explaining encounters in the world. Our aspiration is that these books provide both an introduction for researchers new to a topic, and supplemental and essential reading in classrooms. Thus, *New Approaches* serves a dual purpose that is unique from other large-scale treatments of international history; it applies to scholarly agendas and pedagogy. In addition, it does so against the backdrop of a century of enormous change, conflict, and progress that informed global history but also continues to reflect on our own times.

The series offers the old and new diplomatic history to address a range of topics that shaped the twentieth century. Engaging in international history (including but not especially focusing on global or world history), these books will appeal to a range of scholars and teachers situated in the humanities and social sciences, including those in history, international relations, cultural studies, politics, and economics. We have in mind scholars, both novice and veteran, who require an entrée into a topic, trend, or technique that can benefit their own research or education into a new field of study by crossing boundaries in a variety of ways.

By its broad and inclusive coverage, *New Approaches to International History* is also unique because it makes accessible to students current research, methodology, and themes. Incorporating cutting-edge scholarship that reflects trends in international history, as well as addressing the classical high politics of state-centric policymaking and diplomatic relations, these books are designed to bring alive the myriad approaches for digestion by advanced undergraduates and graduate students. In preparation for the *New Approaches* series, Bloomsbury surveyed courses and faculty around the world to gauge interest and reveal core themes of relevance for their classroom use. The polling yielded a host of topics, from war and peace to the environment; from empire to economic integration; and from migration to nuclear arms. The effort proved that there is a much-needed place for studies that connect scholars and students alike to international history, and books that are especially relevant to the teaching missions of faculty around the world.

We hope readers find this series to be appealing, challenging, and thought-provoking. Whether the history is viewed through older or newer lenses, *New Approaches to International History* allows students to peer into the modern period's complex relations among nations, people, and events to draw their own conclusions about the tumultuous, interconnected past.

Thomas W. Zeiler, University of Colorado Boulder, USA

The United States and the Ends of Empire

Decolonization, Hierarchy, and World Order since 1776

SEAN T. BYRNES

BLOOMSBURY ACADEMIC
LONDON • NEW YORK • OXFORD • NEW DELHI • SYDNEY

BLOOMSBURY ACADEMIC

Bloomsbury Publishing Plc, 50 Bedford Square, London, WC1B 3DP, UK
Bloomsbury Publishing Inc, 1359 Broadway, New York, NY 10018, USA
Bloomsbury Publishing Ireland, 29 Earlsfort Terrace, Dublin 2, D02 AY28, Ireland

BLOOMSBURY, BLOOMSBURY ACADEMIC and the Diana logo are trademarks of
Bloomsbury Publishing Plc

First published in Great Britain 2026

Copyright © Sean T. Byrnes, 2026

Sean T. Byrnes has asserted his right under the Copyright, Designs and Patents Act, 1988,
to be identified as Author of this work.

For legal purposes the Acknowledgments on pp. xiii–xiv constitute
an extension of this copyright page.

Series design by Catherine Wood
Cover image: Photo of Horatio Greenough's *The Rescue* (1837–50) at its long-time site on
the east facade of the U.S. Capitol via Wikimedia commons

All rights reserved. No part of this publication may be: i) reproduced or transmitted in
any form, electronic or mechanical, including photocopying, recording or by means of
any information storage or retrieval system without prior permission in writing from the
publishers; or ii) used or reproduced in any way for the training, development or operation
of artificial intelligence (AI) technologies, including generative AI technologies. The rights
holders expressly reserve this publication from the text and data mining exception as per
Article 4(3) of the Digital Single Market Directive (EU) 2019/790.

Bloomsbury Publishing Plc does not have any control over, or responsibility for, any third-
party websites referred to or in this book. All internet addresses given in this book were
correct at the time of going to press. The author and publisher regret any inconvenience
caused if addresses have changed or sites have ceased to exist, but can accept no
responsibility for any such changes.

A catalogue record for this book is available from the British Library.

A catalog record for this book is available from the Library of Congress.

ISBN:	HB:	978-1-3503-4166-1
	PB:	978-1-3503-4167-8
	ePDF:	978-1-3503-4169-2
	eBook:	978-1-3503-4168-5

Series: New Approaches to International History

Typeset by Integra Software Services Pvt. Ltd.
Printed and bound in Great Britain

For product safety related questions contact productsafety@bloomsbury.com.

To find out more about our authors and books visit www.bloomsbury.com
and sign up for our newsletters.

To Kristi, Liam and—yes—Molly & Rocco too.

CONTENTS

List of Illustrations xi
Acknowledgments xiii

Introduction 1

1 Unleashing the "Empire of Liberty": The Colonization and Decolonization of British North America 23
2 "Afflictions of Longstanding": Native Americans and the Decolonization of the United States 53
3 Reordering the World: The Haitian Revolution, the Decolonization of Latin America, and the Empire of Trade 85
4 Decolonization for Me but Not for You: The United States, the War of 1898, and Establishing an Overseas Empire 125
5 Determining Self-Determination: The United States and Global Hierarchy before and after the Great War 151
6 A Roosevelt Corollary for the World: The United States, World Order, and Decolonization after the Second World War 183
7 "A Structure of Economic Control": The United States and an Independent Global South 219

8 Hyperpower: US Hegemony in the Age of Nation States 247

Conclusion: Hierarchy in a Flat World 277

Bibliography 282
Index 299

ILLUSTRATIONS

Figures

1. "The Rescue," Photograph, 1926, 2016842323, Library of Congress, Prints and Photographs Division 2
2. "The Discovery of America," Photograph, 1867, 2017652607, Library of Congress, Prints and Photographs Division 2
3. "Results of the Revolution—Treaty of Paris 1783," Modern School Supply Company, Chicago, Illinois, 1919, 2009581137, Library of Congress, Geography and Map Division 46
4. "Map of the Indian Tribes of North America," Albert Gallatin, American Antiquarian Society, 1836, 2002622260, Library of Congress, Geography and Map Division 55
5. "Map of the Several Nations of Indians to the Northwest of South Carolina," Deerskin Map, 1724, 2005625337, Library of Congress, Geography and Map Division 86
6. "Map of Territory from Mexico Added to the Southwestern United States," MDE6EH, Alamy 116
7. "The Greater United States," Modern School Supply Company, Chicago, Illinois, 1919, 2009581137, Library of Congress, Geography and Map Division 126
8. "It's Up to Them," Cartoon, Udo J. Keppler, *Puck*, 1901, 2010651486, Library of Congress, Prints and Photographs Division 148

9 "American Troops Marching in the Forbidden City," Photograph, 1900, 514877178, Getty Images 157
10 "Hands Off," Cartoon, Louis Dalrymple, *Judge*, 1904, Wikimedia Commons 165
11 "League of Nations Commission," Photograph, 1919, Wikimedia Commons 180
12 "The United Nations Fight for Freedom," Poster, Leslie Ragan, United States Office of War Information, 1943, Wikimedia Commons 189
13 "Soldiers of the Army of the Republic of Vietnam Interrogate a Captured Soldier," Photograph, AFP, 1965, 2182217466, Getty Images 217
14 "US Ambassador Daniel Patrick Moynihan Addresses the UN Security Council," Photograph, 1976, 515575504, Getty Images 235
15 "USAF Aircraft Fly Over Kuwait," Photograph, US Air Force, 1991, Wikimedia Commons 254
16 "US Troops Patrol in Baghdad," Photograph, Marco Di Lauro, 2003, 2018729, Getty Images 273

Maps

1 Maps showing the decolonization of the Western Hemisphere in the late eighteenth and early nineteenth centuries 94
2 Early twentieth-century US interventions in the Caribbean basin 153
3 Map showing the global decolonization that followed the Second World War 200

ACKNOWLEDGMENTS

Acknowledgments can be an awkward thing to write. You want to, of course, include everyone who helped make the book possible—at the same time, you fear including someone who'd rather not share the guilt of association. With that in mind, let me start with one apology to anyone who I left out and another to those who would have *preferred* to be left out. Certainly, none of either group should feel any responsibility for errors, mistakes, failures, etc. The responsibility there is all my own.

To start on relatively firm ground, I'd like to thank Tom Zeiler for suggesting I pitch a book to the *New Approaches to International History* series, and for all his support for this project and those in the past. Thanks are due as well to Maddie Smith, Niamh Coffey, and the entire team at Bloomsbury for their work in making this book a reality. The same goes for Karthiga Sithanandam and others involved in copyediting and typesetting the manuscript. I'm also grateful to the anonymous reviewers who commented on various stages of the work; their insights considerably improved the final product.

I'd further like to acknowledge all of my fellow historians. A work of synthesis of this sort is only possible because of the efforts others have made producing their own monographs and syntheses. At a time when our collective work is seen as increasingly dispensable, this project has done nothing but remind me how mistaken that view really is. Particular thanks go to Dexter Fergie, Amy Sayward, and Joseph Stieb for various forms of assistance with this project, and Samuel Moyn and Rick Perlstein for supporting my work more generally. I'm also grateful to Tim Shenk for his friendship over many years now. I'd be remiss too if I left out SHAFR, a professional society that does, in fact, actually help people advance in the profession.

Thanks are due as well to Laura Marsh at *The New Republic*, John-Baptiste Oduor at *Jacobin*, and Nick Serpe and the rest of the crew at *Dissent*, for being willing to publish my work—some of which, in the case of *The New Republic*, represented early forms of some of the prose in this book. I'm also grateful to WGU and UMGC for keeping me in funds—it's a privilege to work for both. The UMGC library was essential to the completion of this project, thanks to all who work there.

I'm thankful as well for all my friends, colleagues, and supervisors at both institutions but especially at WGU, where teaching as a team means spending a great deal of time with an incredible group of teachers, scholars, and people. Two of my fellow WGU historians—Alex Tolin Schultz and Katie Eskridge—deserve particular acknowledgment for having the courage to read this manuscript in draft form and for their friendship. Thanks to you both. Other friends outside these institutions due for thanks include: Ned Masek, Dylan Carpenter, Christopher Childers, D-Caff, Wallace Simpson, and all the old Baltimore and Annapolis crowd. To Mom, Dad, and Meg—you got the dedication last time, but your support is as meaningful as ever.

Finally, to Kristi, Liam, and, yes, even the dogs: you guys make it all worth it, so this one's for you.

Introduction

Though now long forgotten, Luigi Persico's *Discovery of America* and Horatio Greenough's *The Rescue* once had legitimate claims to be the most prominently placed sculptures in the United States of America. Commissioned by Congress in 1836, they loomed over the East Front of the United States Capitol for more than a century, from their erection (in 1844 and 1853, respectively) until the mid-twentieth century (see Figures 1 and 2). There they served as the backdrop for, among other events, the inauguration of every US president from the start of James K. Polk's first term in 1845, to the beginning of Dwight D. Eisenhower's second in 1958—silent stewards of that central ritual in American political life, the peaceful transition of presidential power.[1]

While some reviewers faulted one or the other sculpture for artistic execution, thematically, at least, both were initially well received by their intended audience: white US citizens.[2] As a reviewer in the New York weekly *New World* put it in 1845, Persico's *Discovery* had successfully "grouped the history of man" depicting "the beginning of an enterprise, whose results have changed the character and condition of the world," placing the viewer "face to face with ... the march of civilization and Christianity."[3]

---

[1] Inauguration ceremonies were held outside the East Front of the Capitol from 1829 to 1977, switching to the West Front with the inauguration of Ronald Reagan in 1981. See, Library of Congress, "The Inaugural Site," https://www.loc.gov/classroom-materials/inaugurations/an-orderly-transition/the-inaugural-site/.
[2] For more on the statues, their history, and their reception, see Vivien Green Fryd, "Two Sculptures for the Capitol: Horatio Greenough's 'Rescue' and Luigi Persico's 'Discovery of America'," *The American Art Journal* 19, no. 2 (1987): 16–39. The author is also indebted to Walter Hixon's *The Myth of American Diplomacy: National Identity and U.S. Foreign Policy* (New Haven: Yale University Press, 2008) for first alerting him to the history of these statues.
[3] Quoted in Fryd, "Two Sculptures," 21.

FIGURE 1 *A 1926 photograph of Horatio Greenough's* The Rescue, *a statue which stood alongside the main entrance to US Capitol from 1853 to 1958.*

FIGURE 2 *A photo of* The Rescue's *companion,* The Discovery of America *by Luigi Persico. It also stood outside the East Front of the Capitol, in its case from 1844 to 1958.*

Congressman James E. Belser of Alabama grandly proclaimed that Persico's art represented "the power of civilization" which, he believed, would burn "onward and onward" until "it had illuminated this entire continent."[4] The *Bulletin of the American Art-Union*, meanwhile, later praised Greenough's work for "communicating to every spectator ... the natural and necessary superiority of the Anglo-Saxon ... whose destiny is to convert forests into cities, who conquers only to liberate, enlighten and elevate ... the legate of laws, and policy, and morals."[5]

As the latter indicates, the story these sculptures told was, in a word, aggressive. *Discovery* depicted a muscular Christopher Columbus overawing a nude figure intended to represent a Native American woman. *The Rescue* portrayed an oversized white frontiersman in neoclassical garb subduing an equally caricatured Native American, as a cowering white woman snatches her child away in the background. Like much of Washington, DC, *The Rescue* borrowed from the art and architecture of Ancient Rome—in this case, the first-century CE statue group *Laocoön and His Sons*—intentionally tying the United States to the great power of the ancient world.[6] It's perhaps not surprising then that, intentionally or not, the *Art-Union* review had evoked imperial Rome's best remembered propagandist—Virgil—and his exhortation to his fellow Romans "to pacify, to impose the rule of law ... to spare the conquered [and] battle down the proud."[7] Flanking the Capitol's main staircase, celebrating the arrival of Europeans in America, the subjugation of Indigenous peoples, and the supposed spread of "civilization," the two statues could thus also be summed up by another word: imperial.

Indeed, though they had numerous attributes that should shock and appall viewers today, it's the openly imperial motifs of the two sculptures that might be the hardest for many to process.[8] Didn't the very US Congress that commissioned these statues descend directly from the Continental Congress that had declared its independence from an empire in 1776? Did not that very same Declaration of Independence also proclaim—in Thomas Jefferson's famous words—that all men were "created equal" and endowed with "unalienable" rights? Hadn't the American Revolution begun a process that made the hierarchies of empire obsolete? Many of

---

[4]Fryd, "Two Sculptures" 21.
[5]Quoted in Fryd, "Two Sculptures," 34.
[6]Fryd, "Two Sculptures," 24.
[7]Virgil, *Aeneid*, 6.856–857, Robert Fitzgerald trans. (New York: Random House, 1983).
[8]Viewers since 1958 have had to rely upon photographs. The statues are no longer available to the public and *The Rescue* exists now only in fragments, damaged during a move in the 1970s. See: Karis Lee, "'Ground [the statues] into dust!'—The Downfall of Two District Memorials," *Boundarystones: WETA's Local History Website*, July 8, 2020, https://boundarystones.weta.org/2020/07/08/ground-statues-dust-downfall-two-district-memorials.

us are taught that the American Revolution *was* such a step, a significant milestone in the transition from a world of empires to a world of "nation states." Once free from British rule, the independent United States took its first steps into the so-called "Westphalian Order"—a community of equally sovereign polities that originated with the seventeenth-century "Peace of Westphalia."

This settlement, the story goes, helped set the stage for the decline of empire as the dominant political system of the world. It did so by ending Europe's complicated Hundred Years War, halting the Habsburg Dynasty's bid for "universal" control of all Europe in favor of a new continental order, one premised upon the existence of numerous, separate, territorially bound, and fully sovereign states (i.e., states that acknowledged no authority greater than themselves).[9] Beginning in Europe and then slowly spreading outward—with US independence as a key step along the way—the Westphalian system, it is claimed, came to eventually encompass the entire globe, birthing the modern international order. As one scholar put it in 1992, Westphalia established two principles which "to this day ... constitute the norm of international law ... (1) the government of each country is unequivocally sovereign within its territorial jurisdiction and (2) countries shall not interfere in each other's domestic affairs."[10] Regardless of the degree to which the actually existing international system follows these rules, it's certainly the case that the "Westphalian conceit," as the historian Claire Vergerio has put it, is widely accepted, forming "the descriptive foundation of dominant analyses of global politics" today. The problem, however, is that this traditional story—as Vergerio aptly summarizes—is "spectacularly wrong."[11]

As our two Capitol statues reveal, imperial motifs and, more importantly, imperial practices, endured. They did so globally of course, long after Westphalia, but also in the United States, long after it separated from the British Empire. Indeed, the young United States entered not so much a Westphalian world but one where empire retained its ancient status as a ubiquitous form of human social organization, possessing continued vitality both as an idea and as a common method of government. "Far from being an anachronistic political form," the historian Frederick Cooper has written, an "imperial perspective" remained central for the "important states of the nineteenth and twentieth centuries."[12] Some empires contracted after

---

[9] For a summary of this argument's tendencies see: Andreas Osiander, "Sovereignty, International Relations, and the Westphalian Myth," *International Organization* 55, no. 2 (2001): 251–87.
[10] Quoted in Osiander, "Westphalian Myth," 261.
[11] Claire Vergerio, "Beyond the Nation State," *Boston Review*, May 27, 2021, https://www.bostonreview.net/articles/beyond-the-nation-state/. See also Jeremy Adelman, "Empires, Nations, and Revolutions," *Journal of the History of Ideas* 79, no. 1 (2018): 73–88.
[12] Frederick Cooper, *Colonialism in Question: Theory, Knowledge, History* (Berkeley: University of California Press, 2005), 154.

1776, others grew. Instead of regularly being unified in the governments of individual states, sovereignty existed in a variety of forms, divided and qualified as often as unified—not least in the "federal" system established by the US Constitution in 1789.[13]

This is not to say that the US Declaration of Independence doesn't, in retrospect, appear as a watershed moment in a centuries-long transition away from formal imperial rule. It certainly does. America's declaration in 1776 marked, as David Armitage has described it, "the birth of a new genre of political writing," one which became popular across the globe.[14] There was, certainly, no shortage of need. More than one hundred other declarations followed it in the subsequent centuries. Most of the current states of the world were, at one point or another, under imperial rule—as much as 85 percent of the earth's landmass, for example, in 1914. Most of it today is not. Clearly the globe, at some point, transitioned from one dominated by formal empire to one largely divided into individual states. That said, the process was far from predetermined, linear, tidy, or easily summed up by reference to the birth of a "Westphalian system." It was instead complicated, halting—even reversed at times—and thus fraught with conflict and contingency. It is also, in certain respects, far from complete. While formal empire is relatively rare in the contemporary world, so also is true sovereign independence—all the Earth's polities are enmeshed in material, political, and cultural networks that increase the sovereign authority of some while decreasing it for others. A great many of these networks were forged by empire.

Therefore, rather than answering a question about the relevance of empire, US independence merely renewed older ones: when, on what terms, and for what duration, should a given political community gain independence? What even does it mean to be independent and who does that independence serve? Answering such questions has, arguably, been the central foreign policy concern of US history, from its founding through to the present. Speaking to the National Endowment for Democracy, in a 2003 effort to build support for the continued US occupation of Iraq, President George W. Bush, sounded not entirely unlike *The Rescue*'s admirers (and, for that matter, Virgil) when he proclaimed that the United States was not in

---

[13]For relevant discussions of the varying forms of sovereignty see: Edward Keene, *Beyond the Anarchical Society: Grotius, Colonialism and Order in World Politics* (Cambridge: Cambridge University Press, 2002); and Lauren A. Benton, *Law and Colonial Cultures: Legal Regimes in World History, 1400–1900* (Cambridge: Cambridge University Press, 2002).

[14]David Armitage, *The Declaration of Independence: A Global History* (Cambridge, MA: Harvard University Press, 2007), 14, 15–20.

the Middle East to conquer but to elevate and enlighten. "America has put our power at the service of principle," Bush insisted, fighting on behalf of the "essential principles common to every successful society." The United States was not serving itself but a much larger cause, "liberty ... the direction of history."[15] Understanding these continuities in the American approach to empire and its dissolution will be the focus of this book. Though Persico and Greenough's statues were removed in 1958—revealingly, as we shall see—what they suggest about the United States and the ends of empire is as relevant as if they still adorned the Capitol steps.

This book is an introduction to the history of the United States and the end(s) of empire since 1776. It explores how the United States has participated in and navigated "decolonization"—the transition from a world of formal empire to a world of individual states over the past three centuries. It is also therefore a consideration of how the United States has understood the role of empire and hierarchy in world order throughout its history. Its goal is to provide both a narrative overview and an introduction to key themes for understanding how the United States has interacted with the ending of empires, both the processes of decolonization and the status of being "postcolonial" (i.e., being formally independent but still deeply, and unequally, tied into governmental, economic, and cultural structures established by imperial rule).[16] The

---

[15]George W. Bush, "Remarks on the 20th Anniversary of the National Endowment for Democracy," November 6, 2003, Online by Gerhard Peters and John T. Woolley, *The American Presidency Project*, https://www.presidency.ucsb.edu/node/215869

[16]The term "postcolonial" naturally invokes the broad, multidisciplinary academic field of "postcolonial studies." As such, it often carries with it implications and meanings beyond the relatively basic definition used above, ones which would, for example, preclude one from describing the early United States as "postcolonial" because it was a racially exclusive, settler colonial society that practiced imperial expansion and attempted the epistemic erasure of indigenous cultures. Taking inspiration from Sam W. Haynes and Kariann Akemi Yokota, however, we will be using our simpler definition for two purposes (the value of which will, hopefully, be born out over the course of the book). First, it allows us to foreground the way the early United States remained locked in a subordinate relationship to other more powerful states in the world-system—namely, Britain—and then used imperial tools to leverage itself out of that position. Second, by opening an avenue of comparison between the subordination of the postcolonial United States and the subordination of other postcolonial societies, the use of postcolonial in this way helps highlight the hypocritical standards and expectations the United States later had for how other postcolonial states could free themselves from their lower place in the global hierarchy. See: Sam W. Haynes, *Unfinished Revolution: The Early American Republic in a British World* (Charlottesville: University of Virginia Press, 2010); and Kariann Akemi Yokota, *Unbecoming British: How Revolutionary America Became a Postcolonial Nation* (New York: Oxford University Press, 2011).

purpose here is not to exhaust the subject or provide insights based on new research but to review the broader "contours"—to borrow from the historian William Appleman Williams—of a critically important topic in the history of the US interaction with the world.[17] This discussion will therefore focus on providing a narrative interpretation of the United States, decolonization, and related issues of global hierarchy, one developed by drawing on part of the incredibly rich body of historical scholarship on the subject. Given that breadth of available research in the varying fields that touch upon our topic, this discussion will by necessity be incomplete and, perhaps, even somewhat idiosyncratic in its selection of sources. It will hopefully remain, however, broadly representative and of value to those introducing, or reintroducing, themselves to the topic.

The chronological scope of this book, since 1776, may come as a surprise for some readers. After all, discussions of decolonization tend to focus on the twentieth century, particularly the years following the Second World War. This is reasonably so, for that postwar period—when the great wave of decolonization in Asia and Africa largely put an end to the age of formal empire—profoundly shaped the modern world.[18] It will, in due course, occupy a good deal of our attention here. Yet, there is value in looking instead at the "long decolonization" stretching back to 1776, as its early chapters shaped the arrival of the contemporary world order almost as much as its later ones. Moreover, one cannot understand the US response to the seminal events of the twentieth century without understanding how Americans—and the American state, not always the same thing—navigated earlier imperial dissolutions and reconstitutions. Not least of these is, of course, the United States' own decolonization, a process that was far from over in 1776 and one that was as much about *continuing* colonialism as it was about ending it (particularly from the perspective of Indigenous Americans, as we will see). Similarly essential to the story is how the United States responded to the collapse of Iberian—Spanish and Portuguese—authority in Central and South America during the first half of the nineteenth century. These earlier decolonizations reveal what proved to be enduring patterns in the way the United States understood empire and its ends well through the twentieth century.

In brief, what emerges is a United States that—while often skeptical of formal empire and deeply influenced by new concepts of equality and political rights—regularly reserved to itself the authority to control the process of decolonization, both its own (naturally enough) and that of

---

[17]William Appleman Williams, *The Contours of American History* (New York: W.W. Norton and Company, 1988).
[18]See the discussion, for example, in Jan C. Jansesn and Jürgen Osterhammel, *Decolonization: A Short History* (Princeton: Princeton University Press, 2013), 1–34.

others. That is, in practice, the United States claimed the ability to determine the timing, nature, and extent of the independence granted to other political communities. It did so exclusively in the Western Hemisphere at first, but later, as European power over the Eastern Hemisphere waned, the United States assumed this authority across the globe, reaching far-flung places like Vietnam and Afghanistan. Indeed, as the latter indicates, even for states with formal independence, their sovereignty was, in American eyes, partly conditional and open to various forms of abridgement. Despite their country being born of an anti-imperial revolt, therefore, Americans and their leaders tended to believe the United States had a right and/or responsibility to hierarchically order the world, whether by means of formal empire or other less direct forms of American influence. Such determinations about the independence or non-independence of others were thus not made according to allegedly Westphalian concepts of sovereign equality but instead via hierarchies of what we will call "civilization."[19] This ever-pliable concept has had a multitude of meanings and has had other names (including, in President Bush's rendering, "liberty"). However, "civilization" was itself often used explicitly and, even when not, it serves as a useful analytical stand-in for an almost ever-present standard of judgment.

Essential to this standard were shifting American perceptions of a political community's position on scales of economic, cultural, and racial "advancement" toward an idealized vision of the United States. Not unlike Virgil and his fellow Romans, Americans tended to see their society as the cutting edge of human progress, helping to advance the cause of civilization against various forms of "barbarism."[20] Thus, as we will see, another society's perceived distance from the dominant racial, cultural, economic, and religious practices of the United States served regularly as a means for determining the necessity for, and justice of, American abridgement of their independence. Given that this dominant culture was usually organized around varying constructions of racial "whiteness," European cultural practices, Protestantism, and capitalism, it should come as no surprise that the sovereignty of societies seen as falling short of—or deviating from—those characteristics was viewed with the most skepticism.[21] In practice, this meant that while the United States has tended to oppose the creation of empires in Europe—and indeed, has been a symbol if not a force, for republican reform of European political institutions—its record outside Europe is decidedly more mixed.

---

[19]My thinking here is indebted to Ntina Tzouvala, *Capitalism as Civilization: A History of International Law* (New York: Cambridge University Press, 2020).
[20]See, for example, Matthew Frye Jacobson, *Barbarian Virtues: The United States Encounters Foreign People at Home and Abroad, 1876–1917* (New York: Hill and Wang, 2000).
[21]There is a broad literature on the ways white Americans constructed their national identity; for a good introduction see: Anders Stephanson, *Manifest Destiny: American Expansionism and the Empire of Right* (New York: Hill and Wang, 1995).

This is not to say, of course, that the United States abridged the sovereignty of every community deemed lower on the scales of civilization, far from it, but that such thinking suffused US conceptions of world order, particularly when it came to world order outside of Europe. These views of the non-European world were both a product of and a justification for the efforts of individual Americans, and their government, to improve or maintain their position in a highly competitive, hierarchically organized, international socio-economic system that originated in Europe in the sixteenth century and then spread outward across the Atlantic and, eventually, the globe. Scholars have called this system by varying names—from Immanuel Wallerstein's concept of a "world-system" to Sven Beckert's use of the looser term "networks."[22] The debates over these terms needn't detain us in our discussion here. What's important instead is to highlight how it was this competitive economic and cultural system—this world-system or collection of networks—not an expanding Westphalian order, that housed the newly independent United States in the late eighteenth century.

World-Systems, Forced Globalization, and the United States

When Thomas Jefferson penned his lines about human equality into the Declaration of Independence, he was living in a world born of the events mythologized by Persico's *Discovery*: Christopher Columbus's voyage to the Caribbean and the subsequent forced integration of the Eastern and Western Hemispheres. Some of this, of course, is part of an oft told tale, while the rest we will be covering in further detail in the subsequent chapters. However, it's important to sketch some of its outlines here to highlight this important concept for our discussion in this book: the development of an increasingly dominant, increasingly capitalist, world-system, or network of political power and trade, first located around the Atlantic basin but

---

[22] A world-system is Immanuel Wallerstein's term for "a large geographic zone in which there is a division of labor and hence significant internal exchange of basic or essential goods as well as flows of capital and labor." See: Immanuel Wallerstein, *World-System's Analysis: An Introduction* (Durham: Duke University Press, 2004), 23. The hyphen between "world" and "system" here is important as it denotes a system which is a world within itself, rather than something that necessarily encompasses the whole world. Sven Beckert, on the other hand, uses the term "network" in order to highlight the continued differentiation in socio-economic structure between different regions within the system—see: Sven Beckert, *Empire of Cotton: A Global History* (New York: Alfred A. Knopf, 2015), especially ix–xxii, 29–31. We will use both terms interchangeably in this book, for stylistic reasons in part but also because each successfully conveys the essential idea: an expanding and increasingly integrated zone, built around hierarchical arrangement of power and wealth that incentivizes those within it—both states and individuals—to competition and expansion.

eventually global in scope, one which has fundamentally shaped the behavior of Americans and their state.[23] What we find is a United States that was born as an arm of violent European economic and cultural expansion before itself becoming a center of this "enforced globalization"—in A.G. Hopkins's memorable term—as the world-system expanded to encompass more and more of the Earth.[24] The material demands of that expanding economic system—and the cultural practices and assumptions of superiority those demands helped generate—are the essential currents that have guided the interactions between the United States and the world since its founding.

Long residents of a global backwater, the late fifteenth and early sixteenth centuries saw Western Europeans—in a quest both for wealth and for a leg up in their competitions with each other—searching for a means to outflank Venetian and Middle Eastern domination of the spice trade with India.[25] In the process they stumbled across the Americas, triggering what Sven Beckert has called "the world's greatest land grab."[26] Aided by epidemic diseases and the Eurasian world's advantage in military technology, Spanish invaders in the first half of the sixteenth century conquered a vast empire in South and Central America, putting surviving Indigenous Americans to work in extracting resources, silver especially, for the enrichment of their Spanish overlords. The Spanish conquest of the Americas was, to put it bluntly, underwritten by horror. Virgin soil epidemics, triggered by the arrival of Eurasian diseases, combined with ruthless forced labor practices, depopulated large swaths of the Caribbean and the American mainland. This demographic collapse—perhaps the worst in recorded history—was matched by a deliberate program of deculturation, as the European invaders worked assiduously to root out and repress Indigenous cultures. Yet, destructive as it

---

[23]Capitalism is a term most of us use without thinking to refer to the economic arrangement that shapes life in much of the contemporary world. It is, however, worth briefly pausing to consider what we mean by it here, since our narrative is partly a narrative of the American relationship with capitalism. For the sake of simplicity—and to highlight continuities in economic practices across the centuries of history we are exploring in the book—we will rely on Immanuel Wallerstein's admittedly capacious, but still useful definition of capitalism. That is, capitalism is a system which "gives priority to the endless accumulation of capital." By giving priority, he means an economic system that is structured in such a way that those who act in order to accumulate more capital "are rewarded" and those "who act with other motivations are penalized in some way, and are eventually eliminated from the social scene." See: Wallersetin, *An Introduction*, 24 (for quote), and 23–41.
[24]A.G. Hopkins, *American Empire: A Global History* (Princeton: Princeton University Press, 2018), 30.
[25]For more on the relative position of Western Europe in the global economy before 1500, see: Janet Abu-Lughod, *Before European Hegemony: The World System A.D. 1250–1350* (New York: Oxford University Press, 1989); Ronald Findlay and Kevin H. O'Rourke, *Power and Plenty: Trade, War, and the World Economy in the Second Millenium* (Princeton: Princeton University Press, 2007), 43–86.
[26]Beckert, *Empire of Cotton*, 31.

was, empire in the Americas produced great wealth and power for Spain.[27] This led other Western European states, Portugal, England, France, and the Netherlands, to carve out their own space for exploitation.

By the late eighteenth century, there arose what scholars sometimes call the "Atlantic World."[28] This was a relatively integrated socio-economic space tying parts of four continents—both Americas, Europe, and Africa—into a network of trade, voluntary and involuntary migration, and culture. It was also hierarchically organized by violence in the interest of extracting surplus wealth for European elites and their states—"war capitalism" as Beckert calls it.[29] Raw materials extracted from the American colonies were transferred across the Atlantic, where some were transformed into manufactured goods that returned for sale to the colonies, while others helped pay for a growing number of enslaved people from Africa, a new coerced labor force needed to replace the collapsing Indigenous American population and keep extracted wealth flowing. Large numbers of voluntary settlers—whether free or "indentured"—also crossed the Atlantic from Europe, particularly to the thirteen English colonies in North America that would become the United States. There, the "settler colonial" project violently wrested land from the Indigenous inhabitants, transforming it into European-style private property, which was then used to produce both for local consumption and for market exchange back across the Atlantic.[30] Though Indigenous North Americans fiercely resisted the English invasion of their homelands, nearly halting it in a late seventeenth-century counterattack, by the early eighteenth century, the English colonies were well-established fixtures of the new Atlantic World.[31]

This was, again, a hierarchical space, not just in the rankings of race, wealth, and caste within colonial and continental European societies but also in its broad geographic orientation. Imperial policy and, as needed, coercive force were used to ensure that surplus wealth was drawn from the

---

[27]On the Spanish Empire see: J.H. Elliott, *Imperial Spain: 1469–1716* (London: Edward Arnold, 1963); Elliott, *Empires of the Atlantic World: Britain and Spain in America* (New Haven: Yale University Press, 2006); Stanley J. Stein and Barbara H. Stein, *Silver, Trade, and War: Spain and America in the Making of Early Modern Europe* (Baltimore: Johns Hopkins University Press, 2000). For more on the demographic impacts of imperialism in the Americas see: Russell Thornton, *American Indian Holocaust and Survival: A Population History since 1492* (Norman: University of Oklahoma Press, 1990).

[28]For an introduction to the concept of the "Atlantic World," see: Bernard Baylin, *Atlantic History: Concept and Contours* (Cambridge, MA: Harvard University Press, 2005); Jack P. Greene and Philip D. Morgan, eds., *Atlantic History: A Critical Appraisal* (Oxford: Oxford University Press, 2009).

[29]Beckert, *Empire of Cotton*, xv–xvi.

[30]We will be considering the nature of the settler colonial enterprise throughout the first few chapters of the book. For a good introduction see: John C. Weaver, *The Great Land-Rush and the Making of the Modern World, 1650–1900* (Montreal: McGill-Queens University Press, 2003).

[31]On the Indigenous counterattack see: Pekka Hämäläinen, *Indigenous Continent: The Epic Contest for North America* (New York: Liveright, 2002), 145–90.

colonial periphery, through and from colonial urban centers, and across the sea to the European imperial center. Thus, the various empires contained within the Atlantic World were constantly fighting for position, looking to ensure that either Madrid, Paris, London, or the Dutch Republic, accrued the most surplus wealth which, in course, translated to political and military power.[32] This quest for dominance drove two related activities, both of which profoundly shaped the history of the colonies that became the United States: imperial expansion and inter-imperial war.

In the case of the first—imperial expansion—the struggle for supremacy pushed states and individuals to try to incorporate more territory and people into the initially trans-Atlantic economic system. While it was most integrated around and across the Atlantic, the world-system was also critically tied via trade to East Asia. Here, Europeans arriving in the late fifteenth and early sixteenth centuries encountered substantial local populations—unlike the disease-shattered peoples of the Americas—and states powerful enough to resist outright occupation.[33] This did not prevent Dutch, French, and English traders from forcing their way into existing trade networks, however, coming to dominate sea trade between the "East Indies" (which includes in part today's Indonesia, Malaysia, Singapore, Papua New Guinea, and the Philippines), India, China, and the West. These forays around the Cape of Good Hope and across the Indian Ocean initiated two critical developments for the subsequent growth of European power: a diminishing role for the Ottoman Empire as middleman in the trade between Europe and East Asia, and the arrival of Indian cotton textiles in Europe (helping set in motion the Industrial Revolution, which will be discussed further in due course).[34] In North America, meanwhile, the quest for additional land and territory resulted in the American colonists pushing further and further westward into Native American space, forcing out the local population and, eventually, integrating more territory into the larger Atlantic system.

In addition to this push to incorporate more territory and people into the world-system, inter-imperial rivalry in the Atlantic World also, predictably, led to inter-imperial warfare. Increasingly titanic struggles between European powers evolved, by the eighteenth century, into an Anglo-French battle for hegemony. This was settled decisively in the British Empire's favor by two globe-spanning conflicts, the Seven Years

---

[32]For an overview of this competition from a world-systems perspective see: Immanuel Wallerstein, *The Modern World-System II: Mercantilism and the Consolidation of the European World-Economy, 1600–1750* (Berkley: University of California Press, 2011).

[33]On the different regional patterns of interaction with European expansionism, see: J.C. Sharman, *Empires of the Weak: The Real Story of European Expansion and the Creation of the New World Order* (Princeton: Princeton University Press, 2019).

[34]Beckert, *Empire of Cotton*, 136–74; Findlay and O'Rourke, *Power and Plenty*, 143–226.

War (1756–63), and then the French Revolutionary and Napoleonic Wars (1792–1815). The scale of these conflicts, stretching from the North American interior to eastern India, demonstrated the growing reach and scope of the European-centered world-system. Key to British success—and a hallmark of the system's dominant powers—was a strong state. Britain's aristocratic oligarchy, governing via Parliament, proved stronger than their French rivals, better able to draw wealth from its citizens (via both taxing the masses and borrowing from the rich) to fund the conflict while maintaining social order and labor discipline.[35] Yet, even the strength of the British state had its limits. For all the empires, in fact, the power of the imperial writ diminished the further one went from the center. When the center attempted to renegotiate the terms of the empire in order to pay for these conflicts, some on the periphery revolted. This happened with the thirteen North American colonies following the Seven Years War and in Central and South America after the defeat of Napoleon.[36]

But, for the new United States, as we will see, exiting the British Empire did not mean exiting the world-system Britain dominated. The United States remained deeply tied to the same hierarchical division of labor and networks of exchange that it had before independence. The American economy, in effect, needed the British Empire to consume its raw materials, to provide consumer-manufactured goods, and to provide essential capital. This was so much the case that, at root, the major political debates of the Early Republican period were over how to navigate the new state's continued dependance on Britain—or, in other terms, how to maintain and improve its position in the economic system of the Atlantic World—and survive the wars caused by other states trying to defend or improve their own place in the hierarchy.[37] The broader demands of the world-system shaped the decisions of individual Americans just as much as their government, pushing more and more across the frontier in search of land and wealth. This process only accelerated after independence as the removal of British restrictions on settlement in Native American land freed settlers to move across the Appalachians, and the arrival of early industrial textile manufacturing in northwest England gave rise to an almost inexhaustible market for American-grown cotton. The story followed much the same lines as that told by the capitol statues, from *Discovery* to *Rescue*, from arrival to continued conquest in the name of civilization.

---

[35]Immanuel Wallerstein, *The Modern World-System III: The Second Era of Great Expansion of the Capitalist World Economy, 1730s–1840s* (Berkley: University of California Press, 2011).
[36]For an introduction to the global "military-fiscal" crisis of the mid-eighteenth to early nineteenth centuries see, C.A. Bayly, *The Birth of the Modern World, 1780–1940: Global Connections and Comparisons* (Oxford: Blackwell, 2004), 86–100.
[37]On the American quest for "effective independence" from Britain see: Hopkins, *American Empire*, 18–19, 142–90, 287–336.

We will examine this story more closely—and carry it forward to the near present—in the subsequent chapters. What's important to highlight here is that the United States was born of, and fundamentally shaped by, the demands of this globalizing, European-born world-system. This network would shape the American relationship with empire and its neighbors as it became independent in the eighteenth century. It would continue to do so as United States developed into a core manufacturing state itself in the mid-late 1800s, and when it created its own overseas empire at the turn of the century, fought and won the First and Second World Wars in the decades leading to 1945, and then when it transformed into the globe's hegemonic power in the late twentieth and early twenty-first centuries. However, these "structural" concerns (as historians like to call them) did not operate as an exclusive source of the American relationship with the ends of empire. It was also, as the next section will consider, fundamentally shaped by the ideas that those economic and political structures helped generate.

Structure, Ideology, and American Exceptionalism

In his 2022 book, *The Class Matrix*, the sociologist Vivek Chibber noted that "one of the enduring problems in social theory is to explain the sources of stability and conflict in ... society."[38] Until the middle of the twentieth century, he goes on to describe, the prevailing methods for doing so focused on "material" factors, on the underlying "structure" of economic relationships between people in society. That is, how people produced the means for living and who controlled that process and the distribution of those goods, like those we just reviewed in our discussion of world-systems. Starting in the mid-twentieth century, however, scholars began to look more to "culture," or—to provide a simplistic definition of complex ideas—the language and symbols people used for seeing, analyzing, understanding, communicating, and ordering the world around them. Following this "cultural turn," there emerged an oft-substantial divide between those who focused on the material causes for human behavior and those who privileged culture and "ideology."[39]

A similar division is reflected in historical investigations of the impulses behind the United States' interactions with the rest of the world. On the more

---

[38] Vivek Chibber, *The Class Matrix: Social Theory after the Cultural Turn* (Cambridge, MA: Harvard University Press, 2022), 1.
[39] Chibber, *Class Matrix*, 1–21.

structural side are those who advance what is sometimes called the "open door" thesis. Named for Secretary of State John Hay's "Open Door Notes" of 1899 and 1900, and most famously advanced by scholars like William Appleman Williams and Walter LeFaber, this perspective emphasizes the power of economic self-interest—particularly that of wealthy elites and commercial concerns—in US foreign policy.[40] The Notes, where Hay called on the European powers with commercial concessions in China to refrain from transforming those into official colonies, are taken as something of an archetypal American approach to empire and economic interests. What at the surface appear to be anti-imperial documents, encouraging the Europeans to avoid repeating in China their contemporaneous conquest of much of Africa, were in fact lightly disguised attempts to ensure the United States an equal share of the spoils. This was a form of "imperial anticolonialism"—as Williams memorably entitled it—a regular feature of US policy and practice. Regardless of continued protestations of being an anti-imperial state, the United States instead used its power to ensure strategic and commercial advantage or in the interests of powerful segments of society able to capture the ear of government. US interventionism in Central America, as LaFeber acidly noted in his *Inevitable Revolutions*, was "not because of pressure from public opinion," which "could not have identified the five Central American nations on a map, let alone ticked off the region's sins that called for an application of U.S. force."[41] The flag, instead, followed the money.

On the cultural end of the spectrum are those who find more explanatory power in "ideology," or—to borrow from Michael Hunt's definition in his *Ideology and U.S. Foreign Policy*—an "interrelated set of convictions that reduces the complexities of a particular slice of reality to easily comprehensible terms and suggests appropriate ways of dealing with that reality."[42] This means exploring the idea systems that Americans used to comprehend the world, and doing so without necessarily seeing them as rooted in some underlying economic structure. This approach provided a dominant interpretive framework for historians for decades. In the process, it produced valuable insight into how ideologies born of various factors—ranging from nineteenth-century expansionism and racial prejudice to Woodrow Wilson's thought and twentieth-century social science—fundamentally shaped American interactions with other

---

[40] For two classic examples of their work see: William Appleman Williams, *The Tragedy of American Diplomacy*, 50th Anniversary Edition (New York: W.W. Norton and Co., 2009); Walter LaFeber, *The New Empire: An Interpretation of American Expansion, 1860–1898* (Ithaca: Cornell University Press, 1968).

[41] Walter LaFeber, *Inevitable Revolutions: The United States in Central America*, Expanded Edition (New York: W.W Norton and Co., 1984), 13.

[42] Michael H. Hunt, *Ideology and U.S. Foreign Policy* (New Haven: Yale University Press, 1987), xi.

peoples and states.⁴³ Hunt's book remains a touchstone entry in the field, identifying three "core ideas" in US foreign relations that first coalesced in the Early Republic and remained powerful through the latter half of the twentieth century: "visions of national greatness" (the "stunning possibility of Americans reinvigorating a gray, spent world" as Hunt memorably put it), a "hierarchy of race" that placed white Americans at the top, and a skepticism of revolutions (other, of course, than the sacred memory of the United States' own). While Hunt acknowledged the power of class, and indeed, grounds his argument in the reality that a rather small group of white, Anglo-Saxon, Protestant elites dominated the formulation of US foreign policy for much of its history, he faults Williams for too narrow a focus on economic interests. He asks, provocatively, whether "a dramatic alteration in the [U.S.] economic system" would actually "induce any dramatic transformation of foreign policy." Would not, he wonders, "a socialist America ... also pursue a foreign policy that was ... [just as] exploitative and domineering"?⁴⁴

Indeed, recognizing the inherent complexity of the past, historians rarely went so far around the cultural turn as some theorists in other fields. Nor, for that matter, were the "open door" scholars simplistic economic determinists. Williams himself, as Hunt notes, recognized that "ideas persist for a long time after their immediate relevance is gone" and, as such, "may act as an independent variable in later circumstances" separate from their structural origins.⁴⁵ Thus, taking a cue from Williams here—and, admittedly, looking to have our cake and eat it too—in this book, we will turn to the elegantly simple model of the relationship between economic interests and ideology proposed by Chibber in his aforementioned *Class Matrix*.

Chibber's view is more like Williams's than not, remaining fundamentally materialist in orientation and therefore seeing the constellation of economic power relationships within a society as a commanding determinant of human behavior. This is something most of us can understand rather easily. We all know—to varying degrees of severity—the powerful constraints that the need to "make a living" places on our decision-making. This is not to

---

⁴³For a few of many possible examples see: Thomas Hietala, *Manifest Design: American Exceptionalism and Empire* (Ithaca: Cornell University Press, 1985); Richard H. Immerman, *Empire for Liberty: A History of American Imperialism from Benjamin Franklin to Paul Wolfowitz* (Princeton: Princeton University Press, 2010); Michael E. Latham, *Modernization as Ideology: American Social Science and "Nation Building" in the Kennedy Era* (Chapel Hill: University of North Carolina Press, 2000); Frank Ninkovich, *The Wilsonian Century: U.S. Foreign Policy since 1900* (Chicago: University of Chicago Press, 1999); Stephanson, *Manifest Destiny*. For a recent volume reviewing the field see: Christopher McKnight Nichols and David Milne, eds., *Ideology in U.S. Foreign Relations: New Histories* (New York: Columbia University Press, 2022).
⁴⁴Hunt, *Ideology and U.S. Foreign Policy*, 11.
⁴⁵Williams, *Contours of American History*, 21.

suggest that every human is an efficiency-oriented, profit-seeking machine; it's instead to recognize that the quest to avoid starvation and material deprivation is a fundamental orientation of the human animal and thus the activities and relationships whereby starvation is avoided, and material goods are produced, remain an essential framework for social behavior and social thought. Yet, the ideas—the culture—such activities generate can have a great deal of power too (along with a lengthy shelf life). Chibber therefore suggests that we see a process whereby material structure comes first, but is then critically influenced by culture, the two locked in a close, reciprocal embrace.[46]

This too may appear as common sense to some, but for the more skeptical, we might cite two of the many examples of such a process at work, both in this case from the history of prejudice. Alexander Bevilacqua, for example, has noted how European Christian antipathy toward the Islamic world altered with the relative strength of their positions in global trade. A period of relative equality led to the flourishing of a deeply respectful "republic of Arabic letters" in Europe during the seventeenth and eighteenth centuries. As European power relative to the Middle East began to increase in the nineteenth century—thanks to the conquests and processes described earlier—this respect soon devolved into condescension. In the process, the very body of knowledge built by the "republic of Arabic letters," initially born of admiring curiosity, was repurposed, used instead to explain what Europeans increasingly saw as an inherent inferiority in the Muslim world.[47] An even more straightforward example can be found in the history of English, and Anglo-American, attitudes toward people of African descent. As Winthrop Jordan's classic study, *White over Black*, illustrates, European prejudices toward those with darker skin were certainly quite old. Yet, as Robin Blackburn has argued, these prejudices also evolved significantly in interaction with structural forces, hardening into increasingly more rigid boundaries in the environment of colonial America and particularly as slavery increased in importance to the colonial and US economy. Racist ideology clearly had a close relationship to a labor system premised upon racialized slavery; the first facilitated the second, which then only hardened the first.[48] While the relationship between structure and ideology isn't always this clearcut, thinking in this way remains a powerful means for understanding history and, in our case here, for charting the relationship between the United States and the ends of empire.

---

[46]Chibber, *Class Matrix*, 22–45.
[47]Alexander Bevilacqua, *The Republic of Arabic Letters: Islam and the European Enlightenment* (Cambridge, MA: Harvard University Press, 2018), 200–3.
[48]Robin Blackburn, *The Making of New World Slavery: From the Baroque to the Modern, 1492–1800* (New York: Verso, 2010); Winthrop D. Jordan, *White over Black: American Attitudes toward the Negro, 1550–1812* (New York: W.W. Norton and Co., 1968).

Our narrative therefore will proceed framed by these two assumptions: (1) the United States was a community profoundly shaped by its origins in the European-dominated world-system as described above, but (2) was also molded by the ideology that this competitive and hierarchical system developed around it. Americans inherited from the English a sense, in Hunt's terms, of national greatness, the idea that England was a society uniquely blessed by the heavens.[49] A natural enough byproduct of the relentless English competition for power with the Dutch, French, and Spanish, the rebelling colonies retained this English sense of superiority and transformed it during the struggle for independence. Americans saw themselves as, in essence, an improved England in the making.[50] Racially the same, perhaps, but more correctly Protestant and much more advanced politically, having dumped constitutional monarchy for a full-fledged republic.[51] These ideas were contested, of course, and marked by insecurity due to the continuing dependence of American cultural and economic life on the British Empire.[52] While most believed the United States destined to be, in Jefferson's terms, an "empire of liberty," there was also profound disagreement over what that empire might look like. American "exceptionalism" was also arguably more closely tied to race than its English cousin, dependent on constructions of what we today would call "whiteness."[53] The presence of a large population of enslaved people of African descent, and the continuing struggle with Native Americans for control of the North American interior, left white Americans scrambling to justify their efforts to control and subjugate non-whites without undermining the "republican" values so otherwise central to their identity.[54] These ideological wranglings reflected the different economic roles of key constituencies, but they also possessed their own dynamism.

Despite these debates and conflicting pressures, by the time Congress commissioned *Discovery* and *The Rescue* in the mid-1830s, the idea of the United States as a superior civilization, one which was white, Protestant, and republican, had taken firm hold. The exact contents of that ideology of civilization continued to evolve with time. In the decades leading to the US Civil War, for example, there was considerable argument—to put it mildly—over the role that free and unfree labor would play in the future of the United States and humanity. While in the twentieth century, Protestant

---

[49] See also the discussion in Stephanson, *Manifest Destiny*, 3–27.
[50] Hunt, *Ideology and U.S. Foreign Policy*, 19–45.
[51] On the relationship between "Protestant exceptionalism" and American exceptionalism, see: Andrew Preston, *Sword of the Spirit, Shield of Faith: Religion in American War and Diplomacy* (New York: Alfred A. Knopf, 2012).
[52] On American postcolonial insecurity in a British-dominated world see: Haynes, *Unfinished Revolution*; and Yokota, *Unbecoming British*.
[53] Hunt, *Ideology and U.S. Foreign Policy*, 46–91.
[54] For more on how slavery and settler colonialism shaped conceptions of citizenship in the United States see: Christopher Tomlins, *Freedom Bound: Law, Labor, and Civic Identity in Colonizing English America, 1580–1865* (Cambridge: Cambridge University Press, 2010).

Christianity slowly lost price of place to "Christianity" writ large, with "liberalism," "capitalism," and later "human rights," all making their appearance as supposed cornerstones of civilized life, as we will see. Yet, even as Americans continued to change their minds about what exactly it was that made the United States special, the confidence that it was so endured. Indeed, the idea that the United States stands at the forefront of human history remains largely intact in the United States to this day. These ideas provided a powerful means for Americans to justify their interference in other societies, to the extent even of claiming the authority to fundamentally structure the world in the United States' own self-image following the Second World War.

There was, it should be noted, a countercurrent in this exceptionalism, one which suggested that the supposed perfection of the United States meant it should *avoid* interfering with the rest of the world, or at the very least avoid doing so on most occasions. This is the tradition expressed in those widely quoted lines of John Quincy Adams, sixth president of the United States, who as Secretary of State in 1821 asserted that the United States should not: "go abroad, in search of monsters to destroy," but instead be a "well-wisher to the freedom and independence of all" and "champion and vindicator of only her own." This statement was part of a strong history of "anti-imperialism" from the American Revolution to the present. Yet, we should not see anti-imperialism as always meaning non-interference with the outside world. On the contrary, US anti-imperialism has always been an incredibly diverse tradition, one which—as the historians Ian Tyrrell and Jay Sexton have put it—featured "no small amount of hypocrisy … 'do as I say not as I do' denunciations of foreign empires."[55] It has been as much a "shaper of American empire" as it has been a break on it—"far from opposing all forms of empire" US anti-imperialism was "inextricably bound up in imperialist processes and structures."[56] The powerful incentives the world-system placed on individuals and the government tended to override or co-opt whatever restraints were imposed by this anti-imperial tradition. The idea that the United States was opposed to empire was part of the constellation of American exceptionalism, and thus, through it, US anti-imperialism often became a justification *for* US interventionism, if perhaps in a form other than formal empire. Adams himself, after all, was "a tough American imperialist in the name of anti-imperial idealism," particularly when it facilitated the commercial and economic development of the United States.[57] The sometimes-contradictory nature of the anti-imperialist

---

[55]Ian Terrel and Jay Sexton, "Introduction," in *Empire's Twin: U.S. Anti-Imperialism from the Founding Era to the Age of Terrorism*, Ian Terrell and Jay Sexton, eds. (Ithaca: Cornell University Press, 2016), 6.
[56]Terrel and Sexton, "Introduction," 7.
[57]Daniel Walker Howe, *The Political Culture of American Whigs* (Chicago: University of Chicago Press, 1979), 46.

tradition is another reminder of the symbiotic nature of the structural and ideological forces driving the US interaction with the world.

Finally, it's important to remember that American exceptionalism is not in itself particularly exceptional—as Virgil's assertions in *The Aeneid* prove all on their own—it's common for certain humanity communities to tell such stories about themselves. Our goal here therefore is not necessarily to single out the United States—nor to suggest that some past or contemporary counter project, like that, perhaps, of twenty-first-century China—is preferable to the role the United States has played in the world these past three centuries. Many of the alternatives in fact appear to be decidedly worse. The purpose is instead to chart how economic structures and exceptionalist ideology worked together to shape the US approach to the transition from a world of empire to a world of nation states, preserving into the present many of the same hierarchical structures that defined the imperial age. Recognition of the role such hierarchies have played in the construction of modernity seems essential not just to an honest understanding of the present and the sources of power in the world today but also to imagining how that world might be improved in the future.

Chapter Outline

This story will unfold over eight roughly chronological chapters. In the first three, we will review the decolonization of the United States and the Western Hemisphere, seeing how white Americans worked assiduously to build a postcolonial hierarchy in the "New World" with the United States at the top. Chapter 1 will consider the nature of the colonial enterprise that first brought European settlers to the East Coast of North America in the seventeenth century and explore how that project's roots in economic competition and civilizational chauvinism shaped the birth of the independent United States. In particular, we will highlight how the American Revolution did not represent a rejection of the hierarchies of empire generally but was instead a more specific repudiation of where the colonies ranked in the hierarchy being imposed by London in the late eighteenth century. In the second chapter, we will look at how the new United States continued the imperial project of hierarchical ordering as an independent "empire of liberty," using arguments about civilizational progress to justify the subjugation of its Indigenous American neighbors and thus advance its own power. Chapter 3 takes this story further afield, looking at how Americans extended networks of trade, control, and influence across the collapsing Spanish American empire and into the Pacific in the decades prior to the Civil War, with a focus on the US invasion of its largest decolonizing neighbor—Mexico—in 1846.

While these first three chapters tell how the United States took advantage of its neighbors to become a world power, Chapters 4 and 5 review what it did with that power. They show how, using the cause of civilization as its justification, the United States struck out to build its own formal empire by preventing the full decolonization of Cuba, the Philippines, and Puerto Rico in 1898 while extending an informal empire over much of the Western Hemisphere in the years prior to the First World War. When that war threatened to destabilize the European and United States dominated world order, President Woodrow Wilson would step into the breach, offering a reformed vision of a hierarchical world that would temporarily shore up a teetering international system. Key to Wilson's reform was an understanding of history and human progress that allowed for an independent future for some communities across the globe and a long period of tutelage by the "civilized" nations for others. The final three chapters consider what followed when the subsequent failure of Wilson's reformed international system—and the Second World War that resulted—allowed the United States to become the dominant power on the globe. Chapter 6 reveals how the decolonization of much of Asia and Africa posed a challenge to the hierarchies embedded in the United States' new post-Second World War vision for global order, leading Washington to adapt for use worldwide models of informal imperial control employed in interwar Latin America as part of its "Cold War" against communism. Far from allowing postwar decolonization to produce a world of Westphalian sovereign equality, American efforts helped ensure that the basic structure of the world-system established by imperialism remained in place in the mid-twentieth century.

In Chapter 7, we will look at the challenge to those structures that emerged in the 1970s, as the newly independent states of Asia and Africa teamed up with governments in Latin America in the United Nations to question the US-backed postcolonial global hierarchy. Bolstered by their numerical majority in the UN General Assembly and the success of the 1973 Arab oil embargo against the United States, the decolonizing world advanced an alternative and more egalitarian model for global governance. Though this vision for a transformed world-system briefly seemed poised to bring some reform to the international system, it would collapse in the 1980s, as a debt crisis and surging interest in "human rights" bolstered US economic and ideological power. Left without serious challengers for global leadership in the 1990s, the final chapter charts how the United States managed its time as a "hyperpower," asserting a program of world order built around human rights and economic deregulation. Seemingly unassailable as the twenty-first century began, the United States would use its place atop the global hierarchy to aggressively advance its vision of civilization in response to the terrorist attacks of September 11, 2001. The invasions and occupations that followed—in Afghanistan and Iraq—along with the economic chaos of the "Great Recession" would, by the early 2010s, raise the question of whether the US project of postcolonial world-ordering was entering a permanent decline.

The story that follows therefore is one that charts the rise and fall of the United States' ability to determine the ends of empire, shaping the world according to its image of properly constituted hierarchy in the name of the civilizational advancement of all mankind. As such, it is also a story about the birth of the modern world and—to borrow a line from the poet W.H. Auden—the "cement of blood" that binds it.[58] It also hopefully raises questions about whether much of what is described as "inevitable" in contemporary structures of wealth and power was ever indeed so. If nothing else, we might along the way catch glimpses of alternative paths not taken and consider whether they suggest a different way to the future than the one we are currently on.

---

[58]W.H. Auden, "Horae Canonicae," in *The Complete Works of W.H. Auden: Poems*, Vol. 2, Edward Mendelson, ed. (Princeton: Princeton University Press, 2022), 430–43.

CHAPTER ONE

Unleashing the "Empire of Liberty": The Colonization and Decolonization of British North America

In what seemed a miraculous occurrence to many at the time—and to very many more since—July 4th, 1826 ended (on the same day) the long, and accomplished lives of two of the "founding fathers" of the United States: John Adams and Thomas Jefferson. Both men had played indispensable roles in engineering the independence of the United States annually celebrated on the 4th, as well as steering the nation's government in its early years: Adams the second, and Jefferson the third, president of the United States. To many of their countrymen, the near-simultaneous passing of the two former presidents appeared as proof that theirs was a nation blessed by the heavens. As Adam's son—the serving president, John Quincy Adams—recorded in his diary, this was clearly a "visible and palpable" expression of "Divine favor."[1] Not that most citizens of the then young republic needed any further proof of such things. The idea that the United States was a divinely ordained nation, destined to lead humanity and "civilization" into a bright future of liberty, was by this point an indispensable part of the dominant form of American national identity. As Jefferson himself put it in his final public missive—a 4th-of-July message composed in the weeks before his death—the American Revolution had demonstrated, "the mass of mankind" had "not been born

---

[1] David McCullough, *John Adams* (New York: Simon and Schuster, 2001), 647.

with saddles on their backs, nor a favored few, booted and spurred, ready to ride them."² The birth of the United States had undermined those old hierarchies and left "all eyes opened ... to the rights of man."³

Jefferson's last public message is not far off from how Americans today tend to think of the early United States: as a new and powerful agent on the world stage for human freedom. Jefferson's final *private* utterance, however, was of a different and seemingly contradictory nature. As David McCullough, the Pulitzer Prize-winning historian, has described it: "somewhere near four in the morning Jefferson spoke his last words, calling in the servants 'with a clear strong voice' ... which servants he called or what he said to them are unknown."⁴ Known or not, there can be no doubt that some of those Jefferson called for were enslaved Black Americans. People who he, US law, and the majority of his fellow white Americans did in fact see as "born with saddles on their backs": doomed to lives of unrequited toil, the bottom of a hierarchy organized to extract wealth for elites like Jefferson and his creditors in London.

Another discordant note was sounded a few years later, and more than two thousand miles to the south, in Bogota, the capital of the newly independent Republic of Colombia. There, one of the founding fathers of Latin American independence—Simón Bolívar—looked at the North American republic less with admiration than with fear, worrying whether the confluence of divine providence and US history was as salutary for the "mass of mankind" as Jefferson suggested. The United States, he wrote in a letter to a British correspondent in 1829, seemed ready to intervene in Colombian internal politics and, in general, appeared "destined by Providence to plague America with torments in the name of freedom."⁵

One needn't go so far from Jefferson's home in Virginia, however, to find similar skepticism about how beneficial the United States was to the progress of humanity. Speaking in Massachusetts, William Apess, an author and lay Methodist preacher, offered the perspective of those on whom "the torments of freedom" had already been delivered: the once numerous population of Native Americans living east of the Mississippi River. Apess asked his audience to reconsider the American Revolution in the light of his people's forced removal—and near extinction—from their ancestral lands. This, he explained, was the consequence of the colonial project that had created the United States and the "cruelty of those who [claimed they]

---

²McCullough, *John Adams*, 645.
³McCullough, *John Adams*, 645.
⁴McCullough, *John Adams*, 646.
⁵Simón Bolívar, "Letter to Col. Patrick Campbell," in *Latin America and the United States: A Documentary History*, Robert H. Holden and Eric Zolov, eds. (New York: Oxford University Press, 2000), 17–18.

came to improve our race, and correct our errors."⁶ "Let the children of the pilgrims blush," he continued, "while the son of the forest drops a tear, and groans over the fate of his murdered and departed fathers." For Native Americans, the 4th of July was a day "of mourning and not of joy."⁷ American progress was for Apess not a pressing forward toward a promised land, but the erasure of an idyllic past.

We begin our survey of the United States and the end of empire here, with the contradictions embedded in these stories, born of the era when European imperial rule collapsed in most of the Western Hemisphere. On the one hand is the American Revolution, which—divinely ordained or otherwise—did to some degree represent the kind of rupture Jefferson's final message suggested, rejecting some of the hierarchical structures of the British imperial system and initiating a process where the rights of *some* men were with time dramatically expanded. On the other hand, the government and white male citizens of this new United States often then used those rights to perpetuate existing hierarchies and establish new ones. As Apess suggested roughly two centuries ago, the 4th marked not the end of empire, but its unleashing, as the United States broke beyond its colonial borders, expanding westward across North America, bringing destruction to the Native American communities in its way and slavery in its wake. Responding to the imperatives generated by the economic structures in which the thirteen colonies had been housed—which were largely unaltered by US independence—and increasingly confident that their new nation represented the future of civilization, US citizens and their government entered the post-Revolutionary world ready to shape it according to their own wishes by employing old imperial tools in new libertarian packaging.

As England, France, and Spain lost (or sold off) their claimed imperial authority from most of North and South America during the late eighteenth and nineteenth centuries, the United States increasingly asserted its own right to order hemispheric affairs. This was first, and most particularly, at the expense of Native American sovereignty, but it eventually limited Latin American independence as well. Far from marking a firm transition from the imperial era to the Westphalian age of sovereign states, the history of the Early Republic demonstrates how alternative structures of authority and power endured long after the Revolution.

We will develop this story over three chapters. The first will consider the nature of the colonial project that planted England's settlers in North America and how it deeply informed the political and economic structure of the independent nation that emerged from them. Essential here will be noting how the forces that prompted this European invasion of "the

---

⁶Daniel K. Richter, *Facing East from Indian Country: A Native History of Early America* (Cambridge, MA: Harvard University Press, 2003), 238.
⁷Richter, *Facing East from Indian Country*, 244.

New World" did not subside following the Revolution but continued to drive US expansionism. We will see that the American Revolution was not a rejection of empire in general, but simply a repudiation of the way the British Empire was being governed in the late eighteenth century. In the second chapter, we will look at how concepts of civilization, and economic imperatives emerging from the place of the United States in the world-system, shaped the US assault on the Native American communities of North America—a hierarchically conceived, imperial project long disguised under the euphemism of "westward expansion." We will then review in the third how similar impulses drove initial US interactions with the rest of the non-European world and Latin America in particular. Far from embracing the universal rights of man, Americans—whether looking south with dreams of empire, or further abroad with visions of US sails "whitening every sea"— tended to see much of the world as peopled by those, in Jefferson's words, born with saddles on their backs.[8]

The Character of the Colonial Enterprise

It requires—as the historian Daniel K. Richter has noted—a good deal of "imagination" to grasp how some of the seven million or so Native Americans living in North America first learned of the invasion of their homelands.[9] Nothing but oral tradition, often composed generations later, remains to recall the Indigenous half of this momentous event in world history. Richter suggests that the word likely first arrived in the form of shadowy rumor—whispers of strange newcomers in tall ships, often attached to peculiar objects of unknown origin working their way through traditional Native trade networks. Indeed, Richter's own efforts to reconstruct some initial encounters (based on European records) from the Native perspective have aspects of a work of science fiction, or horror. Take, for example, his fictional description of Native hunters on the coast of Newfoundland, discovering "several of the traps they had set" were "missing, along with the needle they need[ed] to mend their fishing nets."[10] Instead of their missing tools, Richter imagines, they find "a smoothly polished upright timber crossed near the top by a second piece of wood, from which hangs the carved effigy of a bleeding man." This, a large Christian crucifix, we know was left behind by John Cabot, the Italian explorer working on behalf of the English crown in 1497—an

---

[8]Brian Roleau, *With Sails Whitening Every Sea: Mariners and the Making of An American Maritime Empire* (Ithaca: Cornell University Press, 2014).
[9]Richter, *Facing East from Indian Country*, 11.
[10]Richter, *Facing East from Indian Country*, 11.

ominous sign of what was to come for Indigenous America.[11] Similarly chilling is Richter's rendering of a documented 1524 encounter of an elderly woman, her daughter, and grandchildren with some of Giovanni da Verrazzano's men. Hiding in the woods, the women "scream as some twenty pale, bearded men, sweating in heavy armor and helmets, stumble upon them," and then snatch away one of the male children. He was never seen by his kinfolk again.[12]

While Native Americans of the fifteenth century could only speculate as to what was bringing these strange signs and pale men to their shores, we can, of course, offer a fuller picture. These were the first forays of an immense trans-Atlantic undertaking—the European effort to build commodity-producing colonies in North America, colonies which in the English case produced the United States. This effort, as we discussed in the introduction, was driven by the centuries-old inter-European struggle for strategic and commercial supremacy. First, Spain and Portugal, then France, England, the Netherlands, and Sweden sent sailors, soldiers, and settlers across the Atlantic in the interest of securing portions of South and North America for their own advantage. In order to understand how the United States approached the decolonization of the Americas in the eighteenth and nineteenth centuries, we must begin with this story, exploring the country's origins in the European effort to *colonize* what they called the "New World" in the fifteenth, sixteenth, and seventeenth centuries. For the nature of that undertaking—and its foundations in commercial endeavor, divided sovereignty, violent conquest, and hierarchy—fundamentally shaped the character of the United States.

Traditionally, the commercial origins of the colonial project were understood to lie in "mercantilism," a way of understanding trade and power that supposedly dominated Western European economic thought prior to the eighteenth century. Mercantilism is usually depicted as a theory which imagines the overall amount of wealth in the world as static and fixed. Trade was thus a "zero-sum" game, whereby any gains of wealth by one monarch, state, or empire meant a corresponding loss in wealth by another. Economic activity did not increase the overall pool of wealth; it just helped determine where that wealth was directed. It was essential for statesmen, the idea went, to ensure that more of that wealth flowed into their lord's coffers, through policies designed to ensure a favorable "balance of trade," whereby more hard currency—primarily gold and silver—entered one's kingdom than exited it.[13]

---

[11]Richter, *Facing East from Indian Country*, 12.
[12]Richter, *Facing East from Indian Country*, 12.
[13]Steve Pincus, "Rethinking Mercantilism: Political Economy, the British Empire, and the Atlantic World in the Seventeenth and Eighteenth Centuries," *William and Mary Quarterly* 69, no. 1 (2012): 3–34; Jonathan Levy, *Ages of American Capitalism: A History of the United States* (New York: Random House, 2021), 9–11.

Colonies, therefore, were beneficial because they brought more land under a kingdom's control, land that could potentially produce gold and silver—as did Spain's American possessions, for example—but also because they might house centers of commodity production that could help ensure a favorable balance of trade. Essential in the latter case is the relative price difference between commodities and manufactured goods. Commodities—produced via agricultural production or extraction from the natural world—generally are at a trading disadvantage with manufactured goods (the latter being commodities that human labor has turned into something else, such as how wool is woven into broadcloth). Mercantilism thus called for structuring an empire's internal trade around a hierarchical relationship between the home country—what we can call the "center"—and the colony—or, the "periphery." The periphery served the center by producing commodities for use in center manufacturing that might not be available at home and then, in turn, provided a captive market where the finished version of those commodities could be re-sold, ensuring the further growth and development of manufacturing and a favorable balance of trade. In that mercantilism called for policies that structured and shaped trade in order to protect the economies of particular states and empires, it is also usually imagined as being diametrically opposed to the "free trade liberalism" associated with figures like Adam Smith and dominant in the economic discourse of the late twentieth and early twenty-first centuries.[14]

Many traditional depictions of the role of mercantilism in the colonization of North America, however, are oversimplifications. For one, there was no clear mercantilist "consensus" among European elites but instead the significant divisions over policy one might expect from any relatively diverse group of people, elite or otherwise. In the English case, for example, some advocates for colonizing North America—like Sir Walter Raleigh, the proprietor of England's first, failed, colony of Roanoke (in today's North Carolina)—believed colonies were valuable because they helped increase the proportion of the world's scarce resources under English control. Raleigh hoped North American colonies might house precious metals like Spanish possessions had, or at the very least, provide bases for English ships to intercept Spanish treasure as it crossed the Atlantic. Others, like John Smith, the colonist and explorer most famous today for his time as the leader of Jamestown, Virginia—England's first successful foray in North America—saw things in a somewhat different light. Smith suggested the possibility

---

[14]For more on English mercantilism, see: Findlay and O'Rourke, *Power and Plenty*, 227–310; David Ormond, *The Rise of Commercial Empires: England and the Netherlands in the Age of Mercantilism* (Cambridge: Cambridge University Press, 2003); Philip J. Stern and Carl Wennderlind, eds., *Mercantilism Reimagined: Political Economy in Early Modern Britain and Its Empire* (New York: Oxford University Press, 2014). For a discussion of the differences between mercantilism and liberalism see: Eric Helleiner, *The Neomercantilists: An Intellectual History* (Ithaca: Cornell University Press, 2021), 1–31.

that colonies might drive dynamic economic growth (economic activity that increased the overall supply of wealth in the world). If the colonists abandoned their "pride and idelnesse [sic]," as Smith put it, the English settlements could develop into vast commercial centers of their own, greatly adding to the wealth of their mother country. Such debates took on a partisan tinge by the seventeenth century in England. Tories, who tended to be from the landed aristocracy, often adopted the Raleigh view, while Whigs (who represented commercial and financial interests) were more open to theories about growth and the value of manufacturing.[15] Most important for our purposes though, is to note that, from the late fifteenth century on, there was a common sense that colonization was a worthwhile undertaking, one that could add to the wealth of the individuals involved and the country that sponsored them.

In the long run, this view proved to be correct for both Whiggish and Tory reasons. Colonies in the Americas both added to the resources under English control and created new dynamic centers of growth and spurs to manufacturing. While we know for certain today that the global economy is not an entirely zero-sum game—the overall amount of wealth can in fact increase—English advocates for empire of both persuasions possessed a fundamental insight into the nature of wealth and power in the world. They correctly perceived that a given community's position in the global exchange of resources helped determine its power and influence, which in turn could help it maintain or increase the favorability of that position. Even if the overall pool of wealth can increase, it's not guaranteed that all will gain an equal share. England's colonies in North America became an essential part of England's rise—as Great Britain, following the 1707 Act of Union with Scotland—to global dominance.[16]

Yet, for all the advantages that North American colonization ultimately brought to England and Great Britain, the English state played a relatively limited role in delivering the first settlers to North America. This hands-off approach was another important influence on the United States. Lacking resources to conduct such operations itself in the sixteenth century, the Crown began to authorize private entities to do so on its behalf, joint stock companies which were collectively owned by wealthy investors, each contributing money and receiving in turn a share of the company. As one might expect, the shareholders anticipated a return on their investment, revealing the fundamentally commercial nature of the colonial enterprise, even in New England. While religious agendas were inarguably a part of the reason for the establishment of the Pilgrims' Plymouth Company, for

---

[15]Steve Pincus. "Rethinking Mercantilism," 14–16, 28.
[16]P.J. Cain and A.G. Hopkins, *British Imperialism: 1688–2015*, 3rd edition (New York: Routledge, 2016), 73–102; Findlay and O'Rourke, *Power and Plenty*, 227–310; Levy, *Ages of American Capitalism*, 14–38.

example, or the Puritans' later Massachusetts Bay Company, each was ultimately a business venture meant to produce a profit. In this, they were not all that dissimilar from the more nakedly commercial Virginia Company (which settled Jamestown). All too, though private companies, took on some of the power of the state, with royal charters granting them vast authority to govern those territories that came under their control. They were in this sense, as the historian Jonathan Levy has described it, "subsovereigns of a composite empire," manifestations of an imperial system where authority was plural and shared.[17] Each colony developed as its own political entity, subordinate to the Crown, but otherwise broadly empowered to order its own affairs. This plurality of authority, where rights to certain aspects of governmental power were owned at different levels, would prove to be a defining feature of the later expansion of the United States.[18]

That expansion would also be defined by violence—a violence exercised in the name of racial and civilizational supremacy—and this too had its origins in the colonial era. Colonialism, it's important to remember, is fundamentally a violent activity. For most of recorded history at least, it's rare for one group of humans to find a desirable piece of land not already at least partly occupied by another group. Therefore, settling that desirable land almost invariably requires displacing or removing the original inhabitants to some degree or another. This was certainly the case in North America, where the arrival of Europeans kicked off what Pekka Hämäläinen has called a "four-centuries-long war" for control of the continent, as "almost every Native nation" fought back at various times against the "encroaching colonial powers."[19] For Native nations there were, and remained, in North America long after the first white settlers arrived. As Hämäläinen reminds us, the "maps in modern textbooks that paint much of early North America with near color-coded blocks" of territory supposedly controlled by Europeans "confuse outlandish imperial claims for actual holdings."[20] Though Native Americans built political communities differently than Europeans, they were no less real than those of the invaders.[21] Only accepting the presumptive claims of the colonists could obscure the fact that the various Indigenous polities of North America were sovereign rulers of the continent's land, as clearly as any nation marked on a map today.

England's colonial boosters realized this, of course—contrary to later myths, it was widely known in Europe that North America was inhabited—and thus a critical first stage of the colonial project was finding a means to

---

[17]Levy, *Ages of American Capitalism*, 22–3.
[18]See: Jack P. Greene, *Peripheries and Center: Constitutional Development in the Extended Polities of the British Empire and the United States, 1607–1788* (Athens: University of Georgia Press, 1986).
[19]Hämäläinen, *Indigenous Continent*, xii.
[20]Hämäläinen, *Indigenous Continent*, xii.
[21]Hämäläinen, *Indigenous Continent*, x, 24.

invalidate the clear rights Native Americans had to their land. In doing so, English colonialists were joining a European discourse on civilization and Indigenous dispossession that began almost the moment that Christopher Columbus arrived on Hispaniola in 1492 and determined to enslave the Taíno people who resided there. Early arguments, emerging from the Spanish conquests that followed Columbus, focused on Christianity and the supposed "rights of conquest" that European nations believed were a part of "natural law." Some European legal minds felt that a failure to be Christian was sufficient in itself to justify the conquest of Indigenous people. Others suggested that, while that wasn't quite enough, any remotely hostile Native response to European efforts to trade with or convert Indigenous populations allowed for a declaration of war. This then—by the law of war—justified their subsequent subjugation. Once conquest was justified, by whatever means, it then became possible to extinguish Indigenous sovereignty and transfer it to European monarchs.[22] Consistent throughout is the idea that the Native peoples of the Americas were insufficiently civilized to retain sovereignty over their land, that they were outside of the community of nations Europeans felt obliged to recognize—whether because their actions in response to the arrival of intruders proved it so, or because they simply had been determined to be so *a priori*. This was particularly the case with the English, who, as the legal scholar Christopher Tomlins has detailed, developed their own distinct discourse justifying colonial seizures.[23]

This uniquely English justification for invading North America was intimately tied up with ideas about human progress born of Renaissance "humanism," a secularizing philosophy that emphasized the power of human reason to order worldly affairs. Many humanists believed that reason, properly applied, could help humanity build ideal commonwealths. This, however, would be difficult to do in the established societies of Europe—a fresh start was required elsewhere. Sir Thomas More's famous 1516 work *Utopia*, for example, imagined an ideal city planted on land taken from a "rude and wilde people" somewhere across the ocean.[24] This city would offer a model of progress for all of humanity, regardless of whether the local inhabitants liked it or not. To be sure, the natives of More's imaginary country would be offered a chance to accommodate themselves to the laws of the new commonwealth established on their land. If they declined, however, "if the inhabitaunts of that lande wyl not ... be ordered by [Utopian] lawes," More wrote, then the Utopians would be justified making "warre against them." Progress justified these land seizures, because in order to retain title to their land, More suggested, its inhabitants needed to be using it in the right way. If "anye people holdethe a piece of ground voyde and vacuant to

---

[22]Tomlins, *Freedom Bound*, 93–132.
[23]Tomlins, *Freedom Bound*, 133.
[24]Tomlins, *Freedom Bound*, 138.

no good nor profitable use," More wrote, then "this is the most juste cause of warre."[25] Though hypothetical, More's vision of Utopia, and the logic it applied to colonial land seizures, came to lay at the heart of English claims to sovereignty in North America. Native people could be denied ownership of their land if their supposedly more advanced brethren determined they were not putting it to proper, economical, and progressive use. This logic would be invoked over and over by England's colonial propagandists.

William Strachey, an English colonial booster writing in 1612, suggested that North America's Natives had long ago lost their rights to the land because they did not "know howe to turne [it] to any benefit," while John Donne, preaching in 1622, described Virginia as having been "utterly derilicted and immemorially abandoned by the former inhabitants." The "whole world," he continued, and "all Mankinde must take care that all places be emprov'd, as farre as may be, to the best advantage of Mankinde in general."[26] In so doing, some argued, the English were merely repaying a debt to empire they had incurred a millennia earlier. Without the Roman invasion of Britain in 43 CE, argued Oxford University's Robert Burton in 1621, Britain would have remained "as unciviill as they in Virginia."[27] By the "planting of [Roman] colonies & good lawes," the island had been transformed. "Had not this violence, and this Injury, bene offred unto us by the Romanis," Strachey explained, the people of England "might yet have lyved [as] overgowne Satyrs, rude and untutred."[28] Now, these writers suggested, it was England's turn to provide the same good service to the inhabitants of North America.

In arguments that will be echoed in different forms and at different times by other figures throughout this book, sixteenth- and seventeenth-century English advocates for colonization insisted that civilizational progress justified conquest and rule, so that, as Richard Haklyut the Elder put it in 1585, "the naturall [Indigenous] people of the country may be made skillfull."[29] None of this should suggest that justifications for Native dispossession always involved such elaborate arguments regarding land use and progress, simple assumptions of inferiority played an important role as well. The assertion of the Anglican Minister, Robert Gray, in 1609 that the inhabitants of North America were mere "brutish sauages," who "participate rather of the nature of beasts then men," is a good example of this.[30] Regardless of the precise form their attitudes took, however, in general, the English approached the colonial project confident in the civilizational

---

[25]Tomlins, *Freedom Bound*, 138.
[26]Tomlins, *Freedom Bound*, 144–5.
[27]Karen Ordahl Kupperman, *Indians and English: Facing Off in North America* (Ithaca: Cornell University Press, 2000), 30.
[28]Kupperman, *Indians and English*, 30.
[29]Tomlins, *Freedom Bound*, 111.
[30]Tomlins, *Freedom Bound*, 143.

inferiority of Native Americans and the corresponding justice of displacing them from their lands.

These civilizational prejudices were further strengthened in the crucible of conquest, as English invaders opened their new theater in the 400-year war for North America. Not all interactions between colonists and Indigenous peoples were defined by violence, of course—there was also considerable peaceful trade and intercourse. For most of the various Algonquin-speaking peoples who lived along the Atlantic Coast, war was usually seen as a last resort when interacting with other communities. They preferred to incorporate the newcomers into their existing trade and kinship networks, to make the Europeans "useful," as Hämäläinen has put it.[31] Over time, however, the nature of English land use—their preference for enclosed private property, intensive agriculture, and animal husbandry—clashed with the existing cultural and ecological patterns of Indigenous North America, leading to growing tensions.[32]

Amidst the confusing mixing of "Old World" and "New," both Natives and newcomers naturally wished to preserve their traditional ways of life from outside influence. Some Algonquin feared the spread of Christianity and the loss of their traditional religious practices. Those Native Americans who looked to slow or reverse the foreign invasion tended to—as an English observer noted—blame all their problems on "the Departure of some of them from their own heathenish Ways and Customs." They "had a great fear to have ani of their Indians... Caled or forsed to be Christian indians."[33] The English, meanwhile, proved particularly, violently, fearful of being corrupted and barbarized by their new homes—of being "contaminated by the influence of America's wilderness and its wild people," as Jill Lepore writes.[34] Required by necessity to partly adapt their lifestyles to the North American environment, the colonists feared any significant accommodation or assimilation with their Indigenous neighbors, lest it cause them to further lose their endangered Englishness and Christianity. Already, warned the New England minister Increase Mather in 1676, there was "a great decay as to the power of godliness amongst us."[35] It was essential, therefore, that the Europeans be perceived as standing atop the new hierarchy created by colonization, anything else was an intolerable affront to English identity as a "civilized" people.[36]

---

[31]Hämäläinen, *Indigenous Continent*, xii.
[32]Ned Blackhawk, *The Rediscovery of America: Native Peoples and the Unmaking of U.S. History* (New Haven: Yale University Press, 2023), 63.
[33]Jill Lepore, *The Name of War: King Phillip's War and the Origins of American Identity* (New York: Vintage Books, 1999), 7.
[34]Lepore, *Name of War*, 7.
[35]Lepore, *Name of War*, 6.
[36]Lepore, *Name of War*, 11.

All of this, and the settlers' voracious appetite for more land, ultimately led to violence and very nearly the early destruction of English North America. Though a series of wars in the seventeenth century—the Pequot War (1636–37) and King Phillip/Metacom's War (1675–78) in New England and the Anglo-Powhatan Wars (1609–14, 1622–32, 1644–46) in Virginia—secured the colonial lodgment, they did so only barely and at considerable cost. As Stonewall John, a Narragansett leader, summarized it to the Puritan Roger Williams, "You have driven us out of our own Countrie and then pursued us to our Great Misere and Your own."[37] Relatively small in scale compared to continental European conflicts of the time, these wars rival any for brutality, featuring the wholesale destruction of villages and cropland as well as the elaborate torture and execution of captives and noncombatants.[38] Hatred was thus stoked on both sides. The leaders of the Connecticut colony, for example, urged their fellow colonists to complete the destruction of the Wampanoag in August 1676. Their "wicked contriveances," the colonial leaders wrote, "will doubtless incite & animate all *true Englishmen* to endeavoure the confusion of such bloodsuckers, as are now, thorow God's mercy to us, totally routed in theses partes & gathered into a net."[39] Already, the Connecticuters gleefully reported, the Native peoples of the New England coast had been reduced to "but the gleanings of sundry nations that were great numbers ere while."[40] These wars asserted English dominance and preserved the colonies as exclusively European-controlled spaces—fundamentally reordering the structures of power in northeastern North America—and in doing so firmly planted anti-Indigenous racism at the heart of colonial culture.

Though these seventeenth-century conflicts made the English colonies a permanent feature of the North American landscape, they did not end Indigenous control of most of the North American interior, nor bring an end to colonial expansionism. The wars instead created the space needed for the economic transformation of the colonies from tenuous coastal enclaves to thriving agricultural and commercial centers with growing populations and a seemingly inexhaustible appetite for more land that could only be acquired through conquest. Empire, and its associated hierarchies, was essential to this economic and physical expansion—not just in terms of Indigenous dispossession but also because of the colonies'

---

[37]Lepore, *Name of War*, 14.
[38]For more on the Pequot War, see: Blackhawk, *Rediscovery of America*, 48–72; for King Phillip's War see: Lepore, *Name of War*; for the Anglo-Powhatan Wars see: Hämäläinen, *Indigenous Continent*, 52–69.
[39]Lepore, *Name of War*, 16.
[40]Lepore, *Name of War*, 16.

membership in the larger British Empire and the trading system of the Atlantic World.

For New England, the critical role was played by British possessions in the Caribbean, primarily sugar-producing islands like Barbados.[41] During the seventeenth century, these islands quickly became the stars of the British commercial empire, producing an extremely valuable commodity at competitive prices that enriched plantation owners and the crown alike. These islands were in effect massive prison camps, wholly given over to export commodity production by slave laborers working under horrific conditions.[42] Unable to feed themselves, Britain's Caribbean possessions looked abroad for foodstuffs and supplies—which is exactly what New England could provide. Beginning then in the 1640s, New England began to offer fish, livestock, and other provisions in return for credit which was then used to purchase manufactured goods, like clothing and firearms, from England.[43] The "triangle trade" was born. New England's commerce, which also included rum, timber, and naval stores, soon began to reach markets across the entire Atlantic World.[44] In the Chesapeake, tobacco was the key to colonial economic success, sold to England in return for the same manufactured goods that New England ultimately received for their food supplies.[45] Overseas trade soon brought considerable wealth to commercial centers like Boston, New York, Philadelphia, and Charleston. Abundant land made available by the collapse of the Native American population through war and disease offered a path to subsistence and prosperity in the expanding rural hinterland as well. All told, on the eve of the American Revolution, the average white colonist was wealthier than his English counterpart.[46]

"White" is, of course, a critical distinction here, for a large and growing minority of the colonial population were enslaved Africans and their descendants. They were brought by force first to Virginia in 1619, almost immediately after Jamestown was settled. Though slavery was a feature of life in all of the colonies—in the mid-seventeenth century, the

---

[41]Richard Dunn, *Sugar and Slaves: The Rise of the Planter Class in the English West Indies, 1624–1713* (Chapel Hill: University of North Carolina Press, 1972), 336.
[42]Blackburn, *Making of New World Slavery*, especially 217–76, 309–430; Dunn, *Sugar and Slaves*; Levy, *Ages of American Capitalism*, 30.
[43]Findlay and O'Rourke, *Power and Plenty*, 233–5; Levy, *Ages of American Capitalism*, 31; Peter Lindert and Jeffery Williamson, *Unequal Gains: American Growth and Inequality since 1700* (Princeton: Princeton University Press, 2016), 47.
[44]Lindert and Williamson, *Unequal Gains*, 47.
[45]Findlay and O'Rourke, *Power and Plenty*, 235–6; Lindert and Williamson, *Unequal Gains*, 48.
[46]Findlay and O'Rourke, *Power and Plenty*, 233–8; Lindert and Williamson, *Unequal Gains*, 43–76.

majority of enslaved people were in New England and the Mid-Atlantic—over the long run, it was in the Chesapeake and the South where they were forced to work in the largest numbers.[47] There were clear economic incentives for this turn to slave labor. Labor shortages were a chronic issue in colonial North America, thanks in part to the destruction of the Indigenous communities of the coast and the continuing dispossession of those of the interior. Bringing settlers to the colonies from abroad was expensive. Meanwhile, what free laborers there were tended to look to the abundant cheap land opened up by war on the frontier as an alternative to working for someone else. Working conditions on a tobacco farm, for example, were difficult and wages were by necessity low—otherwise the crop couldn't compete on the broader Atlantic market. As their operations grew in scale, therefore, the only way for planters to ensure a sufficient workforce was through unfree labor policed by violence. As a result, voluntary—"indentured"—servitude played an important role from the early settlement of the colonies through the mid-eighteenth century, where European immigrants signed a labor contract to serve a colonial master for a given time (usually around 4–7 years) in return for the cost of crossing the Atlantic.[48]

Planters, however, began to move away from indentured servants in favor of a more permanent form of unfree labor—slavery—which in time revealed itself to be more cost-efficient.[49] The very same hierarchies of civilization that justified Native American dispossession reserved this status for non-Europeans. Indigenous slaves were tried, but Native military resistance and the collapsing Indigenous population made this an unsustainable solution, forcing the colonists to look to other sources.[50] Because Europeans also deemed Africans—like Native Americans—to be civilizationally inferior from some combination of their religious, cultural, and/or inherited physical characteristics, they too were eligible to be enslaved, and so Europeans were soon trading for slaves in Western Africa

---

[47]David Brion Davis, *Inhuman Bondage: The Rise and Fall of Slavery in the New World* (New York: Oxford University Press, 2006), 124–40; Tomlins, *Freedom Bound*, 426.
[48]Though a significant part of the forces that brought European immigrants to the colonies, historians still debate exactly how much of an impact indentured servants had on the structure of colonial society, particularly once the American-born population began to grow. See the discussion in Tomlins, *Freedom Bound*, 29–66.
[49]Blackburn, *Making of New World Slavery*, 315–25; Blackburn, *The Overthrow of Colonial Slavery: 1776–1848* (London: Verso, 1988), 11–13.
[50]See: Joseph E. Inikori, "Atlantic Slavery and the Rise of the Capitalist Global Economy," *Current Anthropology* 61, no. 22 (2020): 5166–8; and Tomlins, *Freedom Bound*, 402–3.

to supply colonial markets.⁵¹ This proved the more enduring "solution" to the labor issue. The English crown's approval for slave trading was officially granted in the 1660s—to what would later be named the Royal African Company—an acknowledgment of what was by then an already durable westward leg of the triangle trade. Commerce in enslaved humanity transformed the colonial labor market and, within a century, commodities exported from the colonies were almost overwhelmingly the product of slave labor.⁵²

With so large a portion of the colonial population locked into perpetual slavery, and with so many of the free settlers able to take advantage of Indigenous lands made available by war and disease, it's natural that colonial society began to develop a distinct social hierarchy when compared with the mother country. At the top were free white males who—though divided amongst themselves by lines of wealth and status—were on balance considerably freer than their English brethren across the Atlantic. With more land available in fee simple (i.e., land that could be owned outright and not in tenancy), white colonists were generally better off, more in control of their own affairs, and if wealthy enough, more able to participate in local and colonial government than those in England. There were, as might be expected, significant gradations in white colonial society. Servants, apprentices, women, and the poor were all subject to significant patriarchal restrictions on their freedom.⁵³ Yet, on the whole, there was something to the claim that large sections of colonial North America were "the best poor man's country" in the world at the time.⁵⁴

---

⁵¹There is a longstanding debate among historians about the exact role of cultural prejudice in the origins of slavery in the Atlantic World (which was also briefly discussed in the introduction). There is little doubt that European prejudices toward non-Christians with darker skin long predated Atlantic slavery. At the same time, however, such prejudices only evolved into concepts akin to contemporary understandings of "race" through their use in justifying a slave system that served specific structural needs in the Atlantic economy. Historians disagree about which was more important in the development of slavery in the Americas. Winthrop Jordan in *White over Black*, for example, puts more emphasis on the importance of pre-existing European prejudice, while a study like Robin Blackburn's *Making of New World Slavery*, on the other hand, stresses the structural incentives. For purposes here it's sufficient to suggest that the two were closely related and that existing perceptions of hierarchical difference between Christian Europeans and Africans hardened into categories of "race" as a highly profitable slave system became more established and widespread. Those concepts of race then, in turn, helped reinforce the slave system.
⁵²Blackburn, *Making of New World Slavery*, 459–83; Levy, *Ages of American Capitalism*, 30.
⁵³Tomlins, *Freedom Bound*, 335–40.
⁵⁴James T. Lemon, *The Best Poor Man's Country: Early Southeastern Pennsylvania* (Baltimore: Johns Hopkins University Press, 2002), xxiii.

This remarkable freedom was set against, and in fact predicated upon, the unfreedom of those lower on the hierarchy of civilization.[55] As we have seen, Native Americans were deemed unable to retain sovereignty—hence becoming subjects of the Crown yet only allowed to enter colonial society partially at most (and only if they completely renounced their own culture and communities). They therefore remained largely outside the empire itself while always, at least in European minds, subject to its whims. Enslaved Africans, meanwhile, were kept within the community by force, denied personhood and strictly bound by harsh slave codes—borrowed from Barbados—that licensed torture and death for even the most minor infractions.[56] This North American hierarchy was then in turn wrapped up in the larger pyramidal structure of the British Empire, with the colonies producing commodities which were exchanged for more valuable manufactured goods made back in Britain. That economic hierarchy was paired with a political one—for all the self-government practiced in the colonies, the Crown retained ultimate sovereignty.[57]

Disagreement over the nature of that sovereignty, that is, over the place of the North American colonies in the hierarchy of the British Empire, was the underlying issue that drove the American Revolution—the subject to which we will now turn. Though the Revolution is popularly understood as being animated by egalitarian ideals, it is essential to recognize that it was also far from a complete repudiation of the hierarchical colonial project we've just described. On the contrary, the colonists launched their revolt in order to continue imperial expansion in the form they were used to, rejecting a British effort to restructure the colonial enterprise in a new way. The revolutionaries wanted to shape the course and nature that the empire would take going forward, to ensure that the colonies and their white citizens retained their place near the top of the pyramid of civilization, rather than abolishing it entirely. Decolonization thus somewhat counterintuitively became a tool which allowed Americans to *continue* colonialism, not end it, and to do so on their own terms rather than London's.

The American Revolution and Continuing Imperial Expansion

Though some have a habit of seeing it as singular, the American Revolution was in fact but the opening chapter in a long crisis that transformed the political structures of the Atlantic World over the course of the late eighteenth

---

[55]For the classic statement of this see: Edmund S. Morgan, *American Slavery, American Freedom: The Ordeal of Colonial Virginia* (New York: Norton and Company, 2003).
[56]Tomlins, *Freedom Bound*, 409–508.
[57]Greene, *Peripheries and Center*, 15.

and early nineteenth centuries. By 1826, most of North and South America had severed the formal political ties to Europe that had bound them since Spain had begun its spectacular conquests in Central America three centuries earlier. This long crisis was fundamentally the result of two things: the almost endemic warfare produced by the contest for dominance in the Atlantic world-system and the correspondingly desperate need for money to pay for these conflicts. Though the "military-fiscal" states of Europe, as scholars sometimes call them, had developed increasingly sophisticated means for extracting revenue and organizing manpower to conduct war and project power on a progressively more massive scale, the costs of war always seemed to outpace the means for paying for them.[58] The efforts by British and Spanish governments to extract more revenue from their empires, and by the French monarchy to draw more from France itself, triggered revolutions on both sides of the Atlantic, fueling a half-century of war and upheaval and the first great wave of decolonization.[59] These conflicts all were, therefore, about hierarchies and where particular political groups—ranging from the American colonists to the French "Third Estate"—would fall within them.

That the British Empire was the first to collapse into civil war is not without irony, as it had developed the most intricate and effective structures for raising funds of any of the three dominant "New World" powers. The political and ideological system established following the 1688 "Glorious Revolution" ensured that the average resident of Britain was more heavily taxed than any of their continental counterparts—at the same time, they were also likely to consider themselves among the freest peoples in Europe. British subjects widely believed they were beneficiaries of "English liberty," which was embodied in Parliament and an established Protestant church they tended to contrast favorably with the Catholic and absolutist continent. While the heaviest tax burden fell on the poor and middle class (in the form of tolls and consumption taxes), the Bank of England also provided a means for extracting voluntary contributions from those with excess capital: government bonds.[60] This gave London an ability to generate revenue rivaled only by the sophisticated banking systems of the Dutch. Thanks to its tax structure and the Bank, the British government was soon borrowing much more cheaply than its continental rivals. This ability was key to its ultimate victory in three eighteenth-century wars with France: the War of Spanish Succession (1701–14), the War of Austrian Succession (1740–48),

---

[58]On the military-fiscal state see: John Brewer, *The Sinews of Power: War, Money, and the English State* (Cambridge, MA: Harvard University Press, 1988).
[59]See: Bayly, *The Birth of the Modern World*, 86–120; Hopkins, *American Empire*, 46–94; Wim Klooster, *Revolutions in the Atlantic World: A Comparative History* (New York: New York University Press, 2009).
[60]On the strength of the British tax system see: Findlay and O'Rourke, *Power and Plenty*, 256–62. On the origins of the Bank of England see: David Kynaston, *Till Times Last Sand: A History of the Bank of England, 1694–2013* (New York: Bloomsbury, 2020), 1–58.

and the Seven Years War (1756–63). These left the British with a sprawling global empire to defend and massive costs to defray (the latter two conflicts had increased British public debt by 60 and 80 percent, respectively).[61]

In 1763, a new administration under George Grenville took power in Parliament, one which looked to the colonies—rather than England's landed gentry, as some opposition figures proposed—as a source for more funds to service this debt, setting the stage for confrontation.[62] For Lord Grenville and his ilk, this was about more than just tax policy. As the historian Justin du Rivage has described them, these were "authoritarian reformers" seeking both greater colonial tax revenue and tighter administrative control over the empire. They sought nothing less than the establishment of an "extractive imperial state," one which placed the mother country firmly above the colonies in the empire's hierarchy.[63] This authority even included the ability to restrict colonial expansion into the Native American-controlled interior of North America, something Grenville's government (with good reason) saw as likely to spawn expensive conflict. The Grenville administration advanced its view of colonial relations over the course of the 1760s. The Proclamation of 1763 banned white settlement beyond a line along the Appalachian Mountains, while the Sugar Act of 1764 and Stamp Act of 1765 directly taxed colonial consumption along the lines of taxes in England.

Few in the colonies would have disagreed that the supreme authority of the empire was to be found in London, either in the person of the King or in the power of Parliament.[64] Yet, until Grenville arrived in office, this authority was more theoretical than actual. As a practical matter, power tended to be devolved to the colonies themselves—long habits of colonial self-government had left the exact nature of the imperial constitution unclear and the colonial economy only lightly regulated.[65] Though the empire's mercantilist policies were perhaps draconian on paper, enforcement was relatively lax—smuggling was so rampant, for example, that roughly three-fourths of the tea consumed in North America was uncustomed (bought from the Netherlands rather than Britain).[66] The North American colonists were

---

[61] Justin du Rivage, *Revolution against Empire: Taxes, Politics, and the Origins of American Independence* (New Haven: Yale University Press, 2017), 15. On the significance of British victory in these conflicts see: Fred Anderson, *The Crucible of War: The Seven Years War and the Fate of the British Empire in North America* (New York: Knopf, 2000); and Brendan Simms, *Three Victories and a Defeat: The Rise and Fall of the First British Empire* (New York: Basic Books, 2009).

[62] du Rivage, *Revolution against Empire*, 103–11.

[63] du Rivage, *Revolution against Empire*, 1–24.

[64] On the popularity of the monarchy in colonial America see: Brendan McConville, *The Kings Three Faces: The Rise and Fall of Royal America, 1688–1776* (Chapel Hill: University of North Carolina Press, 2006).

[65] See Greene, *Peripheries and Center*.

[66] Hopkins, *American Empire*, 115.

also subject to a fraction of the tax liabilities that confronted their British cousins—about one-fifth of what was owed in England—and smuggling helped them to evade even those.⁶⁷ Not that the British hadn't benefited from the relationship. As discussed earlier, the relative manufacturing dominance of Britain ensured that the long-term benefits of trade with the North American colonies accrued to the home country, helping it develop and expand a manufacturing sector that would eventually launch the Industrial Revolution.

As a result, some recognized that the colonies didn't need to be heavily taxed to bring benefits to Britain. Members of the opposition Whig party, particularly those who organized under the patronage of the Marquess of Rockingham, for example, argued that while Parliament had the right to further tax the colonies, it should refrain from doing so, as colonial development (potentially hindered by taxation) benefited the broader imperial economy. Rockingham's brief stint as Prime Minister (1765–66) saw his faction put these principles into action, temporarily bringing a reprieve to the conflict by repealing the Stamp Act. However, when the Rockingham administration collapsed in 1766, the authoritarian reformers returned to office.⁶⁸ Tensions were soon raised again by the 1767 Townsend Acts. Though these were nearly all repealed by the new government of Frederick "Lord" North, the latter's arrival in office put the authoritarian reformers firmly in control. Despite the ministerial instability of the era, the would-be authoritarians usually remained the dominant faction in Parliament, able to carry forward the effort to bring North America to heel up to and beyond the point of civil war. North himself completed the famous/infamous litany of Parliamentary Acts—the 1773 Tea Act and the 1774 laws known in the colonies as the "Intolerable Acts"—that led to the outbreak of the Revolution. The Battles of Lexington and Concord in 1775, and the Declaration of Independence in 1776, soon followed.

This break resulted in part because the authoritarian reformers' challenge to colonial autonomy arrived at a time when the colonies were under acute economic, territorial, and social pressure. A long period of growth had come to an end following the conclusion of the Seven Years War. Credit contracted, putting significant pressure on colonial debtors—many of whom were among the most prominent citizens in North America.⁶⁹ The efforts to restrict smuggling, so long a vital part of colonial commerce, also

---

⁶⁷du Rivage, *Revolution against Empire*, 13.
⁶⁸du Rivage, *Revolution against Empire*, 127–46.
⁶⁹See, for example, Woody Holton's discussion of the impact of deflation on the planter elite in Virginia: Woody Holton, *Forced Founders: Indians, Debtors, Slaves, and the Making of the American Revolution in Virginia* (Chapel Hill: University of North Carolina Press, 1999). See also Blackburn's discussion of the role of debt in planting, *Overthrow of Colonial Slavery*, 14–17, 86–7.

threatened both higher prices for all and diminished business prospects for those many influential citizens who earned much from illegal trade. In addition, though white colonial society was still remarkably egalitarian on material terms, inequality was growing in urban centers like Boston, New York, and Philadelphia, creating a swelling lower class quite willing to mobilize against the status quo.[70]

Regional inequality between the poorer frontier and the richer coast contributed to the tensions as well. Frontier settlers—who continued to encroach on Native American land despite the Proclamation of 1763—found themselves subject to Indigenous reprisals, as inland Native communities tried to defend themselves against colonial expansion. The Proclamation had been issued in part to try to prevent these sorts of attacks, a concession to Indigenous power along the shores of Lake Erie and in the northern part of the Ohio River Valley.[71] Earlier that year, Native Americans under an Odawa leader named Obwandiyag (or, more famously, "Pontiac") struck out at the sources of British authority in the region, fighting British troops to a draw and forcing a reluctant imperial government to make peace and grant Indigenous autonomy. This angered many settlers, who saw the British concession as a betrayal by their government in favor of "savages." In the mid-1760s, western Pennsylvanians organized into vigilante militias like the "Black Boys" and "Paxton Boys" in response, attacking British forts, burning peaceful Indigenous villages, and even marching on Philadelphia. They were outraged at the government's desire to reduce conflict with Native Americans and increase trade across the Great Lakes region. They demanded more accountable leaders who were willing to use force to protect settler interests and seize Indigenous land.[72]

As Peter Silver has shown, accusations that high officials had either fomented—or failed to prevent—attacks by Native Americans were, by the 1770s, "dependable tropes ... decades old" for delegitimizing authority in the name of the "people" of the colonies.[73] While colonial elites like Benjamin Franklin and George Washington tended to have a somewhat more benign—if still deeply prejudiced—view of Native Americans, some of them also had their own reasons to oppose British policy toward the Indigenous interior. Washington, for example, had earned considerable grants of land in "the West" from his time serving as an officer in the Virginia militia during the Seven Years War. Other leading revolutionary figures, like Thomas Jefferson

---

[70]The classic discussion of this is: Gary Nash, *The Urban Crucible: Social Change, Political Consciousness, and the Origins of the American Revolution* (Cambridge, MA: Harvard University Press, 1979).
[71]Blackhawk, *Rediscovery of America*, 141.
[72]Blackhawk, *Rediscovery of America*, 139–75; Peter Silver, *Our Savage Neighbors: How Indian War Transformed Early America* (New York: W.W. Norton and Company, 2008), 73–123, 161–226.
[73]Silver, *Our Savage Neighbors*, 252.

and Patrick Henry, also had invested large sums in western lands, lands that would only be valuable if imperial policy made their sale and settlement possible.[74] Thus, as it became clear in the late 1760s and 1770s that the British government was quite willing to ignore colonial preferences and implement its policies by force, there was a broad range of colonists—from urban to rural and poor to elite—who had material reason to resist the expansion (or reassertion) of imperial control over North America.

Yet, the colonists were upset as much about what the Grenville-North program portended as they were its immediate impact. The problem from the colonial perspective is obvious—the authoritarian reformers intended to subordinate the colonial economy to that of Britain. The issue wasn't that the new taxation was particularly onerous—it was not—but that it represented to the colonists a transformation of the relationship between colony and imperial center. They held to a different vision of the empire, one that was closer to the Rockingham Whigs and even more to their "radical Whig" brethren.[75] These saw the American colonies and Britain as equals, or near equals, in a shared imperial undertaking, bringing the benefits of English liberty and Protestant civilization to the barbarous wilderness of North America for the material enrichment of all. The colonists thus resented the implication of policies like the Stamp Act as much as their actual provisions. Writing under a pseudonym in the *Boston Gazette* in 1765, John Adams made this very clear: "we will not be their Negroes ... we are as handsome as old English folks and so should be as free."[76]

Adams's evocation of the racial hierarchy within the empire is a telling one. The colonists did not necessarily reject the idea of an unequally structured, hierarchical society, their issue was with an incorrect hierarchy, one that placed them below Britain in the imperial order. They, as colonists, noted repeatedly, were not slaves. Despite the presence of enslaved people of color in their midst, the majority, wrote the Massachusetts lawyer James Otis Jr., were "white, and there is as good blood flowing in their veins, save the royal blood, as any in the three kingdoms" of Great Britain.[77] As Otis's exception for "royal blood" suggests, properly constituted hierarchy and authority were not the problem. The issue was instead that, in colonial eyes, Parliament was throwing that hierarchy out of whack, elevating *all* of Britain—royal, noble, and commons alike—over the colonies. Silas Downer, a Rhode Island "patriot," lamented how it was "now an established principle in *Great-Britain* that we are subject to the *people* of that country in the same

---

[74]Holton, *Forced Founders*, 3–38.
[75]For more on trans-Atlantic Whig radicalism see: du Rivage, *Revolution against Empire*, 108–9. For more on its American offshoot see: Bernard Bailyn, *The Ideological Origins of the American Revolution* (Cambridge, MA: Harvard University Press, 1967).
[76]T.H. Breen, "Ideology and Nationalism on the Eve of the Revolution: Revisions Once More in Need of Revising," *Journal of American History* 84 (1997): 29.
[77]Breen, "Ideology and Nationalism,' 34.

manner as they are subject to the Crown." It was, he continued, "humiliating and debasing" to "be governed by one part of the King's subjects" when they were in reality "but equals" of their colonial cousins.[78] That London appeared to some to not only value British, but Native American, concerns over those of the colonists only made matters worse.[79]

In essence then, colonial discontent in the 1760s and 1770s was born of a desire to preserve the hierarchical colonial project much as it had been originally constituted, ordered, and imagined by the imperial boosters of the sixteenth and early seventeenth centuries: a collective, imperialist enterprise of the English, and subsequently British, people. Once it was firmly established that a durable majority in Parliament, and in the British public, believed the American colonists to be mere subordinate parts of that undertaking, the Americans began to look for the exits.

Justifying that departure required that they alter the Whiggish rhetoric about liberty and freedom that had previously helped define colonial self-identity within the empire. This had relied upon the idea of *English* "liberty"—that colonial subjects had rights because they were, if not native Englishmen, certainly members of a broader British imperial entity defined by the rights owed to those born in its principal kingdom. Denied access to English rights, the colonists turned to those supposedly granted by nature— the "natural rights" of Enlightenment thinkers like John Locke—rights due to the colonists merely because of their status as human beings.[80] This proved a powerful mobilizing tool, helping to tie the disparate elements of the revolutionary movement together, granting the "patriots" a common ideological identity despite numerous and profound divisions along regional, political, and class lines. The embrace of natural rights "liberalism"—as we call it today—would in the course of time have radical implications for the political society of what was about to become the United States, not least for slaveholders like Jefferson, the most talented natural rights propagandist in the Revolutionary era. At the time, however, the full meaning of the Revolution's egalitarian rhetoric—the idea, as Jefferson put it, that "all men are created equal"—was left undefined.[81]

Though universal in its implied scope, Revolutionary ideology had at its core a relatively limited argument about colonial rights in the face of perceived Parliamentary tyranny—an argument intended almost exclusively for an audience of fellow Europeans, whether they be British antagonists or the audience of potential allies in Western European states like France. This

---

[78]Breen, "Ideology and Nationalism," 30.
[79]Silver, *Our Savage Neighbors*, 227–60.
[80]Breen, "Ideology and Nationalism," 35–9.
[81]Breen, "Ideology and Nationalism," 38–9. On liberalism more generally see: Duncan Bell, *Reordering the World: Essays on Liberalism and Empire* (Princeton: Princeton University Press, 2016), 62–90; Helena Rosenblatt, *The Lost History of Liberalism: From Ancient Rome to the Twenty-First Century* (Princeton: Princeton University Press, 2018).

is not to suggest that the colonists didn't necessarily believe sincerely in the ideas that informed the Revolution. Nor is it to say that the deployment of egalitarian rhetoric in such a way wasn't a critical development leading to the establishment of a relatively unique political culture, one which gave rise within a few decades to a novel mass democracy (however limited it was by race and gender). It is to say instead that—in order to not be surprised by what follows in this chapter and the next—we have to recognize that revolutionary rhetoric had, for most colonists, a much more limited meaning than it might carry to readers today. Outside of some of the most radical revolutionaries, none understood themselves as discussing the rights of, say, Native Americans or enslaved Africans. These were people outside the political community and thus not involved at all in these debates, save as causes of colonial discontent.[82]

This is made abundantly clear in Jefferson's Declaration of Independence itself, where both enslaved and Indigenous peoples are depicted not as fellow inheritors of natural rights but as little more than features of the natural environment, malevolently manipulated by the British tyrant. "He has excited domestic insurrections amongst us," the Declaration complained, accusing the British government of fomenting slave uprisings. The king had also, it continued, "endeavoured to bring on the inhabitants of our frontiers, the merciless Indian Savages, whose known rule of warfare, is an undistinguished destruction of all ages, sexes and conditions." Indeed, one of the key grievances of the revolutionaries was, as we have noted, London's effort to slow the conquest and dispossession of Native American lands, or, as the Declaration puts it, "raising the conditions of new Appropriations of Lands" with the Proclamation of 1763.

The revolutionaries were, therefore, not rejecting *empire* writ large but *an* empire in particular: the British one ruled from London. In its place, they imagined and would build a "genuinely new kind of empire" as du Rivage has described it, ruled by the colonies themselves.[83] To those held to be outside of its communal embrace—slaves and Native Americans—this new empire seemed much the same: hierarchical, aggressive, racist, and expansionist. From within, however, it was relatively novel, a republican empire, collectively ruled by nominally equal, self-governing states. These quickly established provisions to replicate themselves across the North American landscape, in a way not all that different from Thomas More's depiction of Utopia's self-perpetuation among the "rude and wilde" people of his imaginary land across the ocean.

Before we can consider that self-perpetuation in detail—which we will do in Chapters 2 and 3—we first need to review how expansionist imperatives shaped the structure of the state that emerged from the Revolution. When

---

[82]Blackburn, *Overthrow of Colonial Slavery*, 111–12.
[83]du Rivage, *Revolution against Empire*, 4.

FIGURE 3 *A map from 1919 showing the territory claimed by the United States as it began its process of decolonization following the 1783 Treaty of Paris.*

Jefferson called the new United States an "empire of liberty," he was not speaking in contradictions but highlighting the peculiar construction of the new polity, one which reflected the former colonists' desires to construct an improved and idealized version of the old imperial constitution they had once imagined governed the British Empire.[84]

Constituting the Empire of Liberty

All of the historical experiences described thus far in this chapter—from the original public/private colonial project to the trauma of Parliament's attempt to assert centralized imperial control in the mid-eighteenth century—shaped the nature of the new Republic born from the 1783 Treaty of Paris. So too did the contest for hegemony over the Atlantic world-system—a contest that was not halted by the American Revolution and would soon explode into the global conflagration of the French Revolutionary and Napoleonic Wars. Just as important as well was the new state's location on the edge of a still largely Indigenous controlled continent. This history, and the global situation at the time of its birth, pulled the new US state in contradictory directions. The former colonists both needed a strong government to organize their

---

[84]See Peter Onuf, *Jefferson's Empire: The Language of American Nationhood* (Charlottesville: University of Virginia Press, 2000).

efforts to survive collectively in a dangerous world but also feared a system that could disrupt their ability to govern themselves.

Thanks to their origins as separate settlement enterprises, and the painful memories of the pre-Revolutionary crisis, the colonies-turned-states all shared a skepticism of centralized power. This was not a skepticism of *government* power per se—the revolutionaries were not the radical libertarians that we sometimes imagine—but of its concentration in a central authority superior to the states. This skepticism was reflected in the country's first national constitution, the Articles of Confederation, adopted by the Second Continental Congress in 1777 and ratified in 1781. It could be said that the Articles established more a center for coordinating the individual states than it did create a central government of them. Each state retained a great deal of power while at the same time the Confederation government—composed of a unicameral legislature in which each state had an equal vote—had almost no ability to compel the individual states to respect the limited authority it possessed. Unable to raise its own taxes or troops and limited as well in its powers to regulate the nation's commerce, the government established by the Articles perfectly suited the desire for local autonomy that had been at the heart of the Revolution.[85] It did not, however, suit the undertakings many Americans wanted that autonomy for: commerce and expansion. Nor did it seem well designed for survival in a dangerous and highly competitive political and economic environment that threatened the United States with early dismemberment or destruction.

A profound economic slump followed the Treaty of Paris. In a process that will be seen throughout this book, the former colonies discovered that formal independence does not always bring real independence. The economic bonds of an empire are much harder to dissolve than the political ones. The US economy remained in many ways the colonial economy, one that— smuggling aside—had been built for two centuries around trade with other parts of the British Empire. The British blockade during the Revolutionary War had severely handicapped American trade and independence provided no respite. British ports remained closed to American ships and—while a great many American families relied upon their own farms for the bulk of their livelihood—the health of the nation's foreign trade often made the difference between general prosperity and just getting by.[86] Moreover, wartime inflation was followed by peacetime deflation and chaos in public finances as individual states and the Confederation government struggled to defray the debts accumulated during the war. Incomes in the former colonies may have declined as much as 20 percent between 1770 and 1800.[87] With

---

[85]See the discussion of the Confederation government in Greene, *Peripheries and Center*, 153–80.
[86]On the economic impact of the Revolution and independence see: Lindert and Williamson, *Unequal Gains*, 77–95.
[87]Levy, *Ages of American Capitalism*, 67.

the British Empire in control of Canada to the north, the Spanish to the south and west, and France always lurking, the threat of reabsorption into a European empire was quite real. There was too the danger posed by the substantial population of those who held true title to the land in the West—Native Americans—likely somewhere between 600,000 and 1.5 million, a significant number when compared to a US population of about 2.5 million.[88] Thus, the mid-1780s saw increasing calls for some sort of revision to the structure of the central government in order to better preserve the infant Confederation.

The full story of the framing and adoption of the US Constitution needn't occupy us much here. Instead, we simply need to highlight how—despite the formal decolonization of the United States—the new national government was a product both of imperial fears and imperial aspirations. The imperial fears are evident from the paragraph above, there was a clear need for a stronger national government that could coordinate the military and economic policy of the states in such a way that allowed them to retain their political independence and respond to their economic dependance on their former imperial masters. By establishing a strong central government, with the ability to tax, regulate commerce, and establish an army and navy, the Constitution would do just that.[89] The political debates that roiled the United States in the 1790s and afterwards were as much about how to best establish economic independence as they were anything else. Those associated with Thomas Jefferson and the "Democratic-Republican" party tended to favor a limited national economic policy, believing that establishing a nation of independent yeomen farmers would best ensure true independence. The "Federalist" party, meanwhile, and its leading intellectual and political force—Alexander Hamilton—believed positive engagement with the British Empire, and a careful national fiscal and tariff policy, could help the United States develop its own trading and manufacturing advantages and thus replicate Britain's rise. Both parties believed their policies would help the United States establish a true independence, safe from "Old World" meddling.[90]

When it came to imperial aspirations, there was a great deal more unanimity, and it's often forgotten today how much the question of what would later be called "westward expansion" informed the framing of the Constitution. The need for a unified policy for disposing of western lands, and a unified authority capable of administering that disposal, was central to the perceived need for a new government. The Treaty of Paris had granted the United States lands considerably more vast than those it

---

[88]Paul Frymer, *Building an American Empire: The Era of Territorial and Political Expansion* (Princeton: Princeton University Press, 2017), 40.
[89]Greene, *Peripheries and Center*, 181–209.
[90]Hopkins, *American Empire*, 129–35, 142–72.

actually controlled—while most Americans lived east of the Appalachian Mountains, US territory under the treaty stretched west to the Mississippi River, and north and south to today's states of Minnesota and Mississippi. Much of this territory was occupied by Native Americans, particularly in the Great Lakes region, which had welcomed many of the Indigenous refugees who had retreated from the advance of white settlement over the previous century.[91] As Pontiac's War indicated, Native power in the region remained considerable, undermining American claims to sovereignty. All told, contrary to our tendency to imagine the young United States as the only independent polity in North America, it was in fact but one part of a collection of different sovereign communities near as complicated as any in Europe.[92] Despite what the United States' claimed, it inhabited a shared continent. As one Seneca leader complained to New York's leadership, "you tell us your Country is within the line of the States ... this surprises us, for we had thought our Lands were our own."[93]

White settlers, however, had little respect for Native boundaries, as had been the case for centuries. They continued to stream westward in order to secure their own farms and fortunes. Few white Americans, elite or otherwise, felt that it was wrong for them to do so—all believed that the United States' claim to those lands was superior to those of its Native inhabitants and, moreover, many believed that their sale was essential to the financial health of the nation and its citizens. As one Rhode Island legislator put it in 1784, "the western world opens an amazing prospect as a national fund ... it is equal to our debt" and "as source of future population, [and] strength, it is a guaranty of our independence."[94] Yet, the orderly conquest of so vast a territory was a massive undertaking, not least because Native Americans possessed enough power to threaten the new republic's security. Writing as "Publius" in *Federalist 25*, Alexander Hamilton noted that "Indian nations in our neighborhood do not border on particular states but encircle the Union from Maine to Georgia" and might on their own or "instigated by Spain or Britain" strike against its settlements. A strong government capable of mounting a national, rather than state by state, defense was thus an absolute necessity.[95]

In addition to a common defense, a body capable of coordinating the rush westward was essential too. Large landholders on paper like Washington, Jefferson, and Madison had to contend with a maze of contradictory claims and counterclaims. Land speculators staked claims to land regardless

---

[91]On Native communities in the Great Lakes region see: Blackhawk, *Rediscovery of America*, 106–38.
[92]Hämäläinen, *Indigenous Continent*, 318–26.
[93]Blackhawk, *Rediscovery of America*, 184.
[94]Frymer, *Building an American Empire*, 44.
[95]Alexander Hamilton, "The Federalist No. 25," in *The Federalist Papers* (Nashville: Nelson Books, 2014).

of other claimants, while squatters met their would-be landlords with "defiance, under the claim of pre-occupancy," as Washington complained to Henry Knox after touring his lands in the Ohio Valley in 1784.[96] Adding to the confusion was a lack of centralized policy for negotiating with Native Americans. Though the Articles technically granted the national government the sole right of "managing all affairs with the Indians," it could do so only so long as "the legislative right of any state, within its own limits, be not infringed or violated."[97] Given that a number of different states claimed western lands, this contradictory language left Congress with limited real authority. Thus, chaos reigned as settlers claimed land—and states like New York concluded treaties—without reference to the national government. The result was confusion, ignored provisions, and regular outbreaks of violence.[98]

The latter—the potential for dangerous and expensive conflicts with Native Americans—hung over the entire "frontier." While Washington and some other elite easterners did believe that Native Americans had some basic rights to their land that white Americans had to respect (more on this in Chapter 2), they feared violence most of all. Not unlike the British in 1763, they began to look for ways to limit settlement. They did not wish to stop it by any means, but to instead bring more order to a seemingly inexorable wave of migration that saw more than one hundred thousand new settlers move across the Appalachians in the years following the Revolution. The Confederation government seemed entirely unable to control the situation—and this was not for lack of trying.[99] In 1787, the Congress established the Northwest Ordinance, a landmark in the history of American expansion, which established clear rules for converting unincorporated lands into territories and then, eventually, states. In a critical precedent, it suggested that these new states could enter the union on an equal basis with the existing states. This would have a significant impact on the character of US imperial expansion over the subsequent century, yet the legislation initially did little to help improve the situation on the frontier. Settlers were unwilling to grant the national government authority to regulate them—"Congress is not empowered to forbid" settlement, one group told a Congressional representative in 1785.[100] This resistance reached levels where national leaders worried that rural discontent might eventually explode into outright separatism and potentially an alliance with a foreign power. "The touch of a feather would turn them any way," wrote Washington of the Western

---

[96]Blackhawk, *Rediscovering America*, 197.
[97]See the transcription of the Articles provided by the US National Archives and Records Administration: https://www.archives.gov/milestone-documents/articles-of-confederation
[98]Blackhawk, *Rediscovering* America, 187–93.
[99]Blackhawk, *Rediscovering America*, 203.
[100]Blackhawk, *Rediscovering America*, 192.

settlers.[101] Rufus King feared that a nation already separated "by a vast and extensive chain of mountains" would stay separated on the grounds of "interest and convenience." The "feeble policy of our government will not be able to unite them."[102]

Thus, the story of the Constitution begins not only with a desire to form a "more perfect Union"—as the preamble states—but to form a more effective agent of empire. It was part of an effort to transform a country that had long been on the periphery of the British world into, in historian Jack P. Greene's words, "a new center."[103] It was in the chaos of the West that the failures of the Articles of Confederation were made most clear, and it was there that the authority of the new "federal government" established by the 1789 Constitution was perhaps most felt. The Constitution, as Ned Blackhawk writes, "gave the national government centralized powers over land management, taxation, [and] Indian affairs … " while also authorizing "Congress to establish a standing army," all needs the country had principally because of the demands of westward expansion.[104] Indeed, given the habits born from centuries of colonial self-government and the libertarian impulses of the Revolutionary era, it's hard to see the states establishing such a strong central government otherwise. With the establishment of the Constitution, the impulse to continue the original colonial mission won out over the desire for local autonomy. While it would be a mistake to overstate the power of these new institutions—as we will see in the second chapter, the government under the Constitution was stronger, but not necessarily strong—it proved enough to unleash the empire of liberty.

For Native Americans, therefore, the establishment of the Constitution was yet another in a long series of disasters that had befallen them since those strange crosses had first appeared in the forests of the Northeast. It helped ensure that a new power would rise in North America, one which believed it had the right to determine what course the continent's transition from European to local rule would take—one which also believed that it was its mission to bring "civilization" to the wilderness, and in doing so, extinguish the Indigenous world.

It was not just Native Americans who had reason to be concerned. Spain's Ambassador to France, the Count d'Aranda, wrote home worried about the survival of Spain's American possessions. "A day will come," he wrote, when the United States, "will be a giant, even a colossus," and "we shall watch with grief," its "tyrannical existence."[105] The expansion of that would-be colossus is the subject of our next two chapters.

---

[101]Frymer, *Building an American Empire*, 46.
[102]Frymer, *Building an American Empire*, 46.
[103]Greene, *Peripheries and Center*, 131.
[104]Blackhawk, *Rediscovering America*, 204.
[105]Blackhawk, *Rediscovering America*, 191.

CHAPTER TWO

"Afflictions of Longstanding": Native Americans and the Decolonization of the United States

Alexis de Tocqueville, the French aristocrat and scholar, is best remembered today as an early champion of American progress. This he certainly was—his famous 1835 book, *Democracy in America*, is full of praise for the social and political culture of the young United States, seeing in white American society a glimpse of a more egalitarian future for all of humanity. The Frenchman was also an honest chronicler, however, willing to record whatever fell under his gaze as he toured the country between 1831 and 1832, whether flattering to the United States or not. This included a scene from Memphis in the winter of 1831. There, he observed a group of Choctaw refugees attempting to cross the Mississippi River. These Indigenous residents of central Mississippi had recently been forced from their homes by the "Indian Removal Act"—passed by Congress in 1830—and were making for lands promised to them in the trans-Mississippi West. The conditions were brutal. As de Tocqueville described it, the winter:

> that year ... was exceptionally severe; the snow was hard on the ground, and huge masses of ice drifted on the river. The Indians brought their families with them; there were among them the wounded, the sick, newborn babies, and old men on the point of death. They had neither tents nor wagons, but only some provisions and weapons ... the sight

will never fade from my memory. Neither sob nor complaint rose from the silent assembly. Their afflictions were of long standing, and they felt them to be irremediable.[1]

One might naturally wonder how a witness to such suffering could otherwise be so enthused about the society and government that caused it. Yet this de Tocqueville was, and for a relatively simple reason. For him—as for most white Americans—the destruction of Indigenous North America was not some avoidable side effect of human progress; it was the substance of civilizational advance itself.[2]

In this chapter, we will continue our study of how empire, hierarchy, and the idea of "civilization" shaped the history of the United States as it decolonized—separating from the British Empire and then struggling to secure a true independence. As we learned from the last chapter, the United States emerged from the American Revolution not as an opponent of empire, but as its newest practitioner, seeking to consolidate control over the lands granted to it by the 1783 Treaty of Paris. Though there were internal disagreements over the form that this new empire would take, Americans saw expansion as a natural path for both economic and ideological reasons. The primary targets of this project of decolonization through colonization were the Indigenous peoples of North America. Much of the land claimed by the United States was owned on European treaty paper alone and was—in reality—the property of sovereign, self-governing Native American communities. Contrary to our tendency to think of the United States as the only locally governed polity in North America after the Revolution, it was instead but one among many. The new republic and its citizens thus worked assiduously to assert control over these neighbors, relying on claims of their supposedly superior civilizational status for justification.

As this chapter will document, this oft-brutal assault on the Indigenous world played an essential role in the decolonization of the United States. Struggling with many of the problems faced by "postcolonial" states as they gain formal independence, Americans both in and outside of the government routinely saw solutions in attacks on Native American sovereignty.[3] While somewhat more peaceful strategies for absorbing

---

[1] Alexis de Tocqueville, *Democracy in America*, J.P. Mayer and Max Lerner, eds., George Lawrence trans. (New York: Harper and Row, 1966), 298–9.
[2] De Tocqueville would later see US removal policies as a model for French colonialism in Algeria: Claudio Saunt, *Unworthy Republic: The Dispossession of Native Americans and the Road to Indian Territory* (New York: W.W. Norton and Co., 2020), xvi.
[3] For more on the term "postcolonial" see: footnote 16 in the Introduction.

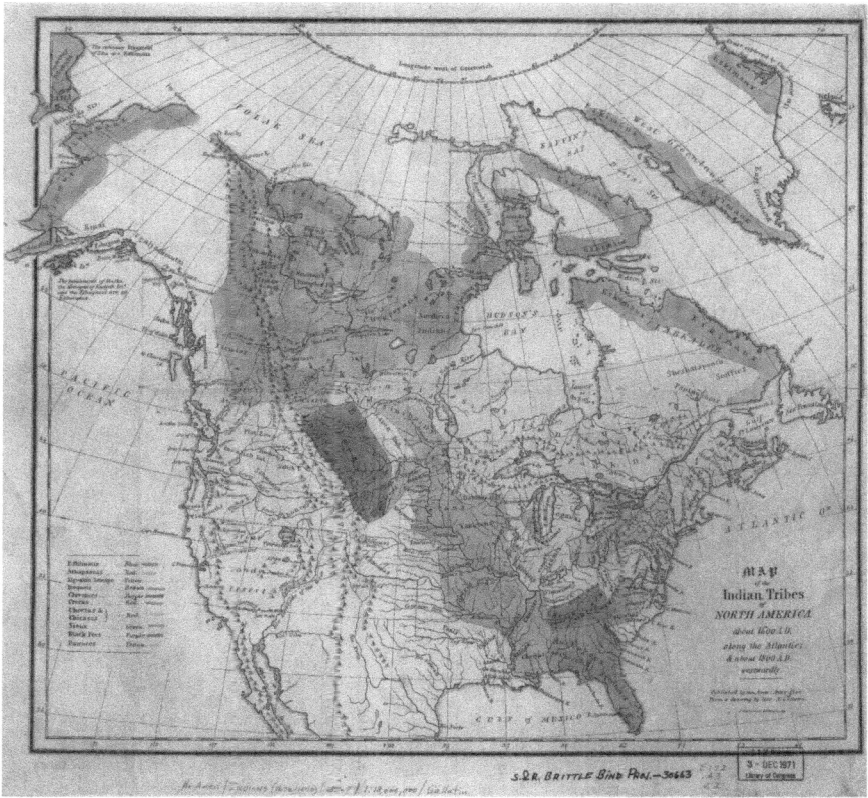

FIGURE 4 *An 1836 map by the ethnologist and politician Albert Gallatin, purporting to depict the various Native American groups of North America. Though imperfect, it effectively reveals the political diversity of the continent in the early nineteenth century, a reality hidden by maps that exclusively show US and European territorial claims.*

Indigenous America were tried, in the end it was "Indian fighting" that provided the essential route to economic, political, and cultural unity for the young republic, helping to establish its place in a competitive world-system. It was only through violent imperial expansion that the United States was able to begin to truly assert its own independence—making the story of its relationship with Native Americans essential to understanding its approach to the ends of empire in later years. For Native Americans—like those weary Choctaws whose suffering so moved de Tocqueville—the American Revolution was therefore less a new departure in the history of human freedom and more another evolution in their afflictions of longstanding.

The United States and an Indigenous Continent[4]

The young United States was in a perilous place during its first decades of existence as an independent country. To start with, it was a relatively weak, primarily agricultural state with almost no permanent military forces in a world dominated by powerful empires with large armies and navies like that of Britain and France. This contrast in power was only enhanced when those two titans of the age resumed their struggle for supremacy over the Atlantic World soon after the end of the American Revolution. Following the outbreak of the French Revolution in 1789, and continuing with Napoleon's rise to power as France's "Emperor," the British and French engaged in nearly a quarter century of globe-spanning warfare.[5] These wars left the United States particularly vulnerable, as both of the great powers of the era saw the new North American state as a potential tool for their advantage—one they were quite willing to see dissolved or dismembered if it suited their purposes. Each too felt it had something of a claim on American sovereignty, the British for obvious reasons and the French because of the 1778 alliance they had formed with the colonies during the Revolutionary War.

Formal independence had not withdrawn the United States from the expanding cultural and economic system that had developed around the Atlantic over the previous three centuries, and this put significant pressure on its leaders to take steps to ensure the United States retained and improved its place within that system's hierarchies.[6] This, of course, had been a key reason for the American Revolution in the first place, a consequence of British efforts to use trade and taxation policy to further subordinate the colonies to London. While American policy toward Britain, and Europe more generally, remained critically important, nothing was more essential to the young republic's efforts to control its destiny than its relations with its Native American neighbors. Few would suffer more as a result.

Roughly one million (and as many as 1.5 million) Native Americans lived in the lands claimed by the United States subsequent to the Treaty of Paris.[7] These ranged from surviving enclaves in the East—amounting to no more than 7,000 people in the early nineteenth century (excluding Georgia)—to the much more populous communities living north of the Ohio River and around the Great Lakes. There were also substantial populations in today's Mississippi, Alabama, Tennessee, and Georgia. Contrary to what many white Americans at the time—and later—would claim, this Indigenous population was no longer in decline. Though the colonial onslaught and the diseases

---

[4]The term is borrowed from Hämäläinen, *Indigenous Continent*.
[5]For more on the global scope of the conflict see: Alexander Mikaberidze, *The Napoleonic Wars: A Global History* (Oxford: Oxford University Press, 2022).
[6]Wallerstein, *The Modern World-System III*, 247–58.
[7]Frymer, *Building an American Empire*, 40.

it brought with it had substantially reduced the overall Native population in North America in the two hundred years following the settlement of Jamestown, this decline had halted and even begun to reverse around the dawn of the nineteenth century.[8] The arrival of the newcomers had irretrievably destroyed the old Indigenous world, to be sure, but the Native American communities of North America had not all simply disappeared. In some ways, America's closest Indigenous neighbors were thriving to a degree not seen in centuries.

In the South, for example, some tribes like the Cherokee had begun to adopt European lifestyles, establishing family farms and, in some cases, even large plantations employing the labor of enslaved Blacks. Many others in the South and across the "Old Northwest" continued to utilize more traditional Native American economic practices adapted to post-European contact realities.[9] Particularly vibrant was the area the historian Ned Blackhawk—borrowing from the Ojibwe-Scotch-Irish poet, Bamewawagezhikaquay—has called the "Native Inland Sea," a region that extended from the Dakotas and the northern banks of the Mississippi to the southern shores of the Great Lakes and the western reaches of the Ohio River Valley. This diverse region encompassed a variety of Siouan- and Algonquin-speaking peoples and villages—as well as descendants of refugees from further east—and was marked both by occasionally devastating inter-tribal warfare and by continued Indigenous self-determination and resistance to European and US rule. This was the heartland of Pontiac's movement against the British, and it still retained much of the autonomy it had gained in that war as the nineteenth century dawned.[10] In fact, life for many Native people in the region was reasonably prosperous, often more so than it was for white settlers back beyond the Ohio River.[11] The same was the case for the Cherokees and the other "five civilized tribes," as they were sometimes called, to the south. Indigenous America was anything but on the road to extinction in the late eighteenth and early nineteenth centuries.

Indeed, we use terms like Native American "communities" or "tribes" here advisedly, as only a prejudice toward European-style forms of government would see them as something other than the sovereign political entities which they were, even if they were not truly "states" in the way we usually understand the term. Indigenous Americans of the time generally practiced a decentralized politics that depended on personal relationships built around kinship, including both biological and imagined family relationships. Rather than having a rigid and unitary hierarchy that ascended toward a single final authority—as was often the case with Europeans—Native Americans

---

[8]Saunt, *Unworthy Republic*, 16.
[9]Saunt, *Unworthy Republic*, 11–16.
[10]Blackhawk, *Rediscovery of America*, 102–38.
[11]Blackhawk, *Rediscovery of America*, 212.

instead had overlapping webs of hierarchy and obligation, with multiple influential leaders rather than an all-powerful "chief" (which was almost invariably a concept invented by Europeans misreading the nature of Indigenous politics). These leaders also did not exert authority in the sense of giving commands and expecting them to be obeyed; they instead asserted influence among their real and fictive kin.[12]

Key to developing this influence was the control of material goods, including food, weapons, and luxury items. These were not stockpiled to be used as payment for services rendered—as one is used to in the European context—but were channeled in the direction of one's followers. Indigenous leaders were, in this sense, patrons whose influence was directly related to their ability to provide clients with material goods. As one seventeenth-century Dutch settler wrote of Algonquin communities on the East Coast, "the chiefs are generally the poorest among them … instead of receiving anything, they were made to give to the populace."[13] This gift-giving created webs of obligation between the leader and his clients, with the latter expected to show some deference to the former's wishes in making communal decisions and potentially also provide a return tribute of goods or labor.[14] Not all such relationships were voluntary, of course. Some—particularly those between different tribal communities—were forged through violence and war, yet within many tribes and confederations political decision-making was communal and participatory.[15] This decentralization was such that it offers part of the explanation for why the post-Columbian history of North America proceeded so differently from that in Central and South America—unlike those more densely populated regions encountered by the Spanish in the sixteenth century, there was no main king or power center for the Conquistadors to invade in North America. Indigenous lands had to be conquered piece by piece and held with force if they were to be controlled at all—a reality that helped slow and eventually stall the Spanish advance beyond Mexico into what is today the Southwest United States.[16]

The arrival of Europeans in the Northeast had, of course, dramatically transformed the Indigenous political world, but it retained many of these same patterns of organization. Newly important for those networks of gift-giving and patronage was access to European markets and manufactured goods. A leader who was able to give European metal tools, glass beads (valued much like branded luxury goods are today), and—especially—firearms to his clients gained considerable prestige and influence, in some cases upending existing distributions of power. The Iroquois League, of today's upstate New York, for example, established a profitable

---

[12]Hämäläinen, *Indigenous Continent*, 24.
[13]Quoted in Richter, *Facing East from Indian Country*, 52.
[14]Richter, *Facing East from Indian Country*, 52.
[15]Richter, *Facing East from Indian Country*, 139–40, 170–1.
[16]Hämäläinen, *Indigenous Continent*, 45–6.

relationship with Dutch traders in the seventeenth century—whom they called "*Kristoni*" or "metal maker"—giving them access to European weapons and other metal goods. This they soon translated to a position of dominance not just in relation to their Native neighbors, but, for a time, over the Dutch colony as well.[17]

Diplomacy and trade, however successful, could not prevent the devastation wrought by diseases like smallpox, which hit the Iroquois hard throughout the seventeenth century. Yet, Iroquoian power in the region was such that, in response, they were able to replenish some of their losses via attacks on their Indigenous neighbors like the Wyandots, many of whom were seized and taken back as captive to the League's villages. These "mourning wars" were part ritual—some of the captives seized were tortured and killed in symbolic assertions of Iroquoian supremacy—and part an effort at repopulating the tribe. Most taken in this way were ritually adopted into the Iroquoian community, swelling its numbers.[18] By the 1660s, Pekka Hämäläinen writes, "war captives ... made up more than half the Iroquoian population," while their power was such that thousands of other Native Americans were left as refugees, fleeing westward to avoid Iroquoian wrath.[19] Even after the Dutch withdrew from North America, the League remained a force to be reckoned with by skillfully managing their relationship with both Britain (which took over the Dutch colony) and France in order to maintain their access to trans-Atlantic trade.[20]

Other Native groups did much the same, allying with France or Britain as proved opportune. French power in North America was in fact almost wholly dependent on their alliances with dozens of tribes—including at various times the Huron, Illini, and Choctaws—without whom the scattered French settlements along the St. Lawrence River were vulnerable to British or enemy Native American attack.[21] In this way, the Native Americans of eastern North America managed to survive the twin disasters of the European invasion and the related spread of smallpox, maintaining their sovereignty, while controlling considerable amounts of territory in area bounded by the Appalachian Mountains, the Mississippi River, the Gulf of Mexico, and the Great Lakes. However, the conditions that allowed for this continued assertion of Native power diminished quickly over the second half of the eighteenth century. First, defeat in the Seven Years War removed France from North America, leaving the French Empire's Indigenous allies in the lurch—some were reportedly "in despair" when they learned the terms of the 1763 Treaty of Paris ceding French claims in North America.[22]

---

[17]Hämäläinen, *Indigenous Continent*, 82
[18]Hämäläinen, *Indigenous Continent*, 100–7.
[19]Hämäläinen, *Indigenous Continent*, 107.
[20]Hämäläinen, *Indigenous Continent*, 212–15.
[21]Hämäläinen, *Indigenous Continent*, 267–8.
[22]Hämäläinen, *Indigenous Continent*, 285.

No longer able to play the Europeans against each other, Native Americans still could rely upon the British government—desperate as it was to avoid expensive colonial wars—to counterbalance the interests of the more aggressive and anti-Indigenous colonists (as it did through the Proclamation of 1763). With the defeat of Britain in the American Revolution and the withdrawal of British power to Canada, therefore, Native Americans saw their room for maneuver diminish even further. Still, despite these setbacks, a substantial and autonomous Native American world remained in the early 1800s, firmly planted on millions of acres of land now claimed by the United States, its future far from determined.[23] The United States, it cannot be stressed enough, was not the sole master of the land Britain had given up after the Revolution.

This did not stop the citizens and leaders of the United States from believing it was theirs to control, however. As we will see, the United States government was committed to eliminating the independence of its Native American neighbors in order to increase its own power and independence. This was attempted first through a process that called for "civilizing" Native people and then—when "civilizing" no longer suited white purposes—via an alternate program to forcefully remove them across the Mississippi River. While we speak of the US government here, it would be a mistake to imagine it as an entity identical to the "nation-states" of today or of Westphalian imaginings. It was closer to an empire in its structure and in its distribution of power, and a relatively weak empire at that. The Constitution of course had famously located ultimate sovereignty over the United States in "the people," and had also planted final political authority in the federal government headquartered (starting in 1790) in Washington, DC. Yet, underneath there remained numerous sub-sovereignties in the individual US states. In addition, there were the citizens themselves and, in particular, the relatively independent settler communities of the frontier, who not infrequently defied the will of their government—a government which some could in turn influence through voting (unlike their colonial predecessors' relationship with the imperial government in London). This influence only increased as political system further opened up to white males in the 1820s and after.

Empire, Civilization, and the Postcolonial United States

As the federal government's lack of authority on the frontier might suggest, the United States faced many of the same difficulties other postcolonial

---

[23]Saunt, *Unworthy Republic*, 3–26.

states would confront later in the nineteenth and twentieth centuries: economic vulnerability along with political and cultural disunity.[24] On the economic front, the people and government of the new United States could not restructure overnight a century of agricultural and business practices premised upon inclusion in the British Empire. The United States thus retained essentially the same subsistence and export economy that it had during the colonial era, making it particularly vulnerable to outside shocks and in a dependent position in relation to European—and especially British—manufacturers. Any decline in the ability to sell excess commodities abroad threatened the country with recession, while the need to purchase manufactured goods from elsewhere meant that capital tended to head eastward back across the Atlantic, leaving the colonies-turned-states chronically short of hard currency. The entire situation gave the British government significant power over its former colonies, a fact clearly demonstrated by the devastating recession that followed the end of the Revolutionary War and the closing of British ports to American commerce.[25]

As a new political entity, the United States lacked the long-established habits of political loyalty that helped ensure that policy divisions didn't lead to the fragmentation of the country along the lines of regional or economic interest. Though the new constitution did create a stronger federal authority to coordinate the various states, it also raised the stakes in the contest for control of that government, with disunion a constant threat from those out of power. With the dissolution of the British Empire, the only remaining political institutions of any respectable age were at the state and local level, which is where the loyalty of many Americans remained. These political realities were reflected culturally as well, as Americans from north to south wondered what practices, rituals, and behaviors unified the country as a whole—other, that is, than those inherited from Britain. As Kariann Yokota writes, Americans "waged" a "struggle to unbecome British without a cohesive sense of what they would become afterwards."[26] Debates over the government, character, and culture of the new republic thus often threatened to pull it apart along fault lines between rich and poor, north and south, and east and west.[27] There was no shortage of separatist schemes floated—and even tried—in the decades following the Revolution, particularly along the frontier. The leaders of the short-lived "state" of Franklin (in today's eastern Tennessee), for example, went so far as to correspond with

---

[24]Haynes, *Unfinished Revolution*; Hopkins, *American Empire*, 142–90; Wallerstein, *The Modern World-System III*, 227–38; Yokota, *Unbecoming British*.
[25]See the discussion in Chapter 1.
[26]Yokota, *Unbecoming British*, 11. See also, Haynes, *Unfinished Revolution*.
[27]Blackhawk, *Rediscovery of America*, 201–4.

Spanish diplomats about a potential alliance in an attempt to secure their recognition from a reluctant federal government.[28]

All these postcolonial difficulties were well illustrated in the negotiations with Britain for what came to be called "Jay's Treaty," signed in London for the United States by John Jay in 1794 and ratified by the Senate in 1795. Sent to London by President Washington (in office: 1789–97) and Secretary of the Treasury Alexander Hamilton, Jay was charged with negotiating a number of issues that had been left outstanding by the Treaty of Paris as well as new problems that arose from the renewal of war between Britain and France. For many Americans the most salient of these—the continued presence of British troops in forts on US territory in the West, and the interception of American commerce and impressment of American sailors on the high seas—were those that seemed an affront to American claims of sovereignty and independence. For Jay and Washington's government, however, the key was opening British ports to American trade, which they—rightly—believed was essential to revitalizing the postcolonial US economy. As British exports continued to dominate North American markets, the US export trade to the Caribbean and the British Isles, so vital to the growth of American wealth in the colonial era, remained stymied by London's trade policies. With his country divided, mired in a recession, and militarily weak, Jay had little to offer the British in return and yet managed to secure the removal of British troops from the West. He also negotiated a commercial treaty granting the United States "most favored nation" status and access to British Caribbean markets (though with some limits on gross tonnage). Much else was left unresolved, however, and to many among the divided public at home, "Jay's concessions smacked of subservience," as the historian George Herring put it.[29] The "damned arch traitor" Jay was burned in effigy across the country, while angry crowds denounced the treaty (Hamilton was even hit by a rock during an appearance in New York). Opposition figures like Thomas Jefferson seethed over an agreement he saw as a "monument of folly and venality," whose negotiators had "had their heads shorn by the harlot England."[30]

Clearly, the American Revolution had not entirely removed the United States from the hierarchies of empire or produced a fully unified and decolonized the United States. The new republic instead remained embedded in a trans-Atlantic economic system that put significant limits on the extent of US independence. As the furor over the Jay Treaty suggests, differing

---

[28]Kevin T. Barksdale, *The Lost State of Franklin: America's First Secession* (Lexington: University of Kentucky Press, 2009), 145–61.
[29]George C. Herring, *From Colony to Superpower: U.S. Foreign Relations since 1776* (New York: Oxford University Press, 2008), 78; Wallerstein, *The Modern World-System III*, 231, 247.
[30]Herring, *From Colony to Superpower*, 77–8.

visions for how to overcome those limits were at the heart of the political divisions of the post-Revolutionary age. The two main political coalitions that developed in the early years of the country, the "Federalists" and the "Republicans" (or "Democratic-Republicans"), represented different regional and economic interests each with their own ideas for how best to secure truer independence for the United States.[31] The Federalists drew their greatest political support from the East and in the North, particularly among those tied to the nation's merchant, financial, and manufacturing sectors. Under the guidance of Hamilton, the Federalists looked to draw the country closer to its old imperial masters in order to follow in Britain's footsteps. They sought to consolidate further power in the federal government and take stronger control of the nation's finances and economy. From there, they could leverage the returns from a restoration of the triangle trade with Britain and trigger what would later be called "Smithian" economic growth. Named for the Scottish philosopher Adam Smith (1723–90), Smithian growth entails an accelerating form of economic development that produces a greater division of labor, increased economic diversity, and growing accumulations of capital. The Federalists hoped that by establishing a permanent public debt, stimulating the domestic banking industry, and using tariffs and infrastructure improvements to spur US manufacturing, they could wean the United States off its reliance on British exports, building a wealthier, more resilient, and more independent economy. This, in turn, would give the government greater ability to raise revenue and borrow at reasonable rates, thus increasing its capacity to build ships, levy troops, and more effectively compete with the European powers.[32]

Republicans like Thomas Jefferson and James Madison, on the other hand, imagined a very different path for the country's decolonization and development. Their party was most popular in the South and West, among both frontiersmen and established large planters. Skeptical of Hamiltonian centralization and wary of tariffs, Republicans wanted to keep trade freer and authority relatively diffused in the hands of state and local officials. For them, greater US independence would come not from diversified growth but from white yeomen farmers overspreading the land westward. As landowners and citizens, the ideal self-reliant Republican farmer would fear neither the supposed tyranny of London nor of Washington. Each would be equal to his fellow white male countrymen and each would be able to rely on the fruits of his own labor for sustenance (insulating him from vagaries of global trade). Collectively, meanwhile, these yeomen farmers would be

---

[31] Hopkins, *American Empire*, 129–35, 142–72.
[32] Helleiner, *The Neomercantilists*, 36–41; Levy, *Ages of American Capitalism*, 5–6, 72–7, 84–6; Gordon Wood, *Empire of Liberty: A History of the Early Republic* (New York: Oxford University Press, 2009), 89–139.

able to defend themselves against any enemy via voluntary militias without resort to a standing army.[33]

Despite these differences, both programs for further securing the independence of the United States had one significant thing in common: neither envisioned a place within the country's borders for Native Americans practicing their traditional lifestyles. While the majority of Republican and Federalist elites had a marginally more humane perspective on Indigenous relations than most white Americans on the frontier—more on this in a moment—all believed that national progress and the survival of the United States required the disappearance of Native peoples. As it had been for the first colonists, the dichotomy of "civilized vs. savage" continued to be a powerful way for white Americans to frame their relationship with Native Americans and define their own identity as a group.[34] The conception of civilization this involved had evolved somewhat since the early seventeenth century. Where it had earlier been tied to Englishness, American concepts of civilization took on an increasingly universalist bent in the eighteenth and into the nineteenth century. Americans saw their own—and broader European—patterns of life as not just particular to their own culture but in fact as representative of an endpoint in development for all humanity. Drawing upon ideas derived from British Enlightenment thinkers like John Locke and Thomas Reid—along with Continental figures like the French international legal theorist, Emer de Vattel—this discourse of civilization saw societies that were built around private property, intensive agriculture, and commerce as the most advanced forms of human life. In European and European-American eyes, therefore, Native Americans were at an earlier stage in the development of civilization, because they practiced communal landownership, low-intensity agriculture, and reserved large areas of land for hunting and gathering (rather than divvying it up into cultivated and fenced-off parcels).[35]

This supposed "failure" to utilize the land efficiently proved a key concept for justifying Indigenous dispossession, just as it had in the sixteenth century. Vattel's 1758 work *The Law of Nations*—which was widely read in the United States and broadly informed the country's political conversation—for example, suggested that nations with growing populations had a right to take land as needed from those people, like Native Americans, who (from a European perspective) had not properly developed their territory.[36] John Sevier, the frontiersman, plantation-owner,

---

[33]Levy, *Ages of American Capitalism*, 77–93; Onuf, *Jefferson's Empire*, 53–79; Wood, *Empire of Liberty*, 140–73.
[34]See the discussion in Chapter 1.
[35]Cynthia Cumfer, *Separate Peoples, One Land: The Minds of Cherokees, Blacks, and Whites on the Tennessee Frontier* (Chapel Hill: University of North Carolina Press, 2007), 43.
[36]Cumfer, *Separate Peoples, One Land*, 42–3.

and first governor of Tennessee, for example, wrote in 1798 of Indigenous lands that "by the law of nations, it is agreed that no people shall be entitled to more land than they can cultivate." No "people will sit and starve," he continued, "for want of land to work, when a neighboring nation has much more than they can make use of."[37]

As the historian Patrick Brantlinger has shown, there was a broad consensus amongst Europeans (and their various expatriate descendants around the world) that for these reasons, "primitive" people were actually destined to disappear from the Earth as a whole. The idea of the "vanishing Indian"—as the concept manifested itself in the United States—possessed a great deal of power well into the twentieth century and served as a means for justifying acts of Indigenous dispossession. The inevitable "demise of savagery throughout the world," as Brantlinger writes, was a "massive and rarely questioned consensus." It was "understood and sometimes celebrated as necessary for social progress" while at the same time being mourned by many of the very people doing the most to bring it about.[38] Indigenous disappearance was seen as a result of vaguely defined and disembodied but unstoppable forces, an inevitable consequence of either natural or historical processes beyond human control. Even those most sympathetic to the plight of Native peoples rarely questioned the idea that such traditional patterns of life were doomed in the long run. The "most ardent humanitarianism" Brantlinger writes, "could speak only of preventing future violence and of saving by civilizing the sad remnants of dying races."[39] The preservation of supposedly primitive communities was understood as an impossibility. Such assumptions thus elided the role that white Americans and their colonial ancestors had played in the disappearance of the Native Americans of the East Coast by suggesting it was Native ways of life—their "savagery"—that brought about their removal.[40]

Benjamin Franklin, for example, demonstrated this pattern of thinking while relating a story in his autobiography about negotiations with Native Americans in Pennsylvania. Apologizing for the drunkenness of some of their company, Franklin reported the Natives as saying "the Great Spirit made everything for some use ... when he made rum, he said 'let this be for Indians to get drunk with'." Franklin agreed, and indeed considered it possible that:

> [if] the design of Providence [is] to extirpate these savages in order to make room for cultivators of the earth, it seems not improbable that rum

---

[37]Cumfer, *Separate Peoples, One Land*, 44.
[38]Patrick Brantlinger, *Dark Vanishings: Discourse on the Extinction of Primitive Races, 1800–1930* (Ithaca: Cornell University Press, 2003), 1–2.
[39]Brantlinger, *Dark Vanishings*, 3.
[40]Brantlinger, *Dark Vanishings*, 1–16.

may be the appointed means. It has already annihilated all the tribes who formerly inhabited the sea-coast.[41]

In Franklin's depiction here, Native Americans are not only "savages," but their lack of civilization marks them out as less worthy compared to European "cultivators," destining them for extirpation by a nonhuman force. In addition, they also destroy themselves through their lack of civilized virtues—in this case through a supposedly unhealthy relationship to alcohol. These personal and cultural shortcomings, Franklin suggests, were why Native Americans had largely disappeared from the East—the European invasion of North America apparently played only a minimal role.[42]

The entire history of war, conquest, and ethnic cleansing carried out by the colonists over the preceding centuries thus disappears in such depictions into either the designs of God or the Native's own supposed lack of civilization—removing any fault from Franklin or his fellow white Americans. While the assumption that God, history, or some other form of fate would eventually destroy the Indigenous world was commonplace, there were many variations within that theme. Some tended to highlight racial differences as a key element, suggesting that Native Americans were somehow less human than Europeans. Henry Schoolcraft, a geographer and early anthropologist who served for a time as an "Indian Agent" for the US government, posited in an 1851 book, for example, that there were "two types of human race": one which advanced, the other which declined. Native Americans declined, therefore, because the more progressive white race was superior.[43] Others felt the differences were more related to cultural practices and relative levels of civilizational progress (or what might be later called progress in "modernization"), leaving the door open for the physical, though not cultural, survival of Native communities. Lewis Henry Morgan, for example, another early American anthropologist from New York, believed that it was the responsibility of the US government to help Native Americans move "towards their final elevation to the rights and privileges of American citizens."[44] Despite admiring traditional Native lifestyles—"it would be difficult to describe any political society in which there was less oppression and discontent", he wrote—Morgan still accepted the inevitability of their disappearance. He just believed that if white Americans behaved responsibly toward their Native neighbors, that disappearance would be via the path to civilized life rather than through violent destruction.[45]

All told, the divisions between "savage" Native Americans and "civilized" European-Americans helped forge a sense of unity among US citizens that

---

[41]Brantlinger, *Dark Vanishings*, 47.
[42]Brantlinger, *Dark Vanishings*, 46–7.
[43]Brantlinger, *Dark Vanishings*, 54.
[44]Brantlinger, *Dark Vanishings*, 54.
[45]Brantlinger, *Dark Vanishings*, 55.

might otherwise have been lacking—a unity only further strengthened by violent confrontations between whites and Natives on the frontier. One of the strands that began to tie the young United States together in the late eighteenth and early nineteenth centuries was what Peter Silver has called the "anti-Indian sublime," an almost rapturous evocation in journalism and art of the slaughter of supposedly innocent white settlers in the West.[46] The sublime provided a powerful common language that, as Silver writes, "excelled at sweeping away context," exaggerating the nature of already violent incidents on the frontier to create a myth of common white victimhood. This imagined community of suffering provided a new way to define the country's identity, bringing together a European-American population that otherwise was divided by class, region, politics, Christian denomination, and country of origin.[47] It also had the effect of shifting debate toward more and more extreme methods of securing American control of Indigenous land.

The Civilization Policy and Frontier Colonization

At first, however, a more moderate perspective tended to govern the federal government's policies toward Native Americans—at least in theory. This is not to suggest that the Washington, Adams (1797–1801), and Jefferson administrations (1801–09) didn't intend to shrink the amount of land under Native control, they did. Again, there was broad consensus among white Americans on the necessity of this for the survival and prosperity of the young country. To white Americans, decolonization—to use the word anachronistically—appeared to require colonization. Official policy was instead initially based around the idea that this colonization was best done by the "civilizing" and eventual absorption of Native American communities into the United States.

The approach, as outlined by one of its key architects, Washington's Secretary of War, Henry A. Knox, would involve first establishing clear federal authority over land transfers: Native Americans would only be able to legally sell their land to the government or federally sanctioned private companies. In return, Native Americans would receive cash, stipends, farm equipment, and other tools. These transfers would supposedly help facilitate a switch from the communal, semi-mobile, hunting and agricultural practices of most North American Indigenous communities to European-style intensive agriculture on individually owned farms. Missionaries would also be sent to help instruct Native Americans on how to transition to their new

---

[46]Silver, *Our Savage Neighbors*, xvi–xxvi.
[47]Silver, *Our Savage Neighbors*, 85.

ways of life.⁴⁸ The move to individual farms, the logic went, would free up additional land (such farms required less room than traditional Indigenous lifestyles) which could then be used by white settlers, producing a carefully managed transition to a settled continent for both whites and Natives. To its architects, the approach had much to recommend it both morally and practically.

The moral reasons were twofold, on the one hand a great many of the country's governing class adopted views like those of Lewis Henry Morgan: Native Americans were fellow humans deserving of decent treatment. "That Indians possess the natural rights of man ... cannot be denied," wrote Knox in 1789. A "nation solicitous of establishing its character on the broad base of justice," he continued in a letter to Washington, "would not only hesitate at, but reject every proposition to benefit itself, by the injury of a neighboring community, however contemptible and weak it might be."⁴⁹ On the other, though the United States claimed ultimate sovereignty over Native lands, many in the government believed that Native American groups still had a "sacred" or otherwise exclusive right to occupy the lands in their possession. As Secretary of State Jefferson put it in a letter to the British Ambassador to the United States in 1792, the United States held exclusive rights over its lands as far as other white states were concerned—"an invasion of those limits by other white nations [would be] an act of war"—yet those claims gave white Americans "no right of soil against native possessors."⁵⁰

In addition to these moral reasons, there were perceived practical benefits to the "civilizing" policy as well. Knox hoped that direct federal control over land transfers would mitigate the frontier chaos described in the last chapter—as individual settlers, private land companies, and states concluded their own land "treaties" with Native Americans, without consulting each other or even taking the time to ensure that the Indigenous leaders they worked with possessed the requisite authority to speak for their communities.⁵¹ The primary concern here was limiting the almost constant settler-Native violence on the frontier, conflicts which threatened to drag the federal government into wars it could ill afford to fight, and which also might easily trigger British, French, or Spanish intervention. As Knox wrote to Washington in August of 1789, the "powerful tribes of Indians" in the Southeast—including the Muscogee, Cherokees, and Seminoles—"amounting to probably fourteen thousand fighting men" were "worthy of serious attention of the government."⁵² Steps had to be taken, he continued,

---

⁴⁸Anthony F.C. Wallace, *Jefferson and the Indians: The Tragic Fate of the First Americans* (Cambridge, MA: Harvard University Press, 1999), 165–70.
⁴⁹Francis Paul Prucha, *The Great Father: The United States Government and the American Indians* (Lincoln: University of Nebraska Press, 1984), 59.
⁵⁰Wallace, *Jefferson and the Indians*, 175.
⁵¹Prucha, *Great Father*, 48–9, 52–6; Wallace, *Jefferson and the Indians*, 165–71.
⁵²Prucha, *Great Father*, 53.

"to attach them firmly to the United States," lest their hostility lead to their partnering with "the Colonies of an [sic] European power, which ... may one day become an enemy of the United States."[53] Even absent European intervention, Knox and Washington worried that frontier violence could explode into a general Native-white conflict that would require the United States to wage a war of extermination against the Native Americans. Such a war would not only be expensive, it would besmirch the honor of the United States.[54] The government thus had to ensure that borders were clearly defined and that violations by Natives or whites were punished by force. "The angry passions of frontier Indians and whites are too easily inflamed by reciprocal injuries, and are too violent to be controlled by the feeble authority of the [local] civil power," Knox wrote, "the sword of the republic only, is adequate to guard a due administration of justice and the preservation of peace."[55] Concerned with showing the European world that the United States was independent, competent, and in control, Washington's government was deeply invested in bringing order to the ever-fractious frontier.

Neither the Washington administration nor its two successors, of course, had any intention of stopping white settlement or preserving Indigenous ownership of their lands. To start, for all its relative increase in power compared to the Articles of Confederation, the Constitutional government still lacked the capacity to halt settlement, nor did its leaders have much will to do so. Many—including Washington, Jefferson, and Madison—were invested in western lands and would only see profit through their further opening to white settlement.[56] All too believed that the nation's future strength lay in the West. For Federalists, white settlers would provide the vast internal market needed to support their planned expansion of domestic manufacturing, while for Republicans those settlers and their independent farms would provide the backbone of the nation's increased independence. Most significantly, none believed that Native ways of life were destined to survive the workings of history and/or God's will for the future. Even those most sympathetic to Native Americans—like Knox—still reflexively believed in the idea that white civilization would inevitably overwhelm and destroy Indigenous peoples wherever it encountered them. "The progress of society, from the barbarous ages to its present degree of perfection," he wrote, showed both that Native Americans were capable of "civilization" but also that, "Indian boundaries ... will be diminished" as "an inevitable consequence of cultivations" by white civilization.[57] The government looked to manage expansion in such a way that it mitigated the costs. "National

---

[53]Prucha, *Great Father*, 53.
[54]Prucha, *Great Father*, 59–60.
[55]Wallace, *Jefferson and the Indians*, 166–7.
[56]See the discussion of this in Chapter 1.
[57]Wallace, *Jefferson and the Indians*, 168.

officials" as the historian Paul Frymer has written, "were self-conscious of their limited authority" and so developed policies "designed to harness the nation's strengths (its increasing population of settlers and citizen soldiers) in order to minimize its weaknesses (a small and weak military and bureaucracy, respectively)."[58]

As should be apparent to the modern reader, the civilization policy, even in its most benign form, was fundamentally a program for what might today be called ethnic cleansing. It dismissed out of hand the idea that Native Americans were entitled to their land or to continue to live as their ancestors had done—civilization had to advance after all, and the United States needed frontier territory to ensure its survival. Native American communities were to be shunted onto smaller and smaller parcels of the least desirable land and surrounding by white settlers and their economic practices. They would either adapt to these new ways of life—their former methods of subsistence no longer possible on such reduced holdings—and disappear into the white population or die out. Knox himself described these as the only two options for the future. Indigenous Americans would civilize or "in a short period the idea of the Indian on this side of the Mississippi will only be found in the pages of the historical."[59] There was no other path US officials were willing to consider.

The overall drift of the civilization policy away from coexistence and uplift and toward the disempowerment and disappearance of Native Americans can perhaps be best seen during the Jefferson administration. Despite his professed concern for Native Americans, Jefferson's primary goal was, as he wrote to General Andrew Jackson, "the preservation of peace [and] obtaining lands."[60] This was necessary in order to secure the independent future of the United States in a hierarchical age. Key to doing so, Jefferson believed, was taking steps to cut Native Americans off from the rest of the world and the potential military or diplomatic support that might come from it. He wanted to, in effect, quarantine Native Americans east of the Mississippi. This was because their ability to resist US expansion was directly tied to their levels of access to manufactured goods they could not usually produce themselves, including firearms and ammunition. While, as we discussed earlier, the strategic situation for Native Americans had deteriorated from the late eighteenth century on, the continued presence at various times of France, Spain, and—especially—Britain in North America meant that Native Americans in the 1790s still had access to weapons, trade, and alliances with countries other than the United States.[61] Thus, in order to try to undersell the British—whose cheaper products were as much a problem

---

[58]Frymer, *Building an American Empire*, 35–6.
[59]Wallace, *Jefferson and the Indians*, 168.
[60]Wallace, *Jefferson and the Indians*, 221.
[61]Hämäläinen, *Indigenous Continent*, 323–6.

for American power on the frontier as they were back east—and tie Native Americans into greater dependency on the United States, the government set up a system of government-financed trading "factories" in Native territory. Generally positioned close to forts, the factory system was an attempt to project federal power into the frontier and steer Native Americans away from non-US sources of trade.[62] As one congressman noted during the 1795 debate over establishing the factories, Native Americans "had common sense enough not to quit [European] allies who supplied them with articles which they wanted, till we also made some effectual establishments of that kind."[63]

Jefferson pushed through a dramatic expansion of the system, increasing both the number of trading posts and their funding. His plan, as he wrote to Governor William Henry Harrison of the Indiana Territory in 1803, was to promote a "disposition to exchange lands" by driving prominent Native Americans into debt. "We shall push our trading houses, and be glad to see the good and influential individuals among them run into debt beyond what the individuals can pay," Jefferson wrote. They would then become, he continued, "willing to lop [their debts] off by a cession of land."[64] This policy frequently bore fruit, for frontier regions were relatively cash poor. As white settlement continued, game became scarcer and scarcer, leaving Native Americans with less to offer in trade. Those who tried to adapt to European-style cultivation, meanwhile, ran into the same problems as their white neighbors: limited frontier infrastructure meant a limited ability to convert any agricultural surplus into cash. With both settlers and Natives competing over the increasingly scarce resources of the frontier, violence continued to be a problem. This too almost inevitably ended up putting more pressure on Natives to make land concessions.[65]

In his quest to further establish the independence of the "empire of liberty," Jefferson pursued such opportunities to gain land via sale and treaty with zeal, and with a clear strategy. He had his representatives focus on obtaining land cessions first along the banks of the major rivers in the West—obtaining over 200,000 square miles through thirty-two treaties—in particular along the eastern bank of the Mississippi and both banks of the Ohio.[66] This helped encircle remaining Native American lands in the East, limiting both their access to international trade and further putting pressure on diminishing reserves of game, all of which were intended to make Indigenous groups more pliant in negotiations. This was, as Anthony Wallace writes, an "essentially military strategy: secure supply lines and encircle the enemy."[67] While Jefferson certainly believed that the civilization

---

[62]See the discussion of the factory system in Prucha, *Great Father*, 115–34.
[63]Prucha, *Great Father*, 116.
[64]Prucha, *Great Father*, 119–25.
[65]Wallace, *Jefferson and the Indians*, 195–205.
[66]Wallace, *Jefferson and the Indians*, 239.
[67]Wallace, *Jefferson and the Indians*, 239.

approach might work, he was also willing to consider more assertive alternatives as long as they satisfied his twin goals of obtaining land and avoiding major wars with Native Americans.[68]

Settlers and the Failure of the Civilization Policy

The wishes of Jefferson and other eastern elites, of course, were far from the only factor determining the success or failure of the civilization policy. Many Native Americans, naturally resisted abandoning their historic ways of living—lifestyles that even some white American observers, as we saw above, believed to be preferable to those in "civilization." On the frontier, European-style agriculture often appeared to be a losing prospect, involving hard work that more often led to debt and poverty than riches and comfort. Some thus shared the sentiment of Onitositah, a leader of the "Overhill" Cherokees of Tennessee, who had remarked in 1777, "much has been advanced on the want of what you term civilization ... we do not yet see the propriety, or practicality of such a reformation, and should be better pleased with beholding the good effect of these doctrines on your own practices."[69] Moreover, when Native Americans, like the Georgia Cherokees, for example, did seek to move toward European-style agriculture, they usually preferred to do so on their own terms, preserving their own cultural distinctiveness, political autonomy, and control of valuable land.[70] The latter undermined the civilization policy's assumptions that civilizing would mean the disappearance of distinct Native American communities and infuriated those whites who continued to believe that Indigenous Americans did not deserve to own good land under any circumstances.

As that might suggest, white settlers too had a strong variety of opinions about the desirability of policies premised on civilizing Native Americans. Some—imbibing the Enlightenment ideas popular among Federalist elites—saw the program as a necessary acknowledgment of a common humanity between Natives and European-Americans. These believed that Native American communities had legitimate claims to sovereignty which needed to be respected, meaning land could only be secured via treaty, sale, or other peaceable agreement. Other settlers, however, carried more negative stereotypes of Indigenous North Americans as irredeemable savages—sometimes informed by personal or ancestral experiences of Native-settler violence as well as the sensationalist accounts of the anti-Indian sublime. This fueled exterminationist rhetoric, where the violent destruction of

---

[68] On Jefferson's views re: the possibility of "civilizing" Native Americans see, Onuf, *Jefferson's Empire*, 18–52.
[69] Cumfer, *Separate Peoples, One Land*, 45.
[70] Blackhawk, *Rediscovering America*, 240–2. Saunt, *Unworthy Republic*, 11–14.

Native Americans was portrayed as the only possible solution to the white need for land. Regardless of their degree of animosity towards their Indigenous neighbors, most settlers saw Native American sovereignty in much the same light as the architects of the civilization policy back in Washington—as fundamentally less than that of white settlers and the United States government. They also felt much more acutely the need to open more land for settlement, leading to frustration with the efforts of the national government, particularly under the Federalists, to slow, structure, and control the settlement of the interior.[71]

Settler encroachment on un-transferred Native land thus proved a significant barrier to the success of the civilization program. While federal law technically prohibited American citizens from settling on Indigenous territory, efforts at enforcement were relatively lax. In 1809, for example, Return J. Meigs, a federal Indian agent, led a column of US troops into Chickasaw land in northern Alabama and removed around 284 white families that were squatting there, while leaving another 5,000 such families undisturbed.[72] This reticence on behalf of federal officials only grew over the course of the Jefferson administration. As Republicans, Jefferson and his allies were much more sympathetic to the settlers than their Federalist predecessors. Relying on votes in the West for success in federal elections, the Republicans showed a natural reluctance to shoot or otherwise molest members of their own political coalition.[73] This was much the case for state governments as well, which were often even more sensitive to popular pressure than was Washington. As a result, some states, like Georgia, for example, proved very aggressive in pursuing their own policies aimed at the elimination of Native landownership, often in defiance of federal officials (more on this in a moment).

For all the differences there were over Indian policy, however, few white Americans dissented from the core assumption that the development and independence of the United States required Indigenous dispossession. Thus, when Jefferson's protégé, James Madison, entered the White House (in office: 1809–17), the chaos on the frontier only worsened and federal will to defy the wishes of settlers correspondingly declined. More and more white Americans headed west, putting greater pressure on the available land. Endemic frontier poverty and continued confusion about treatymaking led to desperation, misunderstanding, and cycles of violence and retribution. In the Indiana territory, the recently concluded Treaty of Fort Wayne (1809) spurred events that followed a predictable pattern. Governor William Henry Harrison managed to force a massive land concession from friendly Lenape and Miami leaders without consulting other Indigenous nations in the area,

---

[71]Cumfer, *Separate Peoples, One Land*, 42–6.
[72]Wallace, *Jefferson and the Indians*, 214.
[73]Wallace, *Jefferson and the Indians*, 217.

the Shawnee in particular. Resentment toward Harrison's treatymaking practices was longstanding—dating back to the Treaty of St. Louis, when Harrison had wrested million acres of land (in today's Missouri, Illinois, and Wisconsin) from Sauk representatives who had not been empowered to negotiate any land cessions at all. Drawing on this anger, a Shawnee who called himself Tenskwatawa or "Open-Door" launched a movement to cleanse Native culture of white influence—rejecting white Americans, according to another Shawnee holy man, as "the scum of the great waters when it was troubled by the evil spirit."[74]

His message soon gained him thousands of followers among the tribes of the Northwest, including Shawnees, Sauks, Lenapes, Kickapoos, Odawas, Wyandots, and others. Joined by his brother Tecumseh—a pragmatic soldier who had been fighting Europeans his whole life—the movement established a base in Prophetstown, a settlement at the junction of the Tippecanoe and Wabash Rivers. They also began negotiating with the British to secure weapons and supplies. Harrison struck first, marching on Prophetstown in 1811 with 1,000 men while Tecumseh was away seeking more followers. Defeating Tenskwatawa in the Battle of Tippecanoe, Harrison burned Prophetstown but did not destroy the movement, which soon came under Tecumseh's influence.[75]

Even before the outbreak of what is sometimes called "Tecumseh's War," and the manifest failure of the civilization policy it represented, the federal government had begun reconsidering its approach to colonizing Indigenous America. In 1803—with the opening of trans-Mississippian land to the United States through the Louisiana Purchase—President Jefferson started to contemplate what would eventually be called "Indian removal." Either civilizing would work, he wrote, and Native Americans "will in time ... incorporate with us as citizens of the United States" or they would have to "remove beyond the Mississippi."[76] As this indicates, what continued to matter most was opening Native territory for white settlement and US economic development. The means for doing so didn't really matter, just so long as they worked. For Jefferson and the other would-be civilizers, therefore, the republican values of the United States did not at all prevent them from viewing the world hierarchically and reserving to themselves the right to determine the future of entire communities of people who did not vote in US elections. The progress of civilization, and US independence, required it.

---

[74]Hämäläinen, *Indigenous Continent*, 367.
[75]Hämäläinen, *Indigenous Continent*, 366–72.
[76]Wallace, *Jefferson and the Indians*, 273.

The War of 1812 and US Decolonization

In 1812 Tecumseh's War became but one theater in a much larger conflict—the War of 1812 (1812–15)—as the entire eastern half of North American descended into the maelstrom of imperialist war. A much more complicated and important conflict than it is usually remembered as today, the War of 1812 was seen in the United States at the time as essentially a "second war for independence," which remains a fair description.[77] Yet, just as the American Revolution was as much a fight *for* empire as it was a battle against empire, the War of 1812 was also just as much about securing imperial supremacy in North America as it was maintaining separation from the British. Before the war, the British Empire, the United States, Native Americans, and to some degree, Spain, competed for control of the continent. By the war's end, the path had been cleared for the United States to become the dominant power in North America.

The full story of the war has been well covered elsewhere, but it's important to note that what began at sea as a question of the rights of American merchant ships and sailors quickly became a battle for control over the frontier in the South and Northwest. Through a combination of luck and skillful diplomacy, the Washington, Adams, and Jefferson administrations had managed to avoid being sucked into the Anglo-French wars discussed at the start of the chapter. However, this had involved enduring numerous insults to American sovereignty and significant damage to vital US overseas trade as both the French and British intercepted American merchant ships. The British added to injury the insult of seizing American sailors and forcing them to serve in the Royal Navy, an act nominally restricted to British subjects hiding on American ships but in reality extending to whomever British officers felt inclined to kidnap. Making matters worse was British support for Native Americans on the frontier, like Tecumseh. The Madison administration hoped that by declaring war on Britain, the United States could solve all these issues in one blow by seizing British Canada and striking against Tecumseh and other British-backed Native Americans. Such steps would weaken British and Indigenous power on the continent and further the quest for full sovereignty for the United States. It was a dangerous gamble. Despite London's preoccupation with Napoleon—and some surprising victories by the infant US Navy—the British ability to assert power in North America remained considerable. The attack on Canada failed, a Royal Navy blockade hampered American commerce, and British forces in Maryland seized and then burned Washington, DC in 1814, forcing

---

[77]J.C.A. Stagg, *The War of 1812: Conflict for a Continent* (Cambridge: Cambridge University Press, 2012), 2; Wallerstein, *The Modern World-System III*, 251.

Madison to flee. In one sense, the United States was very lucky to see the war end with the "status-quo-ante" Treaty of Ghent in December of 1814.[78]

Over the long term, however, the War of 1812 ended up tilting the struggle for control of North America decisively in the United States' favor, highlighting yet again the indispensable role played by war against Native Americans in the American rise to power. The back-and-forth US-Native American conflict in the Northwest was transformed by William Henry Harrison's victory over Tecumseh and an Anglo-Indigenous force in southern Ontario in the Battle of the Thames of October, 1813. Tecumseh was killed in the fighting and his alliance of Northwestern tribes collapsed soon after. In the South, General Jackson used the struggle with Britain as an excuse to intervene in a civil war amongst the Muscogee. There the "Red Sticks"—inspired by Tenskwatawa and Tecumseh's nativism—had rebelled in 1813 against their more pro-American tribal leaders. Violence soon spilled over into white settlements and Jackson marched an army of militia into Muscogee territory, destroying the Red Sticks in the March, 1814 Battle of Horseshoe Bend. He then imposed a victor's peace on the entire tribe, friend and foe alike. The Treaty of Fort Jackson turned over twenty million acres of southern Georgia and central Alabama to the United States, breaking Muscogee power.[79]

Once the war was over, Jackson would pursue Red Stick refugees into Seminole territory in Spanish Florida, where a coalition of runaway slaves and Natives had settled with Spanish acquiescence. Illegally and without Madison's approval, Jackson sacked several Seminole settlements, leading to Spanish protests but little else.[80] These battles in the American interior proved decisive. In the wake of the War of 1812, both the British and the Spanish came to believe that it was best to accommodate the new United States rather than seek North American hegemony. Each abandoned their Native American allies and withdrew. Spain would cede all of Florida to the United States in the 1819 Adams Onis Treaty, while Britain retreated into Canada, beginning a long rapprochement with the United States over the course of the nineteenth century.[81] What remaining ability Native Americans

---

[78]On the War of 1812 see: Herring, *From Colony to Superpower*, 121–33; Donald Hickey, "The Legacy of 1812: How a Little War Shaped the Transatlantic World," *London Journal of Canadian Studies* 28, no. 1 (2021): 1–14; Donald Hickey, *The War of 1812: A Forgotten Conflict* (Chicago: University of Illinois Press, 2012); Stagg, *The War of 1812*; Alan Taylor, *The Civil War of 1812: American Citizens, British Subjects, Irish Rebels, & Indian Allies* (New York: Alfred A. Knopf, 2010).
[79]Michael D. Green, *The Politics of Indian Removal: Creek Government and Society in Crisis* (Lincoln: University of Nebraska Press, 1982), 39–43. Hämäläinen, *Indigenous Continent*, 372–5.
[80]Blackhawk, *Indigenous Continent*, 282–5.
[81]Hickey, "The Legacy of 1812," 10–11.

had after the Revolution to balance Europeans against the United States and maintain access to non-American trade and firearms was now gone. The Indigenous world—as Donald Hickey has summarized it—was now "entirely at the mercy of the expansive young republic."[82]

Democracy, "Indian Removal," and American Power

The War of 1812 therefore proved a watershed moment in the relationship between the United States and its Native American neighbors. US decolonization, and the associated dispossession of Indigenous America, would accelerate in the years following the war, leading to the complete abandonment of the civilization policy and its replacement with a policy of removal through the Indian Removal Act of 1830.

Several material and ideological trends converged in the fifteen years between the Treaty of Ghent and the passage of the Removal Act. One was an increasing consolidation of US national identity as a white, Protestant, republic. The war concluded successfully enough to spur a surge of patriotism, providing heroes, events, and symbols—from Jackson and Harrison, to famous phrases and metaphors like "don't give up the ship" and "Uncle Sam"—around which this nationalism could form. It also handed American politics decisively to the Republicans, largely bringing an end to the Federalists as a relevant force in American politics.[83] While Federalist economic ideas remained in circulation (eventually to be championed by the Whig party in the 1830s) these were now adapted to the more populist, agrarian vision of the Republicans. Protestant religion, an important marker of colonial American identity—though briefly eclipsed by Enlightenment deism among Revolutionary-era elites—regained its political salience, as the revivalist spirit of the "Second Great Awakening" spread widely through the land. These years also saw the further democratization of the political system for white males, as barriers to voting fell across the country. By the end of the 1820s, the United States had built one of the world's first mass democracies. As the political system opened, however ideas about racial and religious eligibility for citizenship tightened around whiteness and Protestantism, making the possibility of Indigenous citizenship—once a core aspiration of the civilization policy—seem all the more remote. "Indian fighting," and the clear line it tended to forge between "red" Native Americans and "white" Americans from

---

[82]Hickey, "The Legacy of 1812," 11
[83]Hickey, "The Legacy of 1812," 8–13.

the United States, played a key role in reinforcing race as part of what culturally defined and unified the country.[84]

The renewed salience of whiteness as a characteristic of US citizenship was also a reflection of the expanding role of slavery in American life, itself a direct result of US policy toward Native Americans. Slavery, as we touched on in the first chapter, had been central to the society and economy of British North America from almost the beginning, a lynchpin of the colonial social hierarchy. For a time around the Revolution there was some speculation about whether slavery was an antiquated system destined to disappear, but this proved a brief and deceptive nadir. With the invention of the cotton gin in 1793 and the restoration of normal trans-Atlantic trade in 1815, US cotton production exploded. The rapprochement with Great Britain following the War of 1812 and the industrialization of the British textile industry then created a seemingly inexhaustible British demand for American-grown cotton and a similarly infinite demand for land to grow it and slaves to harvest it. The expansion of cotton cultivation in the decades following the war thus helped power the confiscation of Indigenous lands.[85] The material pressures this created pushed white Americans to free up more land for cotton production at the same time that ideological systems that highlighted whiteness hardened, making Native Americans appear less entitled to resist encroachment – each impulse, material and ideological, reinforced the other, driving the wheels of American expansion.

No one better exemplified all these trends—slavery, nationalism, frontier expansion, and white male democracy alike—than the leading advocate for "Indian Removal," Andrew Jackson. Elected president in 1828 (and in office until 1837), the former general and frontiersman was also a successful cotton plantation owner, who at the time he was elected was forcing around 100 people to work as slaves on his land near Nashville, Tennessee. Jackson's election represented the triumph of what was sometimes called "the Democracy," or what we know now as the Democratic Party. This was a new coalition of western and southern cotton producing and agricultural interests that took full advantage of increased democratization to appeal to what they called "*the* people" against an imagined, parasitic, and reform

---

[84]On these political and cultural changes see: Hietala, *Manifest Design*, 1–9, 95–131, 173–214; Daniel Walker Howe, *What Hath God Wrought: The Transformation of America 1815–1848* (New York: Oxford University Press, 2007), 164–202, 210, 390–1, 488–92, 836, 850. See also Silver, *Our Savage Neighbors*, which explores the role of settler-Native conflict in the forging of whiteness in the late eighteenth century but informed the discussion here.

[85]On cotton, slavery, and Britain see: Beckert, *Empire of Cotton*, 98–174; Blackburn, *Making of New World Slavery*, 509–80; Howe, *What Hath God Wrought*, 128, 705; Matthew Karp, *This Vast Southern Empire: Slaveholders at the Helm of American Foreign* Policy (New York: Cambridge University Press, 2016); Findlay and O'Rourke, *Power and Plenty*, 330–45; Joseph E. Inikori, *Africans and the Industrial Revolution in England: A Study in International Trade and Economic Development* (Cambridge: Cambridge University Press, 2002); Weaver, *The Great Land Rush*, 123; Wallerstein, *Modern World-System III*, 247–8.

minded eastern and urban elite.⁸⁶ Central to the electoral success of the Democrats was the appeal to white racial solidarity, a whiteness that was relatively open to European immigrants from Ireland to Germany, but one that was otherwise exclusive and defined against non-whites like Native Americans.⁸⁷ Though this racialized nationalism reflected something of a departure from the Enlightenment vision of civilizational advancement common to the Revolutionary generation, Jacksonian Democrats retained many of the same ideas about progress—just repackaged in a new hyper-racialized, democratic populism that helped bring greater unity to the postcolonial United States.

Attacks on Indigenous sovereignty were an essential part of this project. The main political focus of the Democracy during Jackson's first term was the "problem" of Native Americans living east of the Mississippi. Otherwise lacking a clear legislative agenda—Jackson's famous war against the Bank of the United States was still a few years in the future—the cause of Indian Removal was a perfect unifying project for the party. It combined appeals to race, national expansion, the support of slavery, and even attacks on elites (the latter were seen as the authors of the civilization policy and thus race traitors protecting Native American interests over those of the common white man). It also directly reflected Jackson's own views. The famed "Indian fighter" saw the removal of Native Americans, as Daniel Walker Howe has written: as "the key to national development … the tribes not only occupied rich land, they threatened American sovereignty" and "challenged white supremacy."⁸⁸ There "was no measure," wrote Jackson's first Secretary of State—and later Vice President—Martin Van Buren, "in the whole course of his administration of which he was more exclusively the author than this."⁸⁹

The issue had also taken on a new immediacy following Jackson's election victory in 1828, when the state of Georgia moved against the sovereignty of the Cherokees, triggering a constitutional crisis. As mentioned earlier, the Cherokee Nation—which occupied most of northwest Georgia and extended into Alabama, North Carolina, and Tennessee—was by the 1830s remarkably prosperous. It had also seemingly done exactly what the federal government had been encouraging Native Americans to do: adopt European customs. Many Cherokees had turned to European agricultural practices, and they had also established a government and constitution following the US model. They had even developed a new alphabet for writing in

---

[86] Timothy Shenk, *Realigners: Partisan Hacks, Political Visionaries, and the Struggle to Rule American Democracy* (New York: Farrar Straus and Giroux, 2022), 56.
[87] Shenk, *Realigners*, 57-8.
[88] Howe, *What Hath God Wrought*, 347.
[89] Howe, *What Hath God Wrought*, 347.

the Cherokee language, featured in a bilingual newspaper, the *Cherokee Phoenix*.[90] Some of the most prosperous Cherokees took things a step further, owning large plantations worked by slaves. What the Cherokees had not done, however, was disappear into the white population or otherwise further surrender their land and sovereignty. Nor were they inclined to do so. As a Cherokee delegation to Washington protested in 1824, "the Cherokee are not foreigners, but original inhabitants of America; they now inhabit and stand on the soil of their own territory ... defined by the treaties which they have made with the government of the United States."[91] It was, as the Cherokee government had declared the year before, the Indigenous nation's "unalterable determination ... never to cede *one foot* more of our land."[92]

A large number of white Americans—including Jackson's predecessor, President John Quincy Adams (in office: 1825–29)—were sympathetic to the Cherokee's claims and the rights of Indigenous people to their land in general. The egalitarian impulses that had motivated Federalist policy towards Native Americans had not entirely faded. One New York newspaper observed that merely a glance at the *Phoenix* was "sufficient to overthrow a thousand times all the unprincipled declarations ... made by interested white men against the incompetency of all Indians for civilized life."[93] None, of course, believed that Native Americans should continue to live as "savages," few doubted either that ultimate sovereignty over US territory resided in either the individual state governments or the federal government, not Native landholders. Yet, they still believed Native Americans should be treated with some decency, the civilized Cherokees especially. However, the election of Jackson meant that these relatively humane attitudes towards Indigenous land rights would no longer shape policy.

With the White House now decisively on its side, Georgia declared the dissolution of Cherokee authority and the extension of the state's laws over all Indigenous land within its borders.[94] Georgia's justification for this move openly invoked both the rights of civilization and imperial conquest, claiming that the state's title to Indigenous land extended back—through the 1783 Treaty of Paris—to the British Empire and its invasion of eastern North America in the seventeenth century.[95] The British, the Georgia General Assembly proclaimed, had asserted "their claim both to domain and to empire" over the "various wandering tribes of savages" in North

---

[90]Howe, *What Hath God Wrought*, 343–6. For more on the *Cherokee Phoenix*, see: Saunt, *Unworthy Republic*, 16–17, 54–60.
[91]Howe, *What Hath God Wrought*, 345–6.
[92]Howe, *What Hath God Wrought*, 345.
[93]Saunt, *Unworthy Republic*, 59.
[94]Howe, *What Hath God Wrought*, 345; Lisa Ford, *Settler Sovereignty: Jurisdiction and Indigenous People in America and Australia, 1788–1836* (Cambridge, MA: Harvard University Press, 2010), 129–57, 183–203; Prucha, *Great Father*, 192–3.
[95]Ford, *Settler Sovereignty*, 188–96.

America, staking out rights of ownership which were thus "recognised and admitted by the whole civilised world."[96] The import was clear, civilizational hierarchy meant that Native claims to the land were simply not valid. President Jackson moved quickly to support his allies in Georgia, forcing a removal bill through Congress. Introduced in February of 1830 and passed in May despite stiff opposition, the Removal Act authorized the President to take steps to move any Native Americans within the country to federally owned territory in the trans-Mississippi West.[97]

The bill's supporters on Capitol Hill invoked the same hierarchical logic as the Georgians. The House Committee on Indian Affairs, for example, asserted that the US government had an authority to extinguish Native title, "sanctioned by the natural superiority allowed to the claims of civilized communities over those of savage tribes." Indeed, the committee implied, their legislation represented a progressive improvement over British actions because where Britain had used force to take land, the United States was using that most civilized form of power: money. This, the Congressmen congratulated themselves, was "the substitute which humanity and expediency have imposed, in place of the sword."[98] Those claims to the contrary, the sword remained central to the removal policy, as only force could make most Cherokees leave their homes. Armed prospectors had surged onto Cherokee territory following the discovery of gold deposits in 1829, for example, while Jackson had removed federal troops that were in place to protect Cherokee land rights. The Georgia Assembly, meanwhile, ominously hinted of the possibility of using military force if "all other means of redress fail." The message to the Native Americans in Georgia was clear: sell and move west, or else.[99] The state's status as a civilized, sovereign, and white community required it.

The Cherokee Nation responded to this assault on their sovereignty in what was arguably the most civilized manner possible: they took Georgia to court. The legal system, however, would provide them with only a partial and ephemeral vindication. In two cases, the Supreme Court—which under Chief Justice John Marshall remained a vestige of old Federalist attitudes toward Native Americans—made what amounted to a last-ditch effort to restore the civilization policy at the expense of both Jacksonian removers *and* the rights of Native Americans. In the first case, *Cherokee Nation v. Georgia* (1831), Marshall and the Court tossed out the Cherokee's attempt to prevent Georgia's abrogation of their sovereignty on the technical

---

[96]Georgia General Assembly, "Acts of the General Assembly of the state of Georgia, passed in Milledgeville at an annual session in November and December, 1827 [volume 1]," 1827: 241. https://hdl.handle.net/2027/nyp.33433001215882.
[97]Blackhawk, *Rediscovery of America*, 242–7; Howe, *What Hath God Wrought*, 342–57; Prucha, *Great Father*, 183–213.
[98]Prucha, *Great Father*, 196.
[99]"Acts of the General Assembly of the State of Georgia," 1827: 249.

grounds that the Nation lacked standing to sue. In so doing, the Court made clear that civilizational hierarchies retained the same legal force that seventeenth-century colonial theorists had granted them. Sidestepping the issue of whether Georgia's move was a violation of Cherokee rights—while suggesting that it was—the Court rejected Cherokee claims that their Nation was a foreign, independent power. Instead, the Court declared Native American communities were "domestic dependent nations" occupying "territory to which we [the United States] assert a title independent of their will." Native Americans, wrote Marshall for the Court,

> are in a state of pupilage. Their relations to the United States resemble that of a ward to his guardian. They look to our government for protection; rely upon its kindness and its power; appeal to it for relief to their wants; and address the President as their great father.[100]

This was an assertion of the logic behind the old civilization policy in legal form. Cherokees were independent in the way children are to their parents, autonomous but under higher—educational and civilizing—authority. Yet, even such wards of the state had rights in Federalist eyes, and thus the ruling left open the possibility that—could a party with proper standing be found—the Court would be required to vindicate the limited rights it had implied came with being a "domestic dependent nation."[101]

Such standing was found in Samuel Worchester, a missionary and US citizen, arrested for refusing Georgia's order that all whites on Cherokee land had to sign an oath of allegiance to the state government. As a white man, Worchester's standing was clear and so Marshall moved to assert federal power over Georgia and, through that power, to defend the rights of the Cherokees. In *Worchester v. Georgia* (1832), the Court asserted the principle that Jefferson had articulated to the British Ambassador back in 1792: the US national government had inherited from the British the sole right to extinguish Native title via sale or agreement with Native Americans themselves. No one else—including the states—could do so. The Cherokee Nation, the Court wrote, "is a distinct community ... in which the laws of Georgia can have no force, and which the citizens of Georgia have no right to enter, but with the assent of the Cherokees themselves."[102] For the Supreme Court, Native Americans were not yet civilized enough for full sovereignty but still had rights that whites were bound to respect.[103]

---

[100]"Cherokee Nation v. Georgia, 30 U.S. 1 (1831)." *Legal Information Institute*, Cornell Law School. https://www.law.cornell.edu/supremecourt/text/30/1.
[101]Ford, *Settler Sovereignty*, 191–2.
[102]"Worcester v. the State of Georgia, 31 U.S. (6 Pet.) 515 (1832)." *Legal Information Institute*, Cornell Law School. https://www.law.cornell.edu/supremecourt/text/31/515.
[103]Ford, *Settler Sovereignty*, 191–6.

Jackson disagreed. Ignoring existing treaties and embracing a distinctly more racialized concept of civilization, he paid no attention to the Supreme Court and took steps to remove Native Americans anyway. Georgia raffled off Cherokee lands in a lottery, while Mississippi, Missouri, and Alabama—following Georgia's model—also moved to extend white sovereignty over Native American lands in their midst. The Cherokee cases and their aftermath demonstrate clearly what we have been highlighting this entire chapter: white Americans were largely unified in their belief that US independence—its decolonization—required the disappearance of Indigenous America. Jackson's rebuke of Marshall and the Supreme Court merely brought a decisive end to the debate over the proper means for doing so—a debate already trending in the President's direction anyway.

Facing an almost impossible situation, Native Americans from North to South chose different paths forward. Some chose to fight, leading in the North to the Black Hawk War (1832) and in the South to both the Second Creek (Muscogee) War (1836–37) and the Second Seminole War (1835–42). With eastern Native Americans surrounded by the much more populous United States and lacking European allies, the outcome of these conflicts was largely predetermined. In the long run, Jefferson's quarantine strategy proved effective. Other Natives attempted to get the best treaties they could, looking to secure annuities and payments to finance their resettlements, payments that often were never made.[104] Still others, including many Georgia Cherokees, remained on their lands until they were forced into detention camps by the US Army in preparation for relocation to the West. Once thriving towns were left suddenly abandoned: "houses," as Claudio Saunt writes, "stood empty of residents and the objects of everyday life rested in place" until "US citizens moved into Cherokee houses, slept in their beds, and ate out of their pots."[105]

Conditions on these westward marches—the "Trail of Tears" as they are infamously known—were horrific. Food and other necessities were in scare supply, while the soldiers sometimes robbed their Indigenous charges of what property they had managed to bring with them. It's estimated that at least 1,000 (and perhaps as many as 3,500) of the 12,000 forcefully displaced Cherokees died as a result of their deportation over the winter of 1838–39. All—men and women, children and the elderly—suffered horrifically from cold, deprivation, and misery, all under the watchful eye of American troops.[106] As de Tocqueville's *Democracy in America* records, conditions were little better for those who emigrated "voluntarily" like the Choctaws. Within its first eight years, the removal policy had reduced the Indigenous

---

[104]Howe, *What Hath God Wrought*, 416–21.
[105]Saunt, *Unworthy Republic*, 278.
[106]Saunt, *Unworthy Republic*, 279–80.

population east of the Mississippi River to a mere 15,000 living in scattered, often impoverished, enclaves.[107]

Filling in behind were white settlers who brought with them another forcefully deported population: enslaved Blacks. The cotton-producing South soon transformed into a region that was, by 1860, the wealthiest per-capita in the world outside of England—wealth produced by the violent removal of one population and the enslavement of another.[108] In the North, European migration, natural population growth, and nascent industrialization financed by cotton capital also brought significant economic development. In a sense, both the Republican and Federalist visions for the country—which were now championed in somewhat altered form by Jackson's Democrats and the opposition Whigs, respectively—were validated by time. The United States had increasingly made real its independence through self-governing farmers producing commodities for sale overseas *and* an increasingly dynamic and diversified economy of Hamiltonian dreams.[109] It also possessed a new material and cultural unity that—while soon to be sundered by a debate over slavery's expansion—had been forged in large part through war with Indigenous people on the frontier. If not yet a true equal of the British Empire, as we will see in the next chapter, the United States was by the early 1840s a dominant power in the Western Hemisphere, confident in its ability and authority to influence the decolonization of countries to its south. When Congress chose in 1837 to commission *Discovery* and *The Rescue* to flank the main entrance to the US Capitol, they could not have selected better symbols for their country. The arrival of Europeans depicted in *Discovery* had, of course, made the United States possible, while the ethnic cleansing of the frontier symbolized in *The Rescue* had helped constitute it as a newly powerful and more truly independent state.[110]

While large communities of Native Americans west of the Mississippi remained to be dealt with, things were going according to plan for the United States. Decolonization proceed and the imperial mission continued. Huge swaths of North America had been incorporated into the trans-Atlantic system of trade and production that had been first established in the seventeenth century. White Americans—and Europeans like de Tocqueville—could confidently proclaim that civilization was progressing forward. All that had been required was the near annihilation of the Indigenous world east of the Mississippi River.

---

[107]Saunt, *Unworthy Republic*, 316.
[108]Levy, *Ages of American Capitalism*, 159.
[109]Herring, *From Colony to Superpower*, 136–8.
[110]For more on these statues, see the discussion in the introduction.

CHAPTER THREE

Reordering the World: The Haitian Revolution, the Decolonization of Latin America, and the Empire of Trade

In 1721, Francis Nicholson, the governor of the colony of South Carolina, was presented with a deerskin map by members of the Catawba Confederacy, a community of Indigenous Americans who lived along today's border between North and South Carolina. The map, a gift in honor of Nicholson's visit to Catawba territory, depicted the rapidly changing geopolitical world of the North American coast in the early 1720s (see Figure 5). In the center of the map were the villages of the Catawba and their Indigenous neighbors, shown as a series of circles connected by lines representing the kinship relations that were the heart of Indigenous North American politics. Surrounding the Catawba's circles on either side of the map are the sharp, angular contours of the colony of Virginia and the expanding street grid of Charles Town, the main settlement of South Carolina.[1] In so contrasting the organic shapes of the Indigenous world, and the organized grids of the colonies, the unnamed Catawba mapmaker provided a keen insight into the nature of the imperial project that created the United States. It was an effort at "reordering the world," reshaping

---

[1] Hämäläinen, *Indigenous Continent*, 193–4.

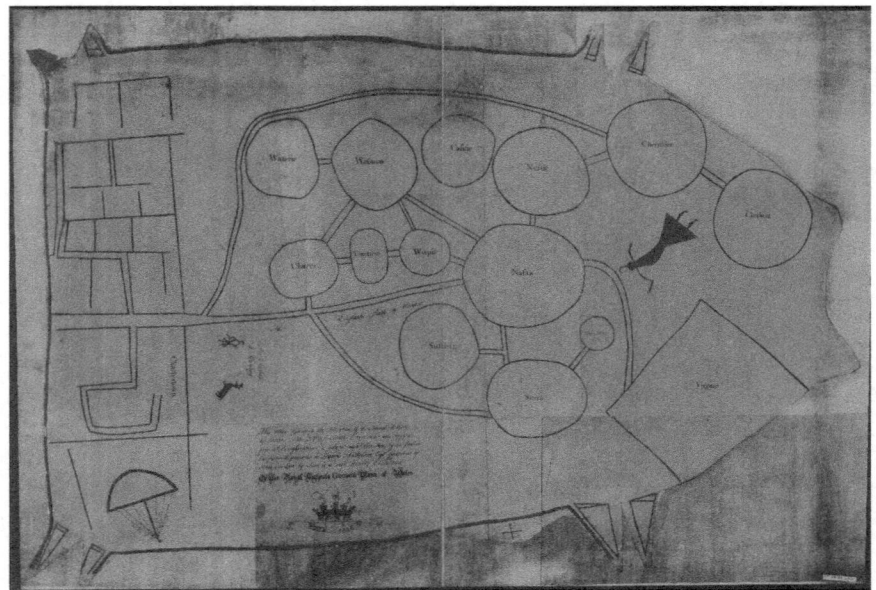

FIGURE 5 *A deerskin map presented to South Carolina Governor Francis Nicholson by the Catawba in 1724.*

other societies to fit patterns that served the elites of the expanding socioeconomic system of Europe.[2]

As we have seen, the American Revolution emerged not from a colonial desire to abandon that project but instead from a dispute over who was to control its North American arm: London, or the colonies themselves. The Revolution and its ideological emphasis on individual rights, political equality, and limited government—ideas born of the intellectual tradition we call "liberalism"—reshaped the undertaking to be sure.[3] Elites across the country and leaders in Washington, DC, soon had to command majorities among an expanding white male electorate in order to stay in power.[4] Liberal ideas also became an important part of how Americans understood what constituted civilization, and therefore joined race, European-American culture, and Protestant religion among the categories by which they evaluated other societies.[5] Yet, Americans otherwise continued to see the world through a similar lens to their colonial ancestors, and so

---

[2] The phrase "reordering the world" here is borrowed from title of Bell, *Reordering the World*.
[3] On the Revolution and liberalism see: Chapter 1.
[4] On expanding suffrage and the empire of liberty see: Chapter 2.
[5] See the discussion in Bell, *Reordering the World*, 91–115.

they worked—not to build a world of sovereign equality—but to instead construct a new global hierarchy, one ordered for the benefit of themselves and what they called the "civilized world."

Few things illustrate this better than our topic for this chapter: the US response to imperial transitions in the Caribbean, Spanish America, and the Pacific in the decades before the American Civil War. As we saw in the last chapter, a key first step in the American project of world-ordering was the subjugation of the Native American neighbors of the new United States. Just as important, however, was the way the US positioned itself vis-à-vis its other neighbors who strove for independence in the years following the American Revolution: those in the French possession of Saint Domingue (today's Haiti) and those in Spanish America—Mexico in particular. Though internal political debates over race and slavery ultimately prevented the most ambitious schemes for imperial conquest until the end of the nineteenth century, it did not prevent the United States from completing its "Manifest Destiny" at Mexican expense.

Meanwhile, American merchants and manufacturers worked to build other hierarchical systems short of formal empire through a network of trade and investment that reached around Cape Horn and across the Pacific. Such forays helped the United States gain a foothold in East Asia—a region experiencing an intensification of European imperial relationships at this time. Though the United States eschewed formal conquests in the Pacific in this period, it participated in the effort to reorganize the Pacific's political and economic power structure all the same, helping facilitate East Asia's unequal incorporation into the world-system. These efforts were a point of pride for many Americans, who tellingly called such ventures a "maritime empire"—one that made the "wilderness" of the world's oceans, as one congressman put it in 1842, "blossom like a rose" and "resound with [the] busy hum … of Civilization" and "its humanizing blessings."[6]

In these years therefore the United States entered a new phase in its relationship with the ends of empire, able to participate in the reorganization of the world not just within the lands granted to it by the Treaty of Paris, but beyond them as well. As a result, by the 1840s, the United States had furthered its own decolonization, leveraging its position to become a more independent "power," if not of the first rate, certainly one that entered into the calculations of all policymakers in Europe.[7] Despite the break with Britain, the commercially oriented, civilizing mission that had founded the thirteen colonies continued—rebranded in the name of American liberty and freedom.

---

[6]Roleau, *Sails Whitening Every Sea*, 3.
[7]Herring, *From Colony to Superpower*, 136–7.

The United States and the Decolonization of Haiti

One can easily see the limits of the egalitarian ideals of the American Revolution—and the ways that hierarchy continued to suffuse conceptions of world order in the United States—in the contrasting responses of white Americans to the French and Haitian Revolutions. The news of the outbreak of revolution in France in 1789 was met with considerable enthusiasm when it reached North American shores. Public speeches and demonstrations, tricolored flags and clothing, newspaper editorials and broadsides, all celebrated what many—Thomas Jefferson and his Republicans among them—saw as a European extension of their own rebellion against monarchy. Even the more skeptical Federalists felt compelled to keep their doubts to themselves amidst the general applause. While the excitement diminished considerably as the French Revolution wound further along its confusing and chaotic course, the initial response revealed a white American public that took the anti-monarchical and liberal ideas of their Revolution seriously.[8] At least, that is, when those ideas were shaping societies that could be considered part of white civilization. When the free and enslaved people of color in French Saint Domingue chose to apply those same principles to themselves—rising up against white rule and the island's brutal plantation system—Americans instead recoiled with horror.

Haiti's war for independence began for reasons common to all the anti-imperial revolts of the late eighteenth- and early nineteenth-century Western Hemisphere: imperial rivalry leading to fiscal crisis. In this case, it was the fiscal crisis of the French monarchical state, which prompted the calling of the Estates General in January of 1789, and the subsequent outbreak of the French Revolution later that year. The turmoil in France, and the liberal ideas that flowed from it—famously articulated in the 1789 "Declaration of the Rights of Man and Citizen"—made their way across the Atlantic to France's richest colony: Saint Domingue, which produced roughly two-thirds of the world's sugar supply and over half of its coffee.[9] It did so through a brutally stratified plantation economy, where an enslaved Black majority was ruled by a minority of wealthy white elites. Rich planters lived alongside less privileged white small holders as well, and a class of free people of color. Disputes between these three groups of free residents of the colony eventually led to violence and, critically, the arming of slaves to advance the cause of each. In 1791, slaves in the north took matters in their own hands, ceased fighting for their masters, and began a general uprising. Led by the talented and charismatic Toussaint Louverture, the former slaves overthrew the planter regime in 1793, and then fought off separate

---

[8]Wood, *Empire of Liberty*, 174–7.
[9]Franklin W. Knight, "The Haitian Revolution," *American Historical Review* 105, no. 1 (February 2000): 103–15, 107–8.

Spanish, English, and French expeditionary forces to maintain control of the colony, eventually declaring independence from France, under Jean-Jacques Dessalines in 1804.[10] Though France refused to recognize Haiti's independence until 1825—and then only in return for a crippling indemnity whereby Haitians were forced to compensate their former masters for their freedom—the Haitian Revolution was most successful large-scale slave revolt in the post-Columbian history of the Western Hemisphere.[11]

It was therefore something of a singular event with singular ramifications for the young United States, one of the largest slave societies in the world at the time, where—as we have seen—whiteness was a key requirement for citizenship. The Haitian slave revolt was, for example, very much on the mind of white Americans in the Southern states as they hardened their slave laws in the first decades of the nineteenth century. Yet, at the same time, the US response to the Haitian fight for freedom should not be understood only through the lens of a slaveholding republic responding to the emergence of a republic of freed slaves.[12] While it was that to be sure, it was also an early example of the larger trends in how the United States understood the ends of empire that we are highlighting in this book. Simply put, Americans did not believe Black Haitians were high enough up the hierarchy of civilization to be legitimate possessors of sovereignty. As a result, the US government at first contributed materially to efforts to suppress the slave revolt, and then—when that effort failed—refused to extend diplomatic recognition to the Haitian state that emerged. Despite briefly engaging with the Haitian regime during the Adams administration, the United States remained firm in its unwillingness to accept Haiti into the community of nations for generations.

The Washington administration was the first to confront the specter of a successful slave revolt so close to US shores. As news reached the United States in the fall of 1791, newspapers began to regularly report on events in the colony, prompting fear and concern across the country. "Most private conversations," wrote Abraham Bishop, a prominent Connecticut farmer and essayist, "have evinced a great zeal in favor of the whites."[13]

---

[10]Louverture had by then died in French captivity in 1803, captured via a false flag of truce a year earlier.
[11]As such, the story of the Haitian Revolution is as essential to understanding the origins of the modern world as that of the United States, and one we will not be able to give its proper due here. A classic account is that of C.L.R. James, *The Black Jacobins: Toussaint L'Ouverture and the San Domingo Revolution* (New York: Penguin Classics, 2022). A narrative of more recent vintage is Laurent Dubois, *Avengers of the New World: The Story of the Haitian Revolution* (Cambridge: Belknap Press, 2004). For good, shorter overviews see: Blackburn, *Overthrow of New World Slavery*, 161–264; and Knight, "The Haitian Revolution."
[12]See: Robert J. Reinstein, "Slavery, Executive Power, and International Law: The Haitian Revolution and American Constitutionalism," *The American Journal of Legal History* 53, no. 2 (April 2013): 141–237.
[13]Timothy M. Matthewson, "George Washington's Policy towards the Haitian Revolution," *Diplomatic History* 3, no. 3 (Summer 1979): 321–36, 324.

James Madison felt the stories filtering north depicted "the distress of the island in the most gloomy colors," while William Vans Murray, a Federalist representative to the US House from Maryland, feared a general "fall into chaos and negroism [sic]."[14] Charles Pickney, the Governor of South Carolina, called on the administration to act in support of the planters, otherwise the "flame" of revolt "will extend to the neighboring islands, and may prove not a very pleasing or agreeable example to the Southern states."[15] President Washington agreed—it was "lamentable!" he wrote, for there to be "such a spirit of revolt among the Blacks."[16] American merchantmen showed a real enthusiasm for keeping the whites supplied—"the [planter's] troops had been fed principally by the American merchants," said one Boston trader—and some Americans even joined the fighting to preserve the slave regime.[17]

Though longshot pleas from French planters for US states to send militiamen to Haiti in their support were rebuffed, Washington did stretch the powers of his newly created office to provide the island's white elites with financial and materiel support.[18] In September of 1791, the French minister to the United States, Jean-Baptiste de Ternant, suggested that the administration might provide $40,000 to purchase weapons and supplies for the planters, which could then be discounted from the United States' debt to France from the Revolutionary War. Though Ternant admitted he did not yet have authorization from Paris for such a scheme, the administration moved quickly to authorize the funds anyway. "There are situations in which forms must be dispensed with," wrote Secretary of State Jefferson of the issue, and a slave uprising against their white masters—"a man attacked by assassins" as he characterized it—was among them.[19] So zealous was the administration about the suppression of the Haitian Revolution that it continued to send larger and larger grants to the island—including two substantial payments of $400,000 and $326,000—without any guarantee from France that the sums would count toward America's debt. This meant too that Washington was doing so without explicit Congressional authorization for this "early version of 'Lend-Lease'," as the legal historian Robert Reinstein has called it.[20] Instead, the administration used an expansive interpretation of the legislation authorizing it to repay the older debt to France to justify the transfers.[21]

---

[14]Matthewson, "Washington's Policy," 324.
[15]Matthewson, "Washington's Policy," 324.
[16]Reinstein, "Slavery, Executive Power, and International Law," 148–9.
[17]It may have been "as high as a few thousand," Matthewson, "Washington's Policy," 325.
[18]On the request for militiamen see: Matthewson, "Washington's Policy," 324–5; on stretching executive power see: Reinstein, "Slavery, Executive Power, and International Law," 147–59.
[19]Reinstein, "Slavery, Executive Power, and International Law," 150.
[20]Reinstein, "Slavery, Executive Power, and International Law," 149.
[21]Reinstein, "Slavery, Executive Power, and International Law," 151–9.

Noteworthy as well is how unified an otherwise divided Washington administration was in its support of the planter regime—both the emerging Republican clique around Jefferson and the Federalists associated with Secretary of the Treasury Hamilton offered their full-throated support of the administration's efforts to help suppress Louverture's self-emancipating army. This attitude reflected both ideological predilections and strategic and commercial interests. The United States had considerable trade connections with Haiti, connections that at first seemed likely to be best preserved by supporting the planters. There was, in addition, the issue of the alliance with France and the desire to keep Britain from taking advantage of the situation to bring Saint Domingue into its orbit.[22] However, as relations with France soured during Washington's second term—and as Louverture's success seemed to offer the possibility of a renewal of trade with the new Black rulers of the island—American enthusiasm for the planters waned. When Adams became president in 1797, for example, US policy began to shift toward active support of the rebel government amidst the Quasi War with France (1798–1800). Cooperation between the United States and the Haitian government even briefly reached a level where US forces directly intervened in fighting between Louverture's troops and those of General Andre Rigaud, a man of mixed ancestry who had broken with the Haitian leader.[23] Full recognition of the Haitian government, however, was not something that even the anti-slavery Adams could approve of—the brief Adams-Louverture partnership was therefore conducted entirely outside formal diplomacy. The possibility of recognizing a regime ruled by people of color as a sovereign equal to the United States continued to be too much to ask, even when it potentially suited American interests to do so.

Vice President Jefferson and his Republican allies meanwhile were horrified by even Adams's limited, unofficial partnership with a Black state—"cannibals of the terrible republic" as the Vice President called its citizens.[24] When Jefferson became president in 1801 therefore, the pendulum shifted in the other direction—largely for good. He cut off the diplomatic contacts established by Adams and began to look at options for suppressing American trade with the Haitians. This is not to say Jefferson's policies toward Haiti were entirely uniform throughout his two terms. When Napoleon ordered his brother-in-law Charles Leclerc and 40,000 men there in 1801 to restore French rule, the President briefly toyed with the possibility of recognizing Haitian independence. He feared that, if successful in Haiti, victorious French troops might be later used to secure

---

[22]Matthewson, "Washington's Policy," 327–9.
[23]Reinstein, "Slavery, Executive Power, and International Law," 172–9.
[24]Reinstein, "Slavery, Executive Power, and International Law," 163.

Napoleon's claims to New Orleans and Louisiana, an intolerable prospect. This made a Haitian victory, and possible steps to help secure it, more appealing. When that victory arrived in late 1803, however—after years of brutal fighting that devastated the Haitian economy—Jefferson was freed to indulge his more natural instincts. He and his Republican allies in Congress first limited trade to Haiti in 1805 and then passed a complete embargo in 1807.[25] Legal trade was restored in 1810, but, by then, the once profitable commercial relationship with Haiti had collapsed, never to meaningfully recover. The US government, meanwhile, was content to act as though Haiti did not exist, refusing to recognize its independence until 1862, pretending it remained a part of France long after even the French had acknowledged otherwise. This was despite the fact that the Haitian government was clearly deserving of basic diplomatic recognition under most conceptions of international relations at the time.[26] As the historian Henry Adams put it in 1889, "the opportunity to declare the negroes [sic] of Hayti [sic] enemies of the human race was too tempting to be ignored."[27] In the first opportunity it had to acknowledge the end of an empire near its shores, therefore, the United States had instead asserted a right to veto, believing that the proper conditions for empire's end had not been met. It was the first such example of many.

Revolution and Decolonization in Spanish America

When it came to Latin America, the United States proved more willing to acknowledge the end of empire when it arrived, but only just. While the United States was the first state to recognize, and in some cases celebrate, the independence of the rebelling communities of Spanish America, it did so warily, as we will see. It also did so with an increasing skepticism of the ability of Spanish Americans to govern themselves, leading to steps to ensure US dominance of the Western Hemisphere.

In order to understand the US response to the decolonization of most of Spanish America in the early nineteenth century, however, we first need to briefly review the dynamics of that process itself, for they would shape the interactions with the United States that followed. Just as the Haitian and

---

[25]For Jefferson's policies towards Haiti see: Tim Matthewson, "Jefferson and Haiti," *The Journal of Southern History* 61, no. 2 (May 1995): 209–48; Reinstein, "Slavery, Executive Power, and International Law," 181–93.

[26]Reinstein, "Slavery, Executive Power, and International Law," 213–17.

[27]Quoted in Reinstein, "Slavery, Executive Power, and International Law," 209.

American Revolutions had some similarities in origin, the collapse of Spanish authority in Central and South America in the early nineteenth century also bears some resemblance to the events that led to the independence of the United States. Both were, at root, the consequence of disputes over how to properly structure the hierarchy of an extractive imperial system under acute fiscal and military pressure due to the imperial competitions of the Atlantic World. Both too resulted in part from the actions of colonial elites who only reluctantly looked to independence as a solution to the structural issues they confronted, turning to liberalism late in the game as a means for justifying those steps. It was fiscal crises and subsequent debates over imperial hierarchies that led to the development of local and liberal identities, not the other way around.[28]

At the same time, it's important not to lose sight of the differences between the two stories of imperial collapse.[29] Spain's American Empire, of course, was much older than the British North American colonies, first established following Christopher Columbus's visit to the Caribbean in 1492. Though the Spanish monarchy had only just consolidated control over most of the territory we associate with modern Spain, technological and organizational advantages over Native Central and South Americans, combined with religious zeal, cruelty, and a disastrous wave of epidemic disease, allowed the Spanish Crown to build a vast empire that stretched from today's Chile to what is now the southern border of Oregon. While the British colonies were born of wars of conquest as well, the nature and organization of that conquest differed significantly. Unlike the decentralized polities of Indigenous North Americans, Native Americans further south lived in imperial structures of their own. Thus, when the Spanish conquered the Aztec Empire of Mexico and Inca Empire of western South America (including parts of contemporary Argentina, Bolivia, Chile, Colombia,

---

[28]Despite the challenges inherent in the task, there is a growing number of single-volume histories of the collapse of Spain's American empire (for those looking for more of the story than is covered here). Some examples include: Jeremy Adelman, *Sovereignty and Revolution in the Iberian Atlantic* (Princeton: Princeton University Press, 2006); Brian R. Hamnett, *The End of Iberian Rule on the American Continent, 1770–1830* (Cambridge: Cambridge University Press, 2017); John Lynch, *The Spanish-American Revolutions, 1808–1826* (New York: W.W. Norton and Co., 1973); Anthony McFarlane, *War and Independence in Spanish America* (New York: Routledge, 2014); and Jaime E. Rodriguez O, *The Independence of Spanish America* (Cambridge: Cambridge University Press, 1998). For a concise historiographical overview see, Hamnett, *The End of Iberian Rule*, 7–11.

[29]Because the Spanish Empire controlled most of Central and South America, and it was Spanish possessions that attracted the most attention from the United States, our narrative here will focus on Spanish America for the sake of brevity and leave out Portuguese Brazil. For those interested in the ways the story of Brazilian independence overlapped with and diverged from that of Spanish America see: Adelman, *Sovereignty and Revolution*, especially, 220–57; and Hamnett, *The End of Iberian Rule*.

MAP 1 *Maps showing the decolonization of the Western Hemisphere in the late eighteenth and early nineteenth centuries.*

and Peru) they did not displace the Indigenous inhabitants—as the English colonists tended to do—they extended their rule over them, replacing local rulers with Spanish rulers. Indigenous Americans were within, rather than outside of, Spanish colonial society, something that over time became true of the descendants of African slaves brought to the colonies as well. Spanish America certainly had its own racial hierarchy that privileged whiteness, but because of these divergent origins it was much less homogenously white than British America.[30]

On the whole, the Spanish Empire was also more tightly regulated along mercantilist lines, meant to ensure that trans-Atlantic treasure fleets filled royal coffers and trade benefited the powerful merchant guilds of Cadiz. For a time, this arrangement—and in particular the gold and silver extracted from Andean mines—made the Spanish Monarchy the dominant power in Europe.[31] This power began to wane in the eighteenth century, however, as imperial military and commercial rivalry wore away at Spanish wealth and authority. French, Dutch, but especially British capital, merchants, and goods began to wend their way around Madrid's mercantile regulations—smuggling was rampant—and into the empire. In the Peace of Utrecht, for example, which brought an end to the War of Spanish Succession (1701–14), Britain secured the *asiento*, the contract to supply slaves to Spanish America. It provided British merchants with the chance not just to sell slaves but also to sell other—British manufactured—goods as well. Though Spain remained a great power in outward appearance, the commercial allowances Britain received in the treaty were, as Stanley and Barbara Stein write, a "persuasive sign of Spanish subordination to English hegemony."[32] Excess revenue increasingly flowed north, as economic power shifted from the Iberian Peninsula to the lands along the English Channel and the North Sea. The resounding British victory in the Seven Years War later revealed Spain's relative weakness for all to see.[33] By the time of the great Anglo-French conflicts that followed the French Revolution, therefore, Spain was more pawn than player, reduced to choosing between a disastrous alliance with

---

[30] For comparative discussions of the origins, nature, and ideology of the British and Spanish empires see: Elliott, *Empires of the Atlantic World*, 3–251; and Anthony Pagden, *Lords of All the World: Ideologies of Empire in Spain, Britain, and France c. 1500–1800* (New Haven: Yale University Press, 2005). For more focused attention on the Spanish imperial system see: Elliott, *Imperial Spain*; Colin M. MacLachlan, *Spain's Empire in the New World: The Role of Ideas in Institutional and Social Change* (Berkley: University of California Press, 1988); Stein and Stein, *Silver, Trade, and War*. See also: Peter Guardino, *The Dead March: A History of the Mexican-American War* (Cambridge, MA: Harvard University Press, 2017), 12.

[31] On Spanish commercial regulations and the importance of silver to the Spanish imperial and broader Atlantic economy see: Adelman, *Sovereignty and Revolution*, 13–55; Carlos Marichal, *Bankruptcy of Empire: Mexican Silver and the Wars Between Spain, Britain, and France 1760–1810* (Cambridge: Cambridge University Press, 2007); Stanley J. Stein and Barbara H. Stein, *Apogee of Empire: Spain and New Spain in the Age of Charles III, 1759–1789* (Baltimore: Johns Hopkins University Press, 2003); Stein and Stein, *Silver, Trade, and War*; John Tutino, "The Americas in the Rise of Industrial Capitalism," in *New Countries: Capitalism, Revolutions, and Nations in the Americas, 1750–1870*, John Tutino ed. (Durham: Duke University Press, 2016), 25–70.

[32] Stein and Stein, *Silver Trade and War*, 106–44, quote on 138.

[33] Adelman, *Sovereignty and Revolution*, 15–22; Marichal, *Bankruptcy of Empire*, 22–5; Stein and Stein, *Apogee of Empire*, 11–24, 48–68; Tutino, "The Americas in the Rise of Industrial Capitalism," 42.

Britain or a disastrous alliance with France (in the end, it maximized the disaster by choosing both at different times).[34]

Thus, when Napoleon's invasion of Spain in 1808 precipitated the collapse of the Spanish monarchy, the Spanish American colonies, increasingly cut off from Madrid, had already been forced to take steps to govern themselves.[35] Local "juntas"—or governing councils—of colonial notables often did so by liberalizing trade, allowing merchants and producers to sidestep Cadiz's monopoly and contract with those who were available (which, in practice, meant the British and, to a lesser degree, those from the United States). Such steps were divisive, however, as they alienated those most allied with the old mercantile system and those who benefited from the price controls for goods that the old regulations had imposed. When the anti-Napoleonic Spanish government, taking refuge in Cadiz, called for all parts of the empire to send delegates to the Cortes—or assembly—of the empire in 1810, these habits of self-government, and divisions, were only further strengthened. Disputes over colonial representation in the Cortes deepened the discord between some in the colonies and the government at home.[36] These divisions led to violence, as colonists feuded with the Peninsular government and each other over how best—and to whose advantage—the empire would be reorganized. Colonists, as Jeremy Adelman puts it, "literally, were forced to choose between more and more polarized sides, between imperium and something else."[37] Such desperate conflicts resulted in more disruption of the social order, as competing elites employed liberal language to make common cause with the populace, eventually disregarding both race and class in their quest for supporters. Independence, however, was still far from inevitable. "Few" as Brian Hamnett writes, "desired or foresaw" independence "in 1808–1810," at most "the preference would have been for some form of home rule" within the empire.[38] It was only after the restoration of the Spanish monarchy in 1814, and King Ferdinand VII's brutal attempt at reestablishing the old colonial system, that the tide turned decisively away from continued attachment to Spain. Royal troops were not completely ejected from the continent until 1824, following Simón Bolívar's victory in the Battle of Ayacucho in southern Peru.[39]

---

[34]Adelman, *Sovereignty and Revolution*, 177–8; Marichal, *Bankruptcy of Empire*, 81–118, 154–212; Mikaberidze, *The Napoleonic Wars*, 179–82; Stanley J. Stein and Barbara H. Stein, *Edge of Crisis: War and Trade in the Spanish Atlantic 1789–1808* (Baltimore: Johns Hopkins University Press, 2009).
[35]For more on the French invasion see: Charles Esdaile, *The Peninsular War: A New History* (New York: Palgrave Macmillan, 2003); Mikaberidze, *The Napoleonic Wars*, 242–81.
[36]Adelman, *Sovereignty and Revolution*, 175–219; Roberto Breña, "The Cadiz Liberal Revolution and Spanish American Independence," in *New Countries*, 71–104; Hamnett, *End of Iberian Rule*, 107–231.
[37]Adelman, *Sovereignty and Revolution*, 268.
[38]Hamnett, *End of Iberian Rule*, 317–18.
[39]Adelman, *Sovereignty and Revolution*, 307; Hamnett, *End of Iberian Rule*, 235–303. McFarlane, *War and Independence*, 283–424; Rodriguez O., *Independence of Spanish America*, 205–37.

The United States and Its New Neighbors

The above is, of course, a vast oversimplification of an important and complicated history, but what is essential for our purposes is to establish the position of the Latin American states as they gained independence and entered into the political calculations of their northern neighbor. Though it would be a mistake to exaggerate the political stability of the young United States—which, of course, had its own difficult revolutionary history and secessionist tendencies—it had two relative advantages over its Latin American counterparts. First, it had a four-decade head start in the process of postcolonial state formation and, second, it had a somewhat stronger foundation to build from. Its revolutionary war had been quicker and somewhat "easier," thanks to decisive outside help from a world power—France—something which was not available to the Latin American revolutionaries. It also had inherited a more diversified economy and stronger local political institutions (the colonies-turned-states) from its divergent imperial history. It possessed too a more homogenous majority population, with both a racial enemy outside the state to organize against (Native Americans), and an internal racial other within the nation to define citizenship against (enslaved Blacks).[40]

Given this relatively more secure position and its revolutionary origins, some Latin American revolutionaries expected that the United States might aid them in their struggle for independence. They were largely disappointed. While the United States was the first foreign country to recognize the independence of the former Spanish colonies—more on this in a moment—official aid never proved forthcoming. Many US sailors did volunteer and serve with distinction in rebel naval forces, particularly after the end of the War of 1812 left a good number without the prospect of employment in their own service. Merchants too were quite willing to sell arms and supplies to pro-independence forces, with tacit US government approval. This was just "as long"—as the historian Piero Gleijeses aptly put it—however, "as the rebels were able to pay, preferably cash."[41] Ever dismissive of the prospect of US support, Bolívar quipped that the North American republic's neutrality was purely "arithmetic" in nature.[42]

This was a generally fair characterization, even though enthusiasm for the Spanish patriot cause was both common and genuine—at least at first. The historian Caitlin Fitz, for example, has documented how many

---

[40]Guardino, *Dead March*, 1–30; Hamnett, *End of Iberian Rule*, 304–13, 320; Timothy J. Henderson, *A Glorious Defeat: Mexico and Its War with the United States* (New York: Hill and Wang, 2007), 3–23; Rodriguez O., *Independence of Spanish America*, 238–46; Part III of Tutino ed., *New Countries*, 233–385; see also Chapter 1–2.
[41]Piero Gleijeses, "The Limits of Sympathy: The United States and the Independence of Spanish America," *Journal of Latin American Studies* 24, no. 3 (October 1992): 481–505, 484.
[42]Gleijeses, "Limits of Sympathy," 484.

Americans celebrated the revolts and their revolutionary leaders, toasting the Spanish-American rebellions, along with the memory of their own, on July 4th. They named towns and even babies after figures like Bolívar (a "Bolívar baby boom" as Fitz calls it).[43] Piero Gleijeses, on the other hand, has pointed to evidence that this initial enthusiasm was relatively muted. US Attorney General William Wirt, for example, remarked of the rebels in 1823 that "there had never been much general excitement in their favor ... some," he continued, "felt warmly for them, but" that feeling "never had been general."[44] Equally, if not more popular, among the US public was the Greek effort to break free from Ottoman rule (1821–29) unfolding around the same time. For all the babies named Bolívar, Gleijeses suggests, Americans seemed much more willing to send their private donations to Greeks rebelling against a Muslim empire than Latin Americans fighting Spain.[45]

"Unlike the Greeks," Gleijeses writes, "Spanish Americans were of dubious whiteness." They "hailed not from a race of giants," as did the Greeks—so closely associated in the American mind with European classical civilization—but "degraded Spanish stock."[46] Their divergent views of the initial US reaction aside, both Gleijeses and Fitz agree that the latter perspective ultimately won out.[47] By the 1820s, most Americans saw to their south civilizational inferiors. In the abstract, some in the United States were able to entertain the possibility that Spanish America might take up the mantle of freedom, and perhaps even one day become part of a single hemispheric republic.[48] Upon any sustained engagement with the issue, however, skepticism of the ability of South Americans to properly govern themselves tended to emerge and overwhelm such feelings of solidarity. To most in the United States, as a writer in the *North American Review* put it in 1821, "it does not appear that there exists in any of these provinces the material and elements of a good national character ... South America will be to North America, we are strongly inclined to think, what Asia and Africa are to Europe."[49] While higher in the civilizational hierarchy than Native Americans or Haitians, Latin Americans still seemed like inferiors in the eyes of their neighbors to the north.

---

[43]Caitlin Fitz, *Our Sister Republics: The United States in an Age of American Revolutions* (New York: W.W. Norton and Co., 2016), 128.
[44]Gleijeses, "Limits of Sympathy," 485.
[45]Piero Gleijeses, "Review of: *Our Sister Republics: The United States and the Age of American Revolutions* by Caitlin Fitz," *Journal of Latin American Studies* 49, no. 1 (2017): 174–6.
[46]Gleijeses, "Limits of Sympathy," 482.
[47]Fitz believes that it only does so by the 1820s, whereas Gleijeses feels it was the dominant perspective from the start.
[48]On the possibilities of hemispheric unionism see: James E. Lewis, *The American Union and the Problem of Neighborhood, 1783–1829* (Chapel Hill: University of North Carolina Press, 1998).
[49]Gleijeses, "Limits of Sympathy," 482, note 5.

These prejudices toward Spanish Americans were born of many sources. They were drawn partly from old English Protestant prejudices toward Catholic Spain, attitudes that predated US independence. They were also, as Gleijesies suggests, due to what North Americans saw as the questionable character of the more racially diverse Latin American population.[50] Even the whitest resident of Spanish America was a descendant of Spaniards—itself a problem for those living in a culture deeply influenced by English Protestantism—while most also had some mix of Indigenous and African ancestry as well, making matters that much worse. Moreover, as the revolutions and civil conflicts in Latin America proceeded, Spanish-American independence leaders resorted to the emancipation and arming of former slaves, something more worrisome still. The US diplomat Joel Poinsett, for example, warned President James Monroe (in office: 1817–25) in 1817 that Bolívar and the revolutionary junta of Caracas had a problematic "connection" with "the authorities of [Haiti]" and commanded a large "number of negroes [sic] in arms," reasons to treat the independence movement warily.[51] To these demerits, some in the United States also added the seeming failure of the new Latin American governments to adopt a properly liberal structure. This was attributed to the supposed defects of national character foisted upon them by centuries of monarchial rule in government and Roman rule in religion. John Quincy Adams, for example, thought that all these factors mixed together to produce "a people heterogeneously composed" with "no spirit of freedom" and "no common principle of reason to form a union of mind."[52]

Even some of the most enthusiastic toward Spanish America—like the legendary Kentucky politician, Henry Clay—were still far from ready to build an egalitarian postcolonial order in the Western Hemisphere. Clay instead saw the United States as destined to be at the top of any future hemispheric hierarchy. His imagined "American System"—essentially a plan for an independent economic order encompassing the Western Hemisphere and excluding Europe—called for US manufacturing to dominate South America. The United States, he believed, would "take the lead in the prosecution of commerce and manufactures," and become the center of industry in the hemisphere, "holding the same position" relative to Latin America, that the factories of New England did "to the rest of the United States."[53] Clay, influenced by what scholars have called "neo-mercantilist" thinking—a system of economic thought that called for high tariffs to protect domestic industrial development—understood that such relationships, while

---

[50]Gleijeses, "Limits of Sympathy," 482.
[51]Arthur P. Whitaker, *The United States and the Independence of Latin America, 1800–1830* (New York: W.W. Norton and Co., 1964), 232.
[52]John Quincy Adams to Richard C. Anderson, May 27, 1873 in *The Writings of John Quincy Adams, Volume VII: 1820–1823*, Worthington Chauncey Ford ed. (New York: Macmillan, 1917), 441–86: 443. See also, Whitaker, *The United States and the Independence of Latin America*, 419.
[53]Lewis, *The American Union*, 141.

mutually beneficial to a degree, ultimately profited the manufacturer more than the buyer.⁵⁴

Given that the general perspective on Latin America in the United States ranged from "deeply prejudiced" to "liberal but profit seeking," it should not be surprising that policy debates tended to focus less on *if* and more on *when* the United States should begin shaping Latin American affairs to its advantage. On one end of the spectrum were those like Clay. He advocated for early recognition and support of the independence movements throughout the 1810s and 1820s (in his various roles as Speaker of the House and Secretary of State) wishing to see the United States take the first steps toward forming his hemispheric American system. He also wanted to see Washington move more assertively toward annexing Texas and adjacent territories in northern Mexico. John Quincy Adams represented the other end of the policy spectrum, not opposed to asserting US control over parts of Spanish America but believing that the international distribution of power mandated patience. The issue was not so much Spain—which most in the US government saw as a terminally weakened power—but Russia, France, and Britain. In Adams' mind, any overly strenuous US intervention risked war with those stronger European states.⁵⁵ Though Adams believed that the status of certain parts of the Spanish American Empire—primarily Mexico, Cuba, and Puerto Rico—was critical to the security of the United States, he also thought there was no need to rush in bringing them under US control. Writing of Cuba in 1823, for example, Adams suggested that while "it is scarcely possible to resist the conviction that the annexation of Cuba to our federal republic will be indispensable to the continuance and integrity of the Union itself" the United States was "not yet prepared" for "this event." It was best, therefore, for the island to remain under Spanish rule for the time being. Eventually, Adams felt, the "laws of political ... gravitation" would join Cuba to the United States, just as "an apple severed by the tempest from its native tree cannot choose but to fall to the ground."⁵⁶ For the moment, however, it seemed safer for Cuba to remain part of the Spanish Empire.

Thus, while more open to the end of empire in Latin America than in Haiti, Americans were also quite willing to countenance an empire's continuation if it furthered the United States' own projects of hierarchy. Rather than applying any universal anti-imperial policy, the United States approached the revolts in Spanish America on a case-by-case basis, a reflection of the cautious ambition expressed by Adams in his comments

---

⁵⁴On Clay's neo-mercantilist influences see: Helleiner, *The Neomercantilists*, 41–3.
⁵⁵Lewis, *The American Union*, 96–125.
⁵⁶John Quincy Adams, "An Apple Severed by the Tempest from Its Native Tree," in Holden and Zolov, *Latin America and the United States*, 9.

on Cuba and an attitude that dominated the Latin American policies of the Madison, Monroe, and Quincy Adams administrations. Though their positions on independence changed from country to country and year to year, in general, the goal remained the same: carefully lay the groundwork for later US hegemony without inciting European intervention in the near term.

The Monroe Doctrine and Ensuring Latin American Disunity

This approach began, first, with a somewhat pro-rebel neutrality. Though the Madison administration briefly considered recognizing some of the rebel movements in the years following the conclusion of the War of 1812, it settled instead on a policy of neutrality as most suited to US interests.[57] At the time recognition seemed as likely to trigger war with Spain as not—and then, more problematically, bring on conflict with the British—while a declaration of neutrality would allow the United States to ignore Spanish imperial restrictions on trade and expand commercial contacts with the breakaway regimes without overly antagonizing Madrid. US representatives fanned out to South America almost as soon as revolutionary juntas were formed—the first arriving in Buenos Aires in 1810.[58] These "consuls" exploited a gray area of diplomatic protocol and international practice, with a status both official and yet not quite, meaning that their arrival allowed the United States to negotiate commercial arrangements with South American rebels without extending them any diplomatic recognition.[59] Seperated by the Napoleonic Wars from the center of the world's firearm industry in Europe, the rebels were desperate for weapons, which afforded the nascent US armament industry a critical market for disposing of its surplus production. In addition to helping US manufacturers survive slumping demand in the years after the War of 1812, weapons also proved a key point of leverage in negotiating favorable trading conditions for other North American products, including textiles.[60]

Even after Monroe formally recognized five breakaway regimes (in Buenos Aires, Chile, Peru, Colombia, and Mexico) in 1822, the goal remained the same: expand favorable commercial relations with Latin America, avoid

---

[57]Lewis, *The American Union*, 69–95.
[58]Lindsay Schakebach Regele, *Manufacturing Advantage: War, the State, and the Origins of American Industry, 1776–1848* (Baltimore: Johns Hopkins University Press, 2019), 114–15.
[59]See: Simeon Andonov Simeonov, "Consular Recognition, Partial Neutrality, and the Making of Atlantic Diplomacy, 1778–1825," *Diplomatic History* 46, no. 1 (January 2022): 144–72.
[60]Regele, *Manufacturing Advantage*, 111–34.

European intervention, and ensure that northern Mexico, Cuba, and Puerto Rico remained available for potential future US annexation. This was the context of the "Monroe Doctrine," the President's now famous proclamation in a message to Congress in December of 1823 that the Western Hemisphere should "henceforth not ... be considered as subjects for colonization by European powers."[61] While Monroe's statement would take on a life of its own in the decades and century after he delivered it—regularly reinterpreted by Americans to suit their purposes—at the time, it fit squarely into the strategy for handling Latin American independence we have been discussing.[62] In the spring and summer of 1823 anti-liberal and monarchical forces in Europe seemed to be on the move. Earlier in 1820 the conservative "Holy Alliance," led at the time by Tsar Alexander I of Russia, declared that it had a right to suppress any revolution in Europe deemed threatening to the alliance's security. While not initially a party to that declaration, France put it into motion in April of 1823 when it invaded Spain to restore the absolute rule of King Ferdinand VII (who had been forced to adopt a liberal constitution in 1820, thanks in part to the ongoing rebellion in the colonies). Rumors began to swirl that the Holy Alliance would take matters a step further and seek to restore the king's authority in the Americas as well.[63]

While no such intervention was actually in the works, American policymakers could not know for sure. Thus, when the British Foreign Secretary, George Canning, made a surprise offer of a joint Anglo-American statement against Russian intervention in the Americas, many of the President's advisors—including his informal, former presidents committee of Jefferson and Madison—feared the worst. Secretary of State Adams, however, was skeptical, both of the sincerity of Canning's motives and of the likelihood of intervention by the Holy Alliance. He believed that the United States had little to gain from the proposal—the Royal Navy would prevent European intervention in the Americas anyway—and risked losing face, coming "in as a cock-boat in the wake of the British man-of-war" as he put it.[64] Moreover, Canning's proposal included a mutual pledge that the United States and Britain would both avoid taking over parts of Spanish America for themselves—potentially preventing future US expansion in southeastern North America and the Caribbean.

Adams proposed instead a unilateral US statement proclaiming the Western Hemisphere off limits from future *European* intervention, while leaving the door open for US expansion when the time came. That time, as

---

[61] James Monroe, "Seventh Annual Message," December 2, 1823, Online by Gerhard Peters and John T. Woolley, *The American Presidency Project*, https://www.presidency.ucsb.edu/node/205755.
[62] Jay Sexton, *The Monroe Doctrine: Empire and Nation in Nineteenth Century America* (New York: Hill and Wang, 2011), 3–14.
[63] Sexton, *Monroe Doctrine*, 49–50; Herring, *From Colony to Superpower*, 151–4.
[64] Herring, *From Colony to Superpower*, 155.

Adams asserted in his comments on Cuba, had not yet arrived. This was not only because the United States could not risk another war with ever-powerful Britain, but also because expansion threatened to prompt a war with itself. With the Missouri Crisis of 1820 only recently resolved, Monroe and Adams were both wary of any annexation that could unpick the carefully wrought compromise between slave state and free forged that year. New territory in Texas, or in Cuba, they feared could do just that. As a result, the cautious statement inserted into Monroe's December message avoided asserting any American right to control what followed decolonization in the hemisphere, while at the same time being intended to keep the field clear for just that sort of activity at some future date.[65]

In addition to trying to keep the Europeans out of the Western Hemisphere, US policy also began to stress the importance of preventing any union among the new Latin American states, something which seemed equally threatening to US interests. While the possibilities were entirely remote, "thoughts of hemispheric union tantalized North American, as well as Spanish American, political theorists"—as the historian James E. Lewis Jr. has put it—throughout the first quarter of the nineteenth century.[66] Most US policymakers, however, hated the idea. Adams, for example, said it should be "disdainfully rejected," a view that informed his approach as president to a planned Pan-American congress held in Panama in 1826.

The brainchild of Bolívar, the meeting was intended to be the first in what the Spanish American liberator hoped might become a permanent assembly of American states. Ever wary of US intentions, Bolívar had not planned to invite the United States to the conference but eventually conceded the inevitability.[67] Adams accepted the invitation largely for symbolic reasons—he thought the meeting could reinforce the message in the Monroe Doctrine—but he also hoped to keep tabs on any project of Spanish American unity. Secretary of State Henry Clay stated the administration's position directly in his instructions to the US delegates, "all notion is rejected of some [pan-American council], invested with power finally, to decide controversies between the American states, or to regulate, in any respect, their conduct."[68] The delegates were also further instructed to prevent the establishment of *any* such union, even a looser one based on trade alone and not predicated on US participation. Such a trade union could, of course, potentially seek to exclude the United States from Latin American markets. The Adams administration believed that racial, religious, and cultural differences made it impossible for the United States to join in any relatively egalitarian hemispheric system.

---

[65]Lewis, *The American Union*, 147–8; Sexton, *Monroe Doctrine*, 47–84; Herring, *From Colony to Superpower*, 154–8.
[66]Lewis, *The American Union*, 210.
[67]Fitz, *Our Sister Republics*, 197–9.
[68]Lewis, *The American Union*, 211.

They also felt any exclusively Spanish American confederation threatened US economic hegemony, meaning it too had to be rejected. In response to Mexican proposals for a series of trade preferences binding all of Spanish America, Clay ordered the delegates to "resist it in every form" and refuse to sign any "treaty which shall admit it."[69]

As this indicates, by the time of the Panama Congress, what excitement there had been for the Spanish-American cause had diminished for many in the US, particularly in Washington. Adams and Clay for their part were increasingly doubtful that their South American neighbors could govern themselves. At one point, Clay even attempted to instruct Bolívar on how to build a good republic, writing to him on why standing armies were a danger to liberty. He also told the Americans in Panama to take every opportunity to explain how the system of government worked in the United States, and the "manifold blessings which the people of the United States have enjoyed" because of it.[70] James Brown, a diplomat and Clay's brother-in-law, summed up the prejudicial views of many in a letter to the Secretary of State, proclaiming that "our South American neighbors are not likely to do us much credit."[71]

This view was in fact so widespread that the Panama delegation was nearly not empowered at all. Adams announced his intention to send representatives to Panama in his first presidential message to Congress, expecting that the Senate would confirm his chosen delegates without any delay. His message instead touched off an explosive debate on Capitol Hill—a debate driven more by partisanship—Andrew Jackson's supporters saw an opportunity to weaken Adams—than any actual difference of opinion on Spanish American affairs. Arguments focused in particular on Cuba and Puerto Rico which many feared might soon be liberated by a combined effort of Mexico and Colombia. Nearly all agreed that this was an undesirable outcome, they just disagreed on whether going to Panama was the best way to prevent it.[72] "Cuba and Puerto Rico must remain as they are," argued one opponent of attending the conference. "It is our interest and duty to keep Cuba as it is" proclaimed another who, in contrast, urged attending the meeting for just that reason.[73] "Is it not reasonable for us to suppose," argued one Adams supporter, "that part of [Cuba's] population would all be declared free?" If so, he continued, "with the black population of Mexico on the frontier of Louisiana, and Hayti [sic] and Cuba for neighbors, what would be the condition of [our] Southern planters?"[74] Opponents of attending similarly

---

[69] Lewis, *The American Union*, 212.
[70] Lewis, *The American Union*, 197.
[71] Lewis, *The American Union*, 204.
[72] Gleijeses, "Limits of Sympathy," 494–500.
[73] Gleijeses, "Limits of Sympathy," 498.
[74] Gleijeses, "Limits of Sympathy," 499.

zeroed-in on on the cultural differences between the United States and Latin America—they "differ from us in every particular" said a Georgia congressman, "language, religion, laws, manners, customs, habits, as a mass, and as individuals"—and refused to countenance any effort at hemispheric cooperation.[75] Adams, as we have seen, thought the same and had no intention of using the Congress for anything other than preventing Latin American cooperation.

Virtually everyone in the US government agreed about Latin American inferiority and the need to preserve opportunities for US expansionism, they just disagreed about the precise means for advancing those causes and—of course—about who should be elected president of the United States in 1828. While Jackson's election that year, marked an important transition in US domestic politics, it did little to change the overall thrust of US policy toward decolonizing Spanish America. Jackson remained cautious, looking for opportunities to expand the United States without triggering a war with either a European power or any of the new states.

Filibustering, Texas, and the Invasion of Mexico

Jackson's consistency here made a good bit of sense, as the policies of his various predecessors had all served the United States well. Indeed, from a purely strategic perspective, the North American republic had so far masterfully managed the decolonization of the Western Hemisphere, preserving its independence while taking steps to ensure it would sit atop the political and economic hierarchy of the Americas. By the 1830s, US manufacturing already had a foothold in South American markets while no new rival—whether of European colonial or independent Latin American origin—had arisen out of the ashes of the Spanish Empire. Yet, perhaps the most critical step in the history of US development as a dominant hemispheric power remained: the conquest of Mexico.

The US war with Mexico (1846–48) proved a decisive one for both countries. In the eyes of future General and President Ulysses S. Grant—who served in Mexico as a junior officer—the war was "one of the most unjust ever waged by a stronger against a weaker nation."[76] Mexico lost more than half of its territory in the conflict, while the United States secured a crucial third of its land (when Texas is included), completing its transcontinental expansion to California. In the short run, victory over Mexico nearly proved disastrous to the United States, as the debate over whether the

---

[75]Gleijeses, "Limits of Sympathy," 501.
[76]Amy S. Greenberg, *A Wicked War: Polk, Clay, Lincoln and the 1846 U.S. Invasion of Mexico* (New York: Alfred A. Knopf, 2012), 274.

newly conquered territory would be made into slave state or free contributed directly to the outbreak of the US Civil War in 1861. Over the long term, however, it was a different story. The war ensured that a continent-spanning United States would be surrounded only by oceans, an increasingly friendly British Canada to the north, and a weakened and economically vulnerable Mexico to the south.

The war with Mexico was not, however, the product of any conscious, long-orchestrated strategy by Americans or their government. Certainly, as we discussed above, the United States responded to Latin American independence with an eye toward securing US advantage and, eventually, northern Mexico, Cuba, and Puerto Rico. Moreover, the war's primary author, President James K. Polk (in office: 1845–49), was an ardent expansionist himself who was quite willing to risk, and even engineer, a war as long as it secured California and most of northern Mexico for the United States.[77] That granted, there was no real unanimity on expansion. The country's politics in the 1840s continued to be divided between the Whigs—who were usually skeptical of further territorial expansion as inheritors of the Hamiltonian vision of using the central government to develop and diversify the existing states—and Democrats, who looked more favorably on expansion as part of a broader program of supporting and maintaining domestic commodity producers. Underlying all of this too was the sectional divide over slavery, which would overwhelm partisan loyalty by the end of the decade. Southerners were more naturally favorable toward action that expanded slavery, while Northerners were more skeptical or hostile. None of these lines were neat and tidy either—there were pro-expansion Northern Whigs as well as Southern Democrats who were wary of adding more new states. There was, therefore, no overwhelming majority in favor of further territorial expansion of the United States into the North American West in the 1840s, particularly if that required a war with either Great Britain or Mexico. The election of 1844, for example, which brought Polk to the White House, was a very close contest. With a few minor twists of fate, Polk's Whig opponent, Henry Clay, could very easily have been elected instead, potentially bringing to an end the territorial expansion of the United States in North America.[78]

Still, despite the real contingency in early nineteenth-century American politics, the empire builders won national office more often than not. It was generally easier to build majorities in favor of expansion than it was to build them against it, a consequence of the broader economic and cultural

---

[77]On Polk see, Walter Borneman, *Polk: The Man Who Transformed the Presidency and America* (New York: Random House, 2008); William Dusinberre, *Slavemaster President: The Double Career of James Polk* (New York: Oxford University Press, 2003); Greenberg, *Wicked War*, 3–110; Guardino, *Dead March*, 34–5; Sam W. Haynes, *James K. Polk and the Expansionist Impulse* (New York: Longman, 1997); Howe, *What Hath God Wrought*, 701–8.
[78]Guardino, *Dead March*, 18–30; Howe, *The Political Culture of American Whigs*, 92–5; Howe, *What Hath God Wrought*, 682–743.

forces we have been tracing in this book. Slavery was part of the story, combining as it did both economic and ideological incentives for expansion. The Constitution was tilted in favor of slaveholders by the infamous 3/5ths clause, allowing Southern states additional representation on the basis of their enslaved populations (which was more than enough to decide close elections). The institution, and the incredible wealth it produced, continued to grease the wheels of westward growth, pushing Americans to bring more and more land into cultivation, while producing enough money for Eastern merchants and manufacturers to make them disinclined to slow it. Many too feared the natural growth of the enslaved Black population and saw territorial expansion as a means of keeping the eastern part of the country more racially homogenous.[79]

Beyond the question of slavery's role in the republic's future, most Americans also remained committed to visions of national greatness—to ensuring that the United States moved up the global hierarchy of wealth and power—even if they disagreed about the best methods for achieving it. Whigs and Democrats alike shared a confidence that civilization followed wherever white Americans settled and entertained doubts about whether Latin Americans were capable of such advancement themselves. In addition, voters had a myriad of material reasons—real or imagined—to support expansion even if they did not personally own slaves. Some elites, for example, were tempted by the potential opportunity for land speculation, while others stood to gain from investment in additional cotton or other commodity production. Other citizens who did not have the wealth to invest in Western business ventures—including urban laborers or small farmers—still saw expansion as in their best interest. New land for settlement meant a potential escape hatch from debt, low wages, stiff job competition, or failed farms back East.[80] This web of material and ideological motivations tipped the balance in favor of the empire builders, which ultimately made it easier for Polk to bring about the war with Mexico and ensure approval of the massive annexations that followed it. Polk's machinations (which we will review presently) were critical, of course, but—again—they came at the end of long term trends that are better understood as part of a process than a plot.

To this point, the evolution from Adams-era caution toward Polk's war of conquest was set in motion not so much by government action, but by individual Americans pursuing the private material interests. From as early as the 1810s, for example, some Americans had been participating in various schemes to disrupt Spanish authority in the rebelling Latin American states, both on behalf of the rebels and in the hope of securing

---

[79]Beckert, *Empire of Cotton*, 105–20; Hietala, *Manifest Design*, 10–54; Howe, *What Hath God Wrought*, 705–6.
[80]Guardino, *Dead March*, 18–22; Hietala, *Manifest Design*, 1–9, 55–131.

more wealth for themselves and/or territory for the United States. These "filibusters" as they were later known—the term first emerged in the 1850s, as a derivative of a Dutch word for "freebooter"—operated mostly in Florida and in Texas. They also usually accomplished little beyond outraging the Spanish Minister to the United States and prompting a series of increasingly strict neutrality laws emanating from Congress.[81] Historians debate the exact position of the federal government on these schemes but it's fair to say that, in general, Washington was more in favor than it let on and less supportive than many filibusters claimed or desired.[82] The government did accept, however, the international legal conventions of the time, which meant that if a state was not at war with another— in this case, the United States was not at war with Spain—then it had a responsibility to make sure its citizens didn't engage in freelance military activity. From time to time, therefore, federal officials would crack down on the most egregious examples, such as when the Monroe administration ordered General Edmund P. Gaines to clear out a vexing privateering base on Amelia Island, Florida in 1817.[83]

Filibustering had its most significant impact on hemispheric history in the 1830s, with the arrival of what the historian Robert E. May aptly called, "the most successful filibuster in American history": the Texas Revolution.[84] US citizens and their slaves had begun settling in eastern Texas legally at the invitation of the Viceroyalty of New Spain in 1821.[85] The arrangement was subsequently upheld by the new Mexican government that achieved independence that year. Though wary of the risks Anglo-American settlement posed to the unity of their state, Mexican leaders saw no other viable means to see the province developed and thus thought it worth the gamble to let the settlers in.[86] The arrangement

---

[81]Henderson, *Glorious Defeat*, 33–5; Robert E. May, *Manifest Destiny's Underworld: Filibustering in Antebellum America* (Chapel Hill: University of North Carolina Press, 2002), 3–7.

[82]See: Frank Lawrence Owsley Jr. and Gene A. Smith, *Filibusters and Expansionists: Jeffersonian Manifest Destiny, 1800–1821* (Tuscaloosa: University of Alabama Press, 1997), 1–6; J.C.A. Stagg, "The Madison Administration and Mexico: Reinterpreting the Gutiérrez-Magee Raid of 1812–1813," *The William and Mary Quarterly* 59, no. 2 (2002): 449–80, https://doi.org/10.2307/3491744.

[83]Owsley and Smith, *Filibusters and Expansionists*, 140.

[84]May, *Manifest Destiny's Underworld*, 9.

[85]Illegal Anglo-American migration had begun earlier. Henderson, *Glorious Defeat*, 35–6, 49–50.

[86]Rightfully concerned that their northern provinces might attract annexation by the United States because they were so lightly populated, Mexican leaders believed that Anglo-American immigrants could help secure Texas for Mexico through settling and developing its economy, leading to further—non-Anglo-American—migration. They were fully aware that the settlers could just as easily bring about an opposite result, of course, but they lacked other options—a "wicked conundrum" as Timothy Henderson puts it. Henderson, *Glorious Defeat*, 35–6.

was made all the more cozy for immigrants from the United States by the liberal, decentralized constitution later adopted by Mexico in 1824, which granted Texas considerable autonomy. However, as the number of Anglo-American settlers rose—and, indeed, flourished, outnumbering Hispanic Texans 10-1 by 1836—so did tensions.[87] Mexico banned slavery in 1829 and further immigration from the United States in 1830. Meanwhile, the Jackson administration brazenly pressured Mexico to sell Texas to the United States, outraging Mexico City and fueling further suspicion of the settlers.[88]

When General Antonio López de Santa Anna repudiated the 1824 constitution following his election to Mexico's presidency in 1833, the settlers in Texas began to organize to preserve their political autonomy—and control over their slaves—many of whom rose up in a bid for freedom in 1835.[89] What began as a settler revolt soon became a filibustering enterprise. As news of the situation in Texas spread north, American adventurers headed south looking for a fight and the potential land and wealth that might come with it. By 1836, roughly three-quarters of the rebel Texans under arms were those who had left the United States in the past year—"violent and desperate men" with "nothing to lose," as one Mexican official put it.[90] Following his defeat and capture in the Battle of San Jacinto in April of 1836, Santa Anna signed agreements promising to withdraw his troops south of the Rio Grande and subsequently push for negotiations to recognize an independent Texas—documents Texans believed settled the war, but the Mexican government refused to honor.[91]

The establishment of the Republic of Texas immediately led to questions about whether the United States would annex the former (and, if you asked Mexicans, *still*) Mexican province. While Jackson had done little to discourage filibustering Americans from crossing into Texas, he also had little interest in courting another Missouri Crisis at the end of his second term.[92] Partisan politics and sectionalism thus kept annexation off the table for nearly a decade, until Polk's election to the presidency in 1844. Polk, as we have mentioned, represented the pro-slavery, arch-expansionist wing of the Democratic Party, yet he was motivated more by a nationalist spirit than a sectional one. He believed that ports on the Pacific coast, a secure Texas, and a North American Southwest free of European influence

---

[87] Henderson, *A Glorious Defeat*, 54–74, 85–6; Howe, *What Hath God Wrought*, 658–60.
[88] On Jackson's pursuit of Texas see: Quinton Curtis Lamar, "A Diplomatic Disaster: The Mexican Mission of Anthony Butler, 1829–1834," *The Americas* 45, no. 1 (July 1988): 1–17.
[89] On Santa Anna's rise to power see: Will Fowler, *Santa Anna of Mexico* (Lincoln: University of Nebraska Press, 2007)
[90] Henderson, *A Glorious Defeat*, 100.
[91] Fowler, *Santa Anna*, 176–9; Greenberg, *Wicked War*, 8–10; Henderson, *A Glorious Defeat*, 84–113; Howe, *What Hath God Wrought*, 662.
[92] Henderson, *A Glorious Defeat*, 121–2.

were essential to American security and economic growth. Moreover, Polk also felt that the national interests of the United States coincided with, as he put it in 1848, "the general interest of mankind."[93] American expansion was essential not just for US wealth and power, but for the progress of humanity as a whole.

In this, he was a true advocate for what became known as "Manifest Destiny," a term coined in 1845 by a New York Democratic magazine—the *Democratic Review*—advocating for Polk's policies in the West. It was, as the *Review* put it, the republic's "manifest destiny to overspread the continent allotted by Providence for the free development of our yearly multiplying millions."[94] In this, Manifest Destiny was merely a new name for the same ideas we have encountered throughout the book, those which saw the settlement and expansion of the United States as representing the advance of civilization itself. As the *Democratic Review*'s editor, John O'Sullivan, put it in another newspaper: a growing United States was "making the desert to bloom in its progress, carrying with it the blessings of civil and religious liberty, and illuminating the night of barbarism with the light of education and science."[95]

While O'Sullivan was using "barbarism" in a general sense, Americans had little issue seeing Mexicans as part of it specifically. In American eyes, their southern neighbors were perhaps above Native Americans and enslaved Black Americans in the hierarchy of civilization, but not by much. James Gordon Bennet, a leading newspaperman of the time, for example, pointed to the mixed racial character of the Mexican population as evidence of the country's supposed degeneration. "Out of seven millions of souls[,] four millions" of the Mexican population "are Indians," he wrote, "and of the remaining three millions but twelve hundred thousand are whites." This he attributed this to a lack of proper wariness about race mixing, a mistake that whites in the United States had avoided. White Americans had "kept aloof from the inferior races," he asserted, and thus, as they moved west, "barbarism had receded before the face of civilization." Mexico, therefore, was likely to suffer a fate "similar to that of the Indians of this country—the race, before a century rolls over us, will become extinct."[96]

Sam Houston, the first president of the independent Republic of Texas, agreed, bluntly claiming that "Mexicans are no better than Indians."[97] Senator (and future President) James Buchanan made clear how he

---

[93] James K. Polk, "Special Message to Congress," July 6, 1848, Peters and Woolley, *The American Presidency*, Project, https://www.presidency.ucsb.edu/node/201637
[94] Howe, *What Hath God Wrought*, 703.
[95] Hietala, *Manifest Design*, x.
[96] Hietala, *Manifest Design*, 155.
[97] Greenberg, *Wicked War*, 57.

understood the hierarchy of North America when he pronounced in 1843 that "our race of men can never be subjected to the imbecile and indolent Mexican race."[98] Levy Woodbury, a US House Democrat from New Hampshire offered much the same view in advocating for the annexation of Texas. It was impossible, he argued, to allow the "Saxon blood" of the Americans in Texas. to be "humiliated, and enslaved to Moors, Indians, and mongrels."[99] It was not just race that made Mexico a backward country in the eyes of white Americans, but religion as well. Though the American Revolution had enshrined freedom of religion as a fundamental aspect of US national character, most Americans interpreted this through a distinctly Protestant lens, limiting the true extent of religious freedom in practice.[100] Roman Catholicism was seen as a form of idolatrous superstition, an older, more irrational and tyrannical form of Christianity that Anglo-Saxons had long since left behind.[101] Such sentiments had only been further inflamed by the vast increase of Catholic immigration to the United States (primarily from Ireland and Germany) in the 1830s, leading to the outbreak of violent anti-Catholic mobs in cities like Philadelphia.[102] Senator Robert J. Walker of Mississippi, summarized the prevailing view when he proclaimed Mexico a nation in thrall to "a cruel, ambitious, and licentious priesthood." [103]

Conveniently, this dubious racial and religious character also made Mexico ripe for conquest. Mexicans would, according to the *Herald*, "melt away at the approach of Anglo-Saxon energy and enterprise as snow before a southern sun."[104] The residents of Mexico were unlike their northern neighbors, Illinois Senator Sidney Breese argued, because the citizens of the United States were of the "glorious Anglo-Saxon race, whose high destiny is to civilize and Christianize the world."[105] Polk offered a similar view after the war—and echoed his colonial forbearers in their justifications for the initial English plantations in North America—explaining that the lands the United States seized from Mexico otherwise "would have continued to remain, almost unoccupied, and of little value to her or any other nation." Under American control, however, they would "be productive of vast benefits to the United States [and] to the commercial world." Thanks to the war, and the territory it had secured for productive use and "development by American energy and enterprise"

---

[98]John C. Pinhiero, "Religion without Restriction: Anti-Catholicism, All Mexico, and the Treaty of Guadalupe Hidalgo," *Journal of the Early Republic* 23, no. 1 (Spring 2003): 69–96, 78.
[99]Pinheiro, "Religion without Restriction," 78.
[100]See: David Sehat, *The Myth of American Religious Freedom* (New York: Oxford University Press, 2010).
[101]Pinheiro, "Religion without Restriction," 73–9.
[102]Pinheiro, "Religion without Restriction," 74.
[103]Pinheiro, "Religion without Restriction," 78.
[104]Hietala, *Manifest Destiny*, 155.
[105]Pinheiro, "Religion without Restriction," 80.

the United States, the President asserted, would have a "destiny without a parallel or example in the history of nations."[106]

Polk's campaign for the presidency was so closely associated with this expansionist vision of American destiny that his election alone was enough to get the ball rolling on Texas. Taking the Tennessean's victory as a mandate for annexation, outgoing President John Tyler (in office: 1841–45) worked with allies in Congress to incorporate Texas into the union before leaving office in March of 1845. Rather than seeking a treaty of annexation, which had long since stalled in front of the Senate's two-thirds requirement, Tyler helped arrange for a resolution accepting Texas as a new state, needing only a simple majority in both houses, which it received in February. When Polk arrived in office on March 4th, Texas was already well on its way to joining the Union, and one part of his expansionist platform was accomplished for him.[107] Polk hoped for much more, however, planning to firmly establish the Rio Grande as the Texas border and secure California and the rest of northern Mexico for the United States, ideally through purchase.

In trying to force Mexico into the sale, Polk employed a concept that would increasingly become important to the United States and the European states near the top of the global hierarchy: "international law." As we have seen, during the revolutionary era in Latin America, American merchants and lenders had practiced "arithmetic neutrality" toward independence, providing loans, munitions, and other supplies in return for cash or promissory notes. Throughout the 1830s and 1840s, some of these merchants and lenders claimed that they had been mistreated or left unpaid, claims that amounted to some millions of dollars. It was widely understood that, as George Herring put it, "many of these claims were inflated, some were patently unjust, and most derived from profiteering at Mexico's expense."[108] Despite this, the US government periodically turned to them as a way of attempting to pressure Mexico, offering to assume the debts as part of some larger payoff for the acquisition of additional Mexican territory. In the nineteenth century, the idea that investors or creditors should expect the property rights they enjoyed in their home country to be respected abroad—regardless of the legal and economic regime in the debtor country—was elevated as a kind of international "legal" principle that all "civilized" states were expected to observe. In practice, it was a tool used by more powerful nations to justify interventions in weaker states, another example

---

[106] James K. Polk, "Special Message to Congress," July 6, 1848, Online by Gerhard Peters and John T. Woolley, *The American Presidency Project*, https://www.presidency.ucsb.edu/node/201637.
[107] Though the annexation resolution became law with Tyler's signature on March 1st, Texas did not formally join the Union until December of 1845. Gene M. Brack, *Mexico Views Manifest Destiny, 1821–1846* (Albuquerque: University of New Mexico Press, 1975), 116; Henderson, *A Glorious Defeat*, 133–47; Howe, *What Hath God Wrought*, 698–700.
[108] Herring, *From Colony to Superpower*, 197.

of the inherently hierarchical structure of what was increasingly called the "civilized world."[109]

Polk believed that the claims issue could serve as a wedge to force Mexico into a sale that—in his eyes—should satisfy both countries, granting the United States its desired territory and helping Mexico with its financial obligations. Like it had the United States in the 1780s, decolonization left Mexico with potentially crippling debt, economic dislocation, and almost no political institutions that could command enduring loyalty across the entire country. As Will Fowler writes, "the constitutional vacuum that resulted from ... separation from Spain" and the "inability of the political class to forge a long-lasting ... order" resulted in decades of "political vigilantism." In its first forty years of independence, Mexico's government was therefore shaped as much by *pronunciamiento*—petitions listing political demands and backed by threats of violence—as it was constitutional provisions.[110] While Mexicans did not welcome foreign domination, they weren't always particularly loyal to their current government either. Mexico's army, meanwhile, was large on paper but ill-equipped to defend its massive border with the United States (not to mention a long coastline in the face of overwhelming US naval supremacy).[111]

Another problem for the Mexican government was that—whether it wanted to negotiate or not—settling with the United States was a domestic political impossibility. By the early 1840s, anti-American sentiment had come to dominate the Mexican political scene. These feelings had, in part, similarly deep origins to American condescension toward Latin Americans: a product of the centuries-long Anglo-Spanish rivalry and the anti-Protestant sentiment that went with it. More decisive though had been recent American behavior. Many Mexicans continued to resent the limited support the United States had provided their movement for independence from Spain. They were also quite aware of the pervasive racism in the United States toward Latin Americans. The vicious characterizations of Central and South Americans that had been part of the US debate over the Congress of Panama had been reported in Mexico—"fanatical intolerance," one editor called it—and disgust with US racism had only grown since.[112] Though no egalitarian paradise itself, Mexico, as mentioned, had banned slavery. Most Mexicans in the 1830s and 1840s viewed the institution with revulsion. As one Chihuahua newspaper writer worried in 1840, if American expansion

---

[109]Charles Sellers, *The Market Revolution: Jacksonian America, 1815–1846* (New York: Oxford University Press, 1991), 420.

[110]Will Fowler, *Independent Mexico: The Pronunciamiento in the Age of Santa Anna, 1821–1858* (Lincoln: University of Nebraska Press, 2016), quote on 249.

[111]Brack, *Mexico Views Manifest Destiny*, 52–6, 79–80, 154–7, 163–6, 174–9; Henderson, *A Glorious Defeat*, 148–9; Guardino, *Dead March*, 7–14; Howe, *What Hath God Wrought*, 745–52.

[112]Brack, *Mexico Views Manifest Destiny*, 45.

was not stopped, Mexican citizens might soon be "sold as beasts" because "their color was not as white as that of their conquerors."[113] The revolt in Texas, which most Mexicans incorrectly (but not unreasonably) saw as a deliberate result of US government policy, only strengthened anti-American sentiment. Tyler's annexation resolution cemented it. Fearing their avaricious neighbor to the north, politically active Mexicans naturally refused to further surrender their land, sovereignty, or national pride.[114]

Therefore, though Mexican officials knew that they had little ability to assert their claims to Texas—or to successfully resist a US invasion if it came—they could not publicly acknowledge these realities without severe risk of being removed from office. Santa Anna, for example, had declared in 1843 that the annexation of Texas would mean war but he was forced from power—following an 1844 *pronunciamiento*—in part because of his failures to recover the rebel province.[115] It thus fell to his successor, José Joaquín de Herrera, to respond when annexation arrived, but he too would struggle to reconcile domestic politics with strategic realities. Hoping to avoid both war and disgrace, Herrera severed relations with the United States without declaring war, but this merely allowed General Mariano Paredes y Arrillaga to use Herrera's supposed weakness as justification for another *pronunciamiento*, seizing the presidency in early January 1846.[116] In office, Paredes y Arrillaga confronted much the same problem as his predecessors, unable to find a solution that didn't involve either losing Texas and California or engaging in a war Mexico was very likely to lose.[117]

Polk was well informed of the Mexican government's predicament, but his patience with stalled diplomacy wore thin all the same. He ordered the US Navy to start provocative patrols of the Mexican coast and then, in July of 1845, sent General Zachary Taylor into disputed territory between the Nueces and the Rio Grande—an act that arguably amounted to an invasion of Mexican territory.[118] When even these efforts failed to push a semi-paralyzed Mexican government into either concessions or war, Polk decided he would proceed to war unilaterally, drafting a war message to Congress in May of 1846. Events, however, made matters simpler for the President. Mexican troops crossing the Rio Grande engaged in a skirmish with US soldiers near today's city of Brownsville on April 25th, prompting

---

[113] Brack, *Mexico Views Manifest Destiny*, 99.
[114] Henderson, *A Glorious Defeat*, especially, 187–91.
[115] Fowler, *Independent Mexico*, 213–15.
[116] Fowler, *Independent Mexico*, 216–17.
[117] Brack, *Mexico Views Manifest Destiny*, 135–66.
[118] The traditional boundary of the Mexican state of Texas had been the Nueces River. Santa Anna had agreed to withdraw south of the Rio Grande after San Jacinto, which Texans had then determined to be the border of their independent state. During subsequent, failed negotiations to recognize the independence of Texas, Mexico had insisted on a boundary at the Nueces. The United States would later unilaterally claim the Rio Grande as its new southern border following its annexation of Texas. Henderson, *A Glorious Defeat*, 98–9, 122–7.

a declaration of war once the news reached Washington.[119] The war that followed was longer, bloodier, and more expensive than most expected—Polk included—but the United States possessed a number of advantages that proved decisive. Not all decolonizations are equal, and the United States had made powerful use of its four-decade head start. US finances were in much better order and the country was significantly wealthier than it had been, making the war easy to pay for despite relatively low taxes. US troops were generally much better fed, equipped, and armed, particularly when it came to artillery. As we have seen, sustained in part by sales to Latin American revolutionaries (including those in Mexico) and by the demand generated by near constant war on the frontier with Native Americans, the United States had an arms industry that already was among the best in the world. Though some Mexicans resisted the US invasion fiercely—both in regular military formations and as partisans—by 1848 their government was forced to accept a humiliating treaty, signed in Guadalupe-Hidalgo on February 2nd, 1848.

Even the huge territorial concessions it contained (all of modern California, Nevada, Utah, and Texas, as well as the majority of Arizona and New Mexico, and roughly half of Colorado) were not necessarily enough for Polk. Late in the negotiations, he pushed for greater territorial concessions (which would have extended US territory to Tampico) and in April, as Congress debated ratification, Polk even recommended sending troops to the Yucatan.[120] Other Democrats went further and pushed for the annexation of "all Mexico," though this was never really a serious possibility. As the occupation of Mexico dragged on, the brutality of American troops ensured continued opposition from the Mexican population, increasing the cost of the war in both blood and treasure, undermining already flagging support at home.[121] Whigs—and anti-slavery Northerners—were opposed to any territorial annexation at all. Many Democrats—like John C. Calhoun—meanwhile, were skeptical of incorporating a large population of Hispanic Catholics into the United States. The very same assumptions of Mexican inferiority that helped justify the war also helped limit the annexations that resulted from it.[122] As a result, Polk was careful to depict the proposed cession as largely uninhabited, a false claim as he well knew. Though lightly populated compared with central Mexico, more than 100,000 Native Americans lived

---

[119]Greenberg, *Wicked War*, 91–110; Guardino, *Dead March*, 71–86; Henderson, *A Glorious Defeat*, 147–56; Howe, *What Hath God Wrought*, 734–43; David M. Pletcher, *The Diplomacy of Annexation: Texas, Oregon, and the Mexican War* (Columbia: University of Missouri Press, 1973), 373–92.
[120]Henderson, *A Glorious Defeat*, 157–78; Howe, *What Hath God Wrought*, 745–6, 796–811; Pletcher, *Diplomacy of Annexation*, 395–402, 439–49, 454–550.
[121]Greenberg, *Wicked War*, 210–11, 246–7.
[122]Howe, *What Hath God Wrought*, 798–9. Pinheiro, "Religion without Restriction," 85–90.

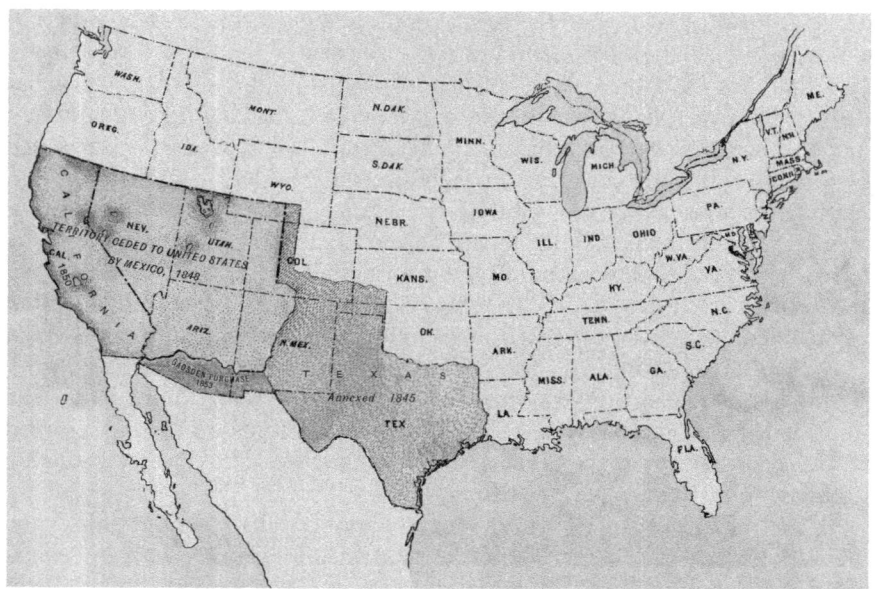

FIGURE 6 *A map showing US territory—amounting to roughly a third of the continental United States—that once belonged to Mexico.*

in the treaty lands, technically enjoying Mexican citizenship, as did nearly 90,000 Mexicans. Ultimately, the treaty was adopted because the Mexicans had little choice, and because its massive transfer of territory stood as a sort of middle ground between the arch-expansionists in the United States and those opposed to any annexations at all. Congress approved the document in March of 1848, Mexico in May. It was formally proclaimed in the United States on July 4th, 1848.[123]

The American war on its largest postcolonial neighbor fundamentally altered the economic and political hierarchy of North America. Mexico's significant disadvantages at the start of the war notwithstanding, the two countries were roughly the same size before Guadalupe-Hidalgo. Mexico's financial issues and political instability—though more acute than those the United States faced in 1783—were not so vastly different as to guarantee that, had war been avoided, it could not have become a peer of the United States in time.[124] Instead, the US-Mexican War made the United States into a territorial colossus, with direct access to both the Atlantic and the Pacific,

---

[123]Greenberg, *Wicked War*, 256–64; Henderson, *A Glorious Defeat*, 179–87; Howe, *What Hath God Wrought*, 809–11; Pletcher, *Diplomacy of Annexation*, 522–71.

[124]See the comparisons of pre-war Mexico and the US in: Henderson, *A Glorious Defeat*, 3–23; Guardino, *Dead March*, 1–30.

as well as significant new mineral resources. Though not known at the time of the war, the later discovery of gold in California (in 1848) revealed the first of several precious metal lodes that would be found in former Mexican land (including large silver deposits in Nevada and Utah). Instead of helping cash-strapped Mexico recover from its fight for independence, these reserves bolstered the US money supply during key phases of its late nineteenth century economic development. American economic power soon translated into dependance for Mexico.[125] As white settlers began to flood into California, their money soon traveled south across the border and into investments in Mexico. Los Angeles became, as Jessica M. Kim has put it, a "imperial metropolis"—a "city empire" that built vast wealth on the "exploitation of Mexican labor and Mexican natural resources."[126] Beginning in the 1870s, American money ensured that pliant, pro-investor governments reigned in Mexico City. By the early twentieth century, US-manufactured goods had gained a dominant share of the Mexican market, while more than a quarter of Mexican territory was owned by citizens of the United States.[127]

In the spring of 1848, of course, all this lay in the future. Rather than building American strength, the Mexican Cession at first nearly proved the country's ruin—the debate over how to split the spoils of war between free-labor North and the slave South led directly to the Civil War. We will deal more with the long-term consequences of that war for the US relationship with empire in the next chapter, but for now, we need to turn instead to another key theater for the antebellum US and global hierarchy: the Pacific.

The Empire of Trade, US Industrialization, and the Great Divergence

"When I contemplate the ardor with which the Anglo-Americans prosecute commercial enterprise," wrote de Tocqueville in 1835, "I cannot refrain from believing that they will one day become the first maritime power of the globe." Americans, he continued, were "born to rule the seas as the Romans were to conquer the world."[128] The perceptive Frenchman was, as

---

[125] Greenberg, *Wicked War*, 268–71; Henderson, *A Glorious Defeat*, 157–78; Alfred Avila and John Tutino, "Becoming Mexico: The Conflictive Search for a North American Nation," in *New Countries*, 266–71; Levy, *Ages of American Capitalism*, 251.
[126] Jessica M. Kim, *Imperial Metropolis: Los Angeles, Mexico, and the Borderlands of American Empire, 1865–1941* (Chapel Hill: University of North Carolina Press, 2019), 5.
[127] Kim, *Imperial Metropolis*, 12.
[128] Alexis De Tocqueville, *Democracy in America*, Volume 1, Henry Reeve trans. (New Rochelle: Arlington House, 1966), 425.

usual, on to something. As he was writing, the United States was already well along the way to such water-born dominance, with a globe-spanning maritime commercial presence second only to the British. Many Americans spoke with pride of this "bright and glorious 'empire of the seas'," as *De Bow's Review* put it in 1849. The magazine further celebrated how "every sea and navigable water under the face of heaven, sees the white wings of our shipping."[129] US vessels had begun the commercial penetration of Spain's collapsing New World from the first available opportunity, while commercial relations across the Atlantic and with the Caribbean were also well established. Therefore, what really swelled the hearts of America's maritime boosters in the early to mid-nineteenth century was expanding US trade in the Pacific.

Previously limited by the British East India Company's (EIC) legal monopoly on trade to Asia, US-based merchants began to explore commercial opportunities in the Pacifc from nearly the moment the Revolutionary War ended. Though the *Empress of China*, the first US ship to reach Asia, produced only a small profit, many more followed, to much greater financial success.[130] These early US commercial ventures in the Pacific Ocean are relevant to our story of the United States and the ends of empire for two reasons. First, nineteenth-century American merchants helped lay the groundwork for a future US empire in the Pacific. Second, in so doing, they played a key role in sustaining trade links between the Atlantic World and Asia during the Anglo-French Wars, maintaining the networks and processes that were slowly reordering global trade at this time, shifting economic power away from Asia and toward the North Atlantic.

As we discussed in the introduction, the centuries after Columbus's arrival in the Americas in 1492 saw European states invade and incorporate the Western Hemisphere into economic systems designed to funnel surplus wealth towards Europe. At the same time, they also aggressively inserted themselves into trade networks in Asia, cutting out traditional Mediterranean and Middle Eastern middlemen and even replacing some intra-Asian networks with their own. Uninterested—and initially unable—to conquer these heavily populated areas, Europeans instead settled for establishing fortified coastal enclaves in places like today's Mumbai, Kolkata, Jakarta, and Macao. Well into the eighteenth century, much of this European-Asian commerce was conducted on relatively equal terms, with Europeans trading Spanish-American silver for finished goods like

---

[129]Roleau, *Sails Whitening Every Sea*, 1.
[130]Dane A. Morrison, *True Yankees: The South Seas and the Discovery of American Identity* (Baltimore: Johns Hopkins University Press, 2014), xi–xiii. Jacques M. Downs, *The Golden Ghetto: The American Commercial Community at Canton and the Shaping of American China Policy, 1784–1844* (Hong Kong: Hong Kong University Press, 2014), 65. James R. Fichter, *So Great a Proffit: How the East Indies Trade Transformed Anglo-American Capitalism* (Cambridge, MA: Harvard University Press, 2010), 45–7.

woven cotton cloth from India or hard-to-obtain luxuries like Chinese tea. Over time however, cumulative European economic advantages began to shift this balance of trade. By the early nineteenth century, European capital and manufactured goods were restructuring economic life in the "East Indies"—as the whole stretch of the globe from India to China was then known to Europeans. The relatively egalitarian trade in luxury goods was eventually overtaken by a more unequal commerce in commodities. The English, French, and Dutch used these trade imbalances—and military force—to extend their political and economic control, becoming the dominant powers of the Asian littoral by the late nineteenth century. The transformation in the global power structure that resulted is sometimes called "the Great Divergence." The name is a reflection of how European and US rates of economic growth and innovation quickly began to outpace an Asian world that—even in the mid-eighteenth century—had been equal to if not richer than the Euro-American one.[131]

Though the United States did not acquire a formal Asian empire until the end of the nineteenth century, it was a participant in, and key beneficiary of, this process of imperial reordering. When the wars between Britain and Revolutionary and Napoleonic France kept the continent's merchant marine shut up in port—and the British East India Company's monopoly kept Britain's shipping relatively uncompetitive—US merchants took up the slack. Because the United States was neutral in the conflict, US flagged vessels could travel relatively unmolested. Soon US trade with Asia—in coffee, tea, spices, cloth, etc.—was second only to Britain. As one US observer commented at the time, the war had thrown "into our hands the greater part of the colonial carrying trade of the world—an economic prize for which European nations had been fiercely struggling for nearly two centuries."[132] French and Dutch carriers returned to the sea following Napoleon's defeat in 1815—and the US percentage of Asian trade duly fell—but in the interim Northeastern US merchants made considerable fortunes. Much of this wealth was in hard currency—silver—creating what the United States had never really had before: a millionaire investor class ready to fund new ventures.[133]

This class proved critical to financing the economic development of the United States. It helped fund in part the expansion of transportation infrastructure, the growth of the US banking industry, and the establishment

---

[131] Kenneth Pomeranz, *The Great Divergence: Europe, China, and the Making of the Modern World Economy* (Princeton: Princeton University Press, 2000). See also: Bayly, *The Birth of the Modern World*, 2–3, 49–83, 134–8; Findlay and O'Rourke, *Power and Plenty*, 143–428; Beckert, *Empire of Cotton*; Wallerstein, *Modern World-System III*, xiii–xvi, 127–89.
[132] Fichter, *So Great a Profitt*, 82 (quote), 56–110.
[133] Previously, most colonial and Early-Republican private wealth was held by Southern planters, whose wealth was based more on access to credit than it was on cash. Fichter, *So Great a Profitt*, 110–48.

of the country's early industrial plant. The famous "Boston Manufacturing Company," for example, was endowed largely by merchant capital earned in Asian trade.[134] This hard currency wealth also proved essential for ensuring foreign, primarily British, investment in American enterprises, as ventures funded partly by specie were more attractive than those which were mostly financed with debt.[135] More broadly significant, by keeping up demand for monoculture commodities—like sugar, coffee, indigo, and cotton—American merchants during the war years helped continue the transition in European-Asian trade we just discussed. American maritime commerce, as the historian James Fichter has put it, played a key role in the "spread of cash crop farming over ever-larger swaths of land, transforming" coastal cities like "Port Louis, Batavia, and Manila from entrepots ... for exotic, high-value Asian products ... into entrepots for cash crops."[136]

Trade with Asia also helped establish a US commercial presence in the Pacific which endured long after the end of the Napoleonic Wars, leading to the establishment of a formal US empire later in the century. Two things principally drew American ships into or across the Pacific: whales and tea. While whaling won't occupy much of our attention here, it deserves mention as American whalers made up most of "nineteenth-century America's largest class of representatives overseas"—sailors.[137] At its 1840s peak, the US whaling fleet was the largest in the world. Tea-ships, on the other hand, were less numerous, but no less important—not least because they left American ports loaded with a something that was scarcer in the United States than whale oil and more precious to its owners: silver. Silver was essential for tea purchases. It was one of the few things that US merchants had which was sufficiently desired by Chinese merchants in Canton (Guangzhou) in order to ensure a full hold on the return journey.[138] Before US trade with Asia was firmly established, silver was hard for Americans to come by and thus many China trips began with stops in South America, where US goods were exchanged for silver that was then shipped across the Pacific.

Yet, it was never enough, which led to merchants relentlessly searching for something else to offer to their Chinese partners, sailing much further afield than a China voyage might otherwise require. These voyages rapidly expanded American commercial interests. In addition to stops in Latin America, US ships soon began traveling regularly to the Pacific Northwest, where one could trade with Native Americans for sea otter pelts.[139] Similar quests for luxuries with a market in China also drew Americans to various islands across the Pacific. When a marooned American sailor reported back

---

[134] Fichter, *So Great a Proffit*, 252–77.
[135] Fichter, *So Great a Proffit*, 278–83.
[136] Fichter, *So Great a Proffit*, 165.
[137] Rouleau, *Sails Whitening Every Sea*, 7.
[138] Fichter, *So Great a Proffit*, 31–55.
[139] Fichter, *So Great a Proffit*, 47–9.

home in 1804 that Fiji contained large reserves of sandalwood—valued in China for its aromatic qualities—it led to the first of what became regular voyages to the South Pacific islands. These trips were later sustained by harvests of "bêche-de-mer," sea slugs, used to enrich a number of traditional Chinese dishes.[140] As natural reserves were quickly exhausted (Fiji's sandalwood groves were essentially depleted by 1810), American merchantment moved on to other sources, from Hawaii to the Marquesas Islands.[141]

Hawaii, for example, had long been a stopover for US whalers and China ships—a welcome respite and resupply point for ocean-weary sailors—but it also became a source for commodities like sandalwood. Sailors would harvest the wood themselves when they could (in effect, stealing it) but they were also forced to deal with locals to acquire the necessary stocks. Much as trade for European made goods had transformed the Indigenous world in North America, the commodity trade in the Pacific had a similarly dramatic impact on Pacific islands. Local rulers regularly attempted to establish trading monopolies, essential for securing access to US-made luxuries and firearms, significantly impacting local power dynamics. As John Richmond Child, a US sailor in the Marquesas, noted in 1810, sandalwood had become so "very rar[e] in this place ... the Natives are most constantly at war."[142] At times, merchant captains would even directly intervene to ensure the best rates of exchange—as Child's captain did, ordering armed sailors and a cannon ashore (in this case to little effect, their powder being too damp from rain).[143]

Sailors brought into the Pacific the standard nineteenth-century American prejudices toward supposedly "primitive" people of color, formed over generations of colonial and frontier warfare. Just as it had on the North American frontier, the idea of progress—and the place of white Americans at its vanguard—shaped how native peoples were depicted. Francis Olmstead, a passenger on a whale ship that traveled much of the South Pacific in 1839, typified this perspective when he commented that native Hawaiians were clearly on an "inevitable" path to "total extinction." The "humble islanders," he continued, "must shrink away before the irresistible march of foreign enterprise" just like "the [Native Americans] of our own country."[144] Whalers were thus often depicted as another class of pioneers, opening a watery frontier for civilization's march. As one New England observer put it, "the master seamen of the young republic [are] as truly pioneers as their kinsmen ... pouring through the passes of the Alleghanies

---

[140]Nancy Shoemaker, *Pursuing Respect in the Cannibal Isles: Americans in Nineteenth Century Fiji* (Ithaca: Cornell University Press, 2019), 1–2.
[141]Fichter, *So Great a Proffit*, 219.
[142]Fichter, *So Great a Proffit*, 220.
[143]Fichter, *So Great a Proffit*, 220.
[144]Rouleau, *Sails Whitening Every Sea*, 95.

to subdue the West."¹⁴⁵ Herman Melville, writing in *Moby Dick*, expressed a similar sentiment: "if American and European men-of-war now peacefully ride in once savage harbors, let them fire salutes to the honor and glory of the whale-ship which … first interpreted between them and the savages."¹⁴⁶ American merchant and whalemen were seen at home—and regularly saw themselves—as the seaborn agents of history.

This prejudice led to plenty of ugly incidents, as merchants and whalers interacted with people they saw as their civilizational inferiors. "Verbal misunderstandings, thefts, and even murders were not unheard of among sailors in all parts of the world"—as the historian Brian Roleau has written—but such issues in the Pacific regularly "took on a special meaning for American men as grievous assaults against civilization."¹⁴⁷ Thus what in a European port may have been handled as a matter of law, in the South Seas was instead addressed through violent retribution. Joseph G. Clark, a merchant sailor, for example, wrote of an 1840 episode where islanders had supposedly robbed members of the crew of some items. In response, the crew proceeded ashore and burned a small village in retaliation—"we wished to show our superiority to the savages," he remembered. William Clark, another crewmember, said that the men were happy to attack the village as "they wanted some sport."¹⁴⁸ In July of 1840, sailors of the United States Exploring Expedition—or "Ex Ex," a cartographical and scientific mission charted by President Andrew Jackson—landed on the Fijian island of Malolo to barter for some hogs. Negotiations soured and the sailors ended up in a fight that left eleven dead, two Americans and nine islanders. The Ex-Ex subsequently deployed two war parties which proceeded to burn buildings, tear up fields, and slaughter every male Fijian they could find. As the mission's commander later explained, "had … the great crime been suffered to go unpunished" the islanders "would in all probability become more fearless and daring than ever."¹⁴⁹

As these examples indicate, in the South Seas, US sailors took it upon themselves to violently enforce what they saw as the hierarchy of civilization and the proper rules for commerce. Given their overwhelming advantages in firepower, Americans usually were able to ensure events went their way, either through the direct application of force or by the careful distribution of firearms to more pliant locals. Violence, therefore, was an essential part of building US commercial networks in the Pacific, ensuring that trade relationships—already unequal given that US merchants could trade manufactured goods—benefited the Americans. By the time the Ex-Ex

---

¹⁴⁵Rouleau, *Sails Whitening Every Sea*, 91.
¹⁴⁶Rouleau, *Sails Whitening Every Sea*, 91.
¹⁴⁷Rouleau, *Sails Whitening Every Sea*, 84.
¹⁴⁸Rouleau, *Sails Whitening Every Sea*, 84.
¹⁴⁹Michael A. Verney, *A Great and Rising Nation: Naval Exploration and Global Empire in the U.S. Early Republic* (Chicago: University of Chicago Press, 2022), 63–4.

sailed, the US government was also developing some capacity to support US whalers and merchantmen in their hierarchical policing of the Pacific. The exploration mission itself was a well-armed effort to show the flag, and it followed the establishment of the US Navy's Pacific Squadron in 1821.[150] Stationed off Chile and charged with protecting US commerce, the squadron in effect was a tool for enforcing the Pacific's new economic hierarchy. In 1830, for example, the residents of the Sumatran town of Kuala Batu revolted against the Salem, Massachusetts merchants who controlled the pepper trade with their island (pepper prices had collapsed, leaving the townspeople desperate). They captured the *Friendship*—a US-flagged merchant vessel—killing three of the crew and seizing its cargo. In response, the Pacific Squadron sailed to Sumatra, landed troops, and sacked the village, leaving more than one hundred islanders dead (including women and children).[151]

Even with its Pacific Squadron, the US government's ability to exert its will upon the Pacific paled in comparison with France and Great Britain before the Civil War, which explains in part why it did not pursue any formal Pacific conquests at this time. The two continental European powers instead took the lead in forcing the unwilling to accept the new—European and American dominated—Asian-Pacific order. Yet, even when Americans did not participate directly, they still benefited from, and participated in, this Anglo-French led reordering of Asian life.

Among the items seized from the *Friendship*'s hold, for example, were twelve crates of opium, bound for China.[152] In the addictive poppy, British merchants had finally found something as good as silver for purchasing Chinese goods, altering the balance of trade between Chinese merchants and the British East India Company. Though illegal in China, the EIC grew the product in India and then smuggled it onto the Chinese mainland in return for sterling, tea, and other Chinese products.[153] American merchants soon followed the company's example—acquiring their opium from Ottoman sources—and by the 1830s addiction had become a widespread problem for the Chinese authorities. When the Chinese imperial government tried to address the issue by cracking down on the trade, the British launched a punitive expedition in response. This was the first of two "Opium Wars" (1839–42 and 1856–60) which forced China to open its borders to British drug merchants. London also demanded and recieved other concessions,

---

[150]Shoemaker, *Cannibal Isles*, 7.
[151]Verney, *A Great and Rising Nation*, 43–4.
[152]Verney, *A Great and Rising Nation*, 43.
[153]Some scholars have suggested that British-exported, Indian-grown cotton had also become sufficiently profitable to balance British trade with China on its own by the late eighteenth century. This did little to stem the flow of opium, however, which remained lucrative for British dealers either way, largely unconcerned as they were with either its lack of macroeconomic necessity or its impact on Chinese society. Findlay and O'Rourke, *Power and Plenty*, 292–4.

including the opening of additional Chinese ports to British trade, lower tariffs, and the establishment of extraterritorial status for all British subjects while in China. Other European powers—and the United States—subsequently demanded and received similar arrangements.[154]

The Opium Wars marked a significant moment in the long reshaping of the global hierarchy begun by Europe's transoceanic expansion in the sixteenth century, forging a final link in the chains locking much of East Asia into a subservient global economic status and ensuring that a large chunk of its surplus wealth would accrue to the states clustered around the North Atlantic. Though still a junior partner when compared to the British and French, the United States nevertheless joined in, developing and policing its own network of unequal, trans-Pacific economic relationships that served US domestic consumption and capital development. It also established a permanent US commercial presence in places like Hawaii, the lynchpin for a formal US empire in Asia later in the century.

All told, by the eve of the Civil War, the United States had ensured for itself a key role in a global process of hierarchy-making that was about to enter its next phase. The progress of "civilization"—the reordering of the world the Catawba mapmaker had so clearly illustrated more than a century earlier—was, with American help, soon to reach nearly every corner of the globe.

---

[154]Britain also gained control of Hong Kong, which it ruled until 1997: Bayly, *The Birth of the Modern World*, 137–8; Downs, *Golden Ghetto*, 105–40, 259–320; Herring, *From Colony to Superpower*, 210–11; Cain and Hopkins, *British Imperialism*, 306–8, 393–4; Fichter, *So Great a Proffit*, 33, 205–6, 223, 227–31.

CHAPTER FOUR

Decolonization for Me but Not for You: The United States, the War of 1898, and Establishing an Overseas Empire

As 1898 dawned, the Spanish Empire seemed on the precipice of yet another—in this case, terminal—wave of decolonization. Its two largest remaining colonies, the Philippines and Cuba, both hosted armed independence movements that were widely expected to bring an end to Iberian rule sooner or later. In Cuba, sooner seemed the more likely option. In the midst of a bloody third war for independence in as many decades, a powerful, mixed-race revolutionary movement had forced a reluctant Madrid to grant the island political and economic autonomy on January 1st, a concession few expected to preserve Cuba's formal ties to Spain for long.[1] In the Philippines, Hispanicized elites led by Emilio Aguinaldo had faced a greater challenge in unifying their archipelago's more physically and culturally divided population for war against Spain. Yet they too had successfully used arms to force Spanish concessions, in this case an 1897 truce which saw Aguinaldo temporarily relocated to Hong Kong, where he continued to raise arms and money for a resumption of the conflict in a year or two.[2]

Though Spanish rule would end in both colonies by year's end, neither Cuba nor the Philippines gained full independence—not in 1898, nor

---

[1] Ada Ferrer, *Cuba: An American History* (New York: Scribner, 2021), 150.
[2] Nicole CuUnjieng Aboitiz, *Asian Place, Filipino Nation: A Global Intellectual History of the Phillipine Revolution* (New York: Columbia University Press, 2020), 74–88.

in 1899, nor in the decades that followed. Both instead would see their processes of decolonization disrupted and hijacked by the United States in the name of civilization through the 1898 "Spanish-American War" (or as we will call it, the "War of 1898"). Significantly more powerful than it had been during the collapse of Spain's continental American empire in the early nineteenth century, the United States by 1898 possessed the ability to ensure Spain's insular empire ended on American terms. Those terms were shaped by a hyper-competitive international political and economic environment, one which saw the world's most powerful states aggressively dividing the globe into spheres of formal control or predominant influence. With its control over its North American territory largely secured, the United States joined this scramble for the world's "unclaimed" space, opening the next phase in its relationship to the ends of empire.

In this chapter, we will explore this new era, looking first at how the American project of world-ordering we have described thus far began bearing fruit in the late nineteenth century, giving the United States a new ability to project power far beyond its shores. From there, we will explore the United States' expanding global influence and how American willingness to suspend the independence of other states became a central part of US foreign policy as it joined the ranks of the world powers. Though Americans never fully embraced the formal empire the war with Spain left them

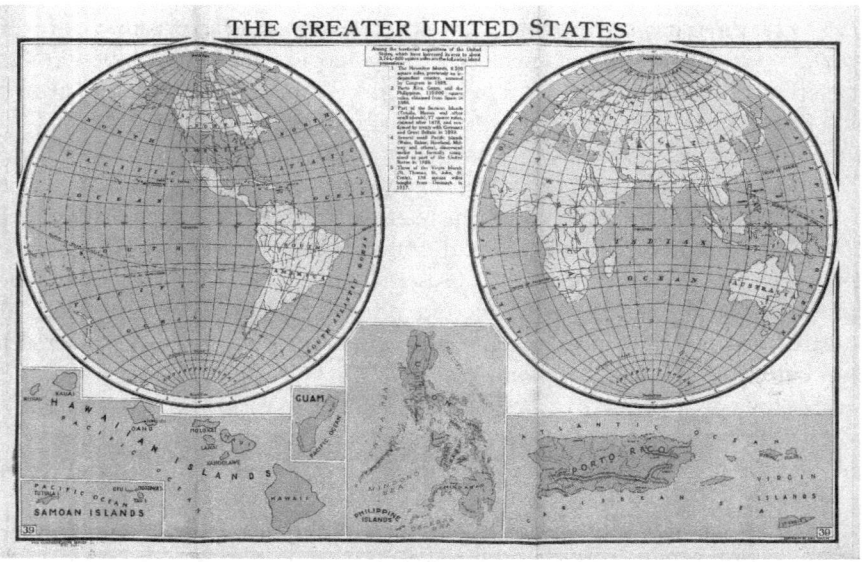

FIGURE 7 *A classroom map from 1919 depicting what was sometimes called the "Greater United States"—America's formal empire established following the War of 1898.*

with—and indeed, resisted the full annexation of Cuba—the War of 1898 marked a key turning point all the same.

The United States and the Global Hierarchy in the Late Nineteenth Century

In order to understand why the United States chose to intervene in, and prevent, the decolonization of the Philippines and Cuba, we first have to explore the economic and political changes in the United States itself that led to its decision to go to war in 1898. Though the economic and ideological forces we have been discussing in this book—the demands of a competitive global economic system and visions of national and civilizational greatness—made such an intervention possible, they did not guarantee that it would occur either. Indeed, one could argue that the 1896 election just prior to the war saw the United States closer than at any point in its history to choosing an alternative path, one away from the ends of empire. Why it did not is naturally, therefore, worthy of further investigation.

As our first three chapters have shown, though the independence of the United States from Britain had given new prominence to Enlightenment ideals about political equality, it did not mark a significant repudiation of the expansionist imperial project that had originally brought the colonists to North America. As a result, Americans—sometimes aided by their government and sometimes merely cheered on by it—continued their territorial and economic expansion, building new states at home and new networks of trade across the continent and into the Caribbean, the South Atlantic, and the Pacific. Though the most violent forms of this expansion faced resistance from Native Americans and Mexicans, the gravest threat to the US imperial project after 1814 was internal, as the divergent "sectional" economic visions of the South and North—those of slave-based wealth versus merchant and early industrial capital—eventually tore the nation apart in 1860. Expansion was at the heart of this dispute, for it was questions over how to divide the spoils of conquest in Mexico that drove the divisions between the two sections. Concern for civilization and progress was also part of the story, as both North and South saw themselves as the true inheritors of the American Revolution and civilizational project it had helped launch. For a time, this sectional discord and the subsequent US Civil War (1861–65) seemed to threaten a dismemberment of the country not dissimilar to that feared by the Revolutionary generation decades earlier. Instead, the Northern "Union" won the war and preserved the unity of the state, ending slavery and ensuring future economic development was free labor in character, following a path that aligned with the Northern vision of progress rather than the Southern one.[3]

The end of the Civil War and the settlement of the slavery question set the stage for two key, and related, developments for our story about the evolving relationship of the United States to empire. The first was the rapid industrial development—indeed, modernization—of the country, which took off in 1870. Americans were already relatively well-off compared with many around the world by that year, with a per-capita income around 74 percent of Britain and 128 percent of Germany.[4] Industrial technologies, particularly steam engines, were beginning to transform the nation, revolutionizing transportation and manufacturing. Capital generated by trade in Latin America and in the Pacific helped provide the seed money for early forms of industrial manufacturing, both through directly financing factories and ensuring a favorable investment climate for British money.[5] Federal policy during the Civil War laid the groundwork for further expansion. With the departure of Southern Democrats during the war, the Republican-controlled Congress was able to pass a bill to establish a transcontinental railroad, a Homestead Act allowing for white settlers to claim federal lands in the West, and a tariff protecting American industry from British competition. In addition, to finance the war, the government had floated 2.6 billion dollars in public debt, helping to firmly tie the state to a new banking industry centered on Wall Street. This "dynamic amalgam" as Jonathan Levy writes, birthed a "new political economy" for the country, "cutting a path for long term economic development."[6] After the war ended, capital owners successfully pushed the government into a policy of "resumption," a deliberately deflationary return to the gold standard, which left Northeastern investors increasingly flush with cash while also attracting further capital from Britain, the international standard bearer for hard money.[7]

Though the South's return to the Union and political divisions within the Republican Party would result in regular challenges to these policies, the tariff and hard money system established in the 1860s would essentially remain in place into the twentieth century. The result was a period of industrial development that transformed the nation, as investment capital followed

---

[3] Few topics have been subject to more historical scrutiny than the US Civil War. On the Civil War as a conflict between two rival visions of American civilization see: Andrew F. Lang, *A Contest of Civilizations: Exposing the Crisis of American Exceptionalism in the Civil War Era* (Chapel Hill: University of North Carolina Press, 2021), especially 7–26, 73–124. In addition to Lang, another good place to start remains: James M. McPherson, *Battle Cry of Freedom: The Civil War Era* (New York: Oxford University Press, 1988). On the Civil War and slave vs. free labor see also Beckert, *Empire of Cotton*, 242–311.
[4] Robert J. Gordon, *The Rise and Fall of American Growth: The U.S. Standard of Living Since the Civil War* (Princeton: Princeton University Press, 2016), 27.
[5] See Chapter 3.
[6] Levy, *Ages of American Capitalism*, 196.
[7] Levy, *Ages of American Capitalism*, 205–14.

the railroads west into the "frontier" and into the coffers of increasingly influential corporations making steel, refining oil, and mass-producing consumer goods on an unprecedented scale. By the early twentieth century, the United States had a booming industrial economy, with growing cities, and a burgeoning industrial labor force fed by waves of European immigrants. Though still junior to more established powers like Britain and France, the late nineteenth-century development of the US economy had granted the country the ability to rely on its own devices in the two critical areas for power: banking and manufacturing. We will return to social tensions generated by these transformations presently, but for now it's enough to note that post-Civil War industrialization helped make the United States into a "great power," one of the small handful of states in the world that posessed real independence of action.[8]

The second development concerning us here was the "closing of the frontier," as settlers and US troops flooded west across North America into lands claimed by the United States but also claimed and occupied by Native Americans. Tighter control over US borders, the laying down of railroad tracks—and strings of recently invented barbed wire—led to growing numbers of white settlements. These, and US cavalry patrols, diminished Indigenous room for maneuver. The blandly titled "Indian Wars" that resulted represented the final phase of the US-backed ethnic cleansing of the North American West, as Lakota, Cheyenne, Comanche, and other groups violently resisted being forced onto reservations. Native triumphs, such as Gen. George Custer's infamous "last stand" in the Battle of Little Big Horn, were more than offset by defeats in conflicts like the Red River War (1874–75) and massacres like the slaughter of hundreds of unarmed Lakota men, women, and children by US Army cavalrymen (many of whom received the Medal of Honor for their actions) at Wounded Knee in 1890. Native American leaders increasingly faced a choice of destruction in war or dispossession and survival through accepting moves to reservations. By the end of the century the grid of European-style modernity overlaid the continent from Atlantic to Pacific, with the last redoubts of millennia-old Indigenous world confined to shrinking plots of often marginal land. In 1890, the US Census Bureau announced that the frontier was "closed," that there was no longer land with a settler population density of less than two people per mile, marking the end of an era and in many ways the fulfillment of the seventeenth-century colonial dream we discussed in Chapter 1.[9]

The end of the nineteenth century was thus an exhilarating time for some Americans, a moment when a more and more advanced civilization seemed

---

[8]Gordon, *Rise and Fall of American Growth*, 25–318; Hopkins, *American Empire*, 287–336; Lindert and Williamson, *Unequal Gains*, 166–93; Elliott West, *Continental Reckoning: The American West in the Age of Expansion* (Lincoln: University of Nebraska Press, 2023), 305–455.
[9]Blackhawk, *Rediscovery of America*, 289–364; Hämäläinen, *Indigenous Continent*, 385–457; West, *Continental Reckoning*, 173–455.

to be on the march and, indeed, well on its way to triumph. Such optimism about the course of human history, and the US role in that history, is also key to explaining why and how the United States intervened in the Philippines and Cuba. White settlement in North America had, of course, been associated with progress and the advance of civilization since the colonial project was a mere twinkle in the eye of colonial boosters like William Strachey. However, the transformations wrought by industrialization and the economic dynamism of the late nineteenth century seemed to provide further proof of this association. Such thinking was reinforced as well by new, supposedly "scientific," ideas about race and progress that had gained widespread currency and popularity in Europe and the United States over the course of the century. Few figures better represent this than Charles Darwin, whose theory about evolution in animal species had quickly—and perhaps predictably—been applied to explanations for human diversity as well. Darwin himself advanced such a perspective, arguing that the differences Europeans and Americans perceived between themselves (the "advanced" peoples of the Earth) and the "savage races" represented peoples at different stages in human evolution. These differences, he suggested in his 1871 treatise *The Descent of Man*, had become so extreme that it was likely "at some future period, not very distant ... the civilized races of man will almost certainly exterminate and replace the savage races throughout the world."[10] Progress and civilization were therefore almost always understood in oppositional terms, requiring clear definitions of the civilized "us" versus the more barbarous or backward "them," though the latter might be ranked as more or less advanced according to their perceived distance from the civilized ideal.

In the United States, that ideal was widely associated with four characteristics: the "Anglo-Saxon" race, Protestant Christianity, political liberalism, and an industrializing market economy. Though the first two excluded a large, and growing, minority of those living in the United States, this did not stop commentators from trumpeting that the country was destined for world leadership. Josiah Strong, a widely read Congregational minister, for example, provided a typical argument when he wrote in 1885 that, Anglo-Saxons had developed two key concepts for human development: civil liberty and a "pure spiritual"—that is, Protestant—"Christianity." These characteristics meant that the Anglo-Saxon race was, as Strong wrote, "divinely commissioned to be, in a peculiar sense, his brother's keeper." This "fact" was, for Strong, further reinforced by US economic development: "add to this the fact of his rapidly increasing strength in modern times, and we have well-nigh a demonstration of his destiny."[11] What was that destiny?

---

[10]Brantlinger, *Dark Vanishings*, 167.
[11]Julius W. Pratt, *Expansionists of 1898: The Acquisition of Hawaii and the Spanish Islands* (Gloucester MA: Peter Smith, 1959), 5.

Nothing less than domination of much of the world, a future seemingly confirmed by Darwinian thinking and quick spread of white settlement across North America:

> this race of unequaled energy, with ... the might of wealth behind it—the representative ... of the largest liberty, the purest Christianity, the highest civilization—having developed peculiarly aggressive traits calculated to impress its institutions on mankind, will spread itself over the earth ... can anyone doubt that the result of [the] competition of races will be the "survival of the fittest"?[12]

John Fiske, as historian and regular contributor to popular magazines like *Harper's*, expressed similar confidence. "The work which the English race began when it colonized North America is destined," he wrote "to go on until ... four-fifths of the human race will trace its pedigree to English forefathers, as four-fifths of the white people of the United States trace their pedigree today."[13] In the future, it seemed, the whole world would end up looking a lot like the United States.

It should come as little surprise therefore that such attitudes led to calls for the United States to start intervening overseas on civilization's behalf. "There is no human right to barbarism," wrote the political scientist John W. Burgess in 1890, and so it was clearly the responsibility of "civilized states" to "answer the call of the unpolitical populations for aid and direction, but also to force organization on them by any means necessary."[14] Westphalian sovereignty was not something that applied to people deemed to be living outside civilization's walls. Yet, it would be a mistake to see the calls for empire, and the empire that developed, as merely the result of civilizational chauvinism and the claimed altruism of "forcing organization" on peoples deemed less civilized. Late nineteenth-century pro-imperial thought was also very clearly motivated by anxiety about maintaining the United States' position amidst a competitive international system. Though the conclusion of the Napoleonic wars had temporarily slowed the pace of imperial competition for territory and economic influence, it began to speed up again as the nineteenth century wore on.[15]

The United States—remarkably durable myths about isolationism to the contrary—played a significant part in this intensification of imperial competition, though the nature of its political system did give it different character than that of its European competitors. The long globalization

---

[12]Pratt, *Expansionists*, 6.
[13]Pratt, *Expansionists*, 5.
[14]Pratt, *Expansionists*, 9.
[15]Jürgen Osterhammel, *The Transformation of the World: A Global History of the Nineteenth Century* (Princeton: Princeton University Press, 2014), 392–504.

which had begun under European imperial auspices in the sixteenth century accelerated dramatically in the second half of the nineteenth century as a consequence of technological advances in communication and transportation. The development of transoceanic steamships facilitated a sharp reduction in the costs of shipping goods around the world as travel and trade became both more regular and predictable. Newly laid ocean-spanning telegraph lines had similar effects in increasing the ease, and lowering the cost, of transmitting information abroad. Already globally integrated markets and production chains—like the trans-Atlantic cotton industry we've discussed in the last few chapters—became more and more tightly bound even as they grew to encompass more territory. Every advance sent capital and business owners looking further afield for new sources of raw material and new markets for their goods.[16] Late nineteenth-century globalization was not merely a peaceful drawing together of the world, however, it was a competitive one. The world's most powerful states sought to pull the world toward themselves for their own benefit. Many in and around government in European capitals and in the United States believed that it was their responsibility to ensure their country gained a significant share of globalization's spoils, either through peaceful means or otherwise.

This apparent need to compete, and the attitudes towards civilization and progress described above, merged into what is often called the "new imperialism" of the late nineteenth and early twentieth centuries. No longer justified by national interest alone, the new imperialism foregrounded the "white man's burden"—more on the very relevant origins of this phrase in a moment—to help deliver the modern world to supposedly backward territories and populations. There was a natural synergy to these claims, as incorporating new lands into the global market system required building modern infrastructure (roads, trains, and telegraph lines) while at the same time such projects appealed to more liberal domestic audiences long in the habit of thinking of European-style civilization as the future for the world.[17]

Beginning in the 1880s, Britain, France, Germany, Belgium, and the Netherlands began aggressively partitioning areas of the globe not yet subject to white rule, particularly in Africa. As these processes played out, a growing group of politicians and writers in and around the Republican Party in the United States began to advocate for the federal government to take the lead in making sure America was well positioned to stake out and protect its own claim. Figures like President Ulysses S. Grant (in office: 1869–77), and sometimes congressman, senator, and Secretary of State,

---

[16]Beckert, *Empire of Cotton*, 274–378; Osterhammel, *Transformation of the World*, 710–43; Jürgen Osterhammel and Niels Peterson, *Globalization: A Short History* (Princeton: Princeton University Press, 2005), 62–9, 76–90.
[17]Cain and Hopkins, *British Imperialism*, 709–14; Osterhammel, *Transformation of the World*, 64–5, 392–468, 826–72.

James G. Blaine, for example, began pushing in the 1870s for policies that reflected what the historian Marc William Palen has called the "imperialism of economic nationalism." A natural evolution of the neomercantilist ideas that had animated Henry Clay's American system, the imperialism of economic nationalism involved a mix of high tariffs to protect domestic industries, along with the pursuit of foreign territory for coaling stations and military bases to allow the United States to project power and protect its trade. It also came to include an interest in acquiring new sources of raw materials for the US industry, and new markets for its products, through restrictive reciprocity agreements with foreign states or through outright annexation.[18] Neomercantilist logic held that such moves were essential to ensuring, and elevating, a state's place in the global hierarchy. The powerful nations of the world, the argument went, were those that manufactured finished goods and sold them to commodity-producing lands abroad. Countries that manufactured goods themselves, wrote the neomercantilist patriarch Friedrich List in 1841, were "richer in capital than agricultural [commodity producing] states." The "power of producing wealth," he argued, was "therefore infinitely more important than wealth itself."[19]

This kind of protectionist program eventually became so closely associated with the United States that it was widely known as "the American system" abroad, yet it did not initially find success at home. While a program of commercial expansion to bolster American industry fit naturally in the generally pro-tariff and neomercantilist Republican party—and had key support from Northeastern manufacturing and financial interests—a confused national political situation helped stymie its supporters' more expansive proposals prior to the 1890s. It also took some time for the idea that restrictive reciprocity agreements were not a form of free trade to settle in, limiting their appeal even among those otherwise predisposed to neomercantilist policies. Grant-era schemes for annexing "Santo Domingo" (today's Dominican Republic), later efforts at building a trans-isthmian canal through Nicaragua, and an 1883 package of reciprocal trade treaties with Mexico and other Latin American states, for example, all failed to secure the necessary Congressional backing.[20]

Support for an imperial or even expansively commercial United States was far from universal among Republicans, while Democrats represented

---

[18]On the imperialism of economic nationalism see: Marc William Palen, *The Conspiracy of Free Trade: The Anglo-American Struggle over Empire and Economic Globalization, 1846–1896* (Cambridge: Cambridge University Press, 2016); Marc William Palen, *Pax Economica: Left-Wing Visions of a Free Trade World* (Princeton: Princeton University Press, 2024), 13–50. On the American system and late nineteenth-century protectionism see also: Helleiner, *The Neomercantilists*, 41–3, 137–69.
[19]For more on the influence of List's thought in the United States see: Helleiner, *Neomercantilists*, 52–79, 137–200, quote on 55–6.
[20]Palen, *Conspiracy of Free Trade*, 84–115; Palen, *Pax Economica*, 14–16.

many white supremacists and Southern and Western commodity producers who saw little advantage in reciprocity with, or annexation of, foreign states that might undersell their products in the domestic market or lead to an increase of the non-white population in the United States.[21] Republican control of the White House for most of the period between 1864 and 1896 was offset by shifting control on Congressional Hill and the two single-term administrations of the anti-tariff and anti-imperial Grover Cleveland (1885–89, 1893–97). Still, the US economy's continued growth generated its own form of pressure, as businessmen scrambled to find outlets for goods the American domestic market was unable to absorb. These contradictory impulses meant that it was initially far from clear who would win—in the economic historian David Pletcher's words—the "contest between a largely self-sufficient, self-satisfied American economy … and an increasing need for the export of goods and capital to relieve pressures at home produced by the very success of that economy."[22]

The political ground began to shift in the 1880s, however, when the Republican Party chose to sell out Black voters in the South in the name of political stability and sectional reconciliation following the financial Panic of 1873. This opened the door to a party realignment.[23] Republican anti-imperial and anti-tariff voices shifted their support to the Democrats in the 1884 election, leaving the GOP as a solely pro-business, pro-tariff, pro-commercial expansion—and empire-curious—nationalist party.[24] None of this would have necessarily been enough to give the Republicans sufficient power to embark on their imperial agenda, however, if not for the social tensions generated by the aforementioned industrialization of the United States. High tariffs, the gold standard, growing factories, and corporate power all led to great dislocation for working- and middle-class Americans, as wages dropped, working conditions grew poorer, and farmers and manufacturers felt the squeeze of more industrialized competition. Labor disputes, strikes, and anti-labor violence by capital owners became a regular feature of life in the late nineteenth-century United States, as did surging immigration from China, and Southern and Eastern Europe. The most powerful expression of agricultural and working-class dissent was the Populist Movement and the party it created, the People's Party (1892–1908).

Unified with the Democrats in the candidacy of William Jennings Bryan during the 1896 election, the Populists briefly sidelined the pro-business

---

[21]Eric T.L. Love, *Race over Empire: Racism and U.S. Imperialism, 1865–1900* (Chapel Hill: University of North Carolina, 2004), 1–72.

[22]David M. Pletcher, *The Diplomacy of Trade and Investment: American Economic Expansion in the Hemisphere, 1865–1900* (Columbia: University of Missouri Press, 1998), 375.

[23]David Blight, *Race and Reunion: The Civil War in American Memory* (Cambridge, MA: Belknap Press, 2001), 98–139. Eric Foner, *Reconstruction: America's Unfinished Revolution, 1863–1877* (New York: Perennial Classics, 1998), 512–601.

[24]Palen, *Conspiracy of Free Trade*, 116–49.

Cleveland Democrats and offered a significant challenge to the emerging industrial order. Bryan's platform called for looser monetary policy (by replacing the gold standard with a bimetallic gold and silver system), lower tariffs, and a promise to rebalance the US political and economic system in favor of workers, farmers, and small craftsmen. He also did not share the Republican enthusiasm for imperial adventures. However—in addition to alienating middle and upper-class voters with his attack on wealth and power—Bryan's Populist-Fusion ticket did not universally appeal to the working class, thanks in part to his decision to jettison his most radical proposals (including an eight-hour workday, government control of the rails, and a progressive income tax) in order to secure the Democratic nomination. A skillful campaign run by Mark Hanna, an Ohio millionaire who ran the Republican National Committee from 1894–1904, took advantage of this—along with the seemingly anti-urban, anti-immigrant, and, in some cases, anti-Black character of the Populist Movement—to grab votes from a sizable number of urban, working-class voters both Black and white. Hanna also managed to consolidate the "fearful elite" vote—"everybody that had a dollar was willing to give fifty cents of it to save himself; not Republicans alone, but all businessmen" commented one Republican operative—to build a coalition that delivered the White House to William McKinley (in office: 1897–1901) and both houses of congress to the Republicans.[25] The election marked a fundamental shift in the balance of power in Washington, establishing the Republicans—the party of empire—as the dominant force in the federal government until the onset of the Great Depression in the late 1920s.[26] The 1896 election thus ensured that the would-be empire builders held the key seats of federal power—keeping the United States on the expansionist, world-reordering, path it had followed since its founding.

Groundwork for Empire

Other events also helped set the course for empire. In the Pacific, the United States deepened its ties to Hawaii. American settlers had begun arriving in the then independent Kingdom of Hawaii as early as the 1820s, and by the latter part of the century there was a small but prosperous and influential group of sugar planters on the island. Under their aegis, the Hawaiian government concluded a reciprocity treaty with the United States in 1875 that effectively made the country an economic dependency of the United States. Planters soon became entirely reliant on the US market for their sugar, as Hawaiian consumers became similarly attached to the American manufactured goods that flooded the islands. In 1893 when Hawaii's queen

---

[25]Shenk, *Realigners*, 132.
[26]Shenk, *Realigners*, 119–63.

attempted to implement a new constitution that would have weakened the planters' power, American settlers led by Sanford Dole convinced the Harrison administration to send the USS Boston and its Marines to Hawaii to "protect American lives and property." It was, in effect, a coup that resulted in Dole becoming president of a provisional government, which sought annexation only to be stymied by Cleveland's election. However, negotiations were resumed upon McKinley's 1896 victory, with Hawaii's new American-led government seeking to become a territory.[27]

In addition to these events in the Pacific, there was also a growing conviction among some Republicans that the United States desperately needed to secure more foreign markets for its goods, particularly in Latin America, where Britain remained the dominant trading power. Blaine and McKinley—then an Ohio congressmen—were key figures here, helping push the short-lived "McKinley" tariff through Congress in 1890. Granting President Benjamin Harrison (in office: 1889–93) power to slap retaliatory duties on countries that did not agree to trade concessions, the McKinley tariff was used to forge agreements with Brazil, Spain (for Cuba and Puerto Rico), the Dominican Republic, the British West Indies, El Salvador, Honduras, Guatemala, and Nicaragua. All of these lowered tariffs on US-manufactured goods entering the other country in return for lower tariffs on primary commodities entering the United States.[28] Though these treaties would be repudiated during the second Cleveland administration, the McKinley bill still marks a key transition, the beginning of what worried European observers called "the American commercial invasion." US manufacturing exports abroad exploded in the following years, from 20 percent in 1890, to 35 percent in 1900, and eventually 50 percent in 1913. The Republican commitment to opening markets would return to the White House with McKinley in 1896, remaining a key part of US policy for decades.[29]

Just as important as these economic developments were new ideas about empire and international competition that increased in circulation in the late nineteenth century—ideas that made expansion in trade and (possibly) in territory appear part of the natural destiny of the United States. In the 1880s and 1890s, writers like US Navy Captain Alfred Thayer Mahan gained national prominence advocating for the United States to take its place in the ranks of the great powers by building a modern navy and the global infrastructure to support it. Early "realist" thinkers like Mahan—found primarily in Germany, Britain, and the United States—developed and

---

[27]Herring, *From Colony to Superpower*, 296–7; Hopkins, *American Empire*, 417–27; Palen, *Conspiracy of Free Trade*, 102–3; David M. Pletcher, *The Diplomacy of Involvement: American Economic Expansion Across the Pacific, 1784–1900* (Columbia: University of Missouri Press, 2001), 46–65, 234–87.
[28]Palen, *Conspiracy of Free Trade*, 194. Pletcher, *Trade and Investment*, 237–79, 378.
[29]For their repudiation see: Pletcher, *Trade and Investment*, 38. On the commercial invasion and subsequent Republican commitment to opening markets, see Palen, *Conspiracy*, 189.

advanced new ideas about geopolitics which suggested that history revealed immutable laws of global competition. Envisioning a geopolitical world not unlike in Darwin's model of the animal kingdom, these laws required great states to either compete and expand to survive or otherwise wither and fall under the sway of more assertive powers.[30] Mahan's ideas attracted powerful supporters and helped pave the way for the modernization of the US Navy over the course of the 1890s. In a process overseen by Mahan disciple Benjamin Franklin Tracy—Secretary of the Navy in the Benjamin Harrison administration—the US Navy built its first modern battleships and cruisers, abandoning a program of coastal defense in favor of developing tools for asserting power abroad.[31] This program ensured that, when the war with Spain began in 1898, the United States—and Mahanite Assistant Secretary of the Navy, Theodore Roosevelt—had a modestly-sized but modern and professional navy to fight it with.

Mahan's work was typical of what Julius W. Pratt (a mid-twentieth-century historian of US overseas expansion) called the "intellectual climate" of the time, a general sense that the moment had arrived for the United States to act more assertively beyond its continental boundaries.[32] This, as Emily Rosenberg has shown, was not merely a common argument among intellectuals, but part of a broader cultural phenomenon. "To many Americans" at the turn of the century, Rosenberg writes, "their country's economic and social history became a universal model."[33] This came with a corresponding belief that "other nations could and should replicate America's own development experience" and that it might be the responsibility of the United States to show them the way directly. Much of this should, of course, sound familiar, as this nineteenth- and early twentieth-century ideology of "liberal developmentalism," as Rosenberg called it, bears many similarities with the ideas that had undergirded US continental expansion in the late eighteenth and early nineteenth centuries.[34]

The years following McKinley's election in 1896 thus saw a convergence of forces—political, economic, and ideological—pushing the United States toward another burst of world ordering, ultimately making choices about the ends of empire not just for Cuba and the Philippines, but for Puerto Rico and Hawaii as well. A powerful, increasingly industrialized, US economy generated pressure to develop new export and raw material markets overseas, while prevailing attitudes about American exceptionalism and America's

---

[30] Matthew Specter, *The Atlantic Realists: Empire and International Political Thought between Germany and the United States* (Stanford: Stanford University Press, 2022), 1–49.
[31] Herring, *From Colony to Superpower*, 303; Hopkins, *American Empire*, 354–5; Palen, *Conspiracy of Free Trade*, 179; Pratt, *Expansionists*, 13.
[32] Pratt, *Expansionists*, 19.
[33] Emily S. Rosenberg, *Spreading the American Dream: American Economic and Cultural Expansion, 1890–1945* (New York Hill and Wang, 1982), 7.
[34] Rosenberg, *Spreading the American Dream*, 7–9.

supposed global mission made it possible—as Rosenberg explains—to see "no fundamental conflict between national advancement and global progress."[35] Meanwhile, the Republican victory had brought to power those ready to view global politics as a zero-sum imperial competition, one in which they believed the United States was destined to compete. Though many Americans, and the Democratic Party in particular, continued to oppose further expansion beyond North America for a variety of reasons, theirs was too thin a reed to stem the burgeoning flood.

The War of 1898

As these trends coalesced in the 1880s and 1890s, many non-American observers watched the United States warily, waiting for what seemed an inevitable break in the dam. Few did so more closely than the Cuban revolutionary leader, José Marti. One of the founders of the *Partido Revolucionario Cubano* in 1892, Marti did much of this surveillance from within the United States itself, where he was based from 1880 to 1895. What he saw—particularly when it came to the tendency of white Americans to see the world through racial hierarchies—filled him with deep concern. "I lived in the monster and I know its entrails," he wrote to a friend. He believed it was imperative to deliver the independence of Cuba as soon as possible, in order "to prevent ... the annexation of Cuba to the United States." Only then, he continued, could Cuba protect the Spanish American world, or as he called it, "*our* America." A free Cuba, he wrote, could "impede, in time ... the extension of the United States throughout the [Caribbean] ... and prevent its full weight from falling upon our American soil."[36] Any delay, he feared, might result in the United States reaching out to reorder the hemisphere to its own designs. "The hour is near," Marti wrote in an 1891 essay, "when our America will be approached by an enterprising and forceful nation that will demand intimate relations with her" even "though it ... disdains her."[37]

Marti wrote to his friend of the "monster and its entrails" from Cuba on May 18th, 1895, the day prior to his death in combat with Spanish troops. He had returned to the island a few weeks earlier to help lead—along with Maximo Gomez and Antonio Maceo—the revolution that had broken out in February of that year. This, the final Cuban war for independence (1895–98), was in many ways a continuation of the so-called "Little War" of 1879–80, which itself was a renewal of conflicts dating back to the

---

[35]Rosenberg, *Spreading the American Dream*, 9.
[36]José Martí, Letter to Manuel Mercado, May 18, 1895, in Holden and Zolov, *Latin America and the United States*, 63.
[37]Ferrer, *Cuba*, 142.

"Ten-Year War" of 1868–78. Though Spain had managed to retain control of the island previously through a mix of force and concessions—including the emancipation of Cuba's enslaved population in 1886—the revolt in 1895 was different. As the historian Louis A. Pérez has written, in 1895 "Cubans were better organized ... they had planned better and were better led" than in previous revolts.[38] Marti himself had helped fashion a more inclusive form of Cuban nationalism, one that helped bring greater unity to a population long divided between those of African or Spanish descent.[39]

Despite Marti's death in May, Gomez and Maceo carried the revolution forward that summer, marching two armies from more restive eastern Cuba into the island's west, long an area of tighter Spanish control. Their efforts inspired a broad cross-class and multiracial uprising, swelling the ranks of the increasingly professional and organized Cuban Liberation Army. What followed was a long and brutal war, which the Spanish first tried to fight through a cruel campaign of repression led by Governor Valeriano Weyler. His scorched earth tactics—burning villages and forcing people into concentration camps—failed to stem the tide. Madrid removed "the butcher" in 1897, promising concessions in the form of limited self-rule and universal manhood suffrage, but few expected this to prevent the eventual separation of the island.[40] Thus, in 1898, the Cuban revolutionaries stood on the precipice of gaining their independence. It was widely believed that "the island must soon slip from Spain's grasp," as William H. Calhoun—a US emissary to Havana—had reported the year before, and there was nothing Madrid could do to stop it.[41]

Calhoun's assessment was based on his conversations with large Cuban planters and Spanish property owners, many of whom, as he told Washington, would welcome "immediate American intervention" to prevent the revolutionary movement from taking control of the island.[42] These elites feared that a popular Cuban regime born of independence from Spain might lead to a fundamental reorientation of the island's racial and class hierarchy, potentially threatening not only elite influence but their control of the island's wealth. This also concerned no small number of Americans—many from the mainland were heavily invested in the island's tobacco and sugar industries. The McKinley administration was far from unsympathetic to these pleas, not simply because of the perceived need to protect American property owners but also because of the increasing clamor in the United States for

---

[38]Louis A. Pérez, *The War of 1898: The United States and Cuba in History and Historiography* (Chapel Hill: University of North Carolina Press, 1998), 7.
[39]Ferrer, *Cuba*, 142–4.
[40]Perez, *War of 1898*, 7. Ferrer, *Cuba*, 145–53.
[41]Louis A. Pérez, *Cuba and the United States: Ties of a Singular Intimacy*, 2nd edition (Athens: University of Georgia Press, 1997), 84.
[42]Perez, *Cuba and the United States*, 84.

intervention to stop the war. Since Weyler's depredations had begun in 1896, "Cuba libre" had become something of a *cause célèbre* for many Americans—and a political football for the Democrats—who were quick to accuse McKinley of not being ardent enough in his support for liberty.[43] Moreover, as Perez has argued, the idea of a fully independent Cuba was not something many Americans, particularly those around McKinley, were comfortable with. From 1823, when John Quincy Adams had written of Cuba as an apple destined to fall toward the North American tree, it had been assumed that the only logical next step for the island after Spanish rule was US annexation, not independence.[44]

The multiracial and populist nature of the revolutionary movement that Marti had helped forge led to deep skepticism in the United States that independence would produce a Cuba that could be trusted to govern its own affairs. "If the Cuban revolutionists gain control," wrote a reporter for the *New York Times*, "there will be a long reign of terror" particularly against Cuba's "higher classes." Another writer for a South Carolina paper agreed, writing that granting Cubans sovereignty "would mean to turn over the island to a worse condition of anarchy [than that] from which we are seeking to rescue it."[45] Many in the government felt similarly. As one State Department report described, intervention would allow the United States to "hold the Cuban territory in trust, until with restored tranquility a government could be constitutionally organized which we could formally recognize and with which we could conclude a treaty regulating our future relations."[46]

Once again, therefore, we find Americans articulating reasons for expansion that reflect a potent mixture of material and strategic interests born of a competitive world-system and hierarchical attitudes toward people deemed to have fallen short of the standards of European/North American civilization. While McKinley was hardly reckless and sought to avoid war if possible, he was also assertive in ensuring a transfer of Cuban sovereignty from Madrid to Washington. In April of 1898, when it became increasingly clear that neither Spain nor the Cuban revolutionaries were willing to see the stars and stripes raised over the island, McKinley asked Congress to authorize a war which, as Perez writes, was "ostensibly … against Spain," but was, "in fact was against Cubans."[47] McKinley was relatively open about this in his war message to the Hill. The note made no mention of bringing independence to Cuba but instead called for establishing

---

[43]This was partly in revenge for Republicans having done the same thing to the Democrats during the Cleveland administration. Hopkins, *American Empire*, 369.
[44]Perez, *Cuba and the United States*, 94.
[45]Perez, *Cuba and the United States*, 99.
[46]Perez, *Cuba and the United States*, 95.
[47]Perez, *Cuba and the United States*, 94.

a "hostile constraint upon both the parties to the contest" in order to ensure "the establishment of a stable government, capable of maintaining order and observing its international obligations." The United States refused to acknowledge Cuban forces as an official belligerent, much less recognize their provisional government (even though, by mid-1898, it controlled most of the country).[48] US operations in Cuba were conducted with a similarly aloof superiority—one which was matched by the prejudices of the US Army's commanders. Despite fighting side by side with the Liberation Army in the siege of Santiago, for example, the Americans prohibited Cuban forces from entering the city following the Spanish surrender on July 17th. Calixto García, the commander of Cuban Liberation Army's forces in the region, wrote to his American counterpart, Major General William Shafter, in protest. "We are not savages," he reminded the American, "we are a poor ragged army as ragged and poor as was the army of your forefathers in their noble war for independence."[49] Shafter, it appears, never bothered to reply, but his views of his Cuban allies were obvious. "Self-government," he scoffed, "why those people are no more fit for self-government than gunpowder is fit for hell."[50]

Similar scenes would soon play out in the Philippines, where Filipino troops under the command of General Emilio Aguinaldo had been fighting the Spanish and keeping order on the main island of Luzon since May. Few things better reveal the imperialist intent of the McKinley administration than the fact that—in a war ostensibly meant to liberate Cuba—the first battle fought by the United States in the conflict was in the Philippines, not the Caribbean. This engagement was the May 1st, 1898 Battle of Manila Bay, which saw the US Navy's Asiatic Squadron soundly defeat Spanish naval forces mere days after the April 25th declaration of war. Commodore George Dewey—ordered to Hong Kong in February by Assistant Secretary of the Navy Theodore Roosevelt—had thus begun to unravel Spanish power in the archipelago but he lacked sufficient ground forces to take the next step and secure possession of the islands. Aguinaldo, who had been in contact with US officials for some months, seemed to offer a solution, so Dewey sent a ship to collect him from Hong Kong. The general had established himself as the leading figure of the Filipino independence movement during the revolution of 1896–97. Filipino nationalists like Aguinaldo and Jose Rizal (whom the Spanish had executed in 1896) had faced significant challenges in unifying opposition to the Spanish under a single banner thanks to the ethnically and religiously divided population of the islands. They had overcome these challenges, however, and had forced the Spanish government

---

[48]Perez, *Cuba and the United States*, 94–5.
[49]Ferrer, *Cuba*, 165.
[50]Perez, *Cuba and the United States*, 100.

in 1897 to sign a truce and pay the rebels a large indemnity.[51] Though not as far down the path towards decolonization as Cuba, the Philippines too was widely seen as nearing its own break with Spain.

When Aguinaldo went ashore at Cavite—his hometown on the southern coast of Manila Bay—his popularity meant he was able to raise an army with remarkable speed. The exact terms of his arrangement with Dewey were disputed from the start, with Aguinaldo claiming that the Commodore had promised independence for the Philippines and Dewey asserting that he'd made no such guarantee. Whatever he had promised initially, Dewey almost immediately began to distance himself from Aguinaldo. His orders from Washington on this were clear: avoid "political alliances with the insurgents ... that would incur liability to maintain their cause in the future."[52] When the Filipino leader declared the archipelago an independent republic on June 12th, Dewey declined to attend the associated ceremonies and offered no public acknowledgement that the declaration had even occured. US coldness toward Aguinaldo's forces only increased as US troops began to arrive in greater numbers over the course of the summer. In a sign of how both the Spanish and the Americans understood the world and the role of hierarchies in it, the two sides negotiated a face-saving surrender of the Spanish garrison in Manila—complete with a partly staged American assault on the city on August 13th. Fundamental to the agreement was ensuring that Aguinaldo's troops played no part, allowing the Spanish to avoid the perceived dishonor of surrendering to non-Europeans and affording the Americans an ability to assert US sovereignty by seizing the Philippine capital on their own. General Thomas Anderson, the commander of the US expeditionary force on Luzon, warned the Filipinos that if their soldiers attempted to enter the city they would be fired upon. Thus when news of the armistice between Spain and the United States arrived a day later, it found US and Filipino troops—each supporting competing claims to sovereignty—eyeing each other ominously across the Pasig River.[53]

Building Hierarchy in America's New Empire

When representatives of the United States and Spain met in Paris in December to conclude a treaty ending the war, no Cubans or Filipinos were invited. There, US negotiators, as a Spanish commissioner complained,

---

[51]Aboitiz, *Asian Place, Filipino Nation*, 32–111; Christopher Capozzola, *Bound by War: How the United States and the Philippines Built America's First Pacific Century* (New York: Basic Books, 2020), 19–21; Paul Kramer, *Blood of Government: Race, Empire, the United States, and the Philippines* (Chapel Hill: University of North Carolina Press, 2006), 35–86.
[52]Kramer, *Blood of Government*, 94.
[53]Kramer, *Blood of Government*, 91–102; Capozzola, *Bound by War*, 19–23.

made the "immodest demands of a conqueror," securing the cession of Cuba, the Philippines, Puerto Rico, and Guam. In return, Spain received a 20-million-dollar payment in compensation for "improvements" they had supposedly made in the infrastructure of the Philippines. Spain's time as a major imperial power was at an end.[54]

Indeed, Spanish diplomats should perhaps be forgiven their pique, as what little modesty was imposed on US acquisitions in 1898 resulted not from negotiations in Paris but those with Washington, DC. The empire builders—McKinley, Roosevelt, and Senator Henry Cabot Lodge—had been forced by Congress to accept some restraint on their sphere of action during the Congressional debate over authorizing the war. This restraint took the form of the "Teller Amendment," a clause introduced to the war resolution by Senator Henry M. Teller and adopted without dissent. The amendment clearly asserted not only that "the people of the island of Cuba are, and of right, ought to be, free and independent" but also that "the United States hereby disclaims any disposition or intention to exercise sovereignty, jurisdiction, or control over said island."[55] The domestic opposition to empire this reflects could also be seen in the close battle in the Senate to ratify the Treaty of Paris and the annexation of the Philippines it contained. Lodge described it to Roosevelt as "the closest, hardest fight I have ever known"—the treaty was approved by only a slim margin of one vote.[56] The anti-imperial minority included numerous prominent figures—Mark Twain, the social reformer Jane Addams, the industrialist Andrew Carnegie, and the sociologist and civil rights advocate W.E.B. Du Bois, among others. All made their case vehemently in the press.[57]

However, it would also be easy to exaggerate the extent of the opposition to annexation, particularly when we keep in mind that the Constitution requires a two-thirds vote in the Senate for ratification of treaties. While the margin for approving the Treaty of Paris was slim, it's also true that many more senators voted for than against (57-27). Congress also further indicated its approval of expansionism by endorsing the annexation of Hawaii as a territory in August.[58] Moreover, McKinley won reelection rather easily in 1900 with his Republicans gaining seats in both the House and the Senate. This seemed to indicate broad approval (or at the very least, tolerance) of the President's conduct of the war. It's also important to note for our purposes that many opponents of imperialism were motivated by the very same hierarchical view of the world that drove the empire-builders. Anti-imperialist Americans feared annexation of the Philippines and Cuba

---

[54]Kramer, *Blood of Government*, 109.
[55]Congress of the United States, "The Teller Amendment," in Holden and Zolov, *Latin America and the United States*, 72.
[56]Capozzola, *Bound by War*, 27.
[57]Capozzola, *Bound by War*, 31.
[58]Herring, *From Colony to Superpower*, 317–18; Pletcher, *Diplomacy of Involvement*, 258–87.

because they feared seeing people they believed to be inferior—Filipinos and Cubans in this case—becoming American citizens. As Carl Schurz, a former Senator from Missouri and anti-annexationist, warned in an August 1898 speech, it was impossible to imagine "a large mass ... of barbarous Asiatics, descendants of Spaniards, mixtures of Asiatics and Spanish blood" becoming part of the United States and governing "the whole Union by participating in the making of its laws and the election of Presidents."[59]

Different from European imperial powers like France and Britain, the United States had prior to 1898 governed its expansion in a somewhat egalitarian way—as far as whites were concerned—creating new political entities (territories) that possessed the ability to gain equality with the existing states, rather than overseas colonies that were seen as permanently subordinate to the mother country. This system was first established by the 1787 Northwest Ordinance, as we saw our opening chapter, and had been premised on an internal hierarchy in those potentially equal territories where Native Americans and Black Americans were deemed to be politically "outside" the communities in which they lived.[60] Despite the marginalization of non-whites, this meant that expansion for the United States had thus far involved bringing new territory into full membership in the state rather than into a relationship of subordination. Matters had been further complicated by the reformist spirit of the Reconstruction Era (roughly 1865–77), where Black males had been granted (on paper) political equality with white males.[61] It was thus possible, as racists like Schurz feared, to imagine that a new American empire might result in large numbers of non-whites gaining citizenship as part of new states joining the Union and thus sharing in the equality theoretically guaranteed by the Constitution.

Yet, rather than preventing the United States from imposing a hierarchy on its newly attained sphere of influence, this history and the fears it engendered simply meant that Americans did so via a variety of methods, including both European-style formal empire and other more indirect forms of control.[62] Hawaii, for example, became part of the United States by the traditional American route, that of being annexed and granted territorial status. This was a reflection of the relatively unique situation of Hawaii, which, unlike the other territories claimed in 1898, possessed an

---

[59] Love, *Race over Empire*, 159–95. Schurz quote on 182.
[60] For more on the Northwest Ordinance and continental expansion, see Chapters 1–3.
[61] Foner, *Reconstruction*, 228–411.
[62] This began at home where the decades before and after the war saw white Americans instituting apartheid laws and practices designed to push Black Americans as far out of the political community as was possible, particularly with the "Jim Crow" laws imposed across the South, but also with more informal forms of segregation which were practiced countrywide. For more on the imposition of Jim Crow see the overview in: Richard White, *The Republic for Which It Stands: The United States during Reconstruction and the Gilded Age, 1865–1896* (New York: Oxford University Press, 2017), 739–46.

American settler community. While they only represented a small part of the archipelago's population, these Americans controlled its government. This allowed the pro-annexationists to argue that Hawaii was a redoubt of white American civilization, one that needed to be brought into the United States both to preserve the power of the white minority and to ensure no foreign power seized the islands. By becoming a territory, Hawaii mirrored the way mainland North America had been incorporated into the Union, but it differed in that it remained in subordinate territorial status for more than half a century—only becoming a state in 1959—much longer than had been common for mainland territories with their white majorities. This prevented Hawaii's residents from having the lawmaking influence on the federal government that Schurz so greatly feared.[63]

This difference aside, Hawaii otherwise followed the standard American practice for adding territory to the Union. As a result, its residents became full US citizens with all the rights and protections provided by the Constitution to those living in territories. The situation was much different in the Philippines, Puerto Rico, Guam, and American Samoa (annexed in 1900). Here American practice followed more along the lines of traditional, European-style imperialism. Unlike in Hawaii, the residents of these islands were not granted full US citizenship, the right to a jury trial, the right to vote, or the ability to trade freely with the rest of the United States. Preventing their full citizenship required the US Supreme Court—through a series of so-called "Insular Cases"—to invent a new Constitutional principle in the form of the "doctrine of territorial incorporation." This maintained a distinction between fully "incorporated territories" (Hawaii) and "unincorporated territories" (the Pacific islands and Puerto Rico). The division between the two categories was sourced to the moment of annexation, which was now seen as merely adding land as a *possession* of the United States rather than adding land *to* the United States. Only a properly worded act of Congress, the Court claimed, could fully incorporate a territory into the United States and therefore extend all the protections of the Constitution to its residents. This "clever plan," as Julius Pratt called it, allowed the United States "to become a colonial power without violating the Constitution," establishing a two-tiered hierarchy of membership in the American polity, a system which echoed that established for Native Americans by the Court's rulings about Indigenous rights in the early nineteenth century.[64]

---

[63]Love, *Race over Empire*, 115–18.
[64]Julius W. Pratt, *America's Colonial Experiment: How the United States Gained, Governed, and in Part Gave Away a Colonial Empire* (New York: Prentice Hall, 1951), 161–4. See also Bartholomew M. Sparrow, *The Insular Cases and the Emergence of American Empire* (Lawrence: University Press of Kansas, 2006). On the court and Indigenous rights, see Chapter 2.

By the time the Supreme Court began to articulate this distinction—which it did between 1901 and 1905—many Filipinos had been fighting for over two years to reject second-class membership in an American empire and to establish an independent state instead. Fighting between Aguinaldo's forces and the United States had broken out in February of 1899, after US sentries had fired on some of the Filipino troops who were stationed outside Manila. American forces quickly overran the Filipino Republic's capital in Malolos and other key positions around the capital city. On the run, Aguinaldo disbanded his regular army and turned to guerilla war. The conflict became progressively more brutal as a result, with American troops resorting to the torture of prisoners, the execution of civilians, deportations to Guam, and—in a sad irony—concentration camps and scorched earth tactics that mirrored the horrors of Weyler's reign in Cuba. In addition to waging war on non-combatants, the United States also employed another common imperialist strategy: divide and rule. American officials attempted, with real success, to win members of the Hispanized elite away from Aguinaldo by offering them positions in the new civilian government of the island, which was established under Governor General—and future President—William Howard Taft in 1902. The United States also organized willing Filipinos into a military force called the "Philippine Scouts" which then fought alongside American forces. Aguinaldo was captured in 1901 and convinced to publicly acknowledge American sovereignty over the islands. The war continued anyway, until 1903, with US troops required to suppress periodic insurrections for years after—fighting a long conflict against the Muslim Moros of Mindanao and Samar, for example, between 1902 and 1913. In total, the Philippine-American War killed more than 4,000 US servicemen, roughly 50,000 Filipino troops, and as many as 200,000 civilians.[65]

This violence, and the American colony of the Philippines it created, was justified through talk of the Anglo-Saxon race and its civilizing mission to the world—the same justification that had been used for English settlement of, and US expansion across, North America. "Take up the White Man's burden," urged the arch-imperialist Rudyard Kipling in an 1899 poem meant to inspire the United States to continue fighting its "savage wars of peace" in the Philippines.[66] Many Americans believed they had done just this. Theodore Roosevelt—who became president following McKinley's assassination in 1901—was rather explicit in using race and civilization as a justification for the war, proclaiming in 1902 that: "warfare that has extended the boundaries of civilization at the expense of barbarism and

---

[65] Kramer, *Blood of Government*, 87–157.
[66] Rudyard Kipling, "The White Man's Burden," 1898, *The Kipling Society*, https://www.kiplingsociety.co.uk/poem/poems_burden.htm

savagery has been for centuries one of the most potent factors in the progress of humanity."[67] Such views naturally required seeing Filipinos as being less civilized than white Americans and thus in need of Anglo-Saxon leadership. US troops, for example, regularly dehumanized their opponents as barbarians. One popular US Army marching song put it this way (referring to the Army's standard issue Krag-Jorgensen rifle): "damn, damn, damn the Filipino ... civilize him with a Krag"[68] Similarly, rebellious Filipinos were routinely depicted as members of a rogue "tribe," rather than soldiers of a recognized army, a "tribalization" of Aguinaldo's republic which, as the historian Paul Kramer writes, "rhetorically eradicate[ed] the Philippine Republic as a legitimate state."[69]

Depicting US colonial rule in the Philippines—as well as in Puerto Rico, Guam, and Samoa—as part of a civilizing mission required infantilizing or barbarizing even those who peacefully acknowledged, or acquiesced, to American sovereignty. Something needed to be lacking in the people in need of tutoring by the United States in order to justify both their forced incorporation into America's empire and their second-class status within it. New imperialist thinking therefore proved an essential part of the justification for US control over its insular empire—while strategic and commercial reasons were cited, it was with much less emphasis than that placed on civilizing. McKinley, for example, announced his plan to fully annex the Philippines with the promise of "benevolent assimilation," later explaining in an interview that the islands "were unfit for self-government."[70] This left the United States with the clear responsibility, the President felt, to "educate the Filipinos, and uplift and civilize and Christianize them."[71] A cartoon printed in the November 20th, 1901 issue of *Puck*—a popular magazine of the time—revealed similar attitudes (see Figure 8). Entitled "it's up to them," the cartoon shows "Uncle Sam" delivering an American teacher and a soldier to a group of confused-looking Filipinos, most of whom are depicted in caricatured forms of traditional dress. These colonial subjects, the caption suggests, faced a clear choice between either learning civilization in a

---

[67]Theodore Roosevelt, "Remarks on Memorial Day in Arlington, Virginia," May 30, 1902, Online by Gerhard Peters and John T. Woolley, *The American Presidency Project*, https://www.presidency.ucsb.edu/node/343493.
[68]Kramer, *Blood of Government*, 139.
[69]Kramer, *Blood of Government*, 122.
[70]"Benevolent assimilation" in: William McKinley, "Executive Order," December 21, 1898, Online by Gerhard Peters and John T. Woolley, *The American Presidency Project*, https://www.presidency.ucsb.edu/node/205913. "Unfit for Self-Government," in Leia Castaneda Anastacio, *The Foundation of the Modern Philippine State: Imperial Rule and the American Constitutional Tradition, 1898–1935* (New York: Cambridge University Press, 2016), 17.
[71]McKinley tellingly ignored the reality that a great many Filipinos were already Christian, the result of centuries of Spanish efforts to spread the Roman Catholic faith. Quote from Anastacio, *The Foundation of the Modern Philippine State*, 17.

FIGURE 8 *This November 1901 cartoon from* Puck *clearly reveals the close relationship between violence and the civilizing mission in the Philippines.*

classroom (from the teacher) or on the battlefield (from the soldier).[72] Either way, many believed America's islands were lucky to be subject to US rule. "In no other Oriental country, whether ruled by Asiatics or Europeans," argued Roosevelt in 1902, "is there anything approaching the amount of individual liberty or self-government which our rule has brought to the Philippines."[73] Insular empire, like continental empire, was an instrument of global progress.

In Cuba, the United States experimented with yet another form of hierarchical ordering, one that—while still dependent on the idea of Americans standing at the vanguard of global progress—eschewed the formal annexations of new imperialism. Sometimes called "neocolonialism" by scholars and critics, it involves allowing a weaker state to possess a nominal independence and sovereignty while also remaining subordinate, required to follow certain rules demanded by supposedly more civilized states. These generally involve ensuring a political environment favorable to foreign property ownership and investment—sometimes even privileging it—regardless of the impact those investments have on the citizens of the country in question. It, in effect, makes a state's independence conditional,

---

[72] Udo J. Keppler, "It's Up to Them", *Puck*, 20 November 1901, Library of Congress, Prints and Photographs Division, https://www.loc.gov/pictures/item/2010651486. See also: Sarah Steinbock-Pratt, *Educating the Empire: American Teachers and Contested Colonization in the Pacific* (New York: Cambridge University Press, 2019), 5.
[73] Julian Go, *The British and American Empires: 1688–the Present* (New York: Cambridge University Press, 2011), 67.

always open to abridgement based on its people and government living up to certain standards. One could begin to see the outlines of such practices emerge during the US military occupation of Cuba that followed the Spanish departure from the island.

Lasting until 1902, the occupation would seem to defy the restrictions the Teller Amendment put on American control of Cuba. However, the occupation government never denied that Cuba was an independent country freed from Spanish tyranny by American beneficence. It instead focused on language in Teller's bill that said "the United States hereby disclaims any disposition or intention to exercise … control over said Island except for the *pacification thereof*."[74] This "pacification" loophole came to be interpreted rather broadly, meaning that the United States could remain in Cuba until it had established on the island, as Congressmen Townsend Scudder of New York put it, "the machinery of true and lasting civilization"—something he personally doubted could be accomplished "by surrendering the destinies of the island to the former insurgent leaders."[75] Over time, as Louis Pérez has written, the pacification requirement eventually underwent complete "transfiguration" coming to mean something along the lines of "ensuring US interests" rather than merely providing public order.[76] General Leonard Wood, the US military governor of Cuba, for example, defined successful pacification, as establishing a "stable" government, something he explained in economic terms. "The people ask me what we mean by stable government in Cuba," he wrote in a letter to the Secretary of War, "I tell them that when money can be borrowed at a reasonable rate of interest and when capital is willing to invest in the island … stability will have been reached."[77] Indeed, one of the most significant acts of the occupation government was a pro-investor "modernization" of Cuban land and tenure law, a reform which in practice opened vast swaths of Cuban territory for sale to Americans and other foreign investors.[78] By 1907, roughly 60 percent of Cuba's rural property was owned by non-residents, with another 15 percent owned by resident Spanish citizens, leaving only a quarter in Cuban hands.[79]

Neocolonial "independence" of this sort is ultimately conditional. It puts limits on the subject government, which are backed either by implicit or explicit threats of intervention and occupation. In the case of Cuba and the United States, that threat of intervention was quite explicit, written directly, lest there be any mistake, into the Cuban constitution. Named

---

[74]Emphasis mine. "The Teller Amendment," in Holden and Zolov, *Latin America and the United States*, 72.
[75]Perez, *The War of 1898*, 32.
[76]Perez, *The War of 1898*, 32.
[77]Perez, *The War of 1898*, 32.
[78]Ferrer, *Cuba*, 175.
[79]Ferrer, *Cuba*, 186–7.

the "Platt Amendment," for its primary sponsor, Senator Orville Platt of Connecticut, this addendum to Cuba's constitution specifically granted the United States the right to intervene "for the preservation of Cuban independence" and "the maintenance of a government adequate for the protection of life, property, and individual liberty." The amendment also denied Cuba the right to make treaties with foreign powers—if the United States deemed that such a treaty might "impair or tend to impair the independence of Cuba"—or to contract debts without American approval. It further required the Cuban government to lease land to the United States for naval bases and coaling stations.[80]

The Platt Amendment in fact put such limits on Cuban independence—making the island, in effect, a protectorate of the United States—that it would be fair to argue that the Cuban-US relationship under it (lasting until 1934) stretches the definition of neocolonialism. Yet, as we will see in the next chapter, the Platt Amendment was merely a codified statement of rights the United States believed it had to ensure its interests—and the interests of its citizens and corporations—in much of the non-European world, whether written or otherwise. Though the formal empire the United States established in 1898 might seem the more spectacular example of American hierarchy making in action, it was its rule in Cuba that provided a more enduring model for how it managed the ends of empire.

---

[80]"Platt Amendment (1903)," *United States National Archives and Records Administration*, "Milestone Documents," https://www.archives.gov/milestone-documents/platt-amendment#:~:text=Approved%20on%20May%2022%2C%201903,the%20enforcement%20of%20Cuban%20independence.

CHAPTER FIVE

Determining Self-Determination: The United States and Global Hierarchy before and after the Great War

Lt. Colonel Theodore Roosevelt, his famous "rough riders," and the other troops of the US expeditionary force, were not the only agents of American power to deploy to Cuba following the outbreak of the War of 1898. As the historian Peter Hudson has described, emissaries of Wall Street began disembarking as soon as July 28th, just over a month after the initial US landings in the island's southeast. Samuel Miller Jarvis, a New York City banker and businessman, for example, quickly established an office for his bank—the North American Trust Company—in Santiago de Cuba. He became, as he later claimed, "the first civilian to raise the American flag on the island after the commencement of the war."[1] The flag of American capital and commerce would remain raised even after US occupation troops left Cuba in 1902. US money flooded the island, as did American manufactured goods, forcing hundreds of Cuban manufacturing interests to close while ensuring that, by 1926, US-owned sugar mills produced 63 percent of Cuba's most valuable product.[2] In fact—as we discussed in the previous chapter—US officials were only willing to end that occupation once it was clear that a government favorable to US businessmen and investors

---

[1] Peter James Hudson, *Bankers and Empire: How Wall Street Colonized the Caribbean* (Chicago: University of Chicago Press, 2017), 18–19.
[2] Ferrer, *Cuba*, 191.

like Jarvis was firmly established. Just in case, the United States had written the "Platt Amendment" into the Cuban constitution, enshrining its right to intervene on the island again, while also securing a perpetual lease on Cuban land surrounding Guantanamo Bay to establish military facilities to that end.

Sure enough, when the vast inequalities of wealth on the island fueled a populist uprising in 1906—threatening to take down Cuba's government and potentially re-order its property regime—US troops were ordered ashore once more. This time it was the former rough rider himself, President Theodore Roosevelt, who gave the order. "I am so angry with that infernal little Cuban republic," snarled the President, "all we have wanted from them was that they would behave themselves and be prosperous and happy so that we would not have to interfere."[3] The United States instead interfered until 1909, preventing the success of what Roosevelt called "an utterly unjustifiable and pointless revolution" and ensuring that Cuba's economic order remained one that overwhelmingly benefited the US and Cuban elites.[4]

In this chapter, we will explore the US relationship to the ends of empire in the first two decades of the twentieth century, a period where the US approach to the non-European world modeled its interactions with Cuba during the years of the Platt Amendment (1902–34) like those described above. Americans in these years increasingly turned away from formal empire, seeing the acquisition of their own as a mistake, part of an older-European style world order that was destined for the scrapheap of history. As Woodrow Wilson would proclaim in 1918, when the United States entered the great war for empire—the First World War—the future was to be shaped by "self-determination," the right of peoples to choose their own form of rule. Yet, this new world of self-determination was still understood in a deeply hierarchical fashion, with some societies closer to having reached a self-determined future, others further, all depending on their perceived proximity to Euro-American conceptions of civilization. These, as always, were determined in part by race and culture but also by a state's "stability" for business investment, its respect for foreign capital, and for foreign ownership of private property. Even if a scrupulous adherence to such rules was manifestly not in the best interest of the people in question—as was the case with Cuba—they were still expected to be followed. Failure to do so immediately called into question a state's sovereignty, opening the door to intervention and occupation, a fate that would befall not only Cuba, but Colombia, the Dominican Republic, Honduras, Haiti, Nicaragua, and Mexico before 1934. The US government did not always undertake such interventions with complete enthusiasm, but the potent combination of

---

[3]Quoted in Louis A. Pérez Jr., *Cuba under the Platt Amendment, 1902–1934* (Pittsburgh: University of Pittsburgh Press, 1986), 97.
[4]Perez, *Cuba under the Platt Amendment*, 97.

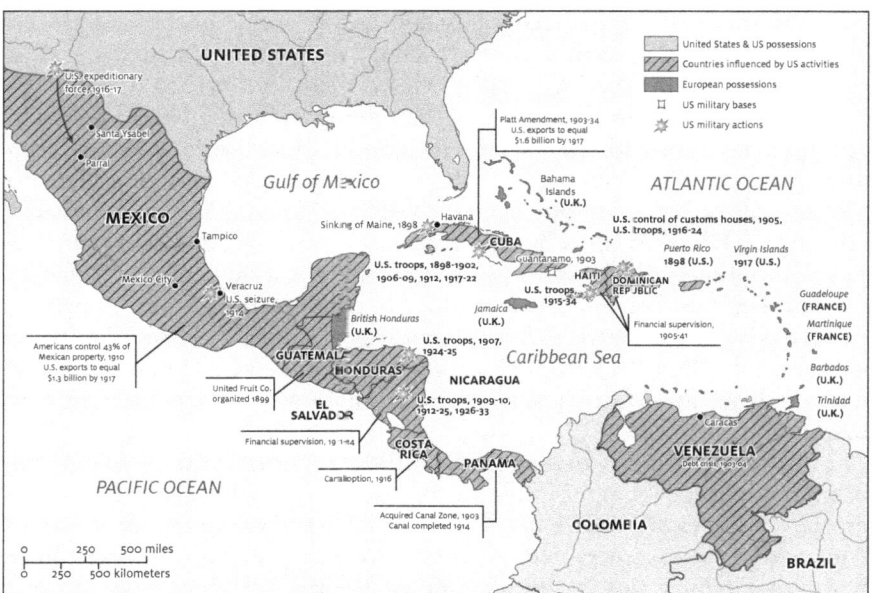

MAP 2 *Early twentieth-century US interventions in the Caribbean basin.*

US business and financial interests, mixed with ideological assumptions about progress and the proper rules for world order, ensured that they happened all the same. Despite starting to step away from the imperial age, therefore, the United States still reserved much of the right of "self-determination" for itself.

Hierarchy without Empire?

As the war in the Philippines wound down—or was made to appear to be winding down thanks to careful work to relabel the insurrection as mere "banditry"—America's new empire faded from popular attention at home.[5] Enthusiastic plans for settling a large number of white Americans in the colonies failed to get off the ground—except in a very limited way in Hawaii, where the well-established settler minority already controlled the government. Even many of the pro-imperialist crowd, like Theodore Roosevelt, experienced some regret about the extent of the annexations. Such sentiments were, however, balanced by contradictory feelings. On the one hand, there was a desire to wind down US control in the Philippines; on the other, there were the very same racial and civilizational prejudices

---

[5]Kramer, *Blood of Government*, 155.

that had made the empire seem possible and desirable in the first place.⁶ These now made it seem contrary to the "new duties thrust on us," as the then-Professor Woodrow Wilson called them in 1901, to dissolve the empire. It would be irresponsible, Wilson thought, for the United States to give up the islands without teaching their populations "order as a condition and precedent to liberty" and "self-control as a condition precedent to self-government."⁷ Governor General William Howard Taft felt similarly, labeling the Filipinos under his rule as a "vast mass of ignorant, superstitious people, well intentioned, light-hearted, temperate, and somewhat cruel … fond of their families and deeply wedded to the Catholic Church"—people, that is, who were far from ready for self-government.⁸ Seeing the world hierarchically had helped facilitate the acquisition of an empire, it also made it hard for Americans in positions of power to imagine its quick dissolution.

This does not mean that there was not a belief that the people of the islands could be "taught" civilization. Many US officials, particularly as the "Progressive Movement" emerged to become a major force in American politics, truly believed that colonized populations, even those with what whites saw as dubious racial origins, could be made to live more like white Americans both for their benefit and the benefit of the world as a whole.⁹ Ideas about assimilation and—what would later be called "modernization"—were broadly popular in US government circles at this time. They were also reflected in late nineteenth-century policies toward Indigenous Americans. The 1887 Dawes Severalty Act, for example, had sought to push Native Americans on reservations away from their traditional patterns of communal land ownership and toward single-family farming on individual parcels of private land. US government-backed "Indian Boarding Schools" were also established with the goal of removing Native American children from their communities and raising them according to European lifestyles. Captain Richard Henry Pratt, the longtime head of one such school in Pennsylvania, promised his approach would "kill the Indian … and save the man." These schools banned students from speaking Indigenous languages or practicing their traditional cultures and religions.¹⁰

---

⁶Hopkins, *American Empire*, 494–504.
⁷Hopkins, *American Empire*, 507.
⁸Hopkins, *American Empire*, 502.
⁹For an overview of the Progressive Movement see: Shelton Stromquist, *Reinventing the People: The Progressive Movement, the Class Problem, and the Origins of Modern Liberalism* (Urbana: University of Illinois Press, 2002).
¹⁰Matthew Bentley and John Bloom, *The Imperial Gridiron: Manhood, Civilization, and Football at the Carlisle Indian Industrial School* (Lincoln: University of Nebraska Press, 2022) quote on 1.

We should recognize today, of course, the vicious chauvinism—the dismissal of the agency, culture, and religions of non-white Anglo-Saxon Protestants—inherent in such thinking. Yet, it would be a historical error not to also recognize that figure like Taft and Pratt saw themselves as doing the right thing by the people they were governing and educating. All the same, even among the well-meaning, these projects were premised upon unequal power dynamics and the violence that sustained them, realities that rather quickly revealed themselves. The Dawes Act in the long run did more to facilitate the sale of Native American land to whites than anything else, further shrinking the already minimal territory granted to tribes by the United States government.[11] The boarding schools became hotbeds of abuse, leading to countless early deaths and generations of traumatized Native American children.[12] In the Philippines, as we saw toward the end of the last chapter, armed force, torture, and forced relocation of civilians were all regularly required to maintain the supposedly tutelary state's control over the archipelago. Most Filipinos, Native Hawaiians, Puerto Ricans, and Cubans, were at best indifferent, and more often hostile, to efforts to "Americanize" them through education and the careful deployment of US national symbols.[13]

Promised American innovations in colonial management never quite emerged. US administrators in the Philippines and Puerto Rico instead came to possess, as A.G. Hopkins has amusingly put it, "a more generous view of their inheritance" from the old Spanish regime.[14] A combination of direct authority and rule through local elites—the classic European imperial pattern—governed the unincorporated colonies. Rule through favored elites also allowed for the assertion of American power over the protectorate in Cuba, while settlers followed American continental practice and controlled government business in Hawaii.[15] In general, while the United States was far from ready to explore a path to decolonization for its empire, it also showed little enthusiasm for expanding it further.

Despite this declining interest in hierarchy-making through formal empire, re-ordering the world in America's image—and for its benefit—had not necessarily lost any of its appeal after 1898. It was just the method of

---

[11]On the Dawes Act see: Emily Greenwald, *Reconfiguring the Reservation: The Nez Perces, Jicarilla Apaches, and the Dawes Act* (Albuquerque: University of New Mexico Press, 2002); Kristin T. Ruppel, *Unearthing Indian Land: Living with the Legacies of Allotment* (Tucson: University of Arizona Press, 2008).

[12]For more on the boarding schools see: Bentley and Bloom, *The Imperial Gridiron*; David Wallace Adams, *Education for Extinction: American Indians and the Boarding School Experience, 1875–1928*, 2nd edition (Lawrence: University of Kansas Press, 2020).

[13]For more on US imperial education see: Steinbock-Pratt, *Educating the Empire*. On the use of national symbols in the empire see: Alvita Akiboh, *Imperial Material: National Symbols in the U.S. Colonial Empire* (Chicago: University of Chicago Press, 2023).

[14]Hopkins, *American Empire*, 502.

[15]Hopkins, *American Empire*, 497–504.

formal annexation that fell out of favor. The United States retained, and continued to build up, its existing sphere of influence, establishing military bases in all of its far-flung islands—from the Philippines and Guam to Puerto Rico—and developed one of the world's largest navies. If, by 1918, the United States was proclaiming a somewhat different perspective on empire than that which held in most European capitals, this difference emerged only slowly and remained within a broader consensus about the hierarchical nature of world order.

In 1900, for example, the United States participated in an expedition clearly meant to assert Euro-American dominance of the globe: the multi-state intervention in China against the Boxer Uprising. Anti-Christian and anti-foreign, the Boxer movement was itself a result of resentment towards the global hierarchy and, in particular, the acceleration of foriegn economic penetration of China following the Qing Dynasty's defeat in the First Sino-Japanese War (1894–95). The "Boxers United in Righteousness," as they were called, were a religious and political movement among peasants in the Shandong province, south of Beijing, where they eventually marched proclaiming "support the Qing, destroy the Foreign." Allying with anti-foreign elements in the Chinese government and eventually gaining the support of the Empress Dowager, the Boxer militias besieged Beijing's "legation quarter," the neighborhood where many foreigners and diplomats resided, in May of 1900. To Americans, as McKinley's Secretary of State, John Hay, noted in July, this development suggested that the rules of civilization were no longer being followed in China. "The condition [in China] is one of virtual anarchy," he wrote, the "furtherance of lawful commerce, and of protection of lives and property of our citizens ... guaranteed under the law of nations" was no longer being respected.[16] This was in some sense true, as the uprising was very much a reaction to the "furtherance" of commerce, a furtherance which the Boxers believed threatened their livelihoods. In response to this threat to European, American, and Japanese interests, eight states—Japan and Russia primarily, but Britain, France, Germany, and United States as well—sent troops to put down the Boxers and install a compliant government in Beijing. Assembling a force of nearly 50,000 men in Tianjin (including 6,300 Americans deployed from the Philippines), the "civilized powers" marched on Beijing, burning villages along the way. They then brutally suppressed the Boxers in the city, killing indiscriminately.[17]

---

[16]John Hay, "Circular Note of July 3, 1900, to the Powers Cooperating in China, Defining the Purposes and Policy of the United States," July 3, 1900, Document 4. United States Department of State, *Foreign Relations of the United States: 1901 Appendix*, https://history.state.gov/historicaldocuments/frus1901China/d4.

[17]For more on the Boxer Uprising, see: Joseph Echerick, *The Origins of the Boxer Uprising* (Berkley: University of California Press, 1987) and Herring, *From Colony to Superpower*, 331–3.

FIGURE 9 *US troops—part of the multinational force deployed to supress the Boxer Uprising—marching in Beijing, China, 1900.*

The eight powers forced new treaties on the Chinese government, requiring it to pay a roughly 300-million-dollar indemnity (of which the United States claimed 25 million) and allow for the stationing of more foreign troops on its territory. Subsequently all, including the United States, demanded and received favorably revised trade rules as well. Britain, France, Russia, and Japan—the latter had vaulted up the global hierarchy thanks to its rapid industrialization in the late nineteenth century—also further expanded their "spheres of influence" in China. These were formal territorial zones within the country where the foreign power's trade was granted exclusive rights. The United States did not possess such a territory and had instead been advocating for an alternative "Open Door" approach. Articulated by Hay in a pair of "notes" in 1899 and 1900, the Open Door policy has sometimes been seen—by the famed diplomat and scholar George F. Kennan, for example—as an instance of American idealism because it called for equalizing foreign trade rights in China and rejected annexations of Chinese territory. The reality, however, was a bit more sordid. The United States was not seeking to elevate Chinese sovereign equality, but to ensure that Chinese subordination proceeded on terms favorable to its own commerce. European and Japanese interests in China were much further advanced than those of the Americans and, coming right after the War of 1898, the United States was not in a position to acquire territory in China anyway. The Open Door was therefore more about keeping the United States in, than keeping the great powers out or maintaining Chinese sovereignty intact. As President McKinley tellingly asked: "may we not want a slice, if it is to be divided?"[18]

What emerges from the US approach to the Boxer Uprising, and the occupations of Cuba, was an alternate, "neocolonial"—a term we identified it in the previous chapter—pattern in enforcing global hierarchy. This involved demanding states follow the rules of "international law" and "civilization" as the United States understood them, which generally meant being willing to accept commercial treaties that favored the United States, along with being open to the stationing of American troops where strategic demands required it. If (and often "when") these unequal relationships generated resentment and political instability in the weaker state, the United States retained a right to intervene with force in order to preserve civilization from the threat of "anarchy." As was the case with Roosevelt's re-occupation of Cuba, such interventions were not always carried out with complete enthusiasm. Instead, the US government often found itself in something of an "empire trap," as the historian Noel Maurer has entitled it, where the vast, government-backed, expansion of private US commercial activity across the world generated immense pressure to intervene if business interests were threatened. Once intervention came to be seen as a possible US government response to appropriations overseas, this facilitated further investment abroad—as capital owners grew used to a form of *de facto* government insurance against potential property losses.[19] Thus, as American businessmen fanned out across the globe seeking to establish hierarchical relationships for their benefit (as is natural to those following the profit motive), they made it increasingly more likely that the US government would feel required to use force to support them.

And fan out the businessmen did. As we touched on in the previous chapter, the late nineteenth century saw the United States develop into a part of the world's manufacturing core, becoming the leading industrial power on the globe by 1914. Despite its huge domestic market, the United States could not absorb all the goods and capital being produced and concentrated within its borders. Commercially-minded Americans thus looked to expand US trade and investment abroad, at first widening the well-worn tracks to the Caribbean and Mexico, and then moving further south into Central and South America. US exports to Latin America would grow by about 600 percent between 1880 and 1913, while the United States also consumed growing amounts of raw materials produced in the region. This dominance of the Latin American market only increased when the First World War

---

[18]Herring, *From Colony to Superpower*, 333–5 (McKinley quote on 334); Williams, *The Tragedy of American Diplomacy*, 45–57.
[19]Noel Maurer, *The Empire Trap: The Rise and Fall of U.S. Intervention to Protect Property Overseas, 1893–2013* (Princeton: Princeton University Press, 2013), 8–10.

increasingly cut Europe—and especially the British—off from Central and South America. By 1917, the United States had supplanted once dominant Britain as the region's main trading partner. Though the US did not extend formal control over the countries it traded with, US industrial might—and, in many cases, the terms of the trade agreements the US demanded—ensured that this commerce followed the ususal hierarchical pattern of trade relations within empires. The United States consumed Latin American raw materials while selling its finished goods to Central and South American consumers, with the long-term benefits accruing in the United States. Direct US investment followed as well, soaring from a modest $308 million in 1897 to $1.2 billion in 1914 (growing further to $3.5 billion by 1929). US companies bought up mining rights, oil concessions, sugar plantations, refineries, fruit farms, and other agricultural interests. Large North American concerns like Standard Oil and the United Fruit Company soon became key players in Central and South American economies.[20]

The United Fruit Company, for example (which was sometimes called in Spanish "el pulpo" or "the octopus") dominated the Western Hemisphere's trade in bananas and garnered considerable political influence along with its growing market share.[21] Many other American businesses also developed close relationships with governments in Latin America, doing their best to ensure friendly environments for their property and investments. In Mexico, the government under President Porfirio Díaz (in office for most of the period 1876–1911) believed foreign capital was the key to the country's development and so offered generous terms for US investment in agricultural, banking, mining, oil, and railroad interests. Influential Los Angelenos, like *Los Angeles Times* publisher Harrison Gray Otis, developed close relationships with Diaz and other Mexican elites, cultivating a cross-border alliance of power that worked to keep investment money flowing south and a steady rate of return headed north. These relationships did much to benefit capital owners in both countries (and compliant Mexican government officials) but less to help the average Mexican, who saw as much as quarter of their country's property pass into foreign hands. The significant rates of inequality that resulted would help lead to the outbreak of the Mexican Revolution in 1910.[22]

US investors, however, believed their partnership was helping bring Mexico into the modern world. When "directed upon a right plane," Otis claimed, US investment "must result for the good of the [Mexican] Republic." After all, he continued, what Mexico "needs more than anything else is

---

[20]Thomas F. O'Brien, *The Century of U.S. Capitalism in Latin America* (Albuquerque: University of New Mexico Press, 1999), 29–31.
[21]For more on the United Fruit Company see Peter Chapman, *Bananas: How the United Fruit Company Shaped the World* (New York: Canongate Books, 2022).
[22]Kim, *Imperial Metropolis*, 12, 48–76.

development…the application of capital, skill, and labor well directed."[23] Otis's comments reflect well the combination of personal financial interest, material hierarchies of wealth, and imagined hierarchies of race and nation, that made Americans willing to abridge the sovereignty of their neighbors. Assigned to one of the Mexican mines of his firm, a young American engineer expressed a typical attitude, writing home in 1918 that, "all Mexicans are children and have to be treated accordingly."[24]

Similar assumptions of superiority governed the US banking houses that gained increasing influence with governments in the Caribbean and Central America at this time. Following the War of 1898, American banks vastly increased their presence in and along the shores of the "American Mediterranean," as one National City Bank of New York employee dubbed the Caribbean.[25] City Bank was the largest but not the only US financial institution to move money south to bankroll trade, fund railroads and other infrastructure projects, underwrite industrial development, and even help manage the currency systems and sovereign debts of cash-strapped Caribbean governments.[26] In so doing, US financial institutions were organized around—and expected borrowers to employ—a "racial chain of command" as Peter Hudson has described it.[27] Funded enterprises were expected to follow practices where Americans or Europeans were in key decision-making positions, with locals seen as whiter or more Europeanized next, and then non-whites serving in the less skilled roles. As the French manager of the soon-to-be-US-controlled Banque Nationale d'Haïti described it in 1913: "as might be expected, the negro and the mulatto [sic]" made up the bulk of his bank's employees, but "all important and responsible positions are held by [white] foreigners."[28]

This echoed the broader order that American money expected the development of the Caribbean basin to follow: manual labor for relatively low pay conducted by non-white laborers, with profits passing upwards through whiter and whiter hands until they reached Wall Street. The overall structure of trade in the Western Hemisphere reinforced this hierarchy as well, as the disparity between the prices paid for manufactured goods and those paid for commodities ensured that capital tended to end up in the United States, requiring governments in Latin America to borrow more from New York. American bankers were far from omnipotent—as we will see, they regularly required the US government to bail them out of sticky situations—but they still exercised considerable influence over life in Latin America.

---

[23] Kim, *Imperial Metropolis*, 57.
[24] Quoted in O'Brien, *Century of U.S. Capitalism*, 25.
[25] Hudson, *Bankers and Empire*, 7.
[26] Hudson, *Bankers and Empire*, 7.
[27] Hudson, *Bankers and Empire*, 81.
[28] Hudson, *Bankers and Empire*, 81.

American businesses were therefore reaping many of the benefits of empire-like hierarchies without an extension of US sovereignty, an approach that gained steam during the administration of Theodore Roosevelt (1901–09). That the United States made something of a break with its age of annexation under the auspices of the once-arch-imperialist Roosevelt is not, perhaps, without some irony. Yet, it's also a reflection of the increasingly negative attitudes toward formal imperialism in the United States following the War of 1898. Even with his most imperial undertaking as president—the acquisition of the Panama Canal Zone in 1903—for example, Roosevelt avoided both full annexation and the appearance of being in a territory "uninvited." In an effort to finally establish the transisthmian canal that had been the dream of many Americans and Europeans since the mid-nineteenth century, Roosevelt pressured the Colombian government into leasing a six-mile-wide zone of land across its long-restive province of Panama. When the Colombian Senate refused to ratify the treaty (holding out for a better deal), the Roosevelt administration gave quiet encouragement to a group of Panamanian separatists. These were largely drawn from the ranks of a nascent Panamanian oligarchy and closely associated with the US-owned Panama railroad. With private assurances that the US would protect any nationalist uprising from Colombian reprisals, the Panamanians revolted and declared an independent state.[29]

Shielded by the US Navy—which Roosevelt deployed to protect "the interests of civilization" in "the peaceable traffic of the world across the Isthmus of Panama"—the new Panamanian government accepted a canal treaty largely written in Washington.[30] In return for sovereign powers over a ten-mile-wide Canal Zone, the United States promised to pay an annual rent of $250,000 and to "guarantee and maintain" the independence of Panama.[31] The US government also undertook to help modernize Panamanian infrastructure—with electric lines, sewers, disease suppression, etc.—a promise subsequently fulfilled.[32] The treaty in effect made Panama a protectorate of the United States, but once again we see a relationship that looked more like that with Cuba than it did US rule in the Philippines.[33]

Roosevelt would elevate this "empire-lite" approach not just to the level of official policy but to that of sacred national mission with his 1904

---

[29]Walter LaFeber, *The Panama Canal: The Crisis in Historical Perspective* (New York: Oxford University Press, 1978), 19–33.
[30]Theodore Roosevelt, "Special Message to the House of Representatives," November 16, 1903, Online by Gerhard Peters and John T. Woolley, *The American Presidency Project*, https://www.presidency.ucsb.edu/node/206241.
[31]"Convention for the Construction of a Ship Canal (Hay-Bunau-Varilla Treaty)," November 18, 1903, Yale University Law School, *The Avalon Project: Documents in Law, History, and Diplomacy*, https://avalon.law.yale.edu/20th_century/pan001.asp.
[32]Lars Schoultz, *In Their Own Best Interest: A History of the U.S. Effort to Improve Latin Americans* (Cambridge, MA: Harvard University Press, 2018), 31.
[33]LaFeber, *The Panama Canal*, 33–9.

"Roosevelt Corollary" to the Monroe Doctrine. The corollary emerged in response to two crises caused by Latin American financial obligations and great power attempts to claim them—one in Venezuela and another in the Dominican Republic. Both nations were struggling to service their sovereign debts, most of which were owned by European and American creditors. A reflection of the hierarchically structured nature of the early twentieth-century world, it was widely assumed that the "civilized" powers had a "right" to protect their own investors by using military force to seize a state's customs houses (tariffs being the primary form of revenue for most governments at the time) and hold them until the debt was paid or otherwise satisfied. Ensuring that foreign investors were protected, and that foreign-owned property was not nationalized, was seen as a requirement of "international law," which continued to be defined in such a way that it almost always protected the interests of richer and more industrialized countries over those of the weaker states in the world-system.[34] As Edwin Boarchard, a leading US international law expert of the time, put it, any abridgement of foreign property rights "transgresses the prescriptions of civilized justice," with the result that the "personal sovereignty of the home state asserts itself."[35] This meant, in essence, that the home state of the foreign investor or property owner then had a right to abridge the sovereignty of the weaker country whenever it deemed necessary.

Some scholars and lawyers in the non-European world had actually begun to push back against this principle of world order, reasoning that a respect for the sovereign equality of independent states required a different, fairer, approach to settling such disputes. The Argentinian jurist Carlos Calvo, for example, argued in 1868 that foreign creditors—and their governments—had no special rights that a domestic lender did not, and thus should endeavor to collect outstanding loans through local courts rather than via the barrel of a naval gun.[36] When Great Britain, Germany, and Italy sent gunboats to blockade Venezuela's coast in 1902, Argentine Foreign Minister Luis M. Drago sent a note to the US government restating Calvo's doctrine, protesting that, "among the fundamental principles of public international law ... is that which decrees that all states, whatever be the force at their disposal, are entities in law perfectly equal one to another." This being the case, Drago continued, the settlement of debt questions must be done "without diminution of [the

---

[34] Schoultz, *In Their Own Best Interest*, 32; Robert Freeman Smith, *The United States and Revolutionary Nationalism in Mexico, 1916–1932* (Chicago: University of Chicago Press, 1972), 23–6.
[35] Smith, *Revolutionary Nationalism in Mexico*, 26.
[36] Lars Schoultz, *Beneath the United States: A History of U.S. Policy Towards Latin America* (Cambridge, MA: Harvard University Press, 1998), 179–80; Smith, *Revolutionary Nationalism in Mexico*, 26–9.

debtor state's] inherent rights as a sovereign entity." The use of force to collect from defaulters would "occasion nothing less than the ruin of the weakest nations, and the absorption of their governments ... by the mighty of the earth."[37]

Drago and Calvo's conception of sovereignty unsurprisingly made little headway in Washington, DC—or in Berlin, London, and Rome, for that matter. The Europeans continued their blockade of Venezuela, bombarding Puerto Cabello and seizing much of the small Venezuelan navy. Under US pressure, the three powers and Venezuela ended the crisis with an agreement whereby 30 percent of Venezuelan customs duties would be committed to debt service. Despite this resolution, however, the Roosevelt administration still feared that the situation could lead to further European intervention and threaten the principles of the Monroe Doctrine.[38] In the Dominican Republic, meanwhile, the situation continued to deteriorate. The Republic had struggled with political instability and financial insolvency since it gained independence from Haiti in 1844. Its place in the global economic hierarchy—producing commodities like sugar and tobacco for export—did not allow the country to generate revenue sufficient for its own economic development and the welfare of its people, not to mention the greed of its rulers and their lending partners in Europe and the United States. The assassination of one such leader, President Ulises Heureaux, in 1899 triggered an intense period of political instability that lasted into the new century. One government after another toppled and the country fell further in arrears on its sovereign debt.[39]

Forces had thus begun to converge in a way that would push the Roosevelt administration into action. First, US owners of Dominican debt and property demanded action to protect their investments. "Surely," wrote one sugar planter to Hay, "it cannot be the purpose of the United States to abandon its citizens and their interests ... to such a condition as exists in Santo Domingo!"[40] Second, the Monroe Doctrine also seemed to demand the United States do something as well. The administration feared Dominican instability could easily lead to European intervention—as it had in Venezuela—and a permanent British, French, or German presence on the island.[41] Third, administration officials were already predisposed to see the states to the south as, in Roosevelt's words, "strange, turbulent,

---

[37]"Señor Luis M. Drago, Minister of Foreign Relations of the Argentine Republic, to Señor Martin Garcia Mérou, Minister of the Argentine Republic to the United States," December 29, 1902, Document 2, United States Department of State, *Papers Relating to the Foreign Relations of the United States, With the Annual Message of the President Transmitted to Congress*, https://history.state.gov/historicaldocuments/frus1903/d2.
[38]For more on the Monroe Doctrine see Chapter 3.
[39]Maurer, *Empire Trap*, 60–5.
[40]Maurer, *Empire Trap*, 64.
[41]Schoultz, *In Their Own Best Interest*, 36.

little half-caste civilizations" in need of North American tutelage.[42] The President's men on the scene—Roosevelt sent a fact-finding commission to the island—reported back in similarly prejudicial tones. The Dominican Republic, they wrote, was "in the grasp of ... irresponsible political brigands ... little better than savages." Albert Dillingham, the commander of the US Navy's Caribbean squadron, thought much the same, writing that "as the great civilizing power of the world, we will be obliged ... to control the finances of the country until every cent of the debt ... has been paid."[43] Administration officials, including the President, agreed but were wary of upsetting domestic opinion with anything that smacked of imperialism during an election year.

With his reelection secured in November, however, Roosevelt felt more freedom to act and thus took advantage of an opening provided by the Dominican Republic's newest dictator, Carlos Morales. Struggling to maintain control of the country—the Dominican civil war had not stopped with his ascension to power in late 1903—Morales looked to US intervention as the surest path for securing his own political future.[44] He invited the US government to take control of Dominican customs houses as long as it promised to provide sufficient revenue for his government. Backed by two of Dillingham's warships, US negotiators secured a treaty to this effect, carefully avoiding any appearance of annexation or formal imperialism, while promising to rationalize Dominican finances and protect the country from any foreign threats. Forty-five percent of Dominican customs revenue was committed to the government's needs with the rest going to debt service.[45] Though the US Senate rejected the treaty for two years (only endorsing it in 1907), Roosevelt used executive authority to implement it immediately. US officials took control of Dominican customs houses in March of 1905 and soon had successfully modernized the country's revenue and tariff collection system, even establishing a frontier patrol and a revenue cutter service.[46] While these efforts went some way to stabilizing Dominican finances and creditworthiness, they also ensured that the Republic remained stuck in the global economic periphery while much of its public revenue went into the bank accounts of United States and European creditors. With a large percentage of its national income siphoned off for debt service, widespread poverty—and the political instability it helped drive—continued to plague America's newest client state.

Roosevelt's Corollary to the Monroe Doctrine, announced as part of his December 6th annual message to Congress, argued that these measures were justified by the need to advance the cause of civilization. In his message,

---

[42]Schoultz, *In Their Own Best Interest*, 31.
[43]Schoultz, *In Their Own Best Interest*, 36.
[44]Maurer, *Empire Trap*, 66–8.
[45]Herring, *From Colony to Superpower*, 372–2, Maurer, *Empire Trap*, 69–70.
[46]Maurer, *Empire Trap*, 70–5.

FIGURE 10 *A March 1904 political cartoon in* Judge—*a popular weekly satirical magazine published in New York—depicting Theodore Roosevelt asserting the Monroe Doctrine over the Dominican Republic.*

Roosevelt expanded the United States' claimed authority over the Western Hemisphere under the Monroe Doctrine. No longer would the United States just protect its half of the globe from outside interference, it would now also maintain order within the sphere itself. The United States, Roosevelt promised, did not feel "any land hunger or entertai[n] any projects as regards the other nations of the Western Hemisphere save such as are for their welfare." Therefore, he continued, "if a nation shows that it knows how to act with reasonable efficiency and decency in social and political matters, if it keeps order and pays its obligations, it need fear no interference from the United States." However, were the United States to perceive a sufficient breakdown in order, one "which results in a general loosening of the ties of civilized society," then that would require the United States as a "civilized nation" to "exercise ... an international police power" to set matters to rights.[47]

In Roosevelt's eyes, the United States was not selfishly acting in its own interests in these cases but serving "the interest of humanity at large." He cited as proof of this not just US actions in the Caribbean but American efforts to "secure the open door in China" as well. "Our interests and those of our southern neighbors are in reality identical," the President claimed, "they have great natural riches, and if within their borders the reign of law and justice obtains, prosperity is sure to come to them." Thus, in what seems almost a direct repudiation of the Calvo and Drago doctrines, Roosevelt argued that the United States retained a clear right to abridge a foreign state's sovereignty if it deemed it necessary, "every nation ... which desires to maintain ... its independence, must ultimately realize that the right of such independence cannot be separated from the responsibility of making good use of it."[48] Even if the United States was no longer interested in a formal empire, Roosevelt implied, much of the world remained unready for a true decolonization.

Dollar Diplomacy

Roosevelt would find himself invoking the newly muscular Monroe Doctrine quicker than he perhaps expected, initiating the aforementioned second occupation of Cuba in 1906.[49] He thus left to his successor, President William Howard Taft (in office: 1909–13), an established pattern of US interventionism in the name of civilization—a "fragile consensus" as the historian Lars Schoultz has put it, "that the U.S. had the right to maintain order in the entire Caribbean region," through all means short of annexation.[50] That consensus was also to become bipartisan with the arrival of Woodrow Wilson (in office: 1913–21) in the White House. Interestingly, both Taft and Wilson claimed that they were moving away from Roosevelt's interventionism—"substituting dollars for bullets" as Taft put it in his 1912 annual message to Congress—but

---

[47]Theodore Roosevelt, "Fourth Annual Message," December 6, 1904, Online by Gerhard Peters and John T. Woolley, *The American Presidency Project*, https://www.presidency.ucsb.edu/node/206208.
[48]Theodore Roosevelt, "Fourth Annual Message".
[49]For more on the occupation see: Perez, *Cuba under the Platt Amendment*, 88–107.
[50]Schoultz, *In Their Own Best Interest*, 42.

such domestic political distinctions were without much difference overseas.[51] Each used force to support their policies as much or more than Roosevelt had. Despite their dissimilar personalities, all three presidents were cut from a similar cloth, each being a distinct reflection of the "Progressive Movement" that played a key role in US politics at the time.

Progressives believed that humanity in the early twentieth century had arrived at a place where, thanks to industrialization and scientific and moral progress, many of the more intractable problems of human life (along with the newer problems created by industry and progress) could in fact be solved. While in many cases genuinely well-meaning, Progressives—who, by and large, were middle, or upper-middle-class white Protestants—were by no means immune to the forms of hierarchical thinking we have been exploring in this book. They often manifested an elitism which looked down upon those they planned on helping, from Catholic immigrants to Black and Indigenous Americans. Progressives were confident that the sober and orderly life of Protestant, middle-class America was the natural and universally desirable endpoint for human development. Many were quite willing to employ coercion upon those who proved unwilling to be helped in that direction—an attitude that, as we have seen, had long been part of the relationship between the United States and the world.[52] Progressive Era foreign policy did not fundamentally alter this longstanding tradition, it merely further adapted it to early twentieth-century American tastes by putting greater emphasis on the supposedly generous and educational aspects of US policy. As Woodrow Wilson would explain to a British official in advance of his intervention in the Mexican Revolution, it was the United States' responsibility to "teach the South American republics to elect good men," a mission he took seriously.[53]

Taft was the most restrained of the three in practice, but he too shared the same commitment to the project of civilizational uplift—an undertaking, it should be noted, that continued to conveniently align with the material interests of wealthy American investors and a US economy in need of markets and raw materials. Taft believed interventions abroad, as he said in 1909, "contributed much to the cause of peace by assisting countries weak in respect to their internal government so as to strengthen... them." By establishing a relationship with Latin American countries like that of a "guardian" to a "ward," he continued, the United States was helping "along the cause of peace" and furthering "progress in civilization."[54] Taft

---

[51]William Howard Taft, "Fourth Annual Message," December 3, 1912, Online by Gerhard Peters and John T. Woolley, *The American Presidency Project*, https://www.presidency.ucsb.edu/node/207239.
[52]Stromquist, *Reinventing the People*, 1–11, passim.
[53]Robert W. Tucker, "Woodrow Wilson's 'New Diplomacy'," *World Policy Journal* 21, no. 2 (2004): 92–107.
[54]Schoultz, *In Their Own Best Interest*, 43.

duly attempted to replicate Roosevelt's Dominican model in Honduras and Nicaragua, with mixed success. In Honduras, where a new government under Miguel Dávila worried the North American banana planters who dominated the economy, the President's effort to establish a US receivership was stymied by both the US and Honduran congresses. The latter in particular did not wish to see their "free country," as they put it, turned "into an administrative dependency of the United States."[55] Subsequently, the American planters, led by Samuel "the banana man" Zemurray, orchestrated their own revolution, bringing a more pliant government to power, one which secured generous financing from New York. Though the US government did not establish control over Honduran finances as Taft planned, US businessmen in essence gained control over the state itself.[56]

A similar situation played out in neighboring Nicaragua, though here the US government did end up taking control of the country's finances. In 1909, US investors, tired of the independence of the country's liberal president, José Santos Zelaya, financed a revolution to overthrow him. When Zelaya executed two US volunteers supporting the revolt, Taft sent in the Marines, leading to the establishment of a pro-US regime in 1910. US banks arranged to take over much of the Nicaragua's debt while Taft dispatched an American—Clifford Ham, fresh from serving in the Philippine colonial government—to oversee the country's customs collection. Though nominally temporary, this arrangement endured for decades. Ham served until 1928, while US Marines remained in the country in varying numbers until 1933, periodically required to put down revolts that threatened US interests. Locked into a subservient economic relationship that ensured that the bulk of the population remained poor, while wealth ended up in the hands of the country's elites and American investors, Nicaragua saw such uprisings regularly, including, for example, a 1912 insurrection that Taft ordered 2,600 Marines to suppress.[57] "In Central America," Taft explained, "the aim has been to help such countries as Nicaragua and Honduras to help themselves."[58]

Despite promises made during the 1912 campaign season about working with Latin American states "on terms of equality and honor," Woodrow Wilson's presidency saw an acceleration of such efforts to "help" those his Secretary of State, William Jennings Bryan, called "our political children."[59] In addition to maintaining and deepening the occupation in Nicaragua, Wilson sent troops to Cuba, Panama, and Honduras (once, twice, and

---

[55] Schoultz, *In Their Own Best Interest*, 49–50.
[56] LaFeber, *Inevitable Revolutions*, 42–6.
[57] LaFeber, *Inevitable Revolutions*, 46–9; Schoultz, *In Their Own Best Interest*, 50–2.
[58] Schoultz, *In Their Own Best Interest*, 51.
[59] Herring, *From Colony to Superpower*, 386.

five times, respectively).⁶⁰ He also initiated a US occupation of Haiti. This brought the entire island of Hispaniola, and thus three of the four largest islands in the Caribbean (Cuba, Hispaniola, and Puerto Rico), under direct or indirect American control.⁶¹ Wilson had a true commitment to the idea of democracy, and believed he was serving its cause abroad, but he also held views—paternalist at best, racist at worst—toward immigrants, foreigners, and people of color that ran counter to his otherwise egalitarian impulses.⁶² He remained wedded to the idea that an ideal human future looked something like the liberal, capitalist society of the United States, and thus saw little problem with a world ordered around economic hierarchies. He was also, to be fair, constrained by the situation he inherited from his predecessors. As Noel Maurer writes, "the United States' prior commitments and its powerful overseas interests ... made disengagement difficult and further entanglements easy."⁶³

In Haiti, the situation followed the predictable pattern: poverty and inequality created political instability, that instability scared American investors, and then those investors began to push the White House for action. Deteriorating conditions in Port-au-Prince and fears of German intervention left Wilson feeling he had little choice but to step in. "We cannot consent," he wrote to Bryan "to stand by and permit revolutionary conditions constantly to exist there."⁶⁴ Once troops were on the ground and US officials were in the customs houses, it was hard for them to leave.⁶⁵ Like Taft's program for Nicaragua, Wilson's arrangements for Haiti endured long after his presidency. The occupation lasted until 1934, while the United States controlled Haitian finances until 1942.⁶⁶

Wilson's moralizing tendencies also further reinforced his interventionism. A former professor, he found it hard to abandon the role of teacher in the White House, particularly when it came to Latin American peoples he, like Bryan, tended to see as childlike. His response to the revolution in Mexico (which toppled Diaz's investor-friendly government in 1911) showed this inclination clearly. When General Victoriana Huerta seized power in 1913, Wilson refused to "recognize a government of butchers," as he saw it, and

---

⁶⁰Herring, *From Colony to Superpower*, 386.
⁶¹Jamaica, the third largest Caribbean island, was a British possession.
⁶²See: Jeffrey Sommers, *Race Reality and Realpolitik: U.S.-Haiti Relations in the Lead Up to the 1915 Occupation* (Lanham: Lexington Books, 2016), 95–112.
⁶³Maurer, *Empire Trap*, 118.
⁶⁴Sommers, *Race Reality and Realpolitik*, 107.
⁶⁵Maurer, *Empire Trap*, 117–25.
⁶⁶Mary A. Renda, *Taking Haiti: Military Occupation and the Culture of U.S. Imperialism, 1915–1940* (Chapel Hill: University of North Carolina Press, 2001), 29–34.

therefore did not officially recognize the new regime.[67] As he told the British Ambassador, he felt a need to make an example of the Mexicans for the hemisphere and "teach [Latin American countries] a lesson by insisting on the removal of Huerta."[68] Unlike the states to its south and east in the Caribbean, Mexico was much too large for the United States to invade without a major national effort, so Wilson was forced to content himself with two smaller scale interventions, including a military occupation of the city of Veracruz in 1914, which did little to advance American objectives and much to inflame Mexican opinion against the United States. After Huerta fell to internal opposition, Wilson withdrew US troops and begrudgingly extended *de facto* recognition to the new government of Venustiano Carranza in October of 1915. Along with that recognition came a written lesson from the professor president: a memorandum warning the new Mexican government that it needed to ensure stability and a good environment for US interests, protecting foreign property rights from any encroachment.[69] The Wilson administration believed more was at stake than just relations with Mexico—Carranza might potentially set a bad example for the whole Latin American classroom. A US oil executive summed up the prevailing view in a message to the State Department in January 1916, warning that "if our government should permit the Mexican government arbitrarily to repudiate [foreign-owned oil] contracts, it will cast a cloud upon the title to all American investments, not only in Mexico but in central and South America" as well.[70]

US troops would be back in Mexico less than two years after their departure from Veracruz. This time they were deployed in the north, primarily in response to a raid by anti-Carranza rebels—under Francisco "Pancho" Villa—on a US border town.[71] Wilson felt an understandable political need to respond to an attack on US soil, but he also tried to use the incursion to teach the Carranza government to better toe the American line. The new Mexican president had indeed overseen some limited, halting steps

---

[67] Wilson was initially unaware of the fact that the Taft administration had helped encourage Huerta's coup. See: Mark Benbow, "All the Brains I Can Borrow: Woodrow Wilson and Intelligence Gathering in Mexico, 1913–15," *Studies in Intelligence* 51, no. 4 (December 2007), https://www.cia.gov/resources/csi/static/Article-All-the-Brains-I-Can-Borrow-Woodrow-Wilson-and-Intelligence.pdf, accessed June 8th 2025; Maurer, *Empire Trap*, 137–8.
[68] Herring, *From Colony to Superpower*, 391.
[69] Hector Aguilar Camin and Lorenzo Meyer, *In the Shadow of the Mexican Revolution: Contemporary Mexican History, 1910–1989*, Luis Alberto Fierro trans. (Austin: University of Texas Press, 1993), 43–61; Maurer, *Empire Trap*, 137–47; Smith, *Revolutionary Nationalism in Mexico*, 23–42.
[70] Smith, *Revolutionary Nationalism in Mexico*, 45.
[71] The raid was itself a direct result of US meddling and Villa's desire to preserve Mexican sovereignty. See: Friedrich Katz, "Pancho Villa and the Attack on Columbus, New Mexico," *The American Historical Review* 83, no. 1 (February 1978): 101–30.

toward reasserting Mexican control over the natural resources that Diaz had allowed to be gobbled up by non-Mexicans. These moves concerned Washington—and US oil companies with concessions in Mexico—as they feared such steps were a prelude for Mexico City to fully adopt the Calvo Doctrine. US troops therefore lingered in Mexico for months and negotiations for their removal stalled thanks to Wilson's insistence on getting firm Mexican guarantees of continued privileges for foreign property owners. War seemed a real possibility—particularly following a June 21st, 1916 skirmish between US and Mexican troops in the Chihuahuan town of Carrizal. However, in the face of Mexican intransigence, and with the war in Europe increasingly on his mind, a defeated Wilson withdrew American forces in January of 1917, the expedition having failed even to capture Villa. Soon after, the Mexican government announced a new constitution which adopted Calvo's ideas and contained a strong assertion of Mexico's rights to its own natural resources. When Carranza was overthrown by a revolt in May 1920, the Wilson administration again withdrew recognition and successfully pressured most European states to do the same. Formal relations were only restored in 1923—by US President Warren G. Harding (in office: 1921–23)—after the Mexican government offered promises of additional protections for US property in return for loans and the opportunity to purchase arms.[72] While Wilson never tried to occupy the whole of Mexico—and largely failed in the end to influence its revolution in the way he intended—his pedantic and domineering approach reveals the persistence of hierarchical conceptions of world order, even among those Americans ostensibly opposed to empire.

For all its experiments with neocolonialism, therefore, it's important to recognize that the United States in the first two decades of the twentieth century still remained within the broader "new imperialist" consensus that held sway in great power capitals at the time.[73] World order was seen as being founded on the authority of those great powers, with each seeking to structure its own hierarchically ordered segment of the world for its benefit and that of civilization. This civilization and that hierarchy were understood in fundamentally Eurocentric and white supremacist terms. As in the nineteenth century, European modes of life were viewed as possessing a universality and superiority that made them the natural end of humanity's historical evolution. Non-European cultures were therefore more or less "primitive" based on their distance from European patterns, an idea often reinforced by racist ideas about whites representing a biologically

---

[72] Camin and Meyer, *Shadow of the Mexican Revolution*, 60–84; Smith, *Revolutionary Nationalism in Mexico*, 43–228; Maurer, *Empire Trap*, 137–47.
[73] For more on new imperialism, see Chapter 4.

more evolved form of the species.⁷⁴ Even many relatively more liberal and egalitarian-minded people—like Wilson—still understood the world in this way. Contrary to what one might assume, a democratic and Progressive outlook did not automatically make one opposed to a hierarchically ordered world, or, for that matter, the occasional empire.⁷⁵

Wilson represented this well. He was, in one sense, truly a reformer. He did not see empire as a permanent feature of the world, as it had long been understood (and still was by many in Europe and elsewhere). Empire was instead to Wilson a somewhat antiquated form of government meant to eventually be replaced by various forms of self-rule. However, the President did not believe that all peoples were ready for this transition just yet, particularly people of color. Self-government was not an automatic right, as he wrote of the Philippines, but one "gained, earned, graduated into from the hard school of life."⁷⁶ Anglo-Saxon citizens of the United States, the President believed, had already earned that right. It was only through "long subjugation to Kings and Parliaments," he argued, that white Americans had learned the skills of self-government.⁷⁷ Other peoples still required that education in self-government, one—luckily—the United States was willing to provide. Un-democratic hierarchies were in Wilson's mind, thoroughly compatible with a belief in democracy and an opposition to empire. Self-government was a skill that only certain people possessed, but a time under imperial rule could help them gain it. Wilson's view of empire was therefore still "new imperialism" just new imperialism in a more Progressive guise. Few, in fact, would do more to ensure that the hierarchies of the imperial age survived the great crisis that nearly brought them down—the First World War (1914–18)—than Woodrow Wilson.

The Great War, Wilson, and the Limits of Self-Determination

When Wilson arrived in office in 1913, the age of empire appeared destined to endure, with the globe dominated by the United States and a handful of powerful European empires. With its defeat of Russia in the Russo-Japanese War (1904–05), industrialized Japan had now also fully joined the ranks of the great powers, adding a new imperial and economic center to the global

---

⁷⁴Osterhammel, *The Transformation of the World*, 746–7, 826–72.
⁷⁵For more on the compatible relationship between liberalism and empire see: Bell, *Reordering the World*, especially 19–61.
⁷⁶Adom Getachew, *Worldmaking after Empire: The Rise and Fall of Self-Determination* (Princeton: Princeton University Press, 2019), 45.
⁷⁷Getachew, *Worldmaking after Empire*, 45.

order, but otherwise only slightly altering its fundamentally Eurocentric character.[78] This age of "high imperialism," as it is sometimes called, was a time of both global integration and global fragmentation. On the one hand, imperial systems and new technologies were accelerating the globalization we have been tracking throughout the book, making the world feel smaller and smaller as more and more territory was tightly integrated into the world-system. With globally integrated supply chains bringing raw materials from the colonial periphery to the industrial core—which then sent the goods back out to the world—it was newly possible in the early twentieth century to speak of a single "global market" of remarkable integrative power. Prices converged globally—the price spread between Liverpool and Mumbai for cotton, for example, dropped from 57 percent in 1873 to 20 percent in 1913—as economic events in one part of the world grew more deeply connected with those in others.[79]

Some were so inspired by this intense phase of globalization that they hoped a new, more peaceful age might be in the offing. Plans were thus advanced for the rationalization of international relations through organizations like the Permanent Court of Arbitration, established in The Hague in 1902.[80] Many also hoped to see economic nationalism and high tariffs replaced with freer trade and interchange—in all, they wanted to establish a reformed version of the world of empire, one that was more pacific, more open, more cooperative, and less hierarchical (though no less fixated on European-style modernity as the ultimate goal for mankind).[81] Such hopes were, however, deeply misplaced, as all of this global integration was occurring as part of a larger process of fragmentation, one where the great powers attempted to pull their spheres of influence closer to themselves and further from their rivals.[82] Integration was happening more *within* each imperial sphere than it was occurring between them. This pulling-apart of the world into competing imperial blocks only intensified over the course of the 1880s–1910s. It eventually reached a point where—as the historian Patrick Cohrs has put it—the "Eurocentric world 'order' of the age of imperialism" might better be called a "war prone 'disorder'," one which soon led to global war.[83] Despite its seemingly

---

[78]Osterhammel, *The Transformation of the World*, 399.
[79]Kevin H. O'Rourke and Jeffrey G. Williamson, "When Did Globalization Begin," Working Paper, *National Bureau of Economic Research*, April 2000, http://www.nber.org/papers/w7632.
[80]Patrick Cohrs, *The New Atlantic Order: The Transformation of International Politics, 1860–1933* (Cambridge: Cambridge University Press, 2022), 112–37. See also the discussion of prewar internationalism in Tara Zahra, *Against the World: Anti-Globalism and Mass Politics between the World Wars* (New York: W.W. Norton and Co., 2023), 3–55.
[81]See Palen, *Pax Economica*, 51–187.
[82]See Chapter 4 and Palen, *Pax Economica*, 13–50.
[83]Cohrs, *The New Atlantic Order*, 1, 41–64.

sturdy appearance, the era of formal empire was about to enter a long final phase of crisis and dissolution.

Part of the story here were the new and consequential challenges to the European-dominated world-system that were developing among the colonized in the early twentieth century. Resistance to the Euro-American reordering of the world was in one respect nothing new. From Indigenous Americans in the seventeenth century, to the Boxers in late nineteenth century China—and many others along the way—numerous communities around the world had fought back against imperial globalization, European modernity, and the subservient status in the global hierarchy of wealth that came with it. However, the developments of the early twentieth century were something different. They involved new and increasingly popular forms of "anti-colonial nationalism"—that is, assertions of national identity that rejected imperial subordination and demanded equal incorporation in a world of equally sovereign states. These nationalist movements would eventually transform much of the globe.

Japan's victory over Russia proved an inspirational watershed in this regard. It demonstrated that a non-European state could industrialize without being colonized. Japan, after all, had never been subject to foreign rule. As one Turkish nationalist put it: "events in the Far East put forth evidence" that "the more isolated and preserved from contact with European invaders and plunderers a people is, the better."[84] The Chinese nationalist Sun Yat-Sen later recalled how prior to Japan's victory, "men thought and believed that European civilization was a progressive one … and that Asia had nothing to compare to it … that Asia could never resist Europe."[85] Arriving at a time when many were already questioning the justice of European rule, Japan's victory helped change that perception. It energized those—from Turkey, to India, Vietnam, and China—organizing and conceptualizing new modes of opposition to European global dominance. This led to increased nationalist agitation in places like British India and French Indochina and even outright revolution, and the toppling of the Qing dynasty, in foreign-dominated China.[86] Such was the diversity of anti-colonial thought at the time—ranging from reactionary anti-modernism, to liberal and left-wing transnationalism—that we

---

[84]Pankaj Mishra, *From the Ruins of Empire: The Intellectuals who Remade Asia* (New York: Farrar, Strauss, and Giroux, 2012), 4.
[85]Mishra, *From the Ruins of Empire*, 7.
[86]See the discussion in Mishra, *From the Ruins of Empire*, 1–11. For more on the response to Japan's victory in India see: T.R. Sareen, "India and the War," in *The Impact of the Russo-Japanese War*, Rotem Kowner ed. (London: Routledge, 2007). On Chinese nationalism see: Rebecca E. Karl, *Staging the World: Chinese Nationalism at the Turn of the Century* (Durham: Duke University Press, 2002). For more on early Vietnamese nationalism see: David G. Marr, *Vietnamese Anticolonialism, 1885–1925* (Berkeley: University of California Press, 1971).

cannot hope to do it justice in our discussion here.[87] It's enough to emphasize, however, that there was a burgeoning intellectual challenge to European global dominance, one that was beginning to bear fruit in anti-colonial organizing and resistance. "The people of the East," said Indian nationalist Mohandas Gandhi in 1905, were "waking up from their lethargy."[88]

The greatest danger to the Eurocentric, early twentieth-century imperial order, however, arose from within its own structure, thanks to the great power rivalries that structure generated and the war those caused. The First World War is in fact best understood as a direct result of the intensifying new imperialist competition we have been discussing. As the African American social scientist W.E.B. Du Bois noted of the war in 1915, "the ownership of materials and men in the darker world is the real prize setting the nations of Europe at each other's throats today."[89] More than a century later, many historians would agree with the spirit of Du Bois's assessment, seeing the Great War as a consequence of overseas imperial competition coming home to Europe "like a poisonous snake," in historian Paul Schroeder's words, "circling back upon itself and sinking its fangs into its own tail."[90]

This was not a matter of simple causation, however. The conflict infamously began in the troubled regions of southeast Europe, not (as with the Seven Years War, for example) on the battlefields of empire abroad. Yet, imperialism drove the key actors towards war all the same. The intensification of imperial competition globally in the late nineteenth and early twentieth centuries—of which the War of 1898, the division of China after the Boxer Uprising, and the Russo-Japanese War are all good examples—made the contest between the great powers seem an increasingly zero-sum game, destined to have an ultimate winner and many losers. Such perceptions were further reinforced by the narratives of progress and development so essential to the new imperialist paradigm. European leaders—particularly in Austria-Hungary and Germany—feared that their own states, not just "backward" colonial subjects abroad, might be left in the dust by the forward march of history. "Modern global imperialism," writes historian Adam Tooze, "was a radical and modern force, not an old

---

[87]See, for example, Aboitiz, *Asian Place, Filipino Nation*, 1–31; Cemil Aydin, *The Politics of Anti-Westernism in Asia: Visions of World Order in Pan-Islamic and Pan-Asian Thought* (New York: Columbia University Press, 2007), 1–14, 71–92; Mishra, *From the Ruins of Empire*, 1–183.
[88]Quoted in Mishra, *From the Ruins of Empire*, 7.
[89]Getachew, *Worldmaking after Empire*, 38.
[90]Paul W. Schroeder, "Stealing Horses to Great Applause: Austria Hungary's Decision in 1914 in Systemic Perspective," in *An Improbable War: The Outbreak of World War I and European Political Culture before 1914*, Holger Afflerbach and David Stevenson, eds. (New York: Berghan Books, 2007), 17–42, quote on 26.

world hangover," and the leaders of the great powers recognized this reality in one way or another.[91] The decades before the outbreak of war in 1914, therefore, saw them become more willing to impose hierarchies not just on colonized peoples but on other European states, hoping to thereby win the contest for power and wealth the structure of the world-system beckoned them to pursue. "The task," for policymakers, as Christopher Clark writes, was "to align oneself with the impersonal, forward momentum of History" and ensure that your country, and not another, took advantage of historical progress.[92] Imperialism helped define the cutthroat rules for international competition that framed the decision-making both before and after the assassination of Austrian Archduke Franz Ferdinand in June 1914, directly contributing to the outbreak of war.[93]

It also made the war longer, more violent, and more globally disruptive. Vast amounts of material wealth—and human lives—were drawn from across the globe to be poured into the European maw, destabilizing the very empires the war was fought to preserve. The First World War collapsed the ruling regimes of four empires—the German, Austro-Hungarian, Russian, and Ottoman—and left the survivors like Britain and France shaken and exhausted. Protests broke out in Egypt, India, China, and Korea soon after the war's end, showing the mounting global opposition to colonial rule.[94] The wasteful destruction of the war—directly witnessed by the many colonial troops deployed to fight in Europe—and the seeming inability of the Europeans to bring it to an end, further undermined the myth of European civilizational superiority so essential to justifying new imperialism. Anticolonial writers and activists—like, for example, the Bengali poet Rabindranath Tagore—articulated a new criticism of empire based on the conflict, a catastrophe which they felt revealed European civilization as far from fit to govern the world.[95] The First World War also amplified the most vehement anti-imperial tradition of European origin: Marxism. With Vladimir Lenin's rise to power in Russia following the collapse of the Tsarist regime and the coup by his communist "Bolsheviks"

---

[91] Adam Tooze, *The Deluge: The Great War, America and the Remaking of the Global Order, 1916–1931* (New York: Penguin Books, 2014), 20.

[92] Christopher Clark, *The Sleepwalkers: How Europe Went to War in 1914* (New York: Harper Perennial 2012), 350.

[93] Cohrs, *New Atlantic Order*, 41–168; Clark, *Sleepwalkers*; Schroeder, "Stealing Horses"; Paul W. Schroeder, "World War I and the Vienna System: The Last Eighteenth-Century War and the First Modern Peace," in *Stealing Horses to Great Applause* (New York: Verso, 2025), 263–355; Adam Tooze, "Capitalist Peace or Capitalist War: The July Crisis Revisited," in *Cataclysm 1914: The First World War and the Making of Modern World Politics*, Alexander Anievas ed. (Boston: Brill, 2015), 66–95.

[94] Getachew, *Worldmaking after Empire*, 38.

[95] Michael Adas, "Contested Hegemony: The Great War and the Afro-Asian Assault on the Civilizing Mission Ideology," *Journal of World History* 15, no. 1 (March 2004): 31–63.

in October of 1917. Marxist anti-imperialism now had a powerful new platform, as Lenin called for a postwar order "without annexations and indemnities and on the basis of the free self-determination of nations."[96] Though Lenin's new Soviet Union almost immediately began to engage in its own, often brutal, form of hierarchy making, the Soviet leader's call for a "democratic peace" and a more equal world resonated powerfully all the same.

The United States entered the First World War in 1917 in part because Wilson recognized, even before the Bolshevik revolution, the growing risk imperial competition represented to the global hierarchies—the world-system—that had helped make the United States into a great power. As a good Progressive, Wilson believed that the modern world of the early twentieth century was a result of commendable progress in culture, technology, and social organization. The economic and political hierarchies of the age of empires were a direct contributor to that progress in that they structured the world in a way that made "modern" life—and the advances in technology and wealth it afforded—possible. Without globalized markets, without regional economic specialization, and without vast commodity chains to feed the industrial center, economic and technological progress could not be maintained. However, the war had also clearly illustrated that modernity carried with it dangers that threatened to undermine all the progress it had thus far delivered. Wilson, as the historian Frank Ninkovich has described it, believed "the very forces that made progress possible—technology, trade, a global division of labor, and interdependence—also made possible the system's destruction if pushed in the wrong direction." The "enormous amount of power concentrated by the global industrial system could lead to disaster" if great power competition remained an essential part of world order.[97] Lenin's triumph was but one example of the potential catastrophes that lurked in the shadows.[98]

Like pre-war, "free trade" reformers, therefore, Wilson wanted to build on the supposed positives of imperial globalization while dispensing with the fragmentation and conflict caused by imperial rivalries. Wilson thus entered the United States in the war, as he famously put it, "to make the world safe for democracy," by which he meant an effort to preserve the global conditions that allowed the United States to exist as it did—hierarchies and all. Globalized, industrialized warfare of the sort which had torn apart Europe since 1914 threatened to delegitimize the economic hierarchies of

---

[96] Getachew, *Worldmaking after Empire*, 39.
[97] Ninkovich, *Wilsonian Century*, 66.
[98] Historians sometimes suggest that Lenin's influence in 1918–19 was equal to Wilson's, which overstates the case. Instead, as we have outlined here, Lenin's revolution exemplified the broad range of threats to global hierarchy Wilson confronted, it was not the primary one, as it would be during the Cold War. See: Tooze, *Deluge*, 21.

capitalism and, in consequence, undermine US-style liberal democracy.[99] Something had to be done to rationalize and restructure the world-system so that great power rivalries would not collapse it completely. As soon as the real issues of the war "became apparent" Wilson would recall in 1919, "we knew that we belonged there."[100] Relatively secure in its dominance of the Western Hemisphere, it at first seemed to Wilson that the United States could wait out the war as a neutral without too much risk. It could then subsequently use its power to shape the peace that followed. It was, in the President's words, "an opportunity such as has seldom been vouchsafed any nation," a pathway to establishing itself as the most influential power on the globe without firing a shot.[101]

As the war dragged on, however, and disruptions to trans-Atlantic commerce continued to mount, maintaining neutrality became almost impossible. The decision to join the Anglo-French side against the Germans was mediated by a number of factors—not least of which were the massive debts the French and British owed to US financial interests— but the most significant was Germany's decision to resume unrestricted submarine warfare in the Atlantic in 1917.[102] This convinced Wilson that "German militarism" was the strongest manifestation of the nationalist rivalries that had caused the war, making Germany the most appropriate target for his war of reform. He did not entirely exempt the British and French though, insisting that the United States remain somewhat aloof from its wartime partners as an "associated" rather than "allied" power.[103] Wilson's challenge was issued, as Adam Tooze puts it, "not to Germany in particular, but to European power as a whole."[104] Winning the war was what was essential in Wilson's mind, not helping one side or the other. The United States had to be able to shape the peace—a peace which the President believed could be used to transform the international system and replace the old politics entirely.

The outlines of this peace were contained in his famous "Fourteen Points," a program that built on the ideas of prewar reformers, calling for free trade on equal terms, arms reductions, and, most radically, a supranational "League of Nations" to help preserve world peace through collective security and collaborative diplomacy. The Fourteen Points also embraced "self-determination," indicating that certain people, particularly in Eastern Europe, should determine their own forms of government and

---

[99]Ninkovich, *Wilsonian Century*, 69–70.
[100]Ninkovich, *Wilsonian Century*, 65.
[101]Tooze, *Deluge*, 34–67, quote on 45.
[102]Germany had temporarily halted unrestricted attacks on shipping in 1915 in response to American protests.
[103]Ninkovich, *Wilsonian Century*, 62.
[104]Tooze, Deluge, 58.

political organization. Wilson's program was in some ways a forward-looking and well-intentioned plan to construct a more equal world, one which excited the hopes of subject peoples across the globe. Petitions from colonized populations in French Indochina, Egypt, India, Korea, Lebanon, and Yemen, for example, would pour into Wilson's offices when he arrived in Paris for the 1919 peace conference.[105]

Yet, Wilson's blueprint for postwar world also had strong elements of a "counterrevolution"—as the historian Adom Getachew has provocatively put it—a moderate reform designed to prevent an even more radical transformation of the international system.[106] The non-European petitioners who reached out to Wilson in Paris were ignored, often dismissively, by the President. In retrospect, one can find hints of this attitude in even his most idealistic language. Unlike the specific articulation of rights to self-determination in the former Austro-Hungarian Empire, for example—"peoples of Austria-Hungary, whose place among the nations we wish to see ... assured, should be accorded the freest opportunity of autonomous development"—the Fourteen Points made no clear promise of decolonization outside of Europe. Indeed, it only vaguely discussed the political status of the non-European world in two places. The first, point five, called for:

> A free, open-minded, and absolutely impartial adjustment of all colonial claims, based upon a strict observance of the principle that in determining all such questions of sovereignty the interests of the populations concerned must have equal weight with the equitable claims of the government whose title is to be determined.[107]

Those in southeastern Europe may have had an assured "place among the nations," but the colonized "populations" here could only hope that their "interests" were given "equal weight" with those of their foreign masters. Wilson believed that in 1919, Europeans alone had sufficient schooling under "Kings and Parliaments" to determine their own political future. Other people—like Filipinos, for example—would need to wait longer. In the second mention of the non-European world, point twelve, a similar hierarchy can be observed. Here Wilson asserted that while "the Turkish portions of the present Ottoman Empire should be assured a secure sovereignty" the "other nationalities" that had been under Ottoman rule—which included most of the Arab Middle East—were

---

[105] Erez Manela, *The Wilsonian Moment: Self Determination and the International Origins of Anticolonial Nationalism* (New York: Oxford University Press, 2007), 59–60.
[106] Getachew, *Worldmaking after Empire*, 37–70.
[107] Woodrow Wilson, "Address to a Joint Session of Congress on the Conditions of Peace ['The Fourteen Points']," January 8, 1918, Online by Gerhard Peters and John T. Woolley, *The American Presidency Project*, https://www.presidency.ucsb.edu/node/206651.

FIGURE 11 *US President Woodrow Wilson stands (center) among his fellow members of the League of Nations Commission—a committee established to draft a charter for the League during the 1919 Paris Peace Conference.*

only guaranteed "an absolutely unmolested opportunity of autonomous development."[108]

While some of Wilson's phrases suggest some right to independence ("autonomous development," for example) others hint at potential delays in the realization of self-rule and reveal a vision of a world divided into tiers, the upper echelons occupied by those Wilson saw as more advanced (more Europeanized) peoples and the lower those who had not yet reached a sufficient level of civilization for democracy. Point five, for example, challenged the long-term legitimacy of imperialism and even implied an eventual right of self-government for colonized peoples.[109] It also made clear, however, that—at that point in the development of global civilization—such a right was at best of equal value with the concerns of the imperial powers. Point twelve also establishes a clear distinction between Turks (seen as more civilized) and those non-Turks that had been under Ottoman rule. This rhetorical distinction took on real-world implications during the peace

---

[108] Wilson, "Address to a Joint Session of Congress on the Conditions of Peace."
[109] Trygve Thronveit, "The Fable of the Fourteen Points: Woodrow Wilson and National Self-Determination," *Diplomatic History* 35, no. 3 (June 2011): 445–81, 470.

conference, when Wilson proposed a form of "trusteeship," managed by the League of Nations—what would become the organization's "mandate" system.

Under this system, territories deemed not yet ready for independence, including former Ottoman lands in the Middle East and surrendered German colonies in Africa, would see their affairs managed by a League-appointed "mandatory" power. Though under foreign rule, the mandates were technically not colonies, but lands in a position of "tutelage" as the League charter put it—"entrusted to advanced nations who by reasons of their resources, their experience, or their geographical position can best undertake this responsibility."[110] Wilson's idea was further revised to have explicit civilizational ranks: A, B, and C. The "A" group was for those peoples who had "reached a stage of development where their existence as independent nations can be provisionally recognized," while "C" was reserved for populations which needed more direct rule, being "best administered under the laws of the Mandatory as integral portions of its territory."[111]

Just as with US policy toward—in Bryan's words—its "political children" in Latin America, the mandate system did not represent an abandonment of the hierarchies of empire but instead their reconfiguration in a seemingly more progressive, neocolonial mode. The same could be said for Wilson's peace as a whole. The President wished to protect American progress from the chaos unleashed by the war, but that progress required global hierarchy. There was need for that hierarchy to be reformed, to be sure—through new institutions to restrain imperial competition and in baby steps toward replacing formal empire with more "modern" arrangements—but it could not be entirely replaced.[112] As the leading historian of the "Wilsonian moment," Erez Manela has put it, Wilson's reforms "did alter the relationship between colonizer and colonized, but it did not do so in the consensual, evolutionary manner" that the President's idealistic language implied.[113]

Whether US participation in the League of Nations—the US Senate infamously rejected the treaty Wilson brought back from Paris—might have prevented another world war is an open question.[114] What one can perhaps

---

[110] The League of Nations, "The Covenant of the League of Nations," Yale University Law School, *The Avalon Project: Documents in Law, History, and Diplomacy*, https://avalon.law.yale.edu/20th_century/leagcov.asp.
[111] "The Covenant of the League of Nations." See also the discussion of the mandates in Cohrs, *New Atlantic Order*, 614–18.
[112] Contrary to what is commonly assumed, the European powers largely endorsed these reforms, at least initially. Tooze, *Deluge*, 22–3.
[113] Manela, *Wilsonian Moment*, 222.
[114] Though, there is certainly little reason to doubt that greater American involvement would have made the postwar political and economic order more stable. See: Tooze, Deluge, 26–30.

assert with more confidence is that, in the end, Wilson's efforts did more to help make the "world safe for empire" than democracy, ensuring the survival of imperial systems—and their rivalries—for decades.[115] What the German empire lost after the war, the British and French empires gained, gains that the imperial powers were quick to maintain with violence. The infamous 1919 Amritsar Massacre in India, for example—where British troops murdered hundreds of Indians gathered in a park—was but one product of the repression used to suppress the anti-colonial dreams Wilson had helped conjure.[116] Only temporarily abated by the peace made in Paris, imperial rivalries would soon lead to another great war and the need to rebuild the international system yet again. As we will see in the remaining chapters of the book, the shift we have described here—away from preserving the world-system through formal empire and toward embracing hierarchical forms of "self-determination"—would continue to shape US conceptions of global order after that next war and beyond.

---

[115] Manela, *Wilsonian Moment*, 197.
[116] Manela, *Wilsonian Moment*, 169–70, 221.

CHAPTER SIX

A Roosevelt Corollary for the World: The United States, World Order, and Decolonization after the Second World War

The international order that Wilson helped establish after the First World War did not long endure, in large part because it was more "safe for empire" than it was for democracy. While the more idealistic and internationalist elements of the arrangement made in Paris inspired hope for a more peaceful future, that system's compromises with imperialism undermined its legitimacy. To many around the world—including, most critically, many in Germany, Italy, and Japan—the League of Nations appeared little more than a front for the imperial interests of the British and French, locking into place a distribution of global power that preserved their interests at the expense of others. Though it remained outside the League, the United States too was seen as part of the same cabal, a "plutocratic and bourgeois alliance," as Italian dictator Benito Mussolini put it, running the world for its own benefit.[1]

The arrival of the Great Depression in 1929, therefore, set the world on the path to what historian Richard Overy has called "the last imperial war": the Second World War. As economic chaos sundered what remained of the peacemaking, internationalist spirit of 1919, the world's powers turned inward to themselves and their spheres of influence—or looked

---

[1]Quoted in Richard Overy, *Blood and Ruins: The Last Imperial War, 1931–1945* (New York: Viking Press, 2021), 22.

abroad to expand those spheres if they seemed insufficient.[2] By 1941, war engulfed the whole world, as the United States, Great Britain, and the Soviet Union fought to prevent the imperial expansion of Germany in Europe, Italy in North Africa, and Japan in China and the western Pacific. At the war's end in 1945, all three of these brutal "Axis" empires lay in ruins while those of the "Allies" teetered on profoundly weakened foundations. Humiliated by defeat and occupation, France, Belgium, and the Netherlands would struggle to restore colonial rule in their old empires, while an ostensibly victorious Britain confronted its own restive imperial possessions with a population and treasury exhausted by years of war.

The last imperial war did indeed prove to be a major turning point in the history of empire, setting the stage for two significant global transformations: the arrival of the United States as the world's dominant military and economic power, and the end of the age of formal imperialism. One might think that these factors are directly related, given that the United States in 1945 stood astride the world like a colossus, able to exert considerable influence in shaping what emerged from the ruins of the war. It was also initially committed to establishing what is sometimes called a "liberal world order," a structure for the postwar world where independent states would engage in increasingly freer trade, cooperative diplomacy, and collective security, all managed by a new "United Nations" organization to replace the old League. As part of this, US President Franklin D. Roosevelt and most of his top advisors also envisioned the beginning of an end to European and US imperialism, with some colonial possessions spending a period as "trust" territories controlled by a foreign power under UN supervision. Wartime statements of principle—such as the 1941 Atlantic Charter and the 1945 United Nations Charter—both contained strong expressions of support for self-determination, statements which were used by anti-colonial nationalists in places like India to question the continuation of empire. However, the end of empire arrived more in spite than because of the United States. Resistance by the colonized and the postwar weakness of the European colonizers were the deciding factors. By the century's end, the broad, single-colored swaths of formal empire had largely disappeared from maps of the world, leaving behind nearly two hundred individual states plus a small scattering of seemingly anachronistic colonial remnants.

As a result of the prevailing attitudes in the United States and Europe, this process of transition was not an easy or direct one, set in motion by the war and then proceeding inevitably forward. Just as the long transition from the eighteenth-century world of empire to the largely nationalist present was non-linear, the same must be said for its final stages in the decades following the Second World War. Despite the war and their precarious

---

[2]Overy, *Blood and Ruins*, xi–xvi, 2–32. On turning inward see also: Zahra, *Against the World*, 133–264.

positions, European states were not yet ready to give up their empires in 1945. The United States, meanwhile, remained unwilling to abandon a world of hierarchy. US policymakers did genuinely want to construct a more cooperative, more open, and more egalitarian world than the prewar order of competitive, protectionist imperialism. Their goals were, in many ways, admirable. At the same time, however, Americans in 1945 still had similar attitudes toward hierarchies of civilization, race, and wealth to those that had undercut Wilson's better instincts. They also needed to preserve a wartime alliance whose key members—including Britain and France—had every intention of restoring their empires after the war. Even at their most idealistic, US postwar planners did not see empire ending quickly—Asians and Africans, in American eyes, could not be expected to govern themselves just yet. They required tutelage. And even when already independent—as Latin American states had long been, for example—it was not always clear to Americans that non-European countries could be trusted to manage the world responsibly.

Many of the hierarchies of the imperial age therefore were grandfathered into the new global regime, built into the institutions of world order in such a way that they ensured the global dominance of the United States and those states it favored. Forgetting the role that violence and imperial expansion had played in their own rise to power, Americans offered a vision of the postwar world that made little accounting for how centuries of imperial globalization had unequally structured the world economy. They also looked to shape the new order on the assumption that US society—its political, social, and economic structure—remained the only just and natural endpoint for human development. Those seeking other, more left-wing, paths to the future were, as we will see, automatically suspect. These tendencies in US policy were only intensified by the emergence of the Cold War with the Soviet Union and the perception of a communist threat to US national security. Much of what idealism there was in 1945 was soon sacrificed on the altar of strategic necessity, as security and economic concerns took precedence. The Cold War pushed policymakers to engage in direct intervention, in the form of development assistance, military aid, and even the deployment of US troops, to ensure the right people remained in charge across what came to be called the "Third" or "developing" world.

This will be our topic for the next two chapters: how the United States understood the ends of empire in the second half of the twentieth century, as the great wave of decolonization in Asia and Africa largely brought an end to the era of formal imperialism. As we will see, despite these transformative changes in the world's geopolitical structure, there were significant continuities in the US approach to world order before and after the Second World War. While the United States recognized that decolonization was the future, and at times took steps to hurry it along, it also did so while trying to control the course the global transition from colony to state took.

This is perhaps far from surprising behavior from a world power seeking to maintain its global status, but it also raises significant questions about whether the mid-twentieth-century collapse of imperialism really ushered in the world of Westphalian sovereignty which we are so often told we live in.

A New Deal for the World?

The United States which oversaw the final defeat of Nazi Germany and Imperial Japan in 1945 was a very different one than that which had helped end the Great War in 1918. It had been transformed first by the Great Depression and then by the presidency of Franklin D. Roosevelt (1933–45). The arrival of the Depression in 1929 had completely scrambled the country's politics, overthrowing the Republican coalition that had mostly dominated national elections since McKinley's victory in 1896. Nationalist, pro-business, pro-Wall Street—and pro-empire—the Republicans had overseen a spectacular period of economic growth, the emergence of the modern corporation and modern consumer culture, along with the arrival of the United States as a world power.[3] The lynchpin of their majority was a promise of economic prosperity, which Republicans had delivered, though at the cost of a growing economic inequality that threatened to undermine their popular support if the gravy train ever ran out. When it did in the fall of 1929, the Republican hold on American politics evaporated, opening a space for what historian Timothy Shenk has called "the strongest and strangest coalition in American history," the New Deal coalition of Franklin Roosevelt's Democrats.[4] While not abandoning capitalism, or capitalists, by any means, Roosevelt's victory in 1932 shifted some power in the United States away from business elites—and Wall Street especially—and toward the working class. It cobbled together a new and ungainly yet remarkably strong alliance of labor unions, urban working-class voters, and immigrants, along with progressive elites and southern conservatives.[5] The New Deal and its varying programs and policies were complex and often contradictory—ranging from new forms of social insurance and protections for unions, to attempts at central state planning of the economy—but they firmly established a more activist role for the federal government in protecting capitalism from its own most self-destructive tendencies.[6]

---

[3]See Chapters 4 and 5.
[4]Shenk, *Realigners*, quote on 163, see discussion, 119–69.
[5]Shenk, *Realigners*, 163.
[6]The literature on the New Deal is, of course, voluminous. For a study that puts the New Deal in a global context see: Kiran Klaus Patel, *The New Deal: A Global History* (Princeton: Princeton University Press, 2016). For a more narrative analysis see: Ira Katznelson, *Fear Itself: The New Deal and the Origins of Our Time* (New York: Liveright, 2013).

The Depression and the New Deal together also undermined much of the support for the most aggressive forms of imperialism and "empire-lite" that the United States had been practicing since 1898.[7] Indeed, the Depression was one of the few periods where the term "isolationist"—once thought to describe much of pre-Second World War US foreign policy—might be somewhat reasonably applied. It forced US business and financial interests to turn inward, focusing on protecting their domestic market share and worrying less about chasing profits overseas. It also broke—for a time—the close connection between the government and the financial institutions which had pushed for and underwritten the era of "dollar diplomacy" in Latin America. Both Roosevelt and his unlucky and unpopular predecessor, Hebert Hoover (in office: 1929–33), made new promises to be "good neighbors" to Latin America, and in fact began to wrap up the occupations in Haiti and Nicaragua, while also largely repudiating the Roosevelt Corollary, refusing to intervene as countries across the US sphere of influence defaulted on their largely American-owned debt.[8]

Franklin Roosevelt himself disliked formal imperialism and thus shifted the United States even further away from the imperial age upon his arrival in office, allowing Cuba to repudiate the Platt Amendment, giving up the clause in the Panama Canal Treaties that allowed the United States to intervene in Panama, and setting the Philippines formally on a ten-year path to independence by signing the Tydings-McDuffie Act in 1934.[9] The New Deal coalition also brought to power figures opposed to trade protectionism and restrictive reciprocity agreements, like Secretary of State Cordell Hull.[10] New liberal trade deals with Latin American states followed, significantly improving the diplomatic climate in the region, while US troops remained at home, even in the face of foreign expropriations of American property, as when Bolivia and Mexico nationalized US-owned oil companies in 1937 and 1938.[11] Though it would be easy to overdramatize the extent of the change, there can be no doubt that the Good Neighbor era marked a significant transition in the American approach to managing its power in the Western Hemisphere.

Still relatively secure in that hemisphere, the United States also appeared to remain aloof and isolationist while war clouds gathered over Europe and Asia, as Nazi Germany, Fascist Italy, and Imperial Japan looked to revise the 1919 settlement for their own imperial advantage. Wary of being sucked into

---

[7]See Chapter 5.
[8]Maurer, *Empire Trap*, 188–90.
[9]On Roosevelt and his views of US imperialism see: Schoultz, *In Their Own Best Interest*, 112. See also: Capozzola, *Bound by War*, 119–22; Herring, *From Colony to Superpower*, 497–501; Hopkins, *American Empire*, 627–9.
[10]Palen, *Pax Economica*, 179–80.
[11]On trade see: Maurer, *Empire Trap*, 259–60. On the oil nationalizations see: Camin and Meyer, *Shadow of the Mexican Revolution*, 150–6, Maurer, *Empire Trap*, 260–96.

war again by economic entanglements abroad—a common explanation at the time for US involvement in the First World War—voters rewarded those who looked to limit them. Congress in turn passed a series of neutrality laws (in 1935, 1937, and 1939) seeking to prevent US businesses and the federal government from aiding belligerents in any conflict. Though Roosevelt—who had served as Assistant Secretary of the Navy under Wilson—was an internationalist at heart, he was also enough of a politician to recognize that domestic sentiment limited his options. In something of a precursor to the policy the United States would later pursue in the Cold War, Roosevelt looked to "contain" the revisionist powers, keeping them out of the Western Hemisphere in particular. He expanded the Navy and then, carefully, worked to find ways around neutrality legislation to get aid to those resisting Axis expansion following the outbreak of war in Europe in 1939. By 1941, the war had grown too large to not draw the United States in directly, particularly in the Pacific, the place where the American empire stretched most broadly beyond its heartland in the Western Hemisphere. Neutrality legislation, it turned out, was not enough in itself to remove the United States from the world. American efforts to contain Japanese expansionism—including crippling economic sanctions—subsequently provoked war, as the Japanese military struck the United States at Pearl Harbor, the Philippines, Guam, and Wake Island in December of 1941. The period of isolation—such as it was—was over.[12]

Just as the Depression had brought new ideas and new influences into the US government, the Second World War brought the United States a new global role. Already a great power, the world's leading manufacturer, and largest creditor in 1918, by 1945 the United States was now the planet's largest economy by far, arming and equipping its own globe-spanning military and the armed forces of its two major wartime allies, the British Empire and the Soviet Union. The United States was the only state to emerge from the war in a stronger economic position than it had entered it, reaching a level of global dominance that required the invention of a new category: superpower. In 1945, the United States controlled 70 percent of the world's gold reserves, held 50 percent of its manufacturing capacity, and three-quarters of its invested capital, while accounting for 35 percent of the world's GDP. Though the Soviet Union had developed one of the most powerful land forces in history, one which by the end of the war occupied the eastern half of Europe, it had nowhere near the global ability to project power possessed by United States' nuclear-armed Army, Navy, and air forces.[13] Many in Washington had come to believe that maintaining that primacy was now essential to

---

[12]German leader Adolf Hitler then declared war on the United States in support of his Japanese ally. See: Overy, *Blood and Ruins*, 72–4, 102–7, 167–84.
[13]Levy, *Ages of American Capitalism*, 462.

FIGURE 12 *A US Office of War Information poster from 1943 depicts the United States leading the "United Nations" to battle during the Second World War.*

preserving American interests.[14] The United States also had at war's end a considerable amount of global prestige—or what might be called "symbolic capital"—not simply for defeating Germany and Japan, but for the broader New Deal and the liberal democratic ideals it went to war to defend.[15] The success of the New Deal state in organizing the war effort, along with idealistic statements of principles like the aforementioned Atlantic Charter as well as Roosevelt's "four freedoms" (freedom of speech and of religion, freedom from want and from fear), suggested to many around the world that the United States was a model for emulation.[16]

Americans themselves tended to agree that it was. Thus, by 1945, there was a broad domestic consensus in support of the United States playing a key role in shaping, and then maintaining, the postwar world order—for delivering a "New Deal for the World," as the historian Elizabeth Borgwardt has called it.[17] Americans believed that just as the New Deal had reordered capitalism without abandoning it, providing greater stability and equality while also protecting political freedom and democracy, a similar program of rationalization could be applied to the international system. This vision for the postwar world was, therefore, in some ways rather egalitarian. It was also clearly grounded in an assumption that humanity was on the cusp of a decidedly less imperial age. Instead of the competitive, tariff-protected, trading blocks that had dominated in the decades before the Second World War, Americans now imagined independent states trading more or less freely with each other, overseen by new international institutions that would coordinate responses to any economic, legal, or political issues that emerged. The heart of this new international infrastructure was to be the United Nations, intended as something akin to a "parliament of man," with a relatively egalitarian, one-country, one-vote General Assembly that its framers imagined could help reveal "world opinion" and then mobilize it against violent aggressors.[18] Adjunct to the UN was to be a collection of new international economic institutions designed to ensure the smooth operation of the global economy. These together became known as the "Bretton

---

[14]See: Stephen Wertheim, *Tomorrow the World: The Birth of U.S. Global Supremacy* (Cambridge, MA: Harvard University Press, 2020).
[15]On the concept of symbolic capital see: Pierre Bourdieu, *Language and Symbolic Power*, Gino Raymond and Matthew Adamson trans. (Cambridge, MA: Harvard University Press, 1991), 163–229.
[16]See the discussion of the Atlantic Charter in Patel, *The New Deal*, 271–8.
[17]Elizabeth Borgwardt, *The New Deal for the World: America's Vision for Human Rights* (Cambridge, MA: Harvard University Press, 2005). See also, Patel, *The New Deal*, 261–300.
[18]For more on the origins and structure of the United Nations see: Borgwardt, *New Deal for the World*; Rowland Brucken, *A Most Uncertain Crusade: The United States, the United Nations, and Human Rights, 1941–1953* (Dekalb: Northern Illinois University Press, 2014); Paul Kennedy, *The Parliament of Man: The Past Present and Future of the United Nations* (New York: Random House, 2006); Mark Mazower, *No Enchanted Palace: The End of Empire and the Ideological Origins of the United Nations* (Princeton: Princeton University Press, 2013).

Woods system," so named for the meeting where they were first crafted, the 1944 UN Monetary and Financial Conference in Bretton Woods, New Hampshire.[19]

The institutions that emerged from Bretton Woods and subsequent UN meetings all reflected the way that the New Deal had transformed the United States and its vision of world order. Despite a brief dalliance with fiat currency during the Civil War, the United States had subsequently returned to the gold standard in 1879. Relatively stable, metallic currency tends to bolster existing hierarchies of wealth, as the low-inflation environment it engenders strengthens the hand of lenders while limiting a government's ability to spend without risk to its gold reserves. This conservative approach to monetary policy seemed increasingly out of touch by the end of the Second World War. Most major economies had suspended the gold convertibility of their currencies during the Depression (the United States was relatively late to do so, leaving gold behind only in 1933) in order to facilitate spending and growth.[20] For a time, in fact, the idea that governments should spend relatively liberally to spur growth, ensure full-employment, and minimize the impacts of inequality was widely accepted as a form of global common sense. This went along with a global, Depression-era vogue for central economic planning, practiced to varying degrees in places as diverse as Mexico, Japan, the United States, Nazi Germany, and the Soviet Union.[21] The US and British planners who took the lead in designing postwar financial institutions built them with this form of spending in mind, calling for the establishment of an "International Monetary Fund," which would oversee a new international currency system based on the US dollar. While the value of the dollar would remain fixed to gold at $35 per ounce, other currencies would be adjustable, making it easier for countries to spend in support of domestic employment and economic development without risking a run on their gold reserves.[22]

There were similar shifts in trade policy as well. Where once the "American system" had been a byword and inspiration for raising tariffs across the world, the United States now pushed for reducing them.[23] A commitment in principle in New Hampshire to lowering trade barriers became over

---

[19] On Bretton Woods see: Barry Eichengreen, *Globalizing Capital: A History of the International Monetary System*, 3rd edition (Princeton: Princeton University Press, 2019), 86–94; Martin Daunton, *The Economic Government of the World, 1933–2023* (New York: Farrar, Straus, and Giroux, 2023), 189–212; Eric Helleiner, *The Forgotten Foundations of Bretton Woods: International Development and the Making of the Postwar Order* (Ithaca: Cornell University Press, 2014); Benn Steil, *The Battle of Bretton Woods: John Maynard Keynes, Harry Dexter White and the Making of a New World Order* (Princeton: Princeton University Press, 2013).
[20] On the rise and fall of the gold standard see: Eichengreen, *Globalizing Capital*, 5–85.
[21] Patel, *The New Deal*, 45–120.
[22] Borgwardt, *New Deal for the World*, 88–113; Daunton, *Economic Government of the World*, 193–206; Eicehngreen, *Globalizing Capital*, 86–94.
[23] For the "American system" see: Chapter 4, also see Palen, *Pax Economica*, 13–50.

the course of 1945–48 the General Agreement on Trade and Tariffs (GATT)—signed in Geneva in 1947—and a proposed International Trade Organization (ITO), chartered in Havana in 1948. GATT was intended to be a provisional framework for gradual tariff reduction, committing all members to non-discrimination in trade. This meant that, unlike the reciprocity treaties the United States had favored in the early part of the century, all reductions in trade would be common to the entire group. The ITO was meant to take matters even further, establishing an institution not just for lowering barriers to trade but also for actively managing the flow of goods and commodities around the world, facilitating freer trade while also encouraging the economic advancement of the world's "developing nations" (as they would start to be called in the 1950s). Indeed, the US approach to the ITO negotiations in Havana showed a surprising, if at times grudging, willingness to accept input from the non-European states, as had American negotiators in New Hampshire. This input (which was by no means uniform) came largely from Latin America—and Mexico in particular—which is where the bulk of independent non-European states were at the time, as well as from India and China.[24] In addition to the ITO's pro-development provisions, it was also expected that the IMF would use its lending capabilities to support development projects. US negotiators at Bretton Woods, as the historian Eric Helleiner has written, "were determined to marry liberal multilateralism with new state-led development policies that had become influential across Latin America and many other poorer regions of the world during the 1930s."[25]

The United States as a "Good Neighbor" had in fact begun to support such programs in Latin America in the mid-1930s, seeking to prevent the spread of German or Japanese influence in the region. The Depression had seriously destabilized the largely export-oriented economies of the Caribbean basin, amplifying longstanding criticisms of what Herminio Portell Vilá—a Cuban historian—called Latin America's "colonial economy."[26] Advancing similar perspectives on the global economy to those that had animated late nineteenth-century US protectionism, Latin Americans argued that they could never escape a subservient economic position without protection and support for manufacturing and industrialization. As Alejandro Carrillo, a Mexican academic put it, "if you believe that Latin Americans wish to continue producing only raw materials for United States manufacturing … and remain in that condition forever, you are certainly mistaken."[27] Hoping to keep its neighbors in the anti-fascist fold, therefore, while also

---

[24]On Mexico's role, and Latin American input more generally, see: Christy Thornton, *Revolution in Development: Mexico and the Governance of the Global Economy* (Berkeley: University of California Press, 2021), 79–98.
[25]Helleiner, *Forgotten Foundations*, 11.
[26]Helleiner, *Forgotten Foundations*, 37.
[27]Helleiner, *Forgotten Foundations*, 37–8.

forestalling more left-wing responses to the Depression that might threaten American property owners, the Roosevelt administration began in 1934 to offer short-term loans to Latin American governments to stabilize their currencies and finance development projects.[28] From the US perspective, these loans also had the added benefit of stimulating trade between the US and Latin America states—keeping commodities flowing north and US exports moving south—while making their governments more dependent on the United States. In fact, so successful was US policy in this regard that the region largely marched in lockstep behind the United States when it finally went to war in 1941.[29]

As this might suggest, though the New Deal had shifted the United States further away from imperialism as a tool of foreign policy, Americans had not entirely left behind their instinct for ordering the world hierarchically either. Even at its most idealistic, the vision of a New Deal for the World retained many of the assumptions of the imperial age, repackaged for a new era. Much of this was already evident before the war. The US approach to Good Neighbor development lending, for example, was not all that far removed from the premises that had both motivated and justified new imperialism: the idea that the United States had some form of global obligation to help other states reach their full potential. In the 1930s, the "white man's burden" was starting to become the "developed state's burden," a responsibility to help the non-European world reach US-style modernity. This was imagined as a tutelary relationship and therefore was inherently hierarchical—while the desire to help was often sincere, the United States also expected that those in its classroom would follow its rules. US loans to Latin America were premised upon the receiving country towing the American line: keeping out US rivals (especially the Germans), suppressing radical forces that might threaten private property or US market access, and staying close to whatever view of political economy was then in vogue in the United States. Considerably more charitable than US policy toward Latin America in the Theodore Roosevelt-Taft-Wilson era, the Good Neighbor approach still retained much of the old interest in control.

Thus, while the Roosevelt administration avoided using troops to manage affairs in Latin America during the 1930s, it enforced its rules all the same. The aforementioned oil nationalizations in Bolivia and Mexico are a good example of this. In both cases, the Roosevelt administration used economic power to force the Bolivian and Mexican governments to the table—withholding trade and development loans in the first case and suspending the purchase of Mexican silver in the second—resulting in financial settlements which paid the oil companies more than fair market value for their seized assets. Though Washington, in effect, helped pay part of the cost of this

---

[28] Helleiner, *Forgotten Foundations*, 44–5.
[29] Schoultz, *In Their Own Best Interest*, 137–62.

compensation (by resuming silver purchases and extending loans), the result was to keep both countries locked in a dependent relationship with the United States and out of the Axis sphere of influence.[30]

This was hardly the first instance of Roosevelt's administration using America's dominant position in the hemisphere to its advantage, either. In Cuba in 1934, for example, the United States had used several means short of armed intervention to destabilize the government of the populist reformer Ramón Grau San Martín. Worried that the new government was "frankly communistic" and seeking to remove "any form of American influence in Cuba"—as US Ambassador Sumner Wells put it in a cable from Havana—the Roosevelt administration refused to extend its recognition, while sending more than two dozen warships to patrol the waters around the island. With American encouragement, Colonel Fulgencio Batista, the de facto leader of the Cuban military, forced Grau to resign, replacing him with a figurehead president, to whom the United States immediately extended recognition.[31] US support helped Batista to officially and unofficially run the country until 1944 (he would be back again in 1952), part of a broader pattern of backing pro-US strongmen across the Caribbean.

In Nicaragua and the Dominican Republic, the United States threw its support behind two dictators who emerged from the political chaos that followed the withdrawal of American troops. The Dominican Republic's Rafael Trujillo took power in 1930 and soon ruled his country with a mix of brutality and venality. His "formula was pragmatic and simple" one US ambassador recalled, "do not quarrel with the United States."[32] Roosevelt reportedly remarked of *"el jefe"*—as Trujillo was known—that, "he may be a sonofabitch, but at least he's our sonofabitch."[33] Much the same principle governed the supportive American relationship with Anastasio Somoza, the ruthless Nicaraguan dictator who had used the country's US-trained National Guard as a springboard to power. As a Peruvian politician complained, "how nice it would be if the president of the United States, faithful to his democratic and pacific principles" could "in the name of suffering people condemn more explicitly the … autocrats who consider Mr. Roosevelt their 'great and good friend'."[34] Of course, this was precisely the point, the commitment to being a "great and good friend" mattered more than any similar relationship with democracy—a pattern which would repeat itself as the century wore on.

Much like the Good Neighbor policy, the institutions for global governance that the United States helped build after the Second World War

---

[30] Camin and Meyer, *Shadow of the Mexican Revolution*, 150–6; Maurer, *Empire Trap*, 260–96; Schoultz, *In Their Own Best Interest*, 140–4.
[31] Ferrer, *Cuba*, 235–47.
[32] Schoultz, *In Their Own Best Interest*, 135.
[33] Herring, *From Colony to Superpower*, 473.
[34] Schoultz, *In Their Own Best Interest*, 135–6.

were genuinely reformist, trying to move away from the age of empire, while remaining hierarchical. The UN General Assembly, for example, certainly represented a vision of sovereign equality, but it could only issue non-binding resolutions—suggestions—to member states. Binding resolutions were the province of a separate, and hierarchically organized, Security Council, on which each of the five "great power" victors of the Second World War—the United States, Great Britain, France, China, and the Soviet Union—held permanent seats and possessed an exclusive right to veto the council's resolutions. Though establishing the veto power was essential to securing Soviet participation (and helped with ratification in the United States), its composition was telling all the same: in addition to the United States, all but one of the permanent members was a European, great power empire. The exception, China, was relatively weak, and long subject to US and European influence, as we have seen. The UN was thus, as one British participant in its planning put it at the time, "an Alliance of the Great Powers embedded in a universal organization."[35]

It's also worthy of note that those involved with framing the UN hardly saw it as incompatible with empire. South Africa's Jan Smuts, for example, a key participant in organizing the new institution, believed that the UN represented a perfect vehicle for ensuring a white supremacist world order, with the United States reinforcing the British Empire's longstanding "civilizing mission" in Africa.[36] The system of UN-approved colonies—"trust territories"—was also clearly framed around assumptions of the organization carrying forth the civilizing mission of new imperialism in a new internationalist guise. All told, though the UN would evolve in a more anti-imperial direction in the 1950s and 1960s, this was as much a result of accident—and advocacy by newly independent states like India—as it was any intention of its framers.[37]

The same could be said about the planned postwar economic order, which was even more hierarchical in its structure than the UN. Both of the two major international finance institutions established after the war—which along with the IMF included the International Bank for Reconstruction and Development, now part of the "World Bank"—were developed with a weighted voting system that gave their largest contributors the largest vote shares. This meant that both funds would be controlled by the world's richest nations and by the United States in particular (which as the world's dominant economic power in 1945 was to have the largest contribution and voting share). In practice, this resulted in a tiered lending system, where some states could access funds without much restriction, while others would be forced to adopt economic austerity cutting domestic spending and/or increasing taxation. Though the IMF's charter was somewhat vague about what

---

[35]Mazower, *No Enchanted Palace*, 7
[36]Mazower, *No Enchanted Palace*, 19–22, 28–65.
[37]Mazower, *No Enchanted Palace*, 141–203.

conditions it could impose upon borrowers, this was as much a gesture to the sensibilities of the British as anything else—economically dependent for the first time in centuries, London disliked the idea of terms being imposed on its policies.[38]

US negotiators, however, had always understood that to be salable at home the fund would have to be able to make demands on borrowing states, in effect, curtailing their sovereignty by requiring them to adopt whatever economic policies the fund's directors thought essential. Despite their reduced influence during the Roosevelt years, US bankers had enough influence over financial matters to ensure this at least—and American dominance of the voting structure guaranteed that this was the interpretation that ended up actually governing lending. The result was an IMF that offered more generous terms to states its governors recognized as more advanced—Australia, for example, was able to borrow in the 1950s without much restriction—and more restrictive terms to those it did not. Lending to Mexico in the late 1940s and 1950s helped set the pattern, where the Mexican government was required to adopt "appropriate" forms of fiscal restraint in order to keep funds flowing.[39] As the historian Jamie Martin has argued, these new international institutions allowed the world's wealthiest states to exert control over the developing world in a way that mirrored imperialism while avoiding "older forms of interference" that were increasingly appearing "anachronistic" after 1945.[40] "It was much easier," he writes, "for a sovereign state to accept the counsel of an international institution than that of a foreign government directly."[41]

Similar tensions were also evident in the new American insistence on free trade. To be sure, idealism was part of the story here, too. A significant contingent of Roosevelt's policymakers—including the aforementioned Secretary of State Hull—were products of an anti-imperialist and anti-protectionist school of thought that believed that freer trade could help lead to global peace. These "Cobdenites"—named for the nineteenth-century British reformer and free trade advocate Richard Cobden—argued that much of the impetus for global conflict came from economic competition engendered by tariffs and the related competition for raw materials and markets. With tariffs reduced to the lowest level possible, and with trade supervised by international institutions like the ITO, they believed, a new global spirit of cooperation could emerge.[42]

At the same time, however, as the leading manufacturing power in the world, the country likely to benefit most from freer trade was the United

---

[38] Daunton, *Economic Government of the World*, 198–200.
[39] Jamie Martin, *The Meddlers: Sovereignty, Empire, and the Birth of Global Economic Governance* (Cambridge, MA: Harvard University Press, 2022), 210–45.
[40] Martin, *The Meddlers*, 250.
[41] Martin, *The Meddlers*, 244.
[42] See Palen, *Pax Economica*.

States. An open global trading system premised upon the protection of existing private property rights and foreign investments—one which lacked any opportunity for developing states to alter the terms of trade in their favor—was destined to preserve the existing global distribution of wealth and economic power. Because they were already well established and well-funded, it was usually much easier for US industries to produce better products more cheaply than manufacturers in developing economies. This meant that, in general, if trade was conducted on free terms without protections for industries in developing economies, it would be almost impossible for those industries to get off the ground and gain significant market share (a challenging prospect even in ideal conditions). The United States had itself confronted a similar problem when trying to compete with superior British manufacturers in the nineteenth century, hence its adoption of the "American system" of protectionism discussed in previous chapters. In so far as industrialization seemed to be the path to global power and true independence, developing states wanted to industrialize as well, which is why Latin American countries pushed for the development provisions of the IMF and ITO discussed above. Mexican officials, for example, complained that initial US positions in trade talks revealed, "the intention of industrialized countries … to have free access to foreign markets for the placement of their products and the easy acquisition of primary materials." Accepting such a policy would, in the Mexican case, they noted, mean "converting ourselves into a semi-colonial country" serving US manufacturing interests.[43] Even once mighty Britain had resisted (unsuccessfully) US efforts to pry open the British Empire by incorporating free trade requirements into wartime Lend-Lease agreements. The British were well aware of the potential risks that such openness might hold for Britain's postwar economic health given the scale of American economic dominance.[44]

On the whole, the new international system that the United States helped establish at war's end represented a true effort at reform—and even gestured toward genuine respect for the sovereign equality of every state—but it was also governed by rules set by the world's most powerful, Americans especially. These rules, the United States insisted, would be good for all, but they were also particularly beneficial to the United States and less so for those in the developing world. As we will see, Americans would struggle to recognize or admit this reality, one that was only too obvious to those who least benefited from this new "liberal world order." Egalitarian in its framing, hierarchical in its structure, the liberal order never attained the universal legitimacy its framers aspired to. As a result, the United States found itself required to bolster and police it from almost the start.

---

[43]See Thornton, *Revolution in Development*, 121–44, quotes on 127.
[44]Daunton, *Economic Government of the World*, 122–31.

Decolonization and the Cold War

The second half of the twentieth century was shaped by two major geopolitical developments: the emergence of the Cold War and the decolonization of Asia and Africa. These both would quickly draw out the hierarchical tendencies inherent in the postwar US approach to world order, creating a situation that seemingly required constant, direct US intervention around the world to sustain both American interests and the liberal international system that served them.

The arrival of the Cold War, on the one hand, resulted in the creation of a rival vision of global governance, one that offered a different path for global progress, ending not in US-style liberal democracy, but in Soviet-style communism. The conflict was in many respects a direct result of the US effort at worldmaking we have been describing so far in this chapter. Though Roosevelt had worked carefully to minimize tensions through personal wartime diplomacy with the Soviet Union's leader, Joseph Stalin, the President's death in April 1945 complicated what would have already been a challenging transition from wartime alliance to peacetime cooperation. His successor, Harry S. Truman (in office: 1945–53), had not been privy to Roosevelt's personal negotiations with Stalin, and thus the two sides quickly fell to misinterpreting each other's goals and actions, which were in some respects already fundamentally at odds—particularly when it came to Eastern Europe. After nearly watching his regime crumble following Hitler's brutal 1943 invasion, Stalin wanted reliable client states to his west, while Truman (and most Americans) wanted to see democratic elections in the territories liberated from the Nazi empire and their incorporation into the liberal world order (when it came to Europeans, the United States was in 1945 a firm supporter of self-determination). Still devastated by a war that killed roughly 27 million of its citizens, Moscow was not in a position to fight a war with the United States, but its armies did control Eastern Europe. A "tit for tat retaliatory system," as Lorenz M. Luthi describes it, soon emerged, leaving the continent divided by what former British Prime Minister Winston Churchill dubbed an "Iron Curtain" in 1946. The establishment of competing alliance systems—the US-backed North Atlantic Treaty Organization (NATO) in 1949 and the Soviet "Warsaw Pact" in 1955—later cemented this division between "the West" and "the East."[45]

---

[45]Lorez M. Lüthi, *Cold Wars: Asia, The Middle East, Europe* (Cambridge: Cambridge University Press, 2020), 24. On Stalin, Truman, and the European origins of the Cold War see: Fraser J. Harbutt, *The Iron Curtain: Churchill, America, and the Origins of the Cold War* (Oxford: Oxford University Press, 1986); Harbutt, *Yalta 1945: Europe and America at the Crossroads* (Cambridge: Cambridge University Press, 2010); Lüthi, *Cold Wars*, 13–36; Sergey Radchenko, *To Run the World: The Kremlin's Cold War Bid for Global Power* (Cambridge: Cambridge University Press, 2024), 17–142; Odd Arne Westad, *The Cold War: A World History* (New York: Basic Books, 2017), 19–127.

Such disputes over postwar spheres of influence were further inflamed by ideological differences. Despite the wartime alliance, there was no denying that the Soviet and American systems were organized around deeply conflicting visions of the proper way to organize human society, both within states and globally. Though Stalin was himself a brutal pragmatist as much as anything else, his regime was committed on paper to a global revolution to overthrow capitalism and the existing hierarchy of wealth and power. The New Deal-era United States, meanwhile, was committed not so much to preserving that global hierarchy but to reforming it enough to prevent any such revolution from occurring—a revolution Americans feared would result in tyranny (which, given the nature of Stalin's regime, was not an entirely unreasonable concern).[46] The gap between the two had been laid bare by the contrasting visions for reconstruction of Wilson and Lenin after the First World War and would soon reemerge following the Second World War. Many Americans—both inside and outside of Washington—certainly took the threat of communism seriously, as revealed by the "Red Scares" that followed each world war. Thus, the emergence of the Soviet Union as a rival "superpower" to the United States, one with its own "bloc" of semi-independent allies in Eastern Europe, deeply influenced how the United States understood its postwar role—facing what they believed to be an inimical threat to US-style freedom, the Cold War made American policymakers more likely to see a need to try to control global events.[47]

The decolonization of Asia and Africa, on the other hand, made this harder to do. It created a whole new world of sovereign states which wanted economic development, higher standards of living, and greater global influence but would struggle to achieve it under the rules the United States established in 1945 and after. As a general phenomenon, the mid-twentieth century wave of decolonization was the result of demands for self-determination that had been growing in the colonized world since the late nineteenth century. As new imperialism failed to deliver the widely distributed growth and development it had seemed to promise, and the world wars eroded perceptions of European cultural supremacy, broad coalitions of colonized peoples embraced independence as the only acceptable path forward.[48]

---

[46]Though most of the sources cited here on the Cold War provide an introduction to how ideology influenced both the Soviet Union and the United States, a particularly helpful one in the context of our focus on decolonization is: Odd Arne Westad, *The Global Cold War: Third World Interventions and the Making of Our Times* (New York: Cambridge University Press, 2007), 8–72.

[47]We will be considering various aspects of the Cold War throughout this chapter and the next. For good general accounts see: Melvyn P. Leffler, *For the Soul of Mankind: The United States, the Soviet Union, and the Cold War* (New York: Hill and Wang, 2007); Luthi, *Cold Wars*; Radchenko, *To Run the World*; Westad, *The Cold War*; Vladislav Zubok, *The World of the Cold War, 1945–1991* (New York: Pelican Books, 2025).

[48]See Chapter 5.

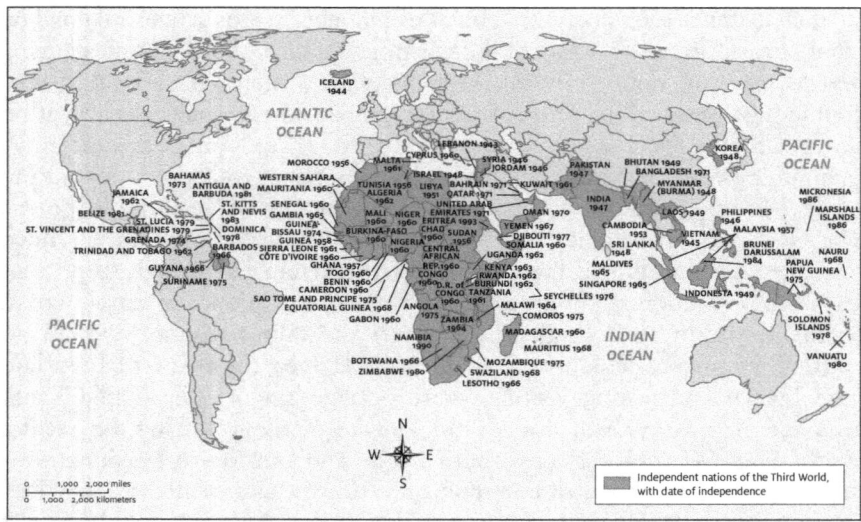

MAP 3 *Map showing the global decolonization that followed the Second World War.*

The European response was a mix of resistance and resignation, a reflection of how diminished Britain, France, Belgium, and the Netherlands were by decades of war but also of the still-persistent asymmetry of world power. The Europeans were not strong enough to retain control of their restive empires, but they were strong enough to try. Even where it became apparent that independence could not be forestalled—they were quickest to realize this with colonies in Asia, much slower in Africa—European leaders still hoped to manage the process of decolonization so as to ensure that the new states were in the hands of parties deemed "responsible" and thus likely to maintain ties to the old colonial center. The result was a process that was often chaotic and violent. Beginning with India and Pakistan's 1947 independence and the subsequent mass slaughter of the partition of its Hindu and Muslim populations, violence spread from Indochina (1946–54) and Algeria (1954–62)—as those populations fought from their freedom from France—to the Dutch East Indies (1945–49) as Indonesians fought for the independence of their archipelago, and Kenya, where the British brutally suppressed the Mau Mau uprising (1952–60). Even as states gained independence, violence frequently continued in the form of civil wars—as in the Congo, Nigeria, Angola, and Mozambique, for example. Populations confusingly mixed by a century of European edict often found it difficult to settle the significant political differences that emerged about how to govern their hard-won independence, while their former colonial rulers used the violence as an excuse to continue to meddle in their affairs, only complicating matters further.[49]

The result was not one US-dominated liberal world as Americans had hoped, but what seemed more like *three* distinct "worlds"—as people did in fact begin describing them in the 1950s. The "First" was that of the United States and the industrialized states of Western Europe. The "Second" was the Soviet sphere, including the USSR itself and its Warsaw Pact allies. The "Third World," was that of the developing states, including now not just Latin America but the vast swaths of Asia and Africa that achieved independence from European and US rule in the period 1946–60.[50] These worlds were not entirely separate, of course, nearly all independent states joined the United Nations, for example, and even at the height of the Cold War commerce resisted the constraints of international politics and its attendant iron curtains. The Third World too remained deeply tied into and dependent upon the networks of commerce and trade they had been yoked to under imperial rule, meaning that it was even less separate from the First World than was the Second (a reality that, as we will touch on in a moment, explains part of the appeal of communism to anti-colonial nationalists). Latin America was often understood as part of the Third World for this reason, though long independent, of course, their largely subservient role in the global economy and vulnerability to outside (especially the United States) interference placed them in a similar category. This situation was later captured by the term "postcolonial"—advanced by theorists in the 1970s—highlighting countries that were nominally independent, but not yet free of all the cultural, economic, and political legacies of the imperial age. At the time, enthused neither by the American nor Soviet models of development, the new countries often tried to pursue their own path, something that the apparent Cold War threat made Americans less and less inclined to tolerate.

---

[49]See the summary in Jansen and Osterhammel, *Decolonization*, 1–22.
[50]The term "Third World" is usually attributed to the French scholar Alfred Sauvy, who used it in much the context we are discussing here in an August 1952 article for the French periodical *L'Observateur*. It quickly became a popular way to refer to what were also called the "developing nations" (a term introduced above): the countries of Latin America, Africa, and Asia that were generally poorer, less industrialized, or "developed" than the "developed" states of North America and Europe (along with Japan, Australia, and New Zealand). The term, as this suggests, is at the same time both vague and relatively specific and—as readers of this book have likely guessed—it quickly became loaded with implications related to civilization and hierarchy. As such, it has long been criticized as, among other things, a potentially insulting oversimplification. However, we will use it advisedly here (along with "developing nations" and the more popular current term, "Global South") because it was widely used at the time in the developed and developing world alike and because it remains a particularly useful term for describing the Third World's peripheral status in the very real hierarchies of the world-system. See the helpful discussion in: Marin Woiciech Solarz, "Third World: The 60th Anniversary of a Concept that Changed History," *Third World Quarterly* 33, no. 9 (October 2012): 1561–73.

It was largely in this postcolonial Third World (or "Global South" as we will sometimes call it) that the contest between the First and the Second would play out—a "Cold War" in that it was a warlike contest for power and influence that did not usually involve direct conflict between the two main parties. With the arrival of the Soviet atomic bomb in 1949, the Cold War in Europe soon became too dangerous for either side to lightly consider serious threats to each other's interests there—all were vital, and all could therefore lead directly to a nuclear confrontation. Competition for influence and allies in the Third World thus became a "safe" place for each side to export their conflict, competing via proxies to avoid overly direct forms of confrontation. Both the Soviet Union and the United States found opportunities in the development needs of the new states to show off the relative merits of their form of political and economic organization, assuring their Third World allies that their programs would lead them to their respective promised lands of industrialized modernity. In so doing, the superpowers—each like a kind of bloodyhanded King Midas—intensified the contests for power that came with decolonization. From Korea, to South Asia, the Middle East, and across Africa, the struggle to control postcolonial states reached new levels of violence and complication as money, guns, and ideology flowed in from the Soviet Union and the United States to the factions they favored. These "proxy wars" would leave millions dead by 1991.[51] If one again sees similarities here with the new imperialism we discussed in Chapter 4, they are right to do so, as once more we are encountering powerful states using the prospect of "helping" the less developed world reach its potential, all while serving their own strategic and economic interests.

Given the track record we have laid out—and the hierarchical structures of the international institutions established in 1945—it's hard to imagine the United States not meddling in the postcolonial world, even if there was no Cold War. The United States, after all, remained a powerful capitalist state, whose influential citizens continued to own property and investments abroad. The collapse of Europe's empires would only increase, not decrease opportunities for Americans to do so. The "empire trap"—to reuse Noel Maurer's term—remained ready to spring of its own accord, the Cold War only oiled the hinges, providing new strategic reasons and ideological justifications for intervention.[52] The superpower conflict also helped bring corporate leaders and Wall Street back into the halls of power. This was a process that was already well underway during the Second World War, which had seen the New Deal state and electoral coalition evolve in a more pro-business direction. The war militarized, corporatized, and unionized the New Deal, as Americans constructed a vast new federal bureaucracy and military industrial complex which relied upon a close (if occasionally

---

[51]See: Paul Thomas Chamberlin, *The Cold War's Killing Fields: Rethinking the Long Peace* (New York: HarperCollins, 2019); Westad, *The Global Cold War*.
[52]See Chapter 5 and Maurer, *Empire Trap*.

uneasy) partnership between the government, corporations, and large labor unions (which roughly doubled their membership between 1939 and 1945). Corporate executives were brought into important positions in the government and the military to oversee war production—as Roosevelt transformed, in his words, from "Dr. New Deal" to "Dr. Win the War."[53]

Victory in the war and the success of American industry in equipping the allies restored the sullied reputation of American business. The early Cold War "Red Scare" only accelerated this process, resulting in the expulsion of the left-leaning groups and leaders—like Vice President Henry Wallace, for example—from the government and the political conversation.[54] While the Cold War New Deal state retained the earlier New Deal's commitment to federal intervention in the economy to ensure more egalitarian outcomes, it took on a decidedly more business-friendly cast during the administrations of Truman and his successor, Dwight D. Eisenhower (in office: 1953–61).

The New Deal for the World followed a similar trajectory away from its most idealistic and egalitarian form to something more militarized, more business-friendly, and more reflective of the hierarchical assumptions of the prewar era. One of the earliest casualties of this change was the ITO, labeled by the US National Association of Manufacturers—a powerful pro-business lobbying group—as a program to "make the world safe for socialistic planning."[55] After failing in Congress in 1948 and 1949, President Truman chose not to submit the ITO's charter again in 1950. "An anticlimatic end" as Martin Daunton writes, "to a project on which so much time and energy had been spent."[56] Shorn of the ITO and its development-related provisions, the postwar global governance regime offered little to the Third World beyond a program for lowering tariffs and the onerously structured development lending described above. At the same time, the United States also showered Europe with reconstruction and development money in the form of the European Recovery Program, or "Marshall Plan" as it is best known. An inarguably brilliant strategic move designed to keep Western Europe in the capitalist fold, the Marshall Plan also reinforced existing global hierarchies by providing 13.4 billion dollars of aid to help Europe recover quickly from the war while offering nothing to a Global South long despoiled by European colonialism. Approved by Congress in 1948—the same year the ITO charter went to the first of its many defeats—the Marshall Plan arrived at much the same time as hopes were dashed for more generous development assistance to the Third World. Latin American

---

[53] Patel, *New Deal*, 261–6.
[54] On the Red Scare see: Richard M. Freeland, *The Truman Doctrine and the Origins of McCarthyism: Foreign Policy, Domestic Politics, and Internal Security* (New York: Alfred A. Knopf, 1972); Michael S. Sherry, *In the Shadow of War: The United States since the 1930s* (New Haven: Yale University Press, 1995), 144–56, 170–7.
[55] New York Times, "ITO Charter Fought by NAM on 6 Points," *New York Times*, March 6, 1949, A39.
[56] Daunton, *Economic Government of the World*, 268.

states, for example, had hoped that their wartime loyalty to the United States, and their significance to North America's wartime economy, would lead to a generous program of postwar aid. Ironically, it was Secretary of State George C. Marshall himself who delivered the bad news at an Inter-American conference in Bogota in 1948: the United States, Marshall told his country's southern neighbors, could provide but a "small portion of the vast development [funds] needed," for Latin America.[57]

The United States would, however, quickly change its tune on development funding as the Cold War intensified and the strength of anti-colonial independence movements became clear. The Truman administration's initially somewhat Eurocentric approach to fighting communism began to shift thanks to two events—each themselves a long-term result of the waning of colonialism: the 1949 victory of Mao Zedong's communists in the Chinese Civil War and the outbreak of the Korean War in 1950. The crisis in Korea, and the deployment of US forces there under the UN's banner, militarized and globalized the US commitment to fighting the spread of communism and reinforced in Washington the idea that the United States had a responsibility to police the entire world.[58]. These—to American eyes—sudden expansions of communism also emerged at much the same time that it became clear that some contraction of Europe's empires was inevitable. By 1950, Burma, India, Pakistan, Sri Lanka, Indonesia, Israel/Palestine, Lebanon, Jordan, and Syria had all gained independence, while French Indochina was embroiled in Ho Chi Minh's war for Vietnam's independence. The decade also saw Malaya, Libya, Sudan, Morocco, and Tunisia join the ranks of independent nations, and by 1960—the "year of Africa," as it was called—much of Sub-Saharan Africa had gained independence as well.[59] Where the UN had only fifty-one member states at its founding in 1945, by 1961 that number had more than doubled to 104.[60]

By the time Algeria won its independence from France in 1962 (after years of violent French resistance), "decolonization," as the historian Todd Shepard writes, had come to be seen globally as "a causal force with all but irresistible momentum," an inevitable final stage in the history of imperialism.[61] Such notions were contested initially—the first French book with "decolonization" in its title, for example, had argued that ending empire was a mistake—yet, the sense that devolutions of authority, and perhaps even sovereignty, were historically necessary was already well established

---

[57]See Thornton, *Revolution in Development*, 121–44, quotes on 143.
[58]Luthi, *Cold Wars*, 26–33.
[59]Latham, *Modernization as Ideology*, 2.
[60]United Nations, "Growth in United Nations Membership," https://www.un.org/en/about-us/growth-in-un-membership.
[61]Todd Shepard, *The Invention of Decolonization: The Algerian War and the Remaking of France* (Ithaca: Cornell University Press, 2006).

in the minds of US policymakers as the 1950s dawned.[62] Paul Nitze, the Director of Policy Planning for the US Department of State, for example, summed up the situation this way in the influential 1950 document NSC-68. "During the span of one generation," he wrote, "the international distribution of power has been fundamentally altered." The "defeat of Germany and Japan," NSC-68 continued, "and the decline of the British and French Empires" had left the United States and the Soviet Union as the only remaining centers of global power. Nitze feared that the Soviet Union was seeking "to impose its absolute authority over the rest of the world," a view that seemed pessimistic to many in the Truman administration before the Korean War, and spot-on after.[63] Believing that they were confronting an implacable communist enemy, capable of fundamentally disrupting the liberal world order, American policymakers therefore recognized a need to pay more attention to the desires of colonized and formerly colonized peoples.[64]

This, however, put the Truman and subsequent Eisenhower administrations in something of a bind. On the one hand, the economic recovery of America's vital Western European, anti-communist allies seemed to require a continuation of colonialism. Senator Henry Cabot Lodge Jr. summed up the prevailing view during a hearing on the establishment of NATO in 1949, saying "we need ... these countries to be strong, and they cannot be strong without their colonies."[65] Overseas possessions were essential sources of raw materials for European—and Japanese—industrial reconstruction. On the other hand, too much support for the Europeans in their effort to retain their empires could easily alienate the Global South from American leadership, driving independence movements to embrace the Soviet Union and communism. The United States could not look at events, as Eisenhower's Secretary of State John Foster Dulles put it, "solely ... from the standpoint of our policies" with "European powers." Doing so risked America's relations with "the great mass of mankind which is non-white and non-European"[66]

The Soviet model of development, and Marxism more generally, already had considerable appeal in the Global South. This was for two main reasons. First, its arguments about the causes of Third World poverty

---

[62]Michael E. Latham, *The Right Kind of Revolution: Modernization, Development, and U.S. Foreign Policy from the Cold War to the Present* (Ithaca: Cornell University Press, 2011), 29.
[63]United States Department of State, "A Report to the National Security Council by the Executive Secretary (Lay)," April 14, 1950, in *Foreign Relations of the United States, 1950, Volume 1: National Security Affairs; Foreign Economic Policy* (Washington, DC: United States Government Printing Office, 1977), https://history.state.gov/historicaldocuments/frus1950v01/d85.
[64]Latham, *Modernization as Ideology*, 2.
[65]Latham, *Right Kind of Revolution*, 29.
[66]Matthew Connelly, *A Diplomatic Revolution: Algeria's Fight for Independence and the Origins of the Post-Cold War Era* (New York: Oxford University Press, 2002), 85.

naturally dovetailed with those of anti-colonial nationalists—namely, that imperialism had provided the violent means for First World capitalists to control the economies of the colonized world, ensuring their own enrichment at the expense of their colonial subjects. This, in the Marxist lens, required a rejection of capitalism wholesale along with foreign rule, not too far from what an anti-colonial nationalist already argued by default. Second, the Soviet Union's own history of rapid industrialization in the 1930s—and its high growth rates in the 1950s—made its command style, centralized economy seem an appealing model to some in the Global South. To its admirers, the Soviet Union appeared to offer the shortest path to modernity of the available Cold War options.[67]

Thus, between the Scylla of neglecting European reconstruction needs and the Charybdis of increasing Marxism's appeal in the decolonizing world, Washington looked to—as Michael Latham writes—"chart an intermediate course."[68] The goal was to avoid rapid decolonization while still appearing sensitive to calls for change from the Global South. Newly independent Third World states could not necessarily be trusted to govern themselves, to be sure, but their demands for self-government had to be acknowledged to some degree, lest independence forces turn to communism. The Truman and Eisenhower administration's therefore began to nudge British, French, and Dutch leaders to grant more authority—and even independence—to their colonial possessions in a careful, controlled, fashion. The Americans wanted to keep the colonies in a close relationship with their former rulers for as long as possible—maintaining the flow of raw materials to European factories—while also ensuring that the new countries, once independent, were ruled by leaders the United States saw as responsible (i.e., those who would not ally with the Soviet Union, cut themselves off from the global economy, or nationalize foreign-owned property).[69] This was a model the United States followed itself in the Philippines, which was granted independence on July 4th, 1946, but quickly descended into violence as significant segments of the population revolted against the new government.

Modernization and Intervention

The United States had granted the Philippines considerable autonomy in 1935—establishing the Philippine Commonwealth—as part of the Tydings-McDuffie promise to establish Philippines independence by 1946, a commitment reaffirmed by FDR during the war. US rule in the Philippines had long relied on Filipino elites, who preserved an economic structure

---

[67]Latham, *Modernization as Ideology*, 27–9.
[68]Latham, *Right Kind of Revolution*, 29.
[69]Connelly, *Diplomatic Revolution*, 34–5, 85–6, 119–20, 199; Latham, *Right Kind of Revolution*, 27–32.

that left much of the population in poverty and thus prone to strikes and demonstrations. These elites helmed the Commonwealth government, which throughout the mid- and late-1930s arrested peasant and communist leaders seen as threatening the state. This governing order had been overthrown by the Japanese occupation (1941–45). The emergence of left-leaning, anti-Japanese militias like the Hukbalahap (a Tagalog acronym for "People's Anti-Japanese Army") seemed to threaten its restoration following the American reconquest of the islands in 1945. The "Huks"—along with the Democratic Alliance (DA), a broadly left-wing political party—reflected discontent with inequality and the working conditions facing most Filipinos as well as anger at elite collaboration with the Japanese occupation during the war. Calling for protections for labor unions, old age and disability pensions, and greater public spending, Huk and DA organizing threatened landlords in Central Luzon, who turned to private militias backed by Commonwealth forces to suppress the peasant left. The situation grew worse in 1946, when the DA scored some successes in the national elections that brought the US-backed candidate, Manuel Roxas, to power. Though carried out on the eve of independence, those elections unfolded against the backdrop of the continued US military occupation of the islands, so Roxas's victory was far from surprising. What was surprising was the election of several DA representatives to the Philippine Congress. When Roxas refused to allow these elected DA congressmen to be seated, the Huks rose in revolt, leading Roxas to adopt what he called a "mailed fist" policy to suppress the uprising.[70]

The United States provided money and arms—both to fight the insurgency and for more general postwar reconstruction—in return for Roxas's support for establishing two US military bases on the islands as well as a trade bill that even US Secretary of State James Byrnes admitted was "inconsistent with our promise to grant the Philippines genuine independence."[71] That trade agreement—the Bell Trade Bill, ratified in 1947—granted US companies an equal right with Filipinos to "develop" the archipelago's natural resources while also ensuring privileged access for American trade goods. It further mandated that the Philippine Peso be pegged to the US dollar. US military assistance, meanwhile, was codified in the 1947 Philippine Defense Act, which provided for ongoing US financial support for the Filipino armed forces and granted the United States numerous territorial concessions for military bases, including what became the massive facilities of Clark Air Base and US Naval Base Subic Bay. The treaties ensured that, while the Philippines gained independence, it remained economically and military subordinated to the United States, locked into a relationship that benefited wealthy Filipinos and the United States more

---

[70]Colleen Woods, *Freedom Incorporated: Anticommunism and Philippine Independence in the Age of Decolonization* (Ithaca: Cornell University Press, 2020), 20–93.
[71]Woods, *Freedom Incorporated*, 88.

than the average Filipino.⁷² Despite American money, advice, and heavy weapons, the war against the Huks dragged on into the early 1950s. As a result, US officials—and Philippine leaders—increasingly defined the war as a battle against global communism, not just disaffected peasants. The conflict only ended following the election of Ramon Magaysay to the Philippine presidency in 1953. Backed by US money and vehemently anti-communist, Magaysay was able to win peasant support with promises of land reform, making the Manila government broadly popular for the first time since independence. Partnering with Edward Lansdale, a US Central Intelligence Agency operative who led Filipino counterinsurgency efforts, Magaysay targeted the material causes of peasant dissent, which proved just enough to undercut Huk support among a war-weary population.⁷³

This focus on the material concerns of the Filipino peasantry reflected—and reinforced—a growing recognition in Washington that preserving the liberal world order, and limiting the spread of communism, required addressing Third World poverty and "underdevelopment," as it was called at the time. Luckily, American universities were beginning to provide a solution for just this problem: "modernization theory." Modernization theory refers to a school of social scientific thinking on development, history, and global inequality that gained prominence and influence in both academic and government circles in the 1950s. It offered what Walt Whitman Rostow—one of its most prominent advocates—called in the subtitle of his 1960 book: a "non-communist manifesto," a counter-narrative to anti-imperial and Marxist explanations for Third World poverty.⁷⁴ Rather than being the result of conquest, imperialism, and capitalist exploitation, modernization theory blamed Third World underdevelopment on the backwardness of supposedly "traditional" societies in the Global South. The idea was that all human societies were theoretically capable of going through what Rostow called "stages of growth," evolving with time into stable "modern" or "advanced" societies (which, naturally enough, looked a lot like the United States). Some around the world had already taken these steps, others had not.⁷⁵

Such differences in the levels of global development were, according to modernization theorists, a result of the fact that different societies were endowed with different cultural inheritances. As the sociologist Talcott

---

[72] Woods, *Freedom Incorporated*, 85–93.
[73] Capozzola, *Bound by War*, 239–47; Woods, *Freedom Incorporated*, 94–129.
[74] W.W. Rostow, *The Stages of Economic Growth: A Non-Communist Manifesto* (Cambridge: Cambridge University Press, 1960). For more on Rostow see: David Milne, *America's Rasputin: Walt Rostow and the Vietnam War* (New York: Hill and Wang, 2008).
[75] For introductions to modernization theory and its influence on US policy see: David Ekbladh, *The Great American Mission: Modernization Theory and the Construction of an American World Order* (Princeton: Princeton University Press, 2010); Nils Gilman, *Mandarins of the Future: Modernization Theory in Cold War America* (Baltimore: Johns Hopkins University Press, 2003); Latham, *Modernization as Ideology*; Latham, *The Right Kind of Revolution*.

Parsons argued in 1960, for example, "the most crucial factor at present in the widespread attempts at industrial development in the 'underdeveloped' societies" was the degree of their exposure to Western and "Judeo-Christian" cultural values. These, according to Parsons, oriented people toward more rational, individualistic, responsible, and self-disciplined approaches to life than did traditional cultural patterns in Africa and Asia.[76] Such cultural differences—not imperial conquest—helped explain why the West had industrialized first. The "resilient forces of tradition," as a 1955 *American Political Science Review* article called them, and "pre-Newtonian attitudes towards the physical world" (in Rostow's words), were the main thing holding back the developing world from achieving the higher level of civilization attained by the United States.[77]

Moving through the stages of development took time, the argument went, and thus frustration with that process made developing societies particularly vulnerable to the temptation to seek what another sociologist, Daniel Lerner, called "new routes and risky bypasses."[78] The most worrisome of these was, of course, communism. In the eyes of modernization theorists, therefore, cultural underdevelopment was the cause of material underdevelopment. The appeal of communism in the Global South was not due to a history of conquest and exploitation. It was instead a consequence of the immaturity of non-European societies, whose people were looking for an easy way out of the hard work of reaching modernity the right way. Such clearly prejudiced and infantilizing views of the peoples of the Global South were born of, and reinforced, well-established and widespread attitudes in the US governing class toward the non-European world. Eisenhower told his National Security Council in a 1957 meeting on Lebanon, for example, that "Arab thinking" was based in "violence, emotion, and ignorance," an argument that would not have been entirely out of place in a contemporary sociologist's journal article about culture and the stages of development.[79] At its most optimistic, however, modernization theory also offered the possibility that the United States could—and, indeed, had an obligation to—help the underdeveloped world transcend its supposed backwardness and reach what Rostow called the "takeoff stage." This could be done by transferring technology, expertise, and massive amounts of foreign aid to the developing country in question. Modernization theorists were aware of what readers of this book no doubt recognize: these arguments have much in common with those that justified imperialism in the late nineteenth and early twentieth centuries. However,

---

[76] Latham, *The Right Kind of Revolution*, 46–7.
[77] Latham, *The Right Kind of Revolution*, 49.
[78] Latham, *The Right Kind of Revolution*, 47.
[79] Douglas Little, *American Orientalism: The United States and the Middle East since 1945*, 3rd edition (Chapel Hill: University of North Carolina Press, 2008), 27.

mid-century experts felt that while imperialists did not always "optimize the development of the pre-conditions for takeoff," as Rostow put it, their better-informed Cold War successors could do just that.[80]

Modernization and related ideas about development thus became part of a broader effort by the United States to win over the decolonizing world to the United States' "side" in the Cold War. This was in one part a program of "public diplomacy," an effort to win "hearts and minds" to the United States through spreading a positive public image of the United States and a negative one of the Soviet Union. Organizations like the US Information Agency (established by Eisenhower in 1953) and the Fulbright Scholars program (a 1946 product of the Truman years), were designed to help spread American cultural products and values across the Global South—an approach perhaps best exemplified by State Department-funded tours for Dizzy Gillespie, Louis Armstrong, and other musicians dubbed "jazz ambassadors" for the United States.[81] While one can doubt the "persuasiveness" of such campaigns, "their pervasiveness was inarguable" as the historian Jason C. Parker has put it.[82]

Material support for development also came along with these propaganda campaigns, first in the form of the "Point Four" program of financial and technical assistance announced by Truman in 1949. While the funding for the program remained trivial when compared to the scale of the Marshall Plan (a mere $27 million when finally appropriated in 1950), it firmly established development aid as one of the four cornerstones of the US anticommunist effort (along with the UN, the Marshall Plan, and NATO).[83] Funding for development projects expanded during the Eisenhower years, but it was not until the John F. Kennedy administration (1961–63) that modernization became the center of American outreach to the Global South. The Peace Corp, for example, established in 1961, was an undertaking that combined modernization and public diplomacy, sending out young Americans to help with development-related projects across the decolonizing world.[84] The most ambitious modernization program of the Kennedy years was the Alliance for Progress, a $20 billion dollar plan for development aid to Latin America. The Alliance was intended, as Kennedy put it, "to demonstrate to the entire world that man's unsatisfied aspiration for economic progress and social justice can be best achieved by free men

---

[80]Latham, *The Right Kind of Revolution*, 53.
[81]See: Jason C. Parker, *Hearts, Minds, Voices: U.S. Cold War Public Diplomacy and the Formation of the Third World* (New York: Oxford University Press, 2016) and Penny M. Von Eschen, *Satchmo Blows Up the World: Jazz Ambassadors Play the Cold War* (Cambridge, MA: Harvard University Press, 2006).
[82]Parker, *Hearts, Minds, Voices*, 3.
[83]Latham, *Right Kind of Revolution*, 10–11, 31–2.
[84]Latham, *Modernization as Ideology*, 109–50.

working within a framework of democratic institutions."⁸⁵ That is, Latin Americans could reach modernity best by aligning with the United States, not the Soviet Union.

All these efforts to shape and control the course of decolonization through means other than force ran into considerable headwinds. To start with, having so recently gained independence, much of the decolonizing world was skeptical of the bipolar Cold War framework offered by both the United States and the Soviet Union. They had little desire to curtail their new independence by falling in line behind one or the other superpower. This was made clear at the first major summit of decolonized states: the 1955 Afro-Asian Conference in Bandung, Indonesia. Sponsored by Burma, India, Indonesia, Pakistan, and Sri Lanka, the meeting invited twenty-nine countries, most with a history of foreign rule. While not all the attendees were neutral in the Cold War, the conference's final communique rejected the "present state of international tension with its danger of an atomic world war" all the same. They demanded instead a reformed international system "free from mistrust and fear."⁸⁶ These sentiments reflected the intentions of some of the most prominent leaders in attendance, in particular Indonesian President Sukarno, India's Prime Minister Jawaharlal Nehru, and Egypt's Gamal Abdel Nasser. All, as the historian H.W. Brands has written, wanted "to avoid ... having simply to react to the moves of the major powers" like the United States.⁸⁷ Such Cold War "neutralism"—as Americans often called it—routinely outraged US policymakers, particularly during the Eisenhower administration. John Foster Dulles, for example, dismissed neutralism as "an immoral and shortsighted conception."⁸⁸ Such statements obscured a somewhat more nuanced US policy response, one that evolved with time and changed country by country. Indian neutralism, for example, was tolerated by Washington, while that of Nasser's Egypt was much more frustrating— Eisenhower himself condemned the Egyptian leader as a mere "puppet" of the Soviets.⁸⁹ By the Kennedy years, American policymakers had also learned to better navigate the postcolonial desire for an independent foreign policy. Yet the tension between aspirations for independence and the United States' desire for anti-communist conformity still remained.

---

⁸⁵Stephen G. Rabe, *The Most Dangerous Area in the World: John F. Kennedy Confronts Communist Revolution in Latin America* (Chapel Hill: University of North Carolina Press, 1999), 3.
⁸⁶See: "Final Communique of the Asian-African Conference," April 24, 1955, Centre virtuel de la connaissance sur l'Europe, University of Luxembourg, https://www.cvce.eu/en/obj/final_communique_of_the_asian_african_conference_of_bandung_24_april_1955-en-676237bd-72f7-471f-949a-88b6ae513585.html.
⁸⁷H.W. Brands, *The Specter of Neutralism: The United States and the Emergence of the Third World, 1947–1960* (New York: Columbia University Press, 1989), 314.
⁸⁸Brands, *Specter of Neutralism*, 5.
⁸⁹Brands, *Specter of Neutralism*, 308–16.

The United States had other baggage to overcome as well. In addition to its close relationship with the European colonial powers, American credibility in the Global South was also undermined by the United States' own long history of discrimination toward people of color. This was an issue regularly in the news in the mid-1950s, thanks to the emergence of the Civil Rights Movement and the US Supreme Court's 1954 *Brown v. Board of Education* decision against "Jim Crow" segregation in public schools. For a country attempting to suggest it was leading the "free world," the regular global headlines about discrimination and violence against peaceful Black protesters in the US South were clearly problematic—particularly since US diplomats had also worked tirelessly to ensure that UN human rights conventions lacked enough teeth to challenge America's domestic racial hierarchy.[90] On the whole, the close relationship between the United States and the global regime of white supremacy established by imperialism tended to taint American appeals abroad. This led to efforts by Washington to try and change the narrative. It was around this time, for example, that the two openly racist and imperialist statues discussed in our introduction—*The Rescue* and *The Discovery of America*—were removed from their prominent perches outside the US Capitol and never restored. They stood as symbols of an imperial narrative of American development which, though accurate in its own way, was no longer convenient to foreground. Despite Eisenhower's own misgivings about desegregation, meanwhile, the same Cold War context also caused him on occasion to take strenuous action against racial discrimination, as when he deployed the 101st Airborne to Little Rock, Arkansas, to enforce a desegregation order in 1957.[91]

Perhaps the greatest problem for the US effort to control the global process of decolonization, however, was its own hierarchically organized international economic order. Because it preserved the existing hierarchies of the imperial age—and, indeed, because the United States had reinforced those hierarchies by aiding the reconstruction of Western Europe and Japan first, before offering development assistance to the Global South— the US-backed system put significant barriers in the way of Third World states seeking to become wealthy via industrialization. US, European, and Japanese manufacturers dominated international markets, while First World interests also controlled access to much of the world's raw materials as well. As empire receded, US and European companies— ranging, for example, from the Anglo-Iranian Oil Company in Iran to the United Fruit Company in Guatemala—remained behind, controlling

---

[90]See: Carol Anderson, *Eyes off the Prize: The United Nations and the African American Struggle for Human Rights, 1944–1955* (Cambridge: Cambridge University Press, 2003).
[91]See the discussion of the relationship between the Cold War and Civil Rights in: Mary Dudziak, *Cold War Civil Rights: Race and the Image of American Democracy* (Princeton: Princeton University Press, 2000).

considerable chunks of the Global South's natural resources. Though the GATT process would lower trade barriers over time, US and European tariffs on outside industrial goods remained relatively high well into the 1960s, making it challenging for Third World manufacturers to compete. On the whole, once significant US aid began to flow south, the paths to global market share had narrowed considerably. Those countries—like Taiwan, Singapore, and South Korea—that were eventually able to take advantage of tariff reductions following the GATT "Kennedy Round" of trade negotiations (1964–67) and penetrate foreign markets with their industrial goods were beneficiaries of uniquely fortuitous circumstances. In most other cases—even for large, resource-endowed countries like India—it made most sense for local industrial interests not to challenge foreign manufacturers, producing for local markets instead, which prevented widespread industrialization and wealth creation.[92]

Indeed, modernization theory was fundamentally flawed in part because it often—if only implicitly—divided the world into separate states which seemed to exist in isolation from each other, contained within their own development histories. This made little sense when imperial globalization had long since established a "global economy"—a world-system—that tied together much of the world's markets, at least in the sense that supranational economic structures and patterns shaped which communities got rich and which did not. Due to US manufacturing dominance (and aid program requirements) American assistance money regularly financed purchases of US-made goods rather than driving manufacturing growth elsewhere. This was particularly the case in the US-dominated Western Hemisphere, where cash would flow out from Washington as development aid and then back into private American hands to purchase US products. This is not to say that the core-periphery structure of the global economy was the only barrier to Third World economic growth—it was not—but that US development spending was unlikely to produce results without the kind of global economic reforms hinted at in the long-abandoned ITO Charter. The same structural issue applied at a more local level as well. Because the United States wanted to support leaders who it saw as responsible—that is, those who resisted communism or any reform remotely approaching it—American aid ended up bolstering existing structures of wealth and power. This in turn stymied development. Even the Alliance for Progress, which was in principle committed to generating equitable growth through local institutional changes such as land reform, failed to deliver on those promises because of the focus on fighting communism and the left. In Brazil, for example, as Felipe P. Loureiro writes, "not even a single dollar loan coming from

---

[92]Vivek Chibber, *Locked in Place: State-Building and Late Industrialization in India* (Princeton: Princeton University Press, 2003), 1–12, 222–43.

USAID ... was provided to Brazilian states governed by what U.S. officials considered to be leftist ... politicians."[93] These, of course, were precisely the types of Brazilian politicians most likely to institute the egalitarian land reforms necessary for broader economic growth and "takeoff." As a result, US aid not only failed to produce the growth modernization theory looked for, it often hindered it—helping in this case to destabilize the democratically elected government of center-left President João Goulart (in office: 1961–64), leading to a military coup.[94]

That outcome was not wholly unappealing to Washington, which tended to take a dim view of modernization programs that didn't closely follow American prescriptions, particularly when they involved land reform or nationalizations. The United States had thus quietly supported the Brazilian coup's plotters and would establish a close relationship with the dictatorship that followed, despite occasional public handwringing about the importance of democracy.[95] In fact, despite the US rhetorical commitment to democracy being a key part of what made the "free world" free, support for dictators who upheld American interests was a regular feature of postwar US foreign policy, a globalized carryover from the Good Neighbor era. To that was added a renewed American willingness to directly intervene in the Global South when it was perceived as necessary. That doesn't mean things hadn't changed from the age of imperialism—they had—for these interventions no longer involved any hint of a formal surrender of sovereignty. Instead, the United States, during the Cold War, deployed troops to support *independent* allies. This was the case during the Korean War, for example, where an American-led UN force protected the regime of South Korean strongman Syngman Rhee from invasion by the communist North.[96]

In Indochina, the United States pushed the French to transfer power to local rulers seen as friendly to Western interests, as with the short-lived puppet "State of Vietnam," nominally under the rule of Bao Dai. When it became clear that even puppet French rule (armed and financed by the United States) was no longer tenable—thanks to the communist Viet Minh's victory in the 1954 Battle of Dien Bien Phu—Eisenhower stepped in, supporting Ngo Dinh Diem's autocratic rule

---

[93] Felipe P. Loureiro, "Making the Alliance for Progress Serve the Few: U.S. Economic Aid to Cold War Brazil (1961–1964)," *Journal of Cold War Studies* 25, no. 1 (2023): 168–207.
[94] Loureiro, "Making the Alliance for Progress Serve the Few," 168–73, 205–7.
[95] Mark Atwood Lawrence, *The End of Ambition: The United States and the Third World in the Vietnam Era* (Princeton: Princeton University Press, 2021), 106–40, 294–7.
[96] On the Korean War see: Bruce Cumings, *The Korean War: A History* (New York: Modern Library, 2010); William Stueck, *Rethinking the Korean War: A New Diplomatic and Strategic History* (Princeton: Princeton University Press, 2002).

over the southern Republic of Vietnam. With firm American political and financial support, Diem ignored the provisions of the 1954 Geneva Accords that called for elections to reunify Vietnam—all expected Ho Chi Minh to win, delivering the country to communism—and attempted to establish a permanent anti-communist bastion in the south.[97] By 1959, several hundred US military personnel had been deployed to advise the new South Vietnamese army in its fight against a growing anti-Diem insurgency, with two Americans dying in a July guerrilla attack on a base outside Bien Hoa, north of Saigon. These were the first of what would eventually become more than 58,000 American causalities in Vietnam.[98] America's relationship with South Vietnam was in one sense clearly colonial, but in another was also markedly different in how it preserved the technical independence of Diem's regime.

When overt intervention would not do, the United States turned to a new tool for exercising its self-assumed veto over Global South sovereignty: covert action. In 1947, the United States had begun to build what became a sprawling civilian and military intelligence "community"—as it is often called today—with the establishment of the Central Intelligence Agency. Eisenhower, in particular, made regular use of the CIA, often to protect US or First World economic interests. In 1953, for example, the CIA and British intelligence collaborated together to orchestrate the overthrow of the democratically elected government of Mohammad Mosaddegh in Iran. An anti-communist nationalist, Mosaddegh had led the effort to nationalize the British-owned Anglo-Iranian Oil Company (which controlled the bulk of Iran's oil production but paid the host country only a modest fee in return).[99] Seeking to control the country's oil wealth to help finance its modernization, Mossadegh thus ran afoul of Washington's "my way or the highway" view of how economic development should proceed. Iran's Shah, whose power was restored by the coup, told Kermit Roosevelt Jr.—head of the operation for the CIA—that he owed his "throne to God, my people, my army ... and to you."[100]

While the CIA's role in the Iranian coup was not publicly acknowledged for decades, Roosevelt (Theodore's grandson) was, in effect, quietly extending a new Roosevelt Corollary over the world on Eisenhower's behalf. More covert interventions soon followed. In 1954, the CIA overthrew the democratically elected president of Guatemala, Jacobo Arbenz. The second

---

[97] Fredrik Logevall, *Embers of War: The Fall of an Empire and the Making of America's Vietnam* (New York: Random House, 2012), 334–701.
[98] Logevall, *Embers of War*, 699–701.
[99] Ali Rahnema, *Behind the 1953 Coup in Iran: Thugs, Turncoats, Soldiers, and Spooks* (Cambridge: Cambridge University Press, 2015).
[100] Rahnema, *Behind the 1953 Coup*, 5.

in a line of reformist presidents—elected after an armed rebellion ended the rule of US-backed dictator Jorge Ubico in 1944—Arbenz had implemented land reform that threatened the holdings of the United Fruit Company, breaking the rules for American-approved modernization and setting off alarm bells in Washington. Already fearful of Arbenz's close ties to the Guatemalan communist party, the Eisenhower administration decided it could not risk honoring the wishes of Guatemalan voters and instead sent in the secret agents—a new pro-US military dictator was soon installed, setting off decades of violence and political instability.[101] A few years later, and north and east across the Caribbean, the United States once again attempted to exercise its covert veto. When Fidel Castro's communist July 26th Movement ended Batista's second stint as Cuba's president in 1959—threatening the extensive US property holdings on the island—Eisenhower instituted trade sanctions designed to cripple Cuba's economy, and the CIA began to plot what became, under Kennedy, the failed "Bay of Pigs" effort to overthrow Castro in 1961.[102]

Meanwhile that year, the number of US military advisors in Vietnam reached into the thousands for the first time, as the effort to sustain an independent, anti-communist South slowly grew in importance to US policymakers. In Vietnam, all the various methods the United States used to try and control the process of decolonization converged. It first supported the continuation of European rule, as we've seen, before turning to pro-Western anti-communists like Diem. In 1960, anti-Diem insurgents in the South formed the "National Liberation Front" [NLF]—which the South Vietnamese Army and its American allies called the "Viet Cong"—in an effort to overthrow the regime and reunify the country. By 1961, the NLF was killing hundreds every month, revealing the weakness of Diem's rule in the countryside. As his unpopular regime began to falter—and Diem himself proved to be stubbornly independent—the Kennedy administration then turned to a CIA-supported military coup. Diem's November 1963 ouster and assassination (Kennedy approved the former, not the latter) did little to stabilize the situation. The government's legitimacy among the South Vietnamese population continued to deteriorate and the power of the NLF-led insurgency grew. After Kennedy's own November 1963 assassination (mere weeks after Diem's), President Lyndon Johnson (in office: 1963–69) turned to the only option left: deploying American combat troops. The first waded ashore at Da Nang in March of 1965, with more than 150,000 deployed by the end of the year and more than half a million by the end of 1968. Operation "Rolling Thunder" kicked off the same

---

[101]See: Piero Gleijeses, *Shattered Hope: The Guatemalan Revolution and the United States, 1944–1954* (Princeton: Princeton University Press, 1991); Richard H. Immerman, *The CIA in Guatemala: The Foreign Policy of Intervention* (Austin: University of Texas Press, 1982).
[102]Ferrer, *Cuba*, 275–368.

FIGURE 13 *Soldiers of the Army of the Republic of Vietnam—equipped with American-supplied weapons and aircraft—question a captured NLF guerrilla in the Tuy Hoa Region, 1965.*

month, as US warplanes began bombing targets in North Vietnam. By 1968, that campaign would kill tens of thousands of Vietnamese civilians, dropping more explosives than were deployed against Japan during the entire Pacific War.[103]

All of America's efforts to control events in the Global South after the Second World War could, of course, be understood through the lens of anti-communism and the Cold War. From Truman to Johnson, US leaders believed they were defending the free world against what they saw as an implacable communist threat to not just American interests, but to the progress of humanity. One might, therefore, be inclined to see postwar interventionism as something peculiar to the rivalry with the Soviet Union. In many ways, it was. However, in the context of what we have been studying in this book, US policy in the decolonizing world also clearly fits into a much older pattern, one where Americans saw themselves as

---

[103]The literature on the Vietnam War is, of course, quite extensive. For a good recent account of the war in the context of the history of Vietnam itself, see: Christopher Goscha, *Vietnam: A New History* (New York: Basic Books, 2016) especially 237–339. For more focus on the North Vietnamese perspective see: Pierre Asselin, *Vietnam's American War: A History* (New York: Cambridge University Press, 2018). On US decision-making during the "long 1964" run up to the deployment of combat troops, see: Frederik Logevall, *Choosing War: The Lost Chance for Peace and the Escalation of the War in Vietnam* (Berkley: University of California Press, 1999).

entitled to interfere in societies—from Native Americans in the nineteenth century, to Filipinos and Latin Americans in the early twentieth—who were seen as on the wrong side of history or in need of American guidance. The United States was continuing, as it always had, to police its perceived sphere of interest in the world-system. That sphere had now taken on global dimensions. As we will see in our remaining chapters, even the mounting casualties in Vietnam would prove insufficient to permanently redirect the United States from this course.

CHAPTER SEVEN

"A Structure of Economic Control": The United States and an Independent Global South

Held from March 23rd to June 16th, 1964 in Geneva, the first United Nations Conference on Trade and Development (UNCTAD I) was, as the historian Edgar J. Dosman has written, "the international event of" the year.[1] One of the largest international conferences ever held, it hosted four thousand delegates and attracted figures as diverse as the Marxist revolutionary Che Guevara (nattily attired in a pinstriped suit and already a global celebrity) and five emissaries of Pope John XXIII (who sang a papal mass to open the conference).[2] As a representative from the World Bank put it, even "old hands at such ... conferences are unanimous in saying they'd never seen such a thing before."[3] Indeed, they had not, for UNCTAD I represented something new in world history: a truly international conference on the global economy, one where the agenda was set largely by the world's poorest states. Many of these, of course, had only just gained independence from colonial rule and thus had not been represented at the foundational meetings for the postwar order held in the 1940s. Their goal, and the goal of UNCTAD, was therefore relatively simple: bring greater fairness to a world economy that was otherwise governed by institutions (like the IMF, the World Bank, and GATT) that most of the world saw as "rich men's clubs" ruled by the United States and its industrialized allies in Europe and

---

[1] Edgar J. Dosman, *The Life and Times of Raul Prebisch, 1901–1986* (Montreal: McGill University Press, 2008), 398.
[2] Dosman, *Raul Prebisch*, 398–9.
[3] Dosman, *Raul Prebisch*, 399.

Japan.⁴ The governments of Latin America, Asia, and Africa came together in a formal caucus—the Group of 77 states or "G-77"— and used their numerical majority to advance their own collective agenda for the first time, challenging the hierarchical structure of the world established by imperial globalization.

UNCTAD I proved but the opening salvo of a two-decade-long effort by the G-77 (whose membership eventually swelled to well over 100) to wrest some control of the global economy away from the industrialized North. Reaching its most radical point with a 1974 UN General Assembly resolution calling for the establishment of a "New International Economic Order" (NIEO), the G-77's campaign used one-state, one-vote international fora like the UN General Assembly to advance a vision of a world without the hierarchies formed in the imperial age. The NIEO, as Adom Getachew writes, proposed "a radical form of economic and political equality between states," one which would make more real the supposed equality granted by sovereignty, offering an economic independence to match the new political independence of the postcolonial world.⁵ Though less well remembered in the United States than the Cold War challenge from the Soviet Union, the G-77's campaign for global economic system reform was an equally direct rejection of the US-backed liberal world order, one that caused significant concern in Washington—and anger among the American public—at the time. Emerging at a moment where American power appeared on the wane, the G-77's program briefly appeared poised to bring about real change, allowing some to imagine a future where the global economic system might begin to move beyond the hierarchies of empire.

The G-77's challenge, and the US response, will be the focus of this next chapter in our study of the United States and the ends of empire. As we will see, despite establishing institutions like the UN to reflect the popular will of the world's governments, US policymakers and voters disliked when those institutions revealed perspectives on world order that ran contrary to their own. While some—most notably, Henry Kissinger—briefly considered some minor accommodation of the Global South's demands, rejecting them outright proved more popular. A "New Right" soon ascended to power in the United States, one which explicitly rejected the Global South's right to shape global economic governance.⁶ Though repackaged in a new language that stressed human rights and economic freedom, the language of civilization remained the means for justifying this denial of true sovereignty for the decolonizing world. By the mid-1980s, an alternative new international economic order was being established instead, one which made little accommodation for

---

⁴Dosman, *Raul Prebisch*, 393.
⁵Getachew, *Worldmaking after Empire*, 144.
⁶Sean T. Byrnes, *Disunited Nations: U.S. Foreign Policy, Anti-Americanism, and the Rise of the New Right* (Baton Rouge: Louisiana State University Press, 2021).

equality—or the historic role of imperial violence in the building of the global economic system.

The Rise of the G-77

As we saw in the last chapter, after the Second World War, the United States had attempted to rebuild the international system along more liberal lines, seeking to leave behind the world of competitive imperialism that had caused the two world wars. While this "New Deal for the World" vision was in one part truly reformist—advancing world order toward a model of cooperative equality between the world's nation states— it also accommodated the continuation of empire and hierarchy. It intentionally reserved special powers for the United States and its closest allies in institutions like the UN Security Council, the IMF, and the World Bank. This US plan for the postwar world immediately confronted two interrelated challenges: the arrival of the Cold War—and the emergence of an alternative, Soviet-led, communist vision of international relations— and the unexpectedly swift collapse of Europe's Asian and Middle Eastern empires. These two developments resulted in a globe seemingly fragmented into three "worlds": the US-dominated "first," the communist "second," and a decolonizing "third" world. The Soviet "Second World" represented to American eyes a nightmare alternative vision of the human future, while the "Third World" held a possible swing vote, one which might be cast for the Soviets, or for the United States, or for something else altogether. As a result, the US government had used its influence and power to try to shape the course of decolonization, working to ensure that the Third World either aligned itself with the United States, or pursued a moderate form of neutralism.

"By the early 1960s," as the historian Ryan Irwin writes, "the United States had reason to view its efforts as a success."[7] Though there had initially been severe setbacks—including the Soviet development of atomic weapons and the "fall of China" to Mao's communist party—in 1960, one could argue that communism was largely contained (at the cost of the constant danger of nuclear war, to be sure, but contained all the same). Meanwhile, to again borrow from Irwin, "Washington still shaped the agenda of the [U.N.] General Assembly, the International Court, and the various economic agencies of the Bretton Woods system."[8] Third World neutralism was certainly an annoyance to US policymakers at times—particularly in the Middle East, where Nasser's Pan-Arab nationalism had a notably pro-Soviet

---

[7]Ryan Irwin, *Gordian Knot: Apartheid and the Unmaking of the Liberal World Order* (New York: Oxford University Press 2012), 11.
[8]Irwin, *Gordian Knot*, 11.

cast—but it hardly represented a real challenge to the US-led international order.

The decolonization of much of Africa—which happened swiftly over the first few years of the 1960s—transformed this picture considerably.[9] The independence of more than forty new countries, almost all majority Black, fundamentally remade the community of nations, firmly establishing a non-European majority of sovereign states. Almost overnight, institutions like the General Assembly became considerably larger, more diverse, and less amenable to American influence. The new majority in the General Assembly was, of course, as diverse a collection of states as the world could produce, drawing as it did from Africa, Asia, and Latin America. Some states were relatively pro-American, others leaned toward the Soviets (positions that could change as individual governments came and went), while many more professed a form of Bandung-style neutralism.[10]

Nevertheless, a distinctly Third World agenda began to emerge over the following decade, one which—though it rejected the Cold War's bipolar framework—was more of a challenge to the US policy than that of the Soviet Union. This Third World solidarity drew in part on common histories of imperial subjugation as well as hostility to the concepts of white racial and cultural supremacy that had undergirded imperial conquest. Those experiences were very different state by state. The Latin Americans, for example, had been independent for more than a century, subject instead in the twentieth century to the various forms of informal US imperialism we have been discussing in this book. What truly helped tie together the G-77 therefore was the peripheral place imperial globalization had left them in the world economy. As the Jamaican politician (and eventual Prime Minister), Michael Manley would write: imperialism and violence had built a global economic structure where much of the Global South had been "geared to produce not what was needed for themselves or for exchange for mutual advantage, but rather ... to be the producers of what other people [in the Global North] needed."[11] Tanzanian President Julius Nyerere analogized the situation of the Third World in the global economy to that of the laboring classes in the industrializing economies of Europe a century earlier. The "poor nations," he wrote, "are now in the position of a worker in nineteenth century Europe" forced to sell their labor "at whatever price [they] could obtain for it."[12] It was both the sense and the reality of sharing this common position of unjust economic exploitation that ultimately underwrote the G-77's solidarity.

---

[9]Irwin, *Gordian Knot*, 11–12.
[10]For more on the Bandung Conference and the vision of world order it advanced see: Chapter 6.
[11]Getachew, *Worldmaking after Empire*, 152; Michael Manley, *The Poverty of Nations: Reflections on Underdevelopment and the World Economy* (London: Pluto Press, 1991), 13–14.
[12]Getachew, *Worldmaking after Empire*, 158.

At first, development economics and modernization seemed to offer the prospect of escaping the global working class, particularly if foreign aid and advice would flow from the Global North to the South. As we saw in the previous chapter, Cold War concerns and a lingering attachment to the New Deal pushed the United States to embrace just this perspective and provide just this type of aid. After all, the modernization narrative did little to threaten American interests. It merely required Third World states to pull themselves up by their bootstraps—perhaps with a handout or two—and develop into wealthy democracies, no dangerous global structural changes required. However, the failures of modernization theory had become manifest by the 1960s, particularly as a drop in global commodity prices began to hollow out G-77 economies mid-decade.[13] A new critique of the global economy thus came into focus and became the foundation of the G-77's work, one which appeared much more threatening to American interests. It didn't help matters either that this critique came from a US-inspired source: the work of Latin American activists, diplomats, and intellectuals. Having struggled for decades to find a way out from under North American economic dominance, Latin America's foreign offices and research institutions helped shape a new global movement against the liberal world order.[14] What emerged was "dependency theory." This theory was based on a recognition that, as Michael Manley wrote, the Global South was locked in "structures of economic control whose roots went as far back as the seventeenth century, to the mercantile system."[15]

States, it turned out, did not develop in isolation from each other but existed in a global economy—a world-system—that was structured in particular ways. This structure put the developing world at a two-fold disadvantage. First, much of the planet's wealth was already concentrated in the Global North—a concentration facilitated by the violence of imperialism. Those wealthy states also dominated the institutions of global governance set up after the war At the same time, their citizens and corporations also privately controlled large swaths of the world's natural resources. Second, most postcolonial economies were vulnerable to a global market for commodities that was at best unstable (commodity prices, and thus, Global South earnings, fluctuated relatively rapidly) and at worst biased in favor of industrial goods. One of the pioneers of dependency theory, the Argentine economist Raul Prebisch had in fact demonstrated just that: the terms of trade for the raw materials produced in the Global South—cotton, cocoa, fruit, tea, sisal, etc.—lost value relative to industrial goods over time.[16] As Nyerere would highlight in the mid-1970s, importing a tractor to Tanzania

---

[13]Getachew, *Worldmaking after Empire*, 146–51.
[14]Stella Krepp, "Fighting an Illiberal World Order: The Latin American Road to UNCTAD, 1948–1964," *Humanity* (Philadelphia, PA) 13, no. 1 (2022): 86–103.
[15]Getachew, *Worldmaking after Empire*, 157. Manley, *Poverty of Nations*, 24.
[16]For more on Prebisch and dependency theory see, Dosman, *Raul Prebisch*.

cost roughly 5.3 tons of sisal in 1965, but by 1972 it required a whopping 17.2 tons.[17] Altering this unbalanced global system thus required more than resource transfers from the industrialized world to the former colonies—the argument went—it required international institutions that would structure world trade in such a way as to balance out its naturally occurring inequities.

Beginning with a 1962 "Conference on Problems of Developing Countries" in Cairo, and then continuing with UNCTAD I—where Prebisch was made UNCTAD's first Secretary General—and the formation of the G-77 in 1964, the Third World countries in the UN began to advocate for this form of structural change. UNCTAD II and III would follow in 1968 and 1972, leading eventually to the banner year of 1974. That year, the Global South majority in the UN General Assembly passed both the Declaration on the Establishment of a New International Economic Order (along with its accompanying Program of Action) and the Charter of the Economic Rights and Duties of States (CERDS). These two resolutions laid out a vision for what historian Johanna Bockman has called a "socialist globalization," in contrast to the hierarchical, neocolonial, globalization of Bretton Woods.[18] This vision of globalization was also in contrast to the competitive, tariff-protected industrialization of the American System discussed in Chapter 4. The G-77 did not call for greater protectionism or cutting off developing economies from global trade but instead for greater liberalization of trade on terms that favored Third World development.[19] Accepting that the globalized world created by empire was an established fact, the NIEO called for making it fairer rather than just pulling it apart.

The program was thus focused on first granting more power to the Global South in determining the shape of the world economy, moving trade policy out of the weighted voting institutions of Bretton Woods and into the majority vote United Nations General Assembly. It then also called for establishing a "Generalized System of Preferences," replacing GATT-style reciprocal tariff reductions with a system that allowed the states in the developing world relatively unfettered access to First World markets while retaining the ability to protect their own economies from foreign goods. Another key element was a proposal for a "Common Fund for Commodities," a UN run, majority vote institution that would pool raw materials and capital in order to moderate fluctuations in global commodity prices. Such a program would, in essence, put a financial safety-net under the commodity-based economies of the Global South.[20]

---

[17]Getachew, *Worldmaking after Empire*, 143.
[18]Johanna Bockman, "Socialist Globalization against Capitalist Neocolonialism: The Economic Ideas behind the New International Economic Order," *Humanity* (Philadelphia, PA) 6, no. 1 (2015): 109–28.
[19]Bockman, "Socialist Globalization," 112.
[20]See, Daunton, *Economic Government of the World*, 533–65. Getachew, *Worldmaking after Empire*, 160–71.

By the time the NIEO and CERDS resolutions were passed, the G-77's efforts in the UN had taken on something of an anti-American aspect. This was not because all the members of the G-77 were necessarily hostile to the United States or supported the Soviet Union. It was instead a natural response to the positition of the United States in the global heirarchy. To start, not only was the United States the clear leader and protector of the global economic system the G-77 wished to change, it was also seen as the key barrier to progress on three other issues that were of central concern to the Global South's majority: the US war in Vietnam, Apartheid in South Africa, and the Arab-Israeli conflict.

As to the first: by the early 1970s, US military support for South Vietnam's government had thoroughly undermined America's global reputation. Where many Americans saw a noble undertaking to protect South Vietnam from communist totalitarianism, much of the rest of the world saw instead an effort to bolster a puppet dictatorship of the United States, one which the technologically advanced US military could protect only by unleashing horrific violence on a largely agrarian people looking for freedom from foreign domination. The Vietnam War therefore became a channel by which older forms of Latin American resentment of US hegemony were given new global dimensions—a reality reflected by Guevara's pinstriped celebrity. His 1967 call for "many Vietnams" had a significant global resonance, not least in the Middle East, where Palestinian Poet Mahmoud Darwash announced in 1973 that "the torch has been passed from Vietnam to us."[21]

Darwash seeing a Palestinian common cause with Vietnam was itself a reflection of the United States' role in the Palestinian conflict with Israel, as the latter country also became a target of the Global South's ire in the late 1960s and early 1970s. The Arab-Israeli conflict emerged as part of the confused decolonization of Britain's "mandate" colony in Palestine. London's hasty 1948 exit had left unclear how power over the territory would be divided between a Jewish settler community set on establishing its own state and the region's historic population of Arab Palestinians. The war that followed left the new Jewish state of Israel in control of much of the mandate's territory, with Arab residents expelled from their lands and confined to enclaves then under Jordanian and Egyptian protection.[22] After a somewhat ambiguous relationship during the Eisenhower years, by the early 1960s the United States increasingly threw its support behind Israel—once again, intervening in a postcolonial struggle in order to support the local rulers seen as most

---

[21]See: Byrnes, *Disunited Nations*, 19–20; Paul Thomas Chamberlin, *The Global Offensive: The United States, the Palestinian Liberation Organization and the Making of the Post-Cold War Order* (New York: Oxford University Press, 2012), 1–42, 175–217.

[22]On the decolonization of Palestine see: Rashid Khalidi, *The Hundred Years's War on Palestine: A History of Settler Colonialism and Resistance, 1917–2017* (New York: Henry Holt and Company, 2020), 17–95.

amenable to US interests. Here, too, we see the United States picking the side that appeared more "civilized" in American eyes: the more European and democratically governed Jewish community.[23] Another decisive Israeli victory—this time in the 1967 Arab-Israeli War—subsequently gave the conflict a new aspect, as Israel was left occupying the Palestinian enclaves in the West Bank and the Gaza Strip.[24] Israel soon appeared to many—not just in the Arab world, but across the Global South—as a dominant regional power using American weapons to crush the self-determination of Palestinians. The cause of the Palestinians became a central preoccupation of the G-77, routinely resulting in an isolated and outvoted United States in the General Assembly, as well as regular use of the American veto in the Security Council.[25]

The United States' first-ever Security Council veto, however, came in 1970 not with regard to Palestine, but southern Africa, where two white supremacist regimes—in Southern Rhodesia (today's Zimbabwe) and South Africa—also drew the condemnation of the UN's majority. Race was already a key vulnerability in the United States' global effort to order the world, as we have seen. A regular feature of Soviet propaganda, America's long history of white supremacy was well known abroad and gained only greater salience as the Civil Rights Movement and urban race riots shook the country throughout the 1960s. US policymakers did little to help alter this image for most of the first two decades of the Cold War. Drawn almost exclusively from the ranks of white elites, US policymakers generally carried the biases common to their race and class, seeing the world through a racial hierarchy that associated greater and lesser degrees of civilized behavior with lighter and darker skin tones.[26] Therefore, their support for the continuation of European rule was both based on strategic motivations and prejudice, as was certainly the case in southern Africa. There the United States remained functionally allied with the white minority regime in South Africa, which maintained control of the country through its brutal system of racial Apartheid. South Africa was both a valuable strategic and economic partner for the United States and its Western European allies.

At first, its internal racial policies seemed a matter of small concern in the context of the global anti-communist crusade. African decolonization transformed Apartheid into a problem for US foreign policy, however, as the "African Group"—a caucus of the continent's states in the General Assembly—demanded stronger international intervention to end white rule in Pretoria. For a time during the Kennedy and Johnson administrations,

---

[23]This was despite widespread anti-Semitism in United States. See Little, *American Orientalism*.
[24]On the 1967 war see: Khalidi, *The Hundred Year's War*, 96–137.
[25]On the evolution of the Palestinian cause, see Chamberlin, *Global Offensive*.
[26]See: Thomas Borstelmann, *The Cold War and the Color Line: American Race Relations in the Global Arena* (Cambridge, MA: Harvard University Press, 2001).

the United States recognized a need to play ball on the issue.²⁷ When the African Group, with support of the broader G-77, passed a resolution for a voluntary arms embargo against South Africa in 1963, the United States announced its compliance. There was an understanding, as Ryan Irwin writes, "that U.S. hegemony flowed from the faith other nations placed in the United Nations," a faith that any American reticence to confront Apartheid undermined.²⁸ This recognition, however, was tempered by a desire to avoid empowering what appeared to the United States to be the most "radical" forces on the continent—as those most loudly calling for an end to foreign rule and white supremacy were most often those with the closest ties to communism. As a result, neither Kennedy nor Johnson was willing to go as far as the G-77 wanted in isolating South Africa, or in opposing the white minority regime in Southern Rhodesia.

The latter had emerged in 1965 from the chaos of Britain's withdrawal from its short-lived Central African Federation (an effort to retain control of several British southern African colonies that had dissolved under African Group pressure two years earlier) and soon became a major global issue itself. Johnson quickly joined the global majority in sanctioning the Rhodesians. The administration feared that the regime was so toxic it could, as one US policymaker put it: "lead to the downfall of responsible, friendly African governments." If they were seen as being too weak in the face of Rhodesian racism, moderates risked losing the political support of their people and eventual "replacement by radical elements" more forceful in pushing for majority rule.²⁹

Over the course of the period 1965–68, however, the Johnson administration grew less concerned with aiding moderate Africans and more restrained in confronting white supremacy in Africa, a position further cemented by the 1969 arrival of Richard M. Nixon to the White House.³⁰ Nixon's administration (1969–73) was initially deeply skeptical of G-77 initiatives and Kennedy-Johnson era efforts to accommodate them. The new President maintained sanctions on Rhodesia but kept open the US consulate there, while also rejecting sterner measures to end white rule. The G-77, however, increasingly demanded such measures, leading to a 1970 UN Security Council resolution that condemned the British for not using military force to depose the white Rhodesians, and an American veto. For nearly a quarter century, US influence in the UN was such that it had been able to avoid exercising this power—the Soviets, for example, had already done so dozens of times—but now that influence was waning.³¹

---

²⁷Irwin, *Gordian Knot*, 3–102.
²⁸Irwin, *Gordian Knot*, 95.
²⁹Irwin, *Gordian Knot*, 98–9.
³⁰Irwin, *Gordian Knot*, 187.
³¹Byrnes, *Disunited Nations*, 33.

The United States in Opposition

The early 1970s thus saw the convergence of a greater G-77 stridency in demanding transformation of the international system and a decreasing American willingness to partner in such a change. The key policy makers in the Nixon administration—Nixon himself and National Security Advisor, Henry Kissinger—in fact believed that American global hegemony was under strain because the United States had been offering *too many* promises of idealistic global transformation, not too little. In a book written during his time as a professor at Harvard, for example, Kissinger argued that the US role in the Global South was "more complicated than engaging in a popularity contest for their favor." Rather than seeking "illusory propaganda victories," Kissinger argued, the United States should instead unashamedly assert its interests.[32] Nixon agreed, dismissing—in a 1967 speech—modernization efforts like the Alliance for Progress as a waste of resources, while suggesting that US aid programs should be more closely tied to advancing American priorities. Nixon also argued that the UN had been made increasingly irrelevant precisely because it now represented the views of the decolonizing world. Some of the "independent countries in black [*sic*] Africa," he complained, "have populations less than the state of Maryland" yet had a UN vote equal to the United States. Worse yet, they did not share American values. "None," Nixon argued, "had a representative government by our standards."[33] The message here was clear: the UN was being taken over by non-white, non-democratic—i.e., uncivilized—societies, in a clear affront to US-backed hierarchies. The UN, and massive modernization programs, were in Nixon's mind no longer useful tools for maintaining American hegemony (if they ever had been).

The Nixon administration instead focused on defending American interests as they understood them, without concern for whether their moves appealed to global sentiment or bolstered American ideological and symbolic hegemony. Nixon also openly embraced dictatorships that were willing to toe the American line—an approach that came to be called the "Nixon Doctrine." This involved asserting US influence in the Global South by supporting local strongmen—like the Shah in Iran or the Saigon regime in Vietnam—with weapons and financial support rather than American troops (and without any American demands for their political reform).[34] In one respect, this was a notable change from the reformist impulses of the New Deal for the World vision—particularly in its most idealistic,

---

[32] Byrnes, *Disunited Nations*, 29.
[33] Richard M. Nixon, "Speech to the Bohemian Club," July 29, 1967, Document 2, Volume 1, *Foreign Relations of the U.S. 1969-1976*, https://history.state.gov/historicaldocuments/frus1969-76v01/d2; Byrnes, *Disunited Nations*, 27–8.
[34] Byrnes, *Disunited Nations*, 30.

modernizing, Kennedy-era form—abandoning any real pretense at positive global transformation beyond a basic toleration of political decolonization. In another, there was no change at all. The United States had long since learned to use authoritarian rulers as partners in maintaining hierarchies in the global periphery, first in Latin America in the interwar period, and then globally after 1945. Whatever idealistic impulses had animated the Kennedy and early Johnson administrations had already faded before Nixon took office. As we saw in the last chapter, for example, Johnson had supported the coup that brought the military to power in Brazil and continued to support it even as the generals thoroughly undermined democracy in the country. The main difference with Nixon was he, "showed little inclination to anguish"—as Mark Atwood Lawrence puts it—about a Global South ally's relationship to democracy, even admitting to Kissinger in 1969 that he in fact did "favor dictatorships" as tools of American power.[35] Nixon's plan to maintain and reinforce a wavering American hegemony was therefore more about shifting, rather than transforming, longstanding US approaches to the world.

That US dominance was under strain—and for reasons well beyond anything the Global South was doing in the UN—was itself without question. The Vietnam War was naturally part of the story. Already deeply divisive and the source of significant protests, by 1968, the war was widely seen in the United States as a mistake best ended as soon as possible. Nearly 17,000 US troops died that year as Johnson withdrew from the presidential race under the pressure. Despite campaign promises to end the war in victory, Nixon entered office without a clear plan for doing so, and so casualties continued to mount (with another approximately 18,000 US service personnel killed in 1969–70) and protests grew in campuses and cities across the nation and the world.[36] Protests against the war were also joined by protests against racism, as the Johnson-era civil rights reforms unwound Jim Crow in the American South but did not bring an end to racial tension.[37] A wave of racial violence gripped American cities in the mid-to-late 1960s—including an April 1968 uprising on Johnson's doorstep in Washington—bringing attention to the heavily policed *de facto* segregation in the American North and West which went along with the *de jure* segregation in its South.[38] Many abroad saw a connection between the hierarchy the United States was attempting to police in the world, and the one it enforced at home, efforts that—as we have seen since the start of our story in this book—did in fact

---

[35]Lawrence, *End to Ambition*, 295.
[36]See: Marilyn Young, *The Vietnam Wars: 1945–1990* (New York: Harper Perennial, 1991).
[37]On the global protest movement see: Jeremi Suri, *Power and Protest: Global Revolution and the Rise of Détente* (Cambridge, MA: Harvard University Press, 2003).
[38]On 1960s urban uprisings and segregation in the north see: Thomas J. Sugrue, *Sweet Land of Liberty: The Forgotten Struggle for Civil Rights in the North* (New York: Random House, 2008).

have common historical origins. In general, the war and domestic political chaos, and the US government's failure to control them, undermined American claims to moral leadership abroad as well as its reputation for competency and problem-solving. It would also lead to revelations about the government's routine mendacity in its quest for power. The 1971 release of the "Pentagon Papers" proved that the White House had long been lying about the war in Vietnam (claiming it was winning while knowing it was losing).[39] Trust in government was only undermined further by the Watergate Scandal (forcing Nixon's resignation in 1974), and a series of revelations regarding the misdeeds of US intelligence services prompted by high-profile Congressional investigations in 1975. When South Vietnam finally collapsed in 1975, it punctuated a disastrous decade for US political stability and its reputation abroad.[40]

The problems with American hegemony ran deeper than that, however. While still the wealthiest society in the world, the United States was no longer in the same dominant economic position it had been in 1945. After partnering with the British Empire and the Soviet Union to destroy much of the world's non-American, industrial core during the Second World War, the United States had then helped to rebuild it through the Marshall Plan. By the 1960s, Western Europe and Japan had begun to catch up to the United States thanks to decades of spectacular economic growth—the *"wirtschaftswunder"* or "economic miracle," as it was known in West Germany. This European and Japanese recovery and the increased economic competition it produced, along with slowing American growth and US overseas spending (in part to finance military deployments), all put significant pressure on the Bretton Woods system. Left teetering by the early 1970s, diplomatic efforts to rebalance its gold-dollar peg failed, and so Nixon—more concerned with the domestic economy than with international finance—brought Bretton Woods to an end. He suspended the dollar's convertibility to gold (temporarily in 1971, permanently in 1973), devaluing the dollar to improve American competitiveness. A clear assertion of American economic power in one sense, the "Nixon Shock,"—as it was called—was also widely seen as a sign of American weakness. It disrupted the relationship between the United States, Western Europe, and Japan for a time—further contributing to the idea that US hegemony was on the wane. As Nixon Treasury John Connelly put it, "the foreigners are out to screw us" so "it's our job to screw them first."[41]

---

[39]See: Daniel Ellsberg, *Secrets: A Memoir of Vietnam and the Pentagon Papers* (New York: Penguin Books, 2002).
[40]Byrnes, *Disunited Nations*, 112.
[41]For quote, see: Levy, *Ages of American Capitalism*, 553. On Bretton Woods and the Nixon Shock see: Daunton, *Economic Government of the World*, 461–91; Eichengreen, *Globalizing Capital*, 119–35. Levy, *Ages of American Capitalism*, 551–60.

American preeminence also appeared eroded because of economic growth in the communist world. While the Soviet Union and its Eastern European satellites were never as wealthy as their opponents in the West, their command economies had managed to produce their own economic miracles, reaching their own—poorer—form of industrial modernity. In the Soviet Union, these decades of growth had underwrote the development of a military-industrial complex that allowed it to keep pace, and even project a degree of parity, with that of the United States, no small accomplishment. Though far from capable of projecting power abroad the way the United States could, the USSR was in the 1970s a nuclear peer able to keep up appearances as the world's second superpower.[42] All together then, the United States no longer had—and no longer appeared to have—the same dominant global economic position it had possessed in 1945.

Even more significant than this story of growth, however, was one of stagnation. The United States might have been better able to manage its relative decline compared to its competition if not for the fact that the entire industrialized world—both communist and capitalist—entered a period of stagnating growth at much the same time in the late 1960s. The factors driving the postwar economic miracle, it turned out, were unique and time limited. A product of war-related reconstruction, cheap energy, and the widespread adoption of industrial consumer goods, the explosive growth rates of the postwar years were, once exhausted, never to return.[43] Both East and West had premised their postwar social contracts on the idea that never-ending rates of growth meant that standards of living would continuously rise as well. A return to slower economic growth, and a much slower increase in the standard of living, meant that there was less new wealth produced each year with which to divide among the various parts of society—in particular, less to divide between wealthy elites and those who worked for them. Stagnation thus helped drive significant political dislocation in the United States, as the promises that undergirded the "consumers republic"—as the historian Lizabeth Cohen has aptly entitled it—began to be left unmet.[44] Facing declining profits and productivity, corporations began to raise prices while showing greater resistance to union demands for higher wages. Unions thus resorted to strikes with increasing regularity in the 1970s, leading to a "wage-price" spiral that accelerated an already problematically high rate

---

[42]Vladislav M. Zubok, *Collapse: The Fall of the Soviet Union* (New Haven: Yale University Press, 2021), 13–18.

[43]For more on why the postwar period was an outlier in productivity growth, unlikely to be replicated, see: Gordon, *The Rise and Fall of American Growth*, 1–23; Thomas Piketty, *Capital in the Twenty-First Century*, Arthur Goldhammer trans. (Cambridge: Belknap Press, 2014), 72–109.

[44]Lizabeth Cohen, *A Consumers Republic: The Politics of Mass Consumption in Postwar America* (New York: Alfred A. Knopf, 2003).

of inflation.⁴⁵ This resulted in "stagflation," a frustrating mix of low growth and high inflation that wore away at the foundations of the industrialized West.

Which is where the G-77 reenters our narrative. The final part of the story of stagflation and weakening American hegemony is a sharp and historic rise in energy costs that began in the mid-1970s, a product of the first serious disruption to the global economic hierarchy established by imperialism. That disruption came at the hands of OPEC—the Organization of the Petroleum Exporting Countries—a cartel of oil-exporting states formed in 1960 by Iran, Iraq, Kuwait, Saudi Arabia, and Venezuela. In October of 1973, when Soviet backed-Egypt and Syria launched a surprise attack on Israel seeking to regain their territory from Israeli occupation, the Nixon administration responded by providing military supplies to its Israeli ally. The oil-producing Arab enemies of Israel replied in turn by imposing an oil embargo on the United States. The results were nothing short of spectacular, not necessarily for the balance of power in the Middle East, but for that between oil producers and the industrial world. The embargo and subsequent OPEC price changes resulted in a fourfold increase in the price of oil from 1973 to 1974, and a tenfold increase from prices in 1970.⁴⁶ As Henry Kissinger (who had become Secretary of State in September) would later write, the embargo "demonstrated the extraordinary leverage of the producing countries," in a world where oil demand had exploded and the United States no longer produced enough to cover its own consumption.⁴⁷ Many Americans, Kissinger included, saw it as an affront to American power and to the global hierarchy: "it is ridiculous that the civilized world is held up by 8 millions savages" he complained in a November 1973 meeting.⁴⁸

The emergence of the "oil weapon" gave the G-77's campaign in the United Nations—then reaching its radical peak—new credibility. If the oil producers could cartelize to control prices, the logic went, why not other commodity producers? Though Kissinger had once dismissed "popularity contests" in the Global South, the humiliation of the oil embargo began change his mind. As British Prime Minister Harold Wilson would put it in a 1974 meeting: there was a danger of "OPEC-syndrome ... catching on" leading to "phosphate-pecs, bauxite-pecs, banana-pecs" and other arrangements that would allow G-77 governments to assert greater control over commodity prices and, through them, the global economy.⁴⁹ This

---

⁴⁵See: Fritz Bartel, *The Triumph of Broken Promises: The End of the Cold War and the Rise of Neoliberalism* (Cambridge, MA: Harvard University Press, 2022).
⁴⁶Bartel, *Triumph of Broken Promises*, 26–7.
⁴⁷For Kissinger quote see: Byrnes, *Disunited Nations*, 86. On oil demand see: Daniel T. Sargent, *A Superpower Transformed: The Remaking of American Foreign Relations in the 1970s* (New York: Oxford University Press, 2015), 131–6.
⁴⁸Byrnes, *Disunited Nations*, 86–7.
⁴⁹Byrnes, *Disunited Nations*, 87–97.

indeed was exactly what the NIEO and its "Program of Action"—adopted in the months after the oil embargo was lifted in March of 1974—called for: commodity cartels, and greater producer control over global commodity prices. The entire structure of the global economy, established via imperialist violence and then reformed and reestablished by the Allies after the Second World War, seemed to be under threat. That structure, of course, was built to ensure a flow of cheap raw materials to the industrial North, while finished goods flowed to the Global South, at increasing rates of return. If it was to survive, as West German Chancellor Helmut Schmidt would put it, the industrial North had to "find a way to break up the unholy alliance between the [developing countries] and OPEC" and "convince the world that there will be no earthquake."[50]

Schmidt and Wilson delivered those comments at a November 1975 meeting that represented part of the US and broader Western effort to ensure that no such earthquake occurred: the formation of the "Group of Seven" or G-7. Emerging from that first meeting in 1975—held outside of Paris—and a subsequent 1976 session in Puerto Rico, the G-7 became the rich countries' response to the G-77, a body for coordinating their positions on the global economy so that they could present a united front against demands for global economic reform. Though the Nixon shocks had undermined Western unity, it was quickly restored in the mid-1970s. Political changes in several capitals—including Nixon's resignation and replacement by Gerald R. Ford (in office: 1974–77)—facilitated the return to cooperation, but it was the specter of Schmidt's "unholy alliance" that really galvanized the developed countries to recognize their common interests.[51] Named for its seven members (Canada, France, Germany, Italy, Japan, the United Kingdom, and the United States) the G-7 soon joined the World Bank and the IMF among central institutions for managing the global economy, as its members largely gave up on the UN as a place for serious discussion.

Kissinger in particular viewed the first summit in France as an essential part of reasserting American hegemony, a means to show—as planning documents put it—that the United States was the "leader of a further evolution in international economic cooperation," and to "secure endorsement of [the U.S.] approach to the developing country commodity problem."[52] While little of substance emerged from the first two meetings, the establishment of

---

[50]Byrnes, *Disunited Nations*, 97.
[51]For the United States and the origins of the G-7 see: Byrnes, *Disunited Nations*, 90–101; Michael Franczak, *Global Inequality and American Foreign Policy in the 1970s* (Ithaca: Cornell University Press, 2022), 36–62. On Western Europe and the G-7 see: Giuliano Garavini, *After Empires: European Integration, Decolonization, and the Challenge from the Global South, 1957–1986* (New York: Oxford University Press, 2012), 201–49.
[52]Byrnes, *Disunited Nations*, 96.

the G-7 and the recognition of common interests "strengthened rich-country cohesion," as Michael Franczak writes, transforming the nature of what was increasingly being called the global "North-South dialogue."[53] Observers in the South didn't miss the significance either, as the *Times of India* put it, the G-7 was "clearly meant to forge a common front ... against" the G-77 "unionism of the developing countries."[54]

The Ford administration, however, was not entirely unwilling to make concessions to the G-77. Kissinger had become convinced that maintaining American power and the international status quo required some effort to mollify growing global sentiment for reform. Over the course of the period 1974–76 he worked to do so. Kissinger's plan, as he put it in a 1974 White House meeting, was "to tell the Third World they must be cooperative and in turn [show] we will try to be cooperative."[55] In a series of speeches that fall, he and Ford announced that the United States recognized the emergence of a new "interdependent world" and that the administration was open to moderate proposals to regulate commodity markets. Without indicating they would accept the types of market controls proposed in the NIEO, the Ford administration nevertheless toned down its opposition to documents like the CERDS. It also announced a willingness to engage in discussions about using pools of commodities—"buffer stocks," as they were called—in an effort to control pricing, a major concession. Kissinger further proposed establishing new IMF funding to help producing states when commodity prices fell. Even more significantly, he also toured southern Africa in the spring of 1976 to demonstrate a new American commitment to ending white supremacy in Rhodesia. Afraid that failing to make concessions would spur further, more radical challenges to the global hierarchy, Kissinger made clear his goal to Ford: "I don't want to accept a New Economic order, but I [also] don't want to confront" the G-77.[56]

Kissinger did much to undermine both the short and long-term viability of his carrot and stick approach to restoring American global hegemony, however, by agreeing to Ford's suggestion to make Daniel Patrick Moynihan the US Ambassador to the United Nations in June of 1975. Moynihan, it would turn out, was all stick. A former official in both the Johnson and Nixon White Houses, the new head of "USUN" had also served a tour as Ambassador to India. While there he had developed strong views on the US relationship with the Third World. As he would explain to the President, Moynihan saw the global situation as one where, "in the early 20th century America—and the world—saw American institutions as those towards which

---

[53]Franczak, *Global Inequality*, 52.
[54]Byrnes, *Disunited Nations*, 101.
[55]Byrnes, *Disunited Nations*, 105.
[56]Quote from Byrnes, *Disunited Nations*, 119. On Kissinger's program see: Byrnes, *Disunited Nations*, 102–36; Franczak, *Global Inequality*, 14–35.

FIGURE 14 *Daniel Patrick Moynihan—seen here sternly addressing the UN Security Council in February, 1976—was among the first to realize the ideological benefits for the United States of a focus on human rights.*

the world was headed." However, since the emergence of the G-77, "the new socialist tradition of the Third World" seemed to be taking precedence. This tradition, Moynihan argued, was misguided because it allowed governments to use the quest for collective justice—the pursuit of independence, equality, and true sovereignty—to override the individiual rights of their citizens. Outlining these views in a widely read piece in *Commentary* magazine, Moynihan called for the United States to "go into opposition," on the global stage, accepting that it had lost the UN, but stridently defending its liberal, free-market vision of world order all the same.[57]

When Ford proposed Moynihan's appointment to the UN in the months following the fall of Saigon, Kissinger agreed despite some misgivings. Believing that the disaster in Vietnam required US diplomacy to be more assertive, he was willing to risk a partnership with Moynihan to give his approach to the G-77 a little more edge. Edge Moynihan provided. His brief tenure at the UN commanded headlines at home and abroad. The Ambassador loudly denounced the General Assembly as a body dominated by dictatorships. In a speech in October of 1975, for example, Moynihan implied that the Organization of African Unity—an anti-colonial

---

[57]Byrnes, *Disunited Nations*, 71–77, 131.

organization of independent African states—was nothing more than a club for dictators. He made further headlines in November with another strident speech, this time against Resolution 3379, an attempt to label Israel and its founding ideology of "Zionism" as racist because of the Jewish state's treatment of Palestinians.[58]

Though he resigned soon after—in February of 1976—Moynihan became a national celebrity for his strident attacks on "Third World dictatorships," landing on the cover of *Time* magazine with the headline "giving them hell at the UN." Soon, some in the United States began speaking of what the American writer Irving Kristol called a "Moynihan Effect," a growing resentment among US voters at attacks on the United States in global fora like the UN. Polls at the time indicated widespread support in the United States for Moynihan's strident style of diplomacy—and declining approval for figures, like Henry Kissinger, who were seen as more moderate.[59] Indeed, Moynihan had touched on what proved to be an important foundation for a revival of American (and "Western") exceptionalism after the struggles of the 1960s and 1970s: human rights.

As scholars like Samuel Moyn have demonstrated, discourse regarding human rights began to surge in the 1970s, as disappointed advocates for justice and liberation across the globe began to confront the reality that neither communism nor anti-colonial nationalism were producing the utopias they promised. Calls for greater respect for human rights—i.e., for the types of basic freedoms from state violence and political oppression enshrined in the US Bill of Rights—seemed to offer a path to a "last utopia" that transcended the era's East-West and North-South divides. Over time, however, the global interest in human rights became an ideological boon for the United States in both those contests. This was because rights discourse tended to focus on political rights.[60] These, though historically limited to white male citizens in imperial centers, had been at the heart of the Euro-American liberal political project since the nineteenth century. The same could not be said for America's main ideological competitors. Both communism—with its focus on economic justice—and anti-colonial nationalism—with its emphasis on foreign non-interference and global economic inequality—had pushed political rights to the side, with oft-dubious results.[61] Meanwhile, as formal imperialism waned, and the Civil Rights Movement helped force an end to legalized racism in the American South, the United States was beginning to shed some of its most problematic ideological baggage. It also benefited

---

[58]Byrnes, *Disunited Nations*, 118–28. Franczak, *Global Inequality*, 76–83.
[59]Byrnes, *Disunited Nations* 128–36.
[60]On the emergence of human rights discourse in the 1970s see: Samuel Moyn, *The Last Utopia: Human Rights in History* (Cambridge, MA: Harvard University Press, 2010). On the failures of human rights to address economic injustice see: Samuel Moyn, *Not Enough: Human Rights in an Unequal World* (Cambridge, MA: Harvard University Press, 2018).
[61]See the discussion in: Roland Burke, *Decolonization and the Evolution of International Human Rights* (Philadelphia: University of Pennsylvania Press, 2010).

from the lingering economic egalitarianism of the New Deal era, allowing Americans to claim their system offered both political freedom and, at that point, no small degree of material equality. The United States was thus well positioned to benefit if human rights became a new international standard of judgment for what constituted civilized politics.

This it did, with even the Soviet Union endorsing rights discourse—on paper at least—in the 1975 Helsinki Accords, a 35-nation treaty on the future of Europe.[62] Moynihan was one of the first to recognize the potential of highlighting human rights as a way to undermine the Third World (and Soviet) cause. As he put it in his *Commentary* piece, "those nations which have put liberty ahead of equality have ended up doing better by equality than those with the reverse priority."[63] This, as we have seen in this book, was a historically dubious claim—the West had for centuries put its own liberty ahead of that of its colonial subjects and had thus done relatively well by equality for itself, while long consigning those in the Global South to political nullity and economic servitude. US agents had also regularly aided in the overthrow of governments looking to provide greater protection for human rights. Yet, the argument proved a powerful one anyway. Its emergence became an essential part of the revival of American economic and ideological hegemony that was to follow in the 1980s. It allowed defenders of American dominance to flip the script, rejecting the G-77's call for the United States to honor its development promises by suggesting that the decolonizing world had failed to honor its own when it came to political freedom.[64] Human rights became part of a new way of defining which parts of the world were civilized—and thus deserving of a role in shaping the course of human history—and which were not.

Reinforcing the Structures of Economic Control

As such, human rights joined a convergence of economic and ideological factors that allowed the United States (and its allies in the G-7) to beat back the G-77 challenge to the international status quo in the 1980s. In fact by the early 1990s, both major socialist challengers to the US vision of the future—in the Soviet led-Second World and in the G-77-led Third—had collapsed. What was left behind was a liberal world order so dominant that it seemed plausible to speak of the "end of history," to suggest that major questions about how the world should be organized economically and

---

[62]For more on Helsinki see: Michael Cotey Morgan, *The Final Act: The Helsinki Accords and the Transformation of the Cold War* (Princeton: Princeton University Press, 2018).
[63]Daniel Patrick Moynihan, "The United States in Opposition," *Commentary* 59, no. 3 (March 1975): 31–2. Also available: https://www.commentary.org/articles/daniel-moynihan/the-united-states-in-opposition/.
[64]Thornton, *Revolution in Development*, 190–2.

politically were more or less permanently settled in favor of the American vision.[65] This was not, however, the same liberal world order as that the US had helped establish in 1945—one that had been built around welfare states, government led-development, modernization, and Bretton Woods-regulated currency markets—but a reconfigured "neoliberal" structure instead. Neoliberalism envisioned a significant but limited role for the state, protecting the market from popular interference, so that newly privileged private actors—corporations, non-governmental organizations [NGOs], and individuals (all endowed with human rights)—could function globally with limited restrictions on the movement of their capital or their earnings.[66] We will explore this new order further in the next chapter. What's essential here is to chart its emergence and how that required the reassertion of the global hierarchies established during the imperial age and a rejection of the more egalitarian NIEO vision.

The global reinvigoration (and, indeed, radicalization) of liberalism was not, however, the result of some vast, carefully planned and executed conspiracy. To be sure, it had advocates who had long been working to see such a change, including neoliberal economists like Friedrich Hayek and Milton Freidman.[67] These wanted to see key national and international institutions of economic decision making—like the Federal Reserve in the United States or the World Bank globally—further insulated from democratic processes. Neoliberals wanted to ensure that elite-aligned experts in the developed world made macroeconomic decisions, not the voting public or the G-77. Their ideas were thus a rejection of the egalitarianisms of both the New Deal and the NIEO.[68] While such intellectuals saw their books and papers finally finding fertile soil in the 1970s—with stagflation and the NIEO sending policymakers scrambling for new ideas—it's important not to overstate their impact. As we have just seen, new institutions of the sort neoliberals advocated for—like the G-7—also emerged organically as a result of the perceived common material interests of the rich nations and not necessarily because Ford, Schmidt, and Wilson were reading neoliberal op-eds. Neoliberal economic thought instead offered policymakers a way to understand and describe a path they were already walking down.

It also blended well with the preexisting Cold War ideology of the "freedom" of the capitalist world as opposed to the "totalitarianism" of

---

[65]Francis Fukuyama, *The End of History and the Last Man* (New York: The Free Press, 1992). See also: Derek Chollet and James Goldgeier, *America between the Wars: From 11/9-9/11* (New York: Public Affairs, 2008), 21–3; Gary Gerstle, *The Rise and Fall of the Neoliberal Order: America and the World in the Free Market Era* (New York: Oxford University Press, 2022), 148–9.
[66]On the role of the state in neoliberal thought see: Quinn Slobodian, *Globalists: The End of Empire and the Birth of Neoliberalism* (Cambridge, MA: Harvard University Press, 2018).
[67]See: Angus Burgin, *The Great Persuasion: Reinventing Free Markets since the Depression* (Cambridge, MA: Harvard University Press, 2012).
[68]Slobodian, *Globalists*.

communism—a Cold War discourse that was itself, of course, a restatement of long-standing ideas about American exceptionalism we have traced in this book. Moynihan, and right-wing figures in the United States who followed in his footsteps, found in human rights a potent way to link these distinct ideological projects together: opposing the freedom loving, human rights respecting West with the violators of rights in both the communist and Third Worlds. The newness of human rights thus restored something of the bloom to the American ideological rose after a withering decade, giving the United States new ground for self-righteousness.[69]

However, even these fortuitous ideological developments were not enough to bring about the restoration of American hegemony in the 1980s on their own. US economic power proved the deciding factor. Matters accelerated during the administration of President Jimmy Carter (1977–81), who replaced Ford (and Kissinger) following a narrow victory in the 1976 election. Carter was very much a transitional figure, one whose presidency reflected both the accommodationist impulses of the later Kissinger years and the neoliberal ascendency that would follow. On the accommodationist side, the Carter administration went out of its way to show an interest in respecting the G-77's wishes for global change. In an important symbolic gesture, he appointed US Civil Rights-era hero Andrew Young to the UN Ambassadorship, while also endorsing the establishment of some form of Common Fund for Commodities to help maintain a price floor for raw materials. The Carter administration in reality had no intention of allowing for even a moderately powerful version of the Fund, but entering the negotiations was still a significant gesture. Carter also signaled greater American opposition to white supremacy in southern Africa, playing a role in finally bringing majority rule to Rhodesia.[70] Arguably more significant was his successful effort to shepherd through Congress two treaties that restored control of the Panama Canal Zone to Panama, removing a potent reminder of the United States' imperial past from the world scene.[71]

At the same time, Carter also began to move the United States toward what would turn out to be its new, individualist, neoliberal future: advancing pro-market reforms at home—including the deregulation of the airline, trucking, and railroad industries—and moving further away from state-oriented developmentalism abroad. The latter was reflected in two key policy initiatives, both of which were at the heart of the administration's response

---

[69]For a discussion of the connections between human rights and neoliberalism see: Moyn, *Not Enough*, 173–211.
[70]See: Piero Gleijeses, "A Test of Wills: Jimmy Carter, South Africa, and the Independence of Namibia," *Diplomatic History* 23, no. 4 (October 1999): 657–85; Simon Stevens, "From the Viewpoint of a Southern Governor: The Carter Administration and Apartheid, 1977–1981," *Diplomatic History* 36, no. 5 (November 2012): 843–80.
[71]Byrnes, *Disunited Nations*, 137–70; Adam Clymer, *Drawing the Line at the Big Ditch: The Panama Canal Treaties and the Rise of the Right* (Lawrence: University of Kansas Press, 2008), 40–139.

to the G-77's call for reform: an embrace of human rights discourse, and an approach to foreign aid that stressed "basic human needs." Both policies were fundamentally individualist in their orientation—a sharp contrast with the G-77's vision of, as Moyn puts it, "the redemption of collective nations ... and an egalitarian welfarism or socialism for the compromise or reconciliation of classes."[72] Human rights focused on an individual's entitlement to basic political rights and freedom from violence and imprisonment. Basic human needs policies, meanwhile, looked to provide the global poor not with a collective path to reach industrialized modernity but merely basic material requirements such as food, shelter, and medical care. However admirable in intent, neither approach represented a challenge to the global hierarchy of wealth and power, a key part of their appeal to US policymakers.[73]

Few policymakers, in fact, were more drawn to finding a way to preserve American hegemony more humanely than Jimmy Carter. As president he embraced both approaches, announcing, in a speech at Notre Dame in May of 1977, that the administration would allow human rights to guide its approach to the world while, as Franczak puts it, "working with Congress to redirect aid away from large scale development projects and towards antipoverty programs" that stressed basic human needs.[74] Despite the concession on the Common Fund, the Carter administration over the long run also proved to be less than forthcoming in negotiations with the G-77 in UNCTAD. The intent was, according to a State Department memo, to "modify the North South dialogue and move it away from [an] emphasis on restructuring the international economic system."[75]

Ronald Reagan's administration (1981–89) would finish that job. Elected via a clear defeat of Carter in 1980, Reagan had a deep, almost religious, belief in the power of markets, making him a natural political vehicle for neoliberal thinking and policy. He was also a deep believer in not just American exceptionalism, but in American historical innocence, unable to understand the history of the United States through any terms other than those that saw its expansion and wealth as the virtuous unfolding of divine providence.[76] So too felt many in his administration. The result was that the G-77's calls for a more egalitarian world order were more than merely suspect to many top Reagan officials, they were fundamentally incomprehensible, save as part of a plot to undermine American freedom.[77]

---

[72]Moyn, *Not Enough*, 120.
[73]Moyn, *Not Enough*, 121.
[74]Franczak, *Global Inequality*, 147–8. On the Notre Dame speech see: Byrnes, *Disunited Nations*, 144–5.
[75]Franczak, *Global Inequality*, 170.
[76]On Reagan's mystical belief in the United States and in the power of markets see: Daniel T. Rodgers, *Age of Fracture* (Cambridge, MA: Harvard University Press, 2011), 15–76.
[77]Byrnes, *Disunited Nations*, 171–89; Franczak, *Global Inequality*, 175–90.

The administration's perspectives on the decolonizing world were therefore deeply hierarchical and framed entirely around a narrow conception of American interests, a view well expressed by the incoming Ambassador to the UN, Jeane Kirkpatrick. In a 1979 *Commentary* piece that brought her to Reagan's attention, Kirkpatrick argued that, under the Ford and Carter administrations, the United States had adopted "a posture of continuous self-abasement and apology vis-à-vis the Third World." By engaging with the G-77, she argued, the United States had shown itself far too willing to admit its own faults—which Kirkpatrick saw as largely imagined—and too unwilling to call out governments for theirs, particularly when it came to human rights. Taking matters further, she suggested that the United States should pick and choose friends in the Third World based on whether or not a government supported American interests and, critically, whether they avoided "Marxist-style liberation." A dictatorship that supported foreign investment and investor property rights—"traditional autocracies," as she called them—should be preferred over those governments that adopted left-leaning economic policies and economic nationalism.[78] The point was clear, the states of the Global South were only entitled to American support for their sovereignty if they adopted policies in line with the free market views of the Reagan administration and accepted a subordinate position in the global economy.

The President—naturally—agreed. He told reporters he was "puzzled," when confronted with Global South anger at parsimonious US aid policies. "We come offering our hand in friendship as your partner in prosperity," he insisted in a 1981 North South meeting in Cancun, Mexico.[79] There was no need for radical transformation of the global economic system, Reagan told the world, because the United States had "a revolutionary idea born more than 200 years ago … it is called freedom, and it works."[80] Building on the idea that the Global South did not respect human rights and freedom—including "economic freedom"—he suggested that its relative poverty was a consequence of this, not because of any history of foreign subjugation or empire. The Reagan solution to Third World development, as one reporter summed it up, was "that the developing nations follow America's example, adopt capitalism … work hard, get loans from the private sector, encourage free enterprise, and help themselves."[81]

The Reagan administration would on occasion back these views with force, showing a renewed willingness to use covert action—and even to deploy US troops—when leftist forces threatened victory. In Nicaragua,

---

[78]Jeane Kirkpatrick, "Dictatorships and Double Standards," *Commentary* 68, no. 5 (November 1979): 34–45. Also available at: https://www.commentary.org/articles/jeane-kirkpatrick/dictatorships-double-standards/.
[79]Byrnes, *Disunited Nations*, 177.
[80]Daunton, *Economic Government of the World*, 584.
[81]Byrnes, *Disunited Nations*, 177.

for example—where the socialist *Frente Sandinista de Liberación Nacional*, or "Sadanistas" had overthrown the US-backed dictatorship of the Somoza family—Reagan had the CIA fund the armed "Contra" opposition, furthering a brutal civil war that would last until the end of the decade.[82] In October of 1983, Reagan sent more than 7,000 US troops to the Caribbean Island of Grenada, deposing its leftist government in the largest US military intervention since the end of the Vietnam War.[83] Widely supported in the United States, the invasion was intended as a clear signal that any lingering American reticence to use force after the disaster in Southeast Asia had since abated.

Despite the return of force as an American tool for policing the Global South, the Reagan administration's ability to blunt the G-77's campaign for reform of the international economic system was possible only because of economic developments largely outside its control—with an assist from none other than Jimmy Carter. In the summer of 1979, as part of a desperate attempt to restore his sagging poll numbers, Carter reshuffled his cabinet, moving Federal Reserve Chairman William Miller to the Treasury Department and asking the President of the New York Federal Reserve Bank, Paul Volcker, to replace him. Volcker was among the school of economists known as "monetarists," those who believed that the money supply—that is the total amount of money in circulation in the economy—was a key driver of economic performance. He was convinced that the high inflation of the 1970s had to be brought under control. It was, as he put it, "a dragon ... eating at our innards." As Fed Chairman, he engineered a dramatic contraction of the money supply by sharply increasing interest rates, with the effective Federal Funds Rate jumping from under 11 percent when he took office, to nearly 18 percent in April of 1980, before eventually topping out over 19 percent in 1981. The "Volcker Shock," as it came to be known, soon crashed the US economy—which fell into its worst downturn since the Great Depression—and all but ensured Carter's defeat in the 1980 election.[84] It did little to help Reagan too at first, as the sudden deflation led to a stark rise in unemployment, business failures, and bankruptcies. The Volcker Shock, along with Reagan's deregulatory and anti-union agenda, brought about a profound political transformation

---

[82]On the Reagan intervention in Nicaragua see: Kyle Burke, *Revolutionaries for the Right: Anticommunist Internationalism and Paramilitary Warfare in the Cold War* (Chapel Hill: University of North Carolina Press, 2018), 118–54; Westad, *Global Cold War*, 331–48.

[83]For a narrative account of the invasion see: Herring, *From Colony to Superpower*, 888–9. On the administration's dubious international legal justifications for the invasion see: Robert J. Beck, "The Grenada Invasion, International Law, and the Scoon Invitation: A Thirty Year Retrospective," in *Grenada: Revolution and Invasion*, Patsy Lewis et al., eds. (Kingston: The University of the West Indies Press, 2015).

[84]Eichengreen, *Globalizing Capital*, 135–41; Levy, *Ages of American Capitalism*, 597–600.

in the United States, ending the relatively egalitarian era that had begun during the New Deal. By the time rates eased and the recession ended in 1983–84, the US economy had entered a new age: one where, as Fritz Bartel writes, "capital firmly regained the upper hand over labor, wages permanently fell behind productivity growth, and inequality dramatically increased."[85] These consequences would only manifest over time, however, and thus, when growth returned, Reagan's popularity recovered. He sailed to reelection in a 1984 landslide.

In addition to upending American political and economic life, the Volker shock, combined with Reagan's tax cuts and defense spending to unintentionally engineer a major reorientation in the movement of capital around the world. Though committed in principle to reducing the size of the government, and to reducing taxes, Reagan was also a devoted Cold Warrior who believed that the United States needed to spend more on defense. His administration thus proceeded in its first term to cut taxes *and* move forward with the largest peacetime expansion of the military in US history. As the government borrowed to fund this defense spending—and as American consumers borrowed more to maintain living standards in an era of declining incomes—money began to rush into the United States in search of the high rates of return. The result was a global scarcity of capital, as US interest rates dragged global capital costs upward, making it harder for governments abroad to borrow. The timing for the states leading the charge against the American-led world order—communist and G-77 alike—could not have been worse. The Soviet-led Eastern Bloc, and many governments across the developing world, especially in Latin America, had borrowed heavily over the preceding decades to fund consumption, social services, and development projects. Their economies were otherwise dependent, as we have seen, on commodity production. Thus, as commodity prices, oil included, entered a period of decline in the early 1980s, the stage was set for a crisis.[86]

In August of 1982, the government of Mexico sent emissaries to Washington, DC to announce that it could no longer service its debts, which had nearly doubled over the course of 1981 alone, from 55 to 80 billion dollars. Aware that a Mexican default risked hurting American creditors—and the global financial system—as much as it did Mexico, the Reagan administration worked with the IMF and private lenders to arrange a bailout. That bailout came with significant conditions, however, requiring Mexico to implement stringent economic reforms, including severe cuts to government spending. So onerous were these requirements for "structural adjustment"—as such austerity measures came to be known—that outgoing

---

[85]Bartel, *Triumph of Broken Promises*, 110–12. On inequality, see also: Gordon, *Rise and Fall*, 605–39; Piketty, *Capital*, 1–35.
[86]Bartel, *Triumph of Broken Promises*, 110–27; Levy, *Ages of American Capitalism*, 600–2.

Mexican President Jose Lopez Portillo refused to consent to them. Rejecting what he called the IMF's "witch doctors," he attempted to nationalize the Mexican banking industry instead.[87] The moment for such efforts at state control of the economy had passed, however, and his effort failed. His successors accepted the IMF's terms.[88] The crisis then quickly spread to Argentina and Brazil, and soon after across the Caribbean. It eventually took on global dimensions reaching African countries like Morocco and Asian states like the Philippines. Before the end of 1984, thirty countries had been forced under the IMF's knife, more would follow in the subsequent years.[89]

Structural adjustment lending not only required cuts in government spending—including cuts to healthcare, education, and development programs—it also required countries to lower barriers to trade and capital inflows, further opening their economies to foreign competition and direct investment.[90] The United States also used its leverage to push borrowing governments to accept international arbitration arrangements and other investment guarantees which allowed foreign property owners to use their home country's court systems to sue governments that nationalized their investments. These arrangements—where it was not uncommon for US appointed World Bank officials to cast deciding votes in arbitration hearings—imposed legal limits on the sovereignty of states. These limits that had long existed of course, but had once required military intervention to enforce. Now, investors had other recourse.[91] In addition to forcing policy changes and adding new legal obligations, the debt crisis also shifted domestic politics across the Global South, moving power away from the left and toward advocates of greater market liberalization, who now had their wishes backed by the international finance institutions. As the historian Christy Thornton writes of Mexico, "IMF prescriptions for the Mexican economy found willing backers among a class of Mexican business leaders who had been skeptical of state intervention for decades," bringing an end to the country's development era.[92]

Such shifts in political power, along with the US and the G-7's resurgent, finance-backed dominance, subsequently brought an end to the G-77's campaign for rebalancing and decolonizing the global economic system. While the new neoliberal world would offer narrow paths for some states to escape economic servitude, it also largely reinforced the global division of wealth and power established in the imperial age. Michael Manley's

---

[87]Franczak, *Global Inequality*, 189.
[88]Thornton, *Revolution in Development*, 192–5.
[89]Franczak, *Global Inequality*, 186–90.
[90]Daunton, *Economic Government of the World*, 596–606, 617–25.
[91]Maurer, *Empire Trap*, 387–432.
[92]Thornton, *Revolution in Development*, 192–5.

"structures of economic control" had not been removed—as once seemed possible—but renovated and reinforced instead. Americans, believing that they had a right to determine the political future of communities deemed insufficiently civilized to fully govern themselves—this time on account of their supposedly insufficient respect for political freedom and (more critically) the freedom of capital—had once again managed to force their vision of a proper international hierarchy on the world.

The Volcker Shock and the debt crisis thus brought the state-led development era to an end—not just for Mexico, but for much of the globe. After facilitating Reagan's political transformation in the United States, it allowed the United States to dictate terms to much of the Global South. Meanwhile, in the Soviet Union, as fossil fuel revenue and international credit markets dried up, the Communist Party was finally forced in the mid-1980s to undertake the reforms the US-led capitalist world had imposed on everyone else. These would prove so destabilizing that the Soviet Empire soon unraveled, with the USSR itself collapsing in 1991.[93] One by one, the alternatives to a US-dominated world order had disappeared. As the last decade of the Millenium dawned, it seemed impossible to imagine anything else.

---

[93]On the collapse of the Soviet Union see: Bartel, *Triumph of Broken Promises*, 169–200; Zubok, *Collapse*.

CHAPTER EIGHT

Hyperpower: US Hegemony in the Age of Nation States

Over the course of this book, we have traced how the United States was born of, and then continued, a project of organizing the world around particular visions of civilization, views derived from what Western Europeans and their colonial American descendants saw as the most advanced elements of their own economic and cultural forms. The exact outlines of this civilization evolved over time, as we have seen. Once it was understood as being more or less a unique possession of those with European racial characteristics, a view which faded (without entirely going away, of course) as less racialized conceptions of Euro-American culture—along with democracy, capitalism, and other concerns—took precedence. Civilization was thus a moving target, its exact composition based on however Americans understood themselves at a given moment. What was constant, though, was its use as a justification for the US attempt to structure the world hierarchically for its own benefit while claiming to be advancing the cause of humanity as a whole.

Arguably, at no other moment was the United States in a better position to do so than where we left off at the end of the previous chapter: the early 1990s. Despite the tribulations of the 1970s, when American power appeared to be on the ebb, the 1990s saw the United States without a clear global rival. Both of the alternative visions for global order that had emerged during the Cold War era—the revolutionary communist program of the Soviet Union and the more reformist, development-oriented vision of the decolonizing Global South—had collapsed. Moreover, the United States appeared to once again be the global hub of innovation and economic growth, with a dynamic, technologically advanced economy and an outsized influence in the global institutions—GATT, the IMF, the World Bank, and the UN Security Council—that shaped the rules of the game. Washington's power was also amplified by a network of partnerships with the advanced economies of Western Europe and Japan (through the G-7, for example) and powerful international corporations which often had close relationships with the US government.

In this chapter, we will explore how the United States used this leverage to continue its project of global organizing over the course of the 1990s and through the first decades of the twenty-first century. Though this was an age in which formal empire had largely—though not entirely—disappeared, it remains important to our story to demonstrate how the United States still believed itself entitled to shape the world no less than the imperial powers had in earlier centuries. Announcing the arrival of the age of American "hyperpower"—as French critics dubbed it—with a spectacularly successful war to turn back Iraq's invasion of Kuwait in 1991, Washington, for a time, seemed ready to wait for the world to come to it. A so-called "third wave of democratization" was sweeping across the planet, as countries adopted democratic institutions of the form championed by the United States.[1] At the same time, states also began to experiment with the forms of market liberalization the US had advocated for since the late 1970s. The holdouts—enemies of the United States including Cuba, Iraq, Iran, North Korea, and Syria—all seemed to be on the wrong side of history. As trade continued to liberalize throughout the world in the 1990s, a new economic order was born, one where it was easier than ever for capital-endowed individuals and corporations to move money and goods around the world.

Following Iraq's ejection from Kuwait, both the administrations of George H.W. Bush (1989–93) and Bill Clinton (1993–2001) were inclined to be relatively restrained in the use of American military power, yet still strong in asserting American interests, expanding the NATO alliance into the old Soviet sphere of influence, maintaining a large defense establishment, and retaining a "pointillist empire"—in Daniel Immerwahr's memorable term—of bases around the world.[2] However, as we will see, some in the United States began to grow impatient with the prospect of letting history work itself out on its own terms, seeking a United States that would work even more actively to expand its vision of civilization. In the caves of Afghanistan, meanwhile, Osama bin Laden, the head of the Al Qaeda terrorist network, surveyed the progress of history in an American-led world with his own form of disapproval. Both of these negative views of American global leadership in the 1990s would soon converge to produce the dramatic events of the

---

[1] The term was coined by Samuel Huntington, *The Third Wave: Democratization in the Late 20th Century* (Norman: University of Oklahoma Press, 1991). See also: Jussi M. Hahnhimäki, *Pax Transatlantica: America and Europe in the Post Cold War Era* (New York: Oxford University Press, 2021), 95–6.

[2] Daniel Immerwahr, *How to Hide an Empire: A History of the Greater United States* (New York: Picador, 2019), 18.

early 2000s, when the United States under the direction of the George W. Bush administration (2001–09) undertook to more aggressively police the global hierarchy following the terrorist attacks of September 11th, 2001. The subsequent invasions of Afghanistan (2001) and Iraq (2003) instead proved disastrous, undermining rather than bolstering American hegemony. Though the presidency of Barack Obama (2009–16) that followed would see some stabilization of the US-led world order, it remains a question whether the forces unleashed by the wars—and by trade liberalization—had fatally damaged the foundations of American power.

The Gulf War and the New World Order

Though the November 1989 fall of the Berlin Wall certainly deserves to be remembered as the "moment" that the Cold War came to an end, one could argue that Iraq's August 1990 invasion of Kuwait is when the post-Cold War era truly began in earnest. In the early morning hours of August 2nd, one hundred thousand members of the Iraqi military—the fourth largest in the world at the time—crossed the Kuwaiti border, completing its conquest in just a few hours. The absorption of Kuwait left Iraqi dictator Saddam Hussein in control of roughly 20 percent of the world's oil reserves, granting him the ability to exert a significant influence on global prices. The Iraqi invasion of its smaller, oil-rich neighbor was a direct response—as the historian Daniel Chardell has argued—to declining Soviet influence and what appeared to be a looming period of unipolar American power, making it one of the first major global responses to the end of the superpower conflict. Saddam feared, as he had told dignitaries in a February 24th, 1990 meeting of the Arab Cooperation Council, "that America has temporarily assumed a predominant position in international politics" one which would allow its Israeli client state to pursue new strikes against Iraq and other Arab states.[3]

Despite the United States' recent support of Iraq in the eight-year Iran-Iraq War (1980–88), events had converged to convince Saddam that the newly installed Bush administration had plans to partner with Israel to assert control over the Middle East, ensuring American dominance of the world's oil reserves. Saddam was ideologically predisposed to see such an "imperialist-Zionist" conspiracy, even when one was not present. An anti-Semite who believed that the United States was controlled in part by Jewish interests, Saddam was also a product of the "Baath Party," an anti-imperial, Arab nationalist movement that sought to reverse the perceived humiliation

---

[3]Daniel Chardell, "The Origins of the Iraqi Invasion of Kuwait Reconsidered," *Texas National Security Review* 6, no. 3 (Summer 2023): 52–78, quote on 52.

the Arab world had suffered because of foreign imperialism. Baathists believed that through greater Arab unity, and state-directed socialist economic development, Arab power could be restored to the heights it had commanded in the Middle Ages. They also saw the Jewish settlers in Palestine as agents of a renewed imperialism under American rule. In this sense, Saddam's invasion represented an interesting confluence of the forces set off by the Cold War and decolonization that we have been exploring in the past two chapters. A brutal dictator, ruthless to his own people, the Iraqi ruler was arguably as committed to his own survival in power as he was to Baathism. Yet, the ideology continued to color his worldview. He thus saw his invasion of Kuwait as a chance to consolidate Arab power in the Middle East under his control, both by taking over Kuwait's oil fields, and—he believed—by solidifying his self-assumed position as "defender of the Arab world." Facing the prospect of unchecked American power, and believing that Israel and the United States would never allow for Arab resurgence in the long term, he chose to strike first.[4] His move can therefore be seen as a deformed, self-serving, and militarized last gasp of the Third World's challenge to the postcolonial global hierarchy in the 1960s and 1970s.

It was also a vast strategic miscalculation that misread global sentiment and American intentions. Whatever Israel may have been planning—the Bush administration was in fact concerned enough about Israeli intentions as to warn Tel Aviv against a strike on Iraq—the United States had hoped to maintain cordial relations with Saddam.[5] The invasion galvanized the Bush administration and immediately transformed the United States into an inveterate opponent of Saddam's regime—an opposition which would not end until US troops removed it from power in 2003. By the end of the day on August 2nd, the United States had helped secure UN Security Council Resolution 660, which denounced the invasion and demanded Iraq "immediately and unconditionally" halt its invasion and withdraw its troops. Resolution 661 followed days later, freezing Iraqi assets and imposing severe economic sanctions. By August 8th, US troops were on the ground in Saudi Arabia at its king's invitation to prevent any further Iraqi expansion.[6] Though filled with instinctively cautious policymakers, from the President on down, the Bush administration moved quickly in response to the invasion. This was partly because of the danger the invasion posed to the global oil market.[7] But it was also because the President "and his cabinet," as Samuel L. Aber writes, "approached the invasion of Kuwait with an acute sense of historical self-consciousness." They saw it not merely as yet

---

[4]Chardell, "Origins of the Iraqi Invasion."
[5]Chardell, "Origins of the Iraqi Invasion," 72.
[6]Joseph Steib, *The Regime Change Consensus: Iraq in American Politics, 1990–2003* (New York: Cambridge University Press, 2021), 21–2.
[7]Stieb, *Regime Change*, 22.

another crisis, but a test of what type of world might emerge following the Cold War.⁸

Bush made these stakes clear in a September 11th, 1990 address announcing that the United States would seek Saddam's unconditional withdrawal from Kuwait. The President indicated that the United States wanted to help create a "new world order," one "quite different from the one we've known. A world where the rule of law supplants the rule of the jungle." He was explicit in his hope that a successful, UN-coordinated resolution to the crisis could help the world overcome its past divisions and inaugurate "an era in which the nations of the world, East and West, North and South, can prosper and live in harmony."⁹

This idea that the world's response to the invasion would shape the international system for decades to come was echoed around the globe— "the sentiment was *de riguer*" at the UN, as Aber puts it, "every foreign minister's remarks contained some statement to similar effect."¹⁰ As a result, Saddam's effort to justify his invasion in the terms of Arab, Third World, anti-Israel, or anti-imperialist solidarity failed to galvanize support for his occupation of Kuwait in the way he had hoped. While his call for using Arab oil on behalf of Arab power and solidarity "struck a responsive chord among oil-poor populations from Jordan and Yemen to the Sudan to North Africa," it also failed to make much headway among elites in Saudi Arabia, Egypt, and even Baathist Syria.¹¹ Saddam had not just misread the room in the Middle East, but also globally, where the dramatic—and largely peaceful— end to communist rule in Eastern Europe, and the still shocking decline in superpower enmity in the late 1980s, suggested that a new world was being born. This attitude made his invasion appear an unwelcome throwback to an earlier time. All told, the Iraqi dictator—widely seen as self-serving, untrustworthy, and ideologically inconsistent—was an unappealing vehicle for a revitalization of Global South activism.

Yet, it would be a mistake to misread the extent of international unity behind the American vision of the crisis all the same, particularly as the United States sought to move from compelling Saddam's withdrawal via sanctions to doing so via military force. While Bush framed the American

---

⁸Samuel L. Aber, "Worldmaking at the End of History: The Gulf Crisis of 1990–91 and International Law," *American Journal of International Law* 117, no. 2 (April 2023): 201–50; Andrew J. Bacevich, *American Empire: The Realities and Consequences of U.S. Diplomacy* (Cambridge, MA: Harvard University Press, 2002), 57–62; Chollet and Goldgeier, *American Between the Wars*, 8–11
⁹George Bush, "Address before a Joint Session of the Congress on the Persian Gulf Crisis and the Federal Budget Deficit," September 11, 1990, Online by Gerhard Peters and John T. Woolley, *The American Presidency Project*, https://www.presidency.ucsb.edu/node/264415.
¹⁰Aber, "Worldmaking at the End of History," 208.
¹¹Quote from: Rex Byrnen and Paul Noble, "The Gulf Conflict and the Arab State System: A New Regional Order?" *Arab Studies Quarterly* 13, no. 1/2 (1991): 117–40, 126. See also: Aber, "Worldmaking at the End of History," 228.

response to the crisis in terms of advancing humanity as a whole into a more pacific future—of defending civilization from the "jungle"—his administration also worked carefully to prevent any resolution that did not directly overlap with American wishes or run through American power.[12] The administration, in effect, insisted on US leadership to the crisis, forestalling any opportunity to develop a more collaborative response.

A number of states, including China, Yemen, Colombia, and Malaysia, raised concern about advancing a UN resolution authorizing the use of force, suggesting it would merely perpetuate the law of the jungle—Chinese premier Deng Xiaoping, for example, supposedly dismissed the American use of force as "big hegemonists beating up on small hegemonists."[13] Wary of authorizing a US-led war that, for all Saddam's perfidy, seemed to conjure up imperialist ghosts, many pushed for continuing the sanctions regime and exploring comprehensive diplomatic solutions to the crisis. Colombia, for example, identified oil as the underlying cause for Saddam's actions and, borrowing from the NIEO playbook, suggested establishing new, collaborative international rules for governing the flow of the critical commodity. Others—including French President François Mitterrand—attempted to link the crisis to other areas where international law was being violated, in particular by Israel, which was at that time violating international law with its occupation of southern Lebanon and the Palestinian territories of the West Bank and Gaza.[14] Despite the apparent unanimity about the stakes of the crisis, and the need to reverse Saddam's occupation, not all were comfortable with the US-centered, military solution the Bush administration advanced.

The United States was uninterested in such efforts at "linkage," however—and for readers of this book, the reason should be clear. To be sure, we should not underestimate the degree to which Bush administration officials truly believed they were serving the cause of civilization. They saw Saddam's actions, as Bush described it to a Veterans of Foreign Wars meeting in August 1990, as "a ruthless assault on the very essence of international order and civilized ideals."[15] That granted, the US response must also be seen as a product of Saddam's direct affront to America's emerging unipolar hegemony. However inconsistent, the Iraqi dictator was still nominally a Third World nationalist, leading a country with a still technically state-directed economy (despite some free-market reforms instituted in the 1980s),

---

[12]Aber, "Worldmaking at the End of History," 7.
[13]Aber, "Worldmaking at the End of History," 209, 229.
[14]Aber, "Worldmaking at the End of History," 210.
[15]George Bush, "Remarks at the Annual Conference of the Veterans of Foreign Wars in Baltimore, Maryland," August 20, 1990, Online by Gerhard Peters and John T. Woolley, *The American Presidency Project*, https://www.presidency.ucsb.edu/node/265243; Aber, "Worldmaking at the End of History," 241.

who sought to take advantage of leverage over oil to advance ostensibly anti-colonial ends. The White House at first even had some concern about such rhetoric catching hold. The United States was, as one report put it at the time, "now locked into a psychological battle with Saddam Hussein ... while he seeks to define the conflict as poor versus rich, Arab versus foreign, Muslim versus non-Muslim."[16] Any success by Saddam in consolidating his hold over Kuwait therefore reflected a danger to a particularly US vision of civilization—one which had as little tolerance for nationalists seizing control of natural resources to alter the global hierarchy as it did for using international fora to force changes in Israeli occupation policy. The crisis thus mandated a swift and overwhelming American response that was, at the same time, limited to confronting Iraq alone.

Such was US power in the wake of Soviet decline and the Third World debt crisis, however, that Bush's program won out. In November, the UN Security Council passed Resolution 678, giving Iraq until January 15th, 1991, to withdraw from its conquests, after which the Security Council authorized "all necessary means" to force Iraqi troops from Kuwait.[17] The United States organized an remarkably multilateral coalition to provide those means, including troops not only from traditional allies such as Great Britain and France, but also from Middle Eastern countries like Egypt, Saudi Arabia, and Syria. However, there was no mistaking the fact that US military power was the backbone of the coalition—particularly following an impressive five-week bombing campaign that demonstrated the technological prowess of American air power. An imposing array of aircraft—from F-117 stealth fighter-bombers and unarmed EF-111 radar jammers to more traditional B-52s launched from Louisiana—entered Iraqi airspace armed with advanced GPS-guided weaponry, alongside ship- and air-launched cruise missiles, disabling the country's air defenses and its power grid within minutes. A relentless air assault against Iraqi targets in Kuwait and Iraq followed—tank "plinking" as US pilots called it—all broadcast on CNN. By the time coalition troops launched their ground attack in February, the once mighty Iraqi army was ready to collapse, which it did over the course of a short, 100-hour, war.[18] The demonstration complete, Bush chose not to send troops onto Baghdad to topple Saddam. He instead opted for a containment strategy, including the maintenance of sanctions and the establishment of "no-fly zones" over large parts of the country.[19]

---

[16]Aber, "Worldmaking at the End of History," 228–9.
[17]Stieb, *Regime Change*, 29.
[18]See Hal Brands, *Making the Unipolar Moment: U.S. Foreign Policy and the Rise of the Post-Cold War Order* (Ithaca: Cornell University Press, 2016), 309–17; Immerwahr, *How to Hide and Empire*, 377–9.
[19]On the choice for containment rather than regime change see: Chollett and Goldgeier, *America between the Wars*, 13–16; Stieb, *Regime Change*, 37–45.

FIGURE 15 *US Airforce jets of the Fourth Fighter Wing fly over burning oil wells in Kuwait, 1991. These F-15 and F-16 fighters were part of the overwhelming array of hi-tech aircraft the United States deployed against Iraqi forces during the Persian Gulf War.*

In all, the "Persian Gulf War" demonstrated the awesome tools of violence at Washington's disposal—the fruits of what was sometimes called the technological "revolution in military affairs"—making the asymmetrical nature of global power clear to all observers. American ideological dominance, meanwhile, received further confirmation later that year in December when the Soviet Union (effectively an American ally during the Iraq crisis) dissolved. In addition to abandoning communist party rule, nearly the entire former Soviet Empire—newly reemerged Russia included—aggressively adopted the free market "shock therapy" urged on it by Western economists. The sudden adoption of the free market, including the swift sale of state assets, proved a disaster in subsequent years—for Russia especially, where standards of living collapsed and male life expectancy declined from sixty-four in 1991 to fifty-seven in 1994. At the time, however, it seemed yet another sign that the world was going America's way.[20] The democratic and capitalist transformation in the former communist world capped off more than a decade of global transition toward democratic rule. Dozens of countries—including Brazil, Chile, Portugal, Spain, South Korea, Taiwan,

---

[20] On the final stages of the disintegration of the Soviet Union see: Zubok, *Collapse*, 365–426. On the failures of shock therapy, see Daunton, *Economic Government of the World*, 677–90; Jonathan Haslam, *Hubris: The American Origins of Russia's War against Ukraine* (Cambridge, MA: Harvard University Press, 2025), 56, 94–8.

and Singapore—had adopted more popular forms of government. As Hal Brands writes, the period "witnessed a major shift in global politics, one in which the democratic values and institutions the United States favored spread far and wide."[21] Riding high on the democratic transition, the global shift toward neoliberal economic policy, and the UN approved defeat of Saddam's revanchist pseudo-Third Worldism, the United States appeared to have a stranglehold on global military, economic, and ideological power.

Clinton, Somalia, and Globalization in the 1990s

There were those, however, who were still unsatisfied with the Bush administration's use of American power. Some believed that the President had abdicated in fulfilling American responsibilities as the global hegemon by not removing Saddam from Baghdad. While not a majority opinion, as historian Joseph Stieb writes, "most major newspapers had at least one prominent writer who called for regime change," including those like the *New York Times*'s William Safire, Charles Krauthammer in the *Washington Post*, and the entire editorial board at the conservative *Wall Street Journal*. There was also a smattering of congressmen and senators who felt similarly, grumbling that Bush had simply not done enough in the Middle East.[22]

Even within the administration, there were those who believed that—Saddam aside—the United States needed to be aggressive and assertive in its use of power. These were the "neoconservatives," a political movement that dated back to debates about arms control negotiations with the Soviet Union in the 1970s. Neoconservatives believed, to varying degrees, that the United States should openly pursue global primacy, assertively using military power to transform the world in America's own image. Insofar as most in Washington—and indeed, most Americans at the time—believed the United States should maintain primacy and felt that the world would be better off if it were more like America, the neoconservative distinction was as much about means and attitude as anything else.[23] In March of 1992, a defense planning document authored by neoconservatives working for Secretary of Defense Richard "Dick" Cheney—and led by Under Secretary of Defense for Policy, Paul Wolfowitz—was leaked to the press. "Chauvinistic" in "vision and tone," as Gary Dorrien has written, the Wolfowitz plan called for the United States to prevent not only the reemergence of a rival superpower, but to deter—as the document read—"potential competitors from even

---

[21]Brands, *Unipolar Moment*, 119.
[22]Stieb, *Regime Change*, 45–6.
[23]For more on the neoconservatives see: Gary Dorrien, *Imperial Designs: Neoconservatism and the New Pax Americana* (New York: Routledge, 2004); and Justin Vaïsse, *Neoconservatism: The Biography of a Movement*, Arthur Goldhammer trans. (Cambridge, MA: Harvard University Press, 2010).

aspiring to a larger regional ... role."²⁴ Despite the recent success in using the Security Council to organize opposition to Iraq, the planning document dismissed collective security, and even America's European allies to a degree, insisting that only the United States could protect "the established political and economic order."²⁵

In the heady atmosphere of the "end of history" in 1992, however, this was a vision that seemed out of step with the times—almost as an anachronistic in appearance as Saddam's invasion of Kuwait. The administration quickly denied it had any influence on US policy—and with all honesty, Bush was no neoconservative—but not in time to prevent it from becoming an election year embarrassment.²⁶ The President could ill afford these, as slow recovery from the 1990–91 recession undermined his once soaring domestic popularity. He was defeated in November by Arkansas Governor, Bill Clinton. The Arkansan brought to the White House a focus on domestic politics—"it's the economy stupid" had been his campaign's internal mantra—and a desire to avoid entangling military engagements. The new administration had a unique form of what was often called the "Vietnam Syndrome," a reticence to use force because of the disaster in Southeast Asia. Clinton had avoided the draft during the war and thus wanted to counter any narrative about his supposed pacifism or cowardice by appearing tough. At the same time, however, he and his cabinet also genuinely wished to avoid any repeat of the Vietnam quagmire.²⁷

Clinton's reticence to deploy US troops was only deepened further by a brewing disaster he had inherited from Bush in the horn of Africa. In December of 1992, Bush had, with UN support, deployed 25,000 US troops to Somalia to protect aid workers attempting to mitigate a disastrous famine there. After emerging from British trusteeship in 1960, Somalia had soon become caught up in the new imperialism of the Cold War, serving first as a Soviet and then second as a US client in a proxy war between the superpowers.²⁸ The conflict had worn away at the traditional foundations of Somali society, and thus when the Cold War ended and US support was withdrawn, the country collapsed into anarchy and civil war.²⁹ As violence escalated, an "essentially humanitarian mission became a police action," with US troops engaging in combat with local warlords.³⁰ When an October 1993 battle in the capital of Mogadishu left eighteen servicemen dead and

---

²⁴Dorrien, *Imperial Designs*, 41.
²⁵Dorrien, *Imperial Designs*, 40.
²⁶Chollet and Goldgeier, *America between the Wars*, 43–7; Dorrien, *Imperial Designs*, 38–43.
²⁷See: M.E. Sarotte, *Not One Inch: America, Russia, and the Making of the Post-Cold War Stalemate* (New Haven: Yale University Press, 2021), 150–3.
²⁸Westad, *Global Cold War*, 250–87.
²⁹On the impact of the Cold War on Somali political structures see: Frederick Cooper, *Africa since 1940: The Past of the Present* (Cambridge: Cambridge University Press, 2002), 186.
³⁰Michael H. Hunt, *The American Ascendency: How the United States Gained and Wielded Global Dominance* (Chapel Hill: University of North Carolina Press, 2007), 285.

downed US helicopters smoldering in the streets, Clinton decided he'd had enough and brought the troops home. The failure of the Somalia intervention colored Clinton's perspective on US troop deployments throughout the rest of his term. As the historian Michael Hunt has put it, "the Somalia syndrome now reinforced the Vietnam syndrome."[31]

Clinton's subsequent reluctance to deploy troops would not prevent him from sending US forces into action again—a topic we will return to in a moment—nor did it stop him from asserting American global dominance through other means. It was on his watch, for example, that the United States pushed forward with plans to expand NATO—the initially anti-Soviet US military alliance—beyond Germany, a move a weakened Russia considered a betrayal but could do little to stop at the time.[32] Clinton also worked assiduously to continue the neoliberal transformation of the world economic system that had begun under Carter in the late 1970s. He did so both at home—where he declared an end to the "era of big government" and partnered with Republicans in Congress to further trim back regulation, the federal budget, and the role of the state in the economy—and abroad.[33] While a late convert to the then-dominant faith in liberalizing trade, Clinton soon became one of its most fervent and impactful acolytes. He helped usher through Congress the North American Free Trade Agreement [NAFTA], a long-developing treaty signed into law with much fanfare in 1993. Effectively eliminating tariffs between Mexico, the United States, and Canada, Clinton believed NAFTA meant the United States was seizing its "opportunity to remake the world," as he put it during the signing ceremony. "The cold war is over," he continued, "the grim certitude of the contest with communism has been replaced by the exuberant uncertainty of international economic competition."[34]

Indeed, the post-Second World War American dream of a world unified in a single capitalist marketplace was coming closer to fruition than it ever had before. NAFTA, for example, was one of numerous new regional free trade agreements across the globe, with roughly 61 percent of the world falling within one or another in 1994. Even more significantly, that year also saw the conclusion of the so-called Uruguay round of trade negotiations under GATT. The Uruguay round's "final act" was arguably the most "comprehensive international trade agreement in history." It applied to 117 countries, lowered tariffs on industrial goods a further third and extended GATT's tariff reduction protocols to agriculture for the first

---

[31]Hunt, *American Ascendency*, 285. See also: Bacevich, *American Empire*, 143–148.
[32]Haslam, *Hubris*, 3–113; Sarotte, *Not One Inch*.
[33]On Clinton's domestic economic policy see: Gary Gerstle, *The Rise and Fall of the Neoliberal Order*, 152–89.
[34]Quotes from: William J. Clinton, "Remarks on Signing the North American Free Trade Agreement Implementation Act," December 8, 1993, Online by Gerhard Peters and John T. Woolley, *The American Presidency Project*, https://www.presidency.ucsb.edu/node/219946. See also: Bacevich, *American Empire*, 95–101.

time.[35] In addition, it established a new, more comprehensive, World Trade Organization [WTO] to supersede GATT. The WTO was designed to be a significantly more powerful organization than GATT (which, if we recall from Chapter 6, was originally meant as a mere temporary arrangement), empowered with new methods to enforce trade rules, while also expanding those rules to areas previously left out, like foreign investments, services, and intellectual property. It was also very much a product of the will of the United States and the other G-7 powers. While developing countries' wishes certainly shaped the Uruguay Final Act and the WTO—there was, if nothing else, a strong collective desire to operate by consensus in such negotiations—they were no longer the decisive force they were in the 1970s. The relatively unified G-7, on the other hand, was able to exert a dominant influence, so that the agreement was, as one observer put it, "a grubby set of global guidelines drawn up at the behest of the powerful for the benefit of the powerful."[36] Indeed, the US-dominated international financial institutions continued to believe in their right to impose economic policies on countries that came to them for money, as South Korea and Indonesia discovered when they accepted IMF bailout packages in the wake of the 1997 Asian Financial Crisis.[37]

The new global guidelines for trade that emerged from the Uruguay round built on the other legal instruments designed to protect foreign investments—arbitration agreements and the like—that we discussed in the last chapter. The result was a global economy where it was easier and safer to move goods and invest money abroad than ever before, a worldwide reign of capital protected not by formal imperial structures but instead by internationally agreed-upon rules and regulations. Capital itself moved around the world with incredible speed, as individual, corporate, and national economic success depended in large part on whether one could attract the attention of a finance industry seeking greater rates of return. Corporations globalized, as companies were able to parlay the new trading regime with improving information technology and lowering transportation costs to build complex, globe spanning supply chains. As a result, US, European, Japanese, South Korean, and other developed world companies increasingly became entities partly unmoored from their national origins, influenced by and influencing communities as far apart as Chicago, Illinois and Chengdu, China —both cities where US basketball star, Michael Jordan, was a household name, or something close.[38] In the mid-1990s, four

---

[35]Norman S. Fieleke, "The Uruguay Round of Trade Negotiations: An Overview," *New England Economic Review* (July/August 1995): 3–14.
[36]Quote in Daunton, *Economic Government of the World*, 640. On the unbalanced nature of the Final Act see, 636–41. On US and European economic dominance see also: Hahnhimäki, *Pax Transatlantica*, 77–84.
[37]Daunton, *Economic Government of the World*, 596–606.
[38]Herring, *From Colony to Superpower*, 918–19.

out of every five bottles of Coca-Cola were sold outside the United States, while Americans drove foreign-made cars home to watch global icons like Jordan on foreign-made televisions.[39] Global prices converged, as it became increasingly plausible to speak of a single global market for goods with regional variations—a process that would intensify further as thousands and thousands of miles of fiber optic cables began to crisscross the globe in the latter part of the decade, laying the groundwork for the online economy of the twenty-first century.[40]

One of Clinton's most consequential decisions in helping to shape the economy of the new century was that he took to improve trade relations with China while supporting Chinese entry into the WTO. Once committed enemies, China and the United States had begun an anti-Soviet rapprochement during the Nixon administration, leading to the complete normalization of relations and the lowering of trade barriers in 1979. Political and economic relations deepened over the course of the 1980s, despite the Chinese Communist Party's [CCP] firm resistance to the global democratization movement, as exemplified by the infamously violent, 1989 repression of pro-democracy activists in Tiananmen Square. The CCP had, however, gone along with the global trend toward market liberalization—though, notably, it resisted the shock therapy that proved so disastrous for Russia in favor of a more gradual liberalization of its economy.[41]

Many Americans believed that with market liberalization came political liberalization. As Clinton himself would put it, "the more China opens its markets, the more it unleashes the power of economic freedom, the more likely it will be to more fully liberate the human potential of its people."[42] The US-China Relations Act of 2000, which permanently normalized trade relations between the two countries, should therefore be seen as a part of the long tradition of the American civilizing mission. The results over the course of the 1990s and into the new millennium were nothing short of spectacular for trade, if not for democracy. By 2010, China was the world's second largest economy, and a manufacturing powerhouse, one locked into a deeply symbiotic relationship with the United States. China's share of world manufacturing exports climbed from 2 to 16

---

[39]Herring, *From Colony to Superpower*, 918–19; Walter LaFeber, *Michael Jordan and the New Global Capitalism* (New York: W.W. Norton and Co., 2002) 14–15, 56, 135.
[40]Levy, *Ages of American Capitalism*, 661–9. On global market integration see also: LaFeber, *Michael Jordan*; Findlay and O'Rourke, *Power and Plenty*, 496–526. Hahnhimäki, *Pax Transatlantica*, 68–84.
[41]Daunton, *Economic Government of the World*, 662–7.
[42]William J. Clinton, "Remarks on Signing Legislation on Permanent Normal Trade Relations With China," October 10, 2000, Online by Gerhard Peters and John T. Woolley, *The American Presidency Project*, https://www.presidency.ucsb.edu/node/228482

percent between 1990 and 2011, while its share of US manufacturing imports grew to 10.9 percent in 2001 before doubling to 23.1 percent in 2011.[43] If the Volcker Shock had transformed the United States into, as Jonathan Levy aptly describes it, the "consumer market of last resort" for the world's manufacturers and a net importer of capital, China became an essential supplier of both.[44]

Neoliberals had promised that their program of liberalization would, in the aggregate, make the world a richer place. They had done so while also being fully aware that the growth that followed their reforms would be unevenly distributed, creating winners and losers in different places throughout the world. This was precisely the reason that they had looked to move as much of the state's management of the economy away from popular political institutions as possible, because they feared that the backlash that might follow from the losers could disrupt the smooth functioning of the market.[45]

They were right, both about the growth and its uneven distribution. In one respect, the economic growth that resulted from the globalizing neoliberal era after 1989 reinforced the existing global hierarchy. It made the rich countries richer, the United States in particular. In addition, just as one could speak of increasingly "multinational" corporations, there also emerged an "international" elite class of capital owners, who shared as much in common with each other as they did with their less wealthy countrymen. Living in "global" cities, like New York, London, and Tokyo, this global elite was drawn predominantly from G-7 states, but not entirely.[46] In the first two decades of the twenty-first century, that elite also gained new members from places like India and China. Even more spectacular though was the growth of the "global middle class," the lucky populations—mostly in China, but also in other Asian countries including India—who had been lifted out of poverty as manufacturing jobs moved out of the Global North and into their own countries.[47] In this limited sense then, the global neoliberal revolution led by the United States did indeed help "transform the world" in the positive way Clinton promised. Yet at the same time, it also did much to reinforce the overall global hierarchy of wealth between the lucky few—which now included many more people in places outside the G-7—and the rest. It also did so at the expense of working- and middle-class Americans, who in the twenty-first century saw their own relative position in the global hierarchy of wealth decline significantly. In time, this would inject levels of instability into the

---

[43]Levy, *Ages of American Capitalism*, 685.
[44]Levy, *Ages of American Capitalism*, 601.
[45]See Slobodian, *Globalists*, 1–26.
[46]Levy, *Ages of American Capitalism*, 661.
[47]Branko Milanovic, *Global Inequality: A New Approach for the Age of Globalization* (Cambridge, MA: Harvard University Press, 2016), 1–45.

US political system severe enough to potentially undermine its position atop the global hierarchy.

Clinton's Unsatisfying Wars

That prospect, however, lay in the future. To return to the 1990s, Clinton's efforts to advance American-led globalization during his term further reinforced American dominance of the international system. In 1999, France's foreign minister summed it up this way: "the United States of America predominates on the economic level, the monetary level, on the technological level, and in the cultural area in the broadest sense of the word." It was, he continued, "not comparable, in terms of power and influence, to anything known in modern history."[48]

Yet, for certain groups of Americans, this historic global influence—and Clinton's style of global leadership—remained insufficient. They wanted to see the mighty US military put to greater use—a military that remained the strongest in the world. Despite talk after the Soviet collapse of a "peace dividend" and potential cuts to defense spending, reductions in American military power were never as severe as expected. This was in part due to the nature of the "military-industrial complex" that had built up over the Cold War. Defense spending was too deeply wound into the fabric of American life to be reduced very easily. Jobs and regional development were closely tied to the location of defense plants and military bases, meaning their closure threatened the supply of lobbying money, and voter support, on which politicians in Washington relied.[49] The instinct for military primacy was also deeply wound into American political culture as well, with the result that US defense spending in the 1990s still dwarfed all its competitors. The United States also continued to control a sprawling network of hundreds of bases around the world, stretching from Puerto Rico and Greenland in the Western Hemisphere, to Germany and Italy in Europe, Saudi Arabia and Bahrain in the Middle East, tiny Diego Garcia in the Indian Ocean, and Okinawa in the Pacific. This empire "of points" might not look as impressive on the globe as the broad swaths of color-coded territory on maps of old empires, but it allowed the US military an unprecedented global reach.[50] Critics of Clinton believed he was not making sufficient use of the military power that all that money and all those bases supported.

---

[48]Quote in: Ahsan I. Butt, "Why Did the United States Invade Iraq in 2003," *Security Studies* 28, no. 2 (2019): 250–85, 269.
[49]See the discussion in Michael Brenes, *For Might and Right: Cold War Defense Spending and the Remaking of American Democracy* (Amherst: University of Massachusetts Press, 2020) especially 236–48.
[50]Bacevich, *American Empire*, 117–40; Immerwahr, *How to Hide an Empire*, 336–90.

Neoconservatives continued to see the world in the same light as was reflected in Wolfowitz's 1992 defense planning document, believing that one could not just trust the forces of history to bring about an American dreamworld of peace, justice, and seamless global trade. In 1996, two prominent neoconservative intellectuals, William Kristol and Robert Kagan, wrote a widely read article in the journal *Foreign Affairs*, which called for a new, "neo-Reaganite foreign policy."[51] By this, they meant a foreign policy that more aggressively used force to assert a "benevolent hegemony" across the globe. Such an approach, they wrote, would be "good for America, and good for the world," because it would push back against "relativistic multiculturalism" and remind all that American principles, and "core elements of the Western tradition," were "not merely the choices of a particular culture but ... universal, enduring, 'self-evident' truths."[52] Calls for a more assertive use of American power in the name of universal principles, however, were not entirely the preserve of those like Kagan and Kristol who identified as conservatives. While they did not share the openly chauvinistic neoconservative obsession with the "Western tradition"—nor the related fixation with American unilateralism—there were those in the American center and center-left who believed the United States needed to be doing more to stop gross violations of human rights abroad. As the then-journalist Samantha Power would write in a 2002 tract that exemplified this line of thinking, "Americans are extremely slow to muster the imagination needed to reckon with evil" and therefore were doing too little to stop it.[53]

Over the course of the 1990s, there emerged a new international focus, particularly in the Global North, on "crimes against humanity." Building on the interest in international human rights that had emerged in the 1970s (as we saw in the last chapter), there were now a bevy of bodies, from the UN Human Rights Commission to committees in the US Congress and international NGOs like "Human Rights Watch," which were committed to revealing and coordinating responses to violations of human rights. "Ordinary Americans" at this time, Samuel Moyn writes, "lived through a profound shift toward a morality attentive to human life ravaged by war."[54] A new focus on civilian suffering during wartime—which developed along with a surging popular interest in the history of the Second World War's

---

[51] Dorrien, *Imperial Designs*, 125–79.
[52] Robert Kagan and William Kristol, "Toward a Neo-Reaganite Foreign Policy," *Foreign Affairs* 75, no. 4 (June/July 1996): 18–32.
[53] Samantha Power, *"A Problem from Hell": America in the Age of Genocide* (New York: Harper Perennial, 2002), xvii.
[54] Samuel Moyn, *Humane: How the United States Abandoned Peace and Reinvented War* (New York: Farrar, Straus, and Giroux, 2021), 218.

Holocaust—brought new attention to gross violations of human rights at much the same moment post-Cold War struggles were producing no shortage of them.[55]

The key events in this evolution occurred in southeastern Europe and in central Africa. In the Balkans, the end of the Cold War severed the last ties holding together an ethnically divided Yugoslavia, which began to break apart in 1991. Serbian President Slobodan Milošević took advantage of the chaos to try and secure an outsized chunk of territory for the plurality population of Serbs, waging war on Yugoslavia's non-Serbian population, including Muslims in Bosnia. Slaughter of civilians soon followed, including the 1995 mass killing of Bosnian civilians in Srebrenica, a city supposedly under UN protection.[56] This followed the horrific 1994 genocide in Rwanda, where postcolonial power struggles had led to the organized slaughter of hundreds of thousands Rwandan Tutsis.[57] Much as with Srebrenica, the international community, and UN peacekeepers on the ground, did nothing to stop the killing until it was too late. Subsequently, there began to evolve from these events new ideas about the supposed responsibilities of the international community to prevent or halt genocidal killings of this sort—what would later be entitled the "responsibility to protect."[58] Such sentiments blended well with prevailing attitudes in the world of "international humanitarianism." This mix of NGOs, UN offices, and agencies was well-meaning in their desire to help global victims of poverty, war, and oppression, but often imposed hierarchies over those they helped in a way that echoed the old imperial order.[59] Indeed, the arguments for international intervention ran directly counter to the sentiments that prevailed among the G-77 in the 1970s, which had usually stressed non-intervention as *the* essential right of their hard-earned, postcolonial sovereignty.[60]

The combination of neoconservative sniping, humanitarian sentiment, and TV news stories about horrible violence against the innocent all

---

[55]Moyn, *Humane*, 217–23.
[56]A vulnerable minority themselves in certain parts of the country, the Serbs, as Jonathan Haslam writes, "sought to save themselves at the expense of everyone else." Haslam, *Hubris*, 42. See: Chollet and Goldgeier, *America Between the* Wars, 127–8; Hahnhimäki, *Pax Transatlantica*, 46–49; Haslam, *Hubris*, 42–51, 84–6; Herring, *From Colony to Superpower*, 924.
[57]See: Cooper, *Africa since 1940*, 1–2, 6–9, 191–2.
[58]This belongs first to the government of an individual state but then defaults to the international community if events prove that government is falling short of fulfilling it. See: United Nations Office on Genocide Prevention, "About the Responsibility to Protect," https://www.un.org/en/genocide-prevention/responsibility-protect/about. See also: Chollet and Goldgeier, *America Between the* Wars, 213–19.
[59]For a discussion of the neocolonial aspects of humanitarianism, see Jill Rosenthal, *From Migrants to Refugees: The Politics of Aid Along the Tanzania-Rwanda Border* (Durham: Duke University Press, 2023).
[60]See: Burke, *Decolonization and the Evolution of International Human Rights*.

generated intense pressure for Clinton to act. The President had brought this on himself to some degree, as his original campaign strategy against Bush involved painting his opponent as insufficiently concerned about human rights.[61] Eventually, therefore, political pressure overcame his post-Mogadishu reluctance to use force. Though he sent troops to Haiti in 1994 to oversee the departure of a military government that had ousted the democratically elected Jean-Baptiste Aristide a few years earlier, Clinton preferred to rely on the incredible airpower the United States had first demonstrated during the Gulf War. In August of 1995, soon after the Srebrenica massacre, for example, Clinton organized NATO airstrikes against Serbian positions in Bosnia, leading eventually to the Dayton Accords, which were enforced by a UN Peacekeeping force that included 20,000 US troops. When the Serbian government again began to engage in ethnic violence—this time against Albanians in Kosovo—Clinton again resorted to airpower in the late spring of 1999, with a monthslong bombing campaign that forced a Serbian withdrawal. American troops were deployed to the region as part of a NATO peacekeeping force that protected Kosovo from any further Serbian incursions. Clinton had also used airstrikes to enforce the containment of Iraq, launching cruise missiles into Baghdad in 1993 and then overseeing more comprehensive Anglo-American strikes in December of 1998. All of these uses of force—however reluctantly undertaken—were intended to demonstrate American preeminence and enforce the global hierarchy. As the international relations scholars Derek Collet and James Goldgeier have written of the 1999 strikes on Serbia, the intent was "not simply to end the bloodshed" in Kosovo, "but also to send a message to other dictators who might have similar designs."[62]

For Clinton's critics, however, his military efforts at enforcing American hegemony were insufficient. For them, the end of history—whether it was understood as a world without enemies of the United States, or one without gross violations of human rights—was not arriving quickly enough. Beyond the problems in the Balkans, there was also the issue of what the United States called "rogue states," which were those governments seen as threatening the international order through their supposed support for terrorism and/or their desire to secure "weapons of mass destruction" [WMDs] (usually understood as nuclear, chemical, or biological weapons).

---

[61]Chollet and Goldgeier, *America between the* Wars, 25–52; Haslam, *Hubris*, 28; Stieb, *Regime Change Consensus*, 102.
[62]For quote see: Chollet and Goldgeier, *America between the* Wars, 216. On Clinton's wars see: Bacevich, *American Empire*, 141–66; Hal Brands, *From Berlin to Baghdad: America's Search for Purpose in a Post-Cold War World* (Lexington: University of Kentucky Press, 2008) 128–262; Chollet and Goldgeier, *America between the* Wars, 29–145, 177–243; Hahnhimäki, *Pax Transatlantica*, 46–52; Haslam, *Hubris*, 41–109; David Halberstam, *War in a Time of Peace: Bush, Clinton and the Generals* (New York: Scribner, 2001).

The rogue states—which at the beginning of the Clinton administration included Saddam's Iraq, along with Muammar Gaddafi's Libya, Cuba, Iran, and North Korea—were all still around (and still rogue) as his time in office came to a conclusion. Whereas in the early 1990s it had been easy to imagine that such outlaw regimes would struggle to survive in the "new world order" atmosphere of rights, international law, and commerce, by the end of the decade they had instead demonstrated a vexing durability.[63]

They had also undermined confidence in another tool of American power: economic sanctions. Because of the central position of the United States—and the US dollar—in the global economy, the United States had an ability to impose sanctions on states that defied its will all but unilaterally, especially when its Western European allies were onboard (as they often were).[64] These restrictions on the movement of money and goods into and out of the target country were supposed to use economic power to bring that state to heel—or, ideally, cause its problematic government to collapse and be replaced by one more pliant to US interests. In practice, however, sanctions routinely caused significant suffering among the sanctioned population, while the rogue governments that were the real targets of the economic restrictions usually survived. The UN-backed sanction regime in Iraq had followed just this pattern—sharp increases in infant mortality, for example, were just one sign of the distress caused by the trade restrictions, resulting in as many as 227,000 excess deaths, all while Saddam remained firmly ensconced in Baghdad.[65]

The growing, and notably bipartisan, impatience in Washington with Iraq's dictator is a good example of the shifting mood. As Joseph Stieb has demonstrated, by the end of the Clinton years, a "regime change consensus" had emerged that saw Saddam's removal—by one means or another—as a necessary step for securing the international order.[66] Saddam's survival was itself an affront to US power, and the possibility that he might pursue the development of weapons of mass destruction raised the perceived risks further. Regime change became the stated goal of US policy with the passage of the "Iraq Liberation Act" by Congress in 1998, even though Saddam was at this point far from a serious threat to anyone but his own people.[67]

---

[63]On faith in the transformative power of a US-backed world order see John J. Mearsheimer, *The Great Delusion: Liberal Dreams and International Realities* (New Haven: Yale University Press, 2018).
[64]For more on US sanction power in a dollar-dominated world see: Ntina Tzouvala, "Sanctions, Dollar Hegemony, and the Unraveling of Third World Sovereignty," *Yale Journal of International Law*, June 10, 2024, https://yjil.yale.edu/posts/2024-06-10-sanctions-dollar-hegemony-and-the-unraveling-of-third-world-sovereignty.
[65]Hunt, *The American Ascendency*, 285.
[66]Stieb, *Regime Change Consensus*, 1–13.
[67]Stieb, *Regime Change Consensus*, 3, 9–11.

Though the CIA was, and had been, attempting to facilitate Saddam's departure, any more strenuous action was prevented by what Clinton had instinctively understood all along: outside Washington, Americans were not particularly enamored with the idea of going to war again in the Middle East.[68] Containment was, as Senator Joseph Biden put it in 1998, "a very unsatisfying policy at an emotional level" but "the best of [the] bad options available to us."[69]

September 11th, the War on Terror, and the Return to Iraq

Thus, even when the 2000 presidential election returned many neoconservatives to the White House as part of George W. Bush's new administration, a major military undertaking to remove Saddam appeared out of the question.[70] The terrorist attacks of September 11th, 2001, changed all that, and much else besides. Al Qaeda's strikes on the World Trade Center—a symbol of American economic supremacy—and the Pentagon—the symbol of US military power—were the most direct and spectacular attacks on America's place atop the global hierarchy since the end of the Cold War. They also appeared to threaten the increasingly open and interconnected global society the United States had been leading the world in building since 1991. A shadowy network of terrorist operatives, Al Qaeda seemingly preyed on just that openness, moving money and people around the globe, coordinated by their leader, Osama bin Laden, and his satellite phone.[71] When dawn broke on September 11th, American global hegemony "may not have been popular," as Ahsan Butt writes, "but neither was it challenged, a general deterrence held."[72] Despite the ongoing defiance of international norms by rogue states, and a growing desire to challenge American dominance in places like Russia and China, all knew the dangers of challenging US rule too directly, and thus none truly did.[73]

Suddenly, this sense of impregnability had been challenged by a "rag-tag cabal of Middle Eastern terrorists" without an army, high-tech weaponry,

---

[68]For more on the CIA's regime change efforts see, Steven Coll, *The Achilles Trap: Saddam Hussein, the C.I.A., and the Origins of America's Invasion of Iraq* (New York: Penguin, 2024).
[69]Stieb, *Regime Change Consensus*, 187.
[70]Stieb, *Regime Change Consensus*, 187–8.
[71]Immerwahr, *How to Hide an Empire*, 381.
[72]Butt, "Why Did the United States Invade Iraq," 268.
[73]Butt, "Why Did the United States Invade Iraq," 269.

or the full control of a state.⁷⁴ Operating from bases in rural Afghanistan, whose Islamic fundamentalist Taliban government provided them safe harbor, Al Qaeda operatives had managed to seize control of four civilian aircraft, kill three thousand American citizens, level a significant chunk of lower Manhattan, and slam a plane into the headquarters of the US military. It also at the time appeared to be poised to strike again and again, and there seemed to be little the United States could do to stop it. As the *Wall Street Journal* lamented in October of 2001, "this is the harsh reality of life after September 11, when Americans learned that their own homeland is now vulnerable to attack."⁷⁵ As the focus on the "homeland" here suggests, Americans could accept that US troops, diplomats, and facilities overseas might become targets of the country's enemies, but not the United States itself.

It was by striking some of those forward deployed "points" of American hegemony, in fact, that Al Qaeda had begun to make its name. The organization was born amidst the US-backed campaign of the Afghan "mujahideen" against the Soviet Union's occupation of their country (1979–89) during the final decade of the Cold War.⁷⁶ The scion of a wealthy Saudi family—his father owned and ran a successful construction firm—Bin Laden represented a movement that merged an extremist form of Saudi Islam with the Islamic, anti-colonial thought of the Egyptian Sayyid Qutb (1906–66). Bin Laden had gone to Afghanistan, therefore, to help protect the Muslim world from what he perceived as the godless, Western imperialism of the Soviet Union, before turning his attention to the (in his mind) equally godless perfidy of the United States following the Gulf War. Just like Saddam's Baathist party, Al Qaeda therefore was very much a response to the project of imperial ordering we have traced in this book, a reflection of outrage over the lower place the Muslim world had been afforded in the global hierarchy.⁷⁷ As the leading power defending that hierarchy, with its troops supposedly defiling the holy soil of Saudi Arabia, and its money and guns supporting what Islamists saw as Israel's Western settler beachhead in the Middle East, the United States was a natural target. Though many Americans first learned of the threat of radical Islam following the February 1993 bombing of the World Trade Center's parking garage—carried out by associates of Bin Laden—Al Qaeda's first major strike on US assets was

---

⁷⁴Butt, "Why Did the United States Invade Iraq," 268. At the time, it was believed that Al Qaeda had operated on 9-11 without the direct support of any state institutions, later reporting challenged that assumption. See: Daniel Benjamin and Steven Simon, "New 9-11 Evidence Points to Deep Saudi Complicity," *The Atlantic*, May 20, 2024, https://www.theatlantic.com/ideas/archive/2024/05/september-11-attacks-saudi-arabia-lawsuit/678430/.
⁷⁵Butt, "Why Did the United States Invade Iraq," 269–70.
⁷⁶On the proxy war in Afghanistan see: Westad, *Global Cold War*, 299–330, 348–57, 372–8.
⁷⁷Mishra, *From the Ruins of Empire*, 278–9.

the 1998 bombings of the American embassies in Kenya and Tanzania, killing hundreds. In response, Clinton had ordered cruise missile strikes on a pharmaceutical facility in Sudan—believed to be making chemical weapons—and on suspected Al Qaeda camps in Afghanistan.[78] Another Al Qaeda attack followed in October of 2000, this time on a US Navy destroyer refueling in Yemen's port city of Aden. It killed seventeen sailors, wounded dozens more, and disabled the ship, requiring it to be towed home.[79]

None of these, of course, compared with September 11th, which seemed to confirm to critics of the relative American restraint of the 1990s that everything they had been saying about the use of US power had been correct. The Bush administration moved quickly in the aftermath of the attacks to reassert America's place in the global hierarchy, looking to make it clear that Al Qaeda had not shaken American power, but reawakened it. In October, the United States launched an operation—entitled "Enduring Freedom"—to overthrow the Taliban and oust Al Qaeda from its Afghan bases. It was, initially, an overwhelming success, thanks to an unconventional, high-tech campaign that mixed special forces, airpower, and allied anti-Taliban Afghans to quickly conquer a country long seen as a "graveyard of empires." By November, the United States had set up a new provisional government under Hamid Karzai, which was intended to oversee Afghanistan's transition to a US-style liberal democracy.[80] Though Bin Laden evaded capture, few expected he would be able to remain on the run for long. In addition to toppling the Taliban, Bush also made aggressive use of America's network of bases and alliances with governments and intelligence organizations across the globe to round up suspected terrorists and allies of Al Qaeda. Desperate to prevent another attack on American soil—and, increasingly, to find Bin Laden—the administration authorized US intelligence agencies to employ a number of methods in violation of US and international law. These included "extraordinary rendition"—which involved kidnapping terrorist suspects and moving them to CIA "black site" prisons in allied countries to evade US law—and the torture of those moved to those sites.[81] Though the CIA's torture chambers remained secret, a publicly acknowledged prison for what were called "enemy combatants" would become the symbol of America's

---

[78]The missile strikes did little beyond destroying the source of roughly half of Sudan's drug supply. Immerwahr, *How to Hide an Empire*, 381.

[79]On the emergence and escalation of Al Qaeda's war on the United States see: Steven Coll, *Ghost Wars: The Secret History of the CIA, Afghanistan, and Bin Laden from the Soviet Invasion to September 10, 2001* (New York: Penguin Books, 2004); Lawrence Wright, *The Looming Tower: Al Qaeda and the Road to 9/11* (New York: Vintage Books, 2007).

[80]For more on the US war in Afghanistan see: Carter Malkasian, *The American War in Afghanistan: A History* (New York: Oxford University Press, 2023).

[81]Many of those captured and tortured in this way turned out to be innocent of any association with terrorism. For an overview of the US treatment of detainees during the War on Terrorism see: David P. Forsyth, *The Politics of Prisoner Abuse: The United States and Enemy Prisoners after 9/11* (New York: Cambridge University Press, 2011).

"war on terrorism": "Camp X-Ray" located at Naval Station Guantanamo Bay in Cuba. Built on land seized, of course, during the Spanish-American War, the "GTMO" prison illustrated clearly how each generation of American hierarchy-making was built on that which came before.

However, for the neoconservatives—including Cheney and Wolfowitz, now Vice President and Undersecretary of Defense, respectively—and their allies in the administration, like Secretary of Defense Donald Rumsfeld, it was plain that the war in Afghanistan was not going to be a strong enough reassertion of US dominance. As early as the evening of September 11th, in fact, Rumsfeld was already convinced, as he said privately, that "we need to bomb something else to prove that we're, you know, big and strong and not going to be pushed around by these kinds of attacks."[82] Writing to the President later in the month, Rumsfeld continued "if the war does not significantly change the World's political map, the US will not achieve its aim." The administration, he suggested, "should envision a goal along these lines: New regimes in Afghanistan and another key State (or two) that supports terrorism."[83] The import was clear, the humiliation of September 11th required the United States to demonstrate its continued control of the global hierarchy by knocking some rogue states down a peg. Afghanistan, already quite low in the hierarchy after all, wouldn't be an effective demonstration on its own. What the Bush administration decided was needed to preserve American hegemony was—to use Ahsan Butt's apt term—a "performative war."[84]

With that goal in mind, it was only natural that Bush officials would quickly focus on Iraq as Americas' next target, despite it having no meaningful connection to Al Qaeda beyond some tenuously common ideological roots in Arab anti-imperial thought. As we have seen, in official Washington a "regime change consensus" had already begun to settle in the late 1990s. Saddam remained an irritating reminder of the limits of American power and a potential lynchpin for forcing a strategic realignment in the Middle East— the heartland of rogue states. In July of 2001, Rumsfeld had suggested in a memo "if Saddam's regime were outed, we would have a much-improved position in the region and elsewhere."[85] A friendly, pro-American regime in Iraq would put further pressure on Iran and Syria, while Saddam's fate if removed would stand as a warning to Libya and even rogue regimes further afield like North Korea and Venezuela (which had elected a president in 1999, Hugo Chavez, who was resurrecting the anti-American rhetoric of the 1970s Global South). Neoconservatives in particular embraced the idea

---

[82]Butt, "Why Did the United States Invade Iraq," 270–1.
[83]Butt, "Why Did the United States Invade Iraq," 272.
[84]Butt, "Why Did the United States Invade Iraq," 251.
[85]Memo: Donald Rumsfeld to Condoleezza Rice, "Iraq," July 27, 2001, *The National Security Archive*, George Washington University, https://nsarchive2.gwu.edu/NSAEBB/NSAEBB326/doc06.pdf.

of global transformation. They saw an opportunity not only to eliminate a longstanding foe of the United States, but also a means to further remake the world in America's image—to bring "an end to evil," as two neoconservative Bush staffers would put it after leaving the administration in 2004.[86]

Bush himself got caught up in this sentiment, believing that his administration had a chance to advance the cause of American-style civilization. As he put it in a speech two weeks after 9-11, "freedom and fear are at war. The advance of human freedom, the great achievement of our time and the great hope of every time, now depends on us."[87] Moreover, though the administration would present the image of Iraq as a dangerous threat to the United States, its appeal as a target had as much to do with its weakness and isolation as anything else. Unlike many of the other rogue states that defied American power, as Jeffrey Record writes, in the early 2000s, "Iraq was both helpless and friendless."[88] It was the low-hanging fruit among the last bastions of resistance to America's long project of global reordering.

In his January 2022 State of the Union Address, Bush thus announced that the United States intended to confront not just Iraq, but all the rogue states—rhetorically assembling them in an imaginary alliance: the "Axis of Evil." This axis was purportedly led by Saddam's Iraq and joined by Iran and North Korea. Aware that strategic arguments on behalf of a performative war for hierarchy might not produce enough support among an American public concerned mostly with the threat of terrorism, Bush also did everything he could to suggest that not only was Saddam producing WMDs, but that he might give them to Al Qaeda or other terrorist groups for a strike on the United States.[89] As he would put it in October—at a time when debate over whether Saddam actually had a weapons program was undermining the administration's case for war—"we cannot wait for the final proof, the smoking gun, that could come in the form of a [nuclear] mushroom cloud."[90] The administration also emphasized—especially once the invasion

---

[86] David Frum and Richard Perle, *An End to Evil: How to Win the War on Terrorism* (New York: Random House, 2003).

[87] George W. Bush, "Address before a Joint Session of the Congress on the United States Response to the Terrorist Attacks of September 11," September 20, 2001, Online by Gerhard Peters and John T. Woolley, *The American Presidency Project*, https://www.presidency.ucsb.edu/node/213749.

[88] Jeffrey Record, *Wanting War: Why the Bush Administration Invaded Iraq* (Washington, DC: Potomac Books, 2010), 25.

[89] George W. Bush, "Address before a Joint Session of the Congress on the State of the Union," January 29, 2002, Online by Gerhard Peters and John T. Woolley, *The American Presidency*, Project, https://www.presidency.ucsb.edu/node/211864; Butt, "Why Did the United States Invade Iraq," 252–63.

[90] George W. Bush, "Address to the Nation on Iraq From Cincinnati, Ohio," October 7, 2002, Online by Gerhard Peters and John T. Woolley, *The American Presidency Project*, https://www.presidency.ucsb.edu/node/215740.

began and WMDs failed to emerge—another form of the civilizational argument: democratization. They suggested that through the occupation of Iraq (and of Afghanistan as well), the United States could bring into the fold a Middle East that had resisted the post-Cold War wave of democratization and economic liberalization.

In a speech before the National Endowment for Democracy in November of 2003, for example, Bush offered his own history of decolonization in the Middle East, one that suggested that it was the very defiance of US-backed political and economic norms that had kept the Arab world out of the friendly confines of civilization:

> As the colonial era passed away, the Middle East saw the establishment of many military dictatorships. Some rulers adopted the dogmas of socialism, seized total control of political parties and the media and universities. They allied themselves with the Soviet bloc and with international terrorism. Dictators in Iraq and Syria promised the restoration of national honor, a return to ancient glories.

Rejecting the hierarchical vision of the world offered by the United States, Bush argued, these dictatorships had instead opted to align with its two main competitors—Soviet and Third World alike—with grim results. "They've left instead a legacy of torture, oppression, misery, and ruin," he asserted. Making matters worse, the President continued, these regimes still clung to those visions even after the "end of history" had seemingly foreclosed them as true rivals to US authority. Despite all the changes in the world since 1991, Bush said, "the great wave of democracy has … 'barely reached the Arab states'." The Iraq invasion was going to change that, he suggested, bringing not only democracy and economic liberalism to the Middle East, but equal rights for women and religious freedom as well.[91]

While there was opposition in Washington to Bush's plan to strike Iraq, it was, for the most part, more about method and timing than ultimate necessity. The Congressional resolution authorizing the President to use force against Saddam received notable bi-partisan support, while editorialists and public intellectuals from across the political spectrum—from liberal humanitarians to neoconservatives and their allies—justified the need to remove the Baathist regime from power.[92] Many Democrats—and figures within the administration like Secretary of State Colin Powell—wanted

---

[91]Bush, "Remarks on the 20th Anniversary of the National Endowment for Democracy."
[92]Butt, "Why Did the United States Invade Iraq," 284; Stieb, *Regime Change Consensus*, 216–28, 231–3.

to see the Bush administration move more slowly and work carefully to build a broad international coalition for the war with explicit UN Security Council endorsement.[93] This endorsement proved not to be forthcoming, both because of Bush's impatience to get the war underway and because there was broad global skepticism about the necessity of an invasion. The heart of the administration's case for war under international law was the supposed existence of a WMD program in Iraq, and the fact that Saddam had expelled UN weapons inspectors in 1998. Both the governments and the public in traditional American allies like France and Germany did not see the immediate necessity for an invasion to address this, a perspective shared by wary would-be rivals like China and Russia. The French, Chinese, and Russians—all permanent members of the Security Council—were willing to authorize resolutions that confronted Saddam and threatened serious consequences if he failed to comply but were unwilling to approve of the use of force, particularly once Saddam allowed the inspectors back into the country.[94] Unable to produce the international authorization it demanded, the United States proceeded to war more or less unilaterally, leading what the Bush administration called a "coalition of the willing" into Iraq in March of 2003. Though this coalition claimed dozens of countries as members, only a handful actually contributed troops to the invasion, with the vast majority of combat forces coming from the United States and Great Britain.

The full story of the war in Iraq is beyond our scope here, save to note that after an initially spectacular success for the American-led coalition, the subsequent occupation quickly turned to disaster. US troops entered Baghdad in less than a month. Saddam fled and his regime collapsed (he was captured in December and then executed following trial in 2006). In May 2003, President Bush loudly proclaimed the "mission accomplished" during a dramatic speech from the flight deck of the aircraft carrier, USS Abraham Lincoln. However, thanks to poor planning, limited resources, and the administration's desire to quickly withdraw US troops, the US occupation government—the "Coalition Provisional Authority"— struggled to govern America's newest imperial possession.[95] Indeed, as Bush was giving his speech to the Lincoln's crew an insurgency was forming in Iraq against American rule and the security situation in the country subsequently collapsed. Soon more than 100,000 US troops were battling to maintain control of the country, reaching a peak of nearly 160,000 during the so-called "surge" that began in 2007. Though Iraq began to stabilize enough following the surge to allow a drawdown of US troops,

---

[93]Stieb, *Regime Change Consensus*, 216–28.
[94]Stieb, *Regime Change Consensus*, 235–47.
[95]On the Coalition Provisional Authority see: James Dobbins et al., *Occupying Iraq: A History of the Coalition Provisional Authority* (Santa Monica: RAND Corporation, 2009).

FIGURE 16 *US Soldiers from the 3rd Platoon, A-Company, 2nd regiment, 7th Infantry patrol the streets of Baghdad in May of 2003—around the time the security situation in the country rapidly deteriorated.*

the war killed more than four thousand Americans and wounded tens of thousands more, while killing somewhere between 100 and 200,000 Iraqis, mostly civilians.[96]

Increasingly distracted in Iraq, the United States allowed a resurgence of the Taliban in Afghanistan, which launched its own insurgency in 2003–04 against US forces and the American-backed government in Kabul. By the end of Bush's second term in 2009, it was clear to most observers that the war in Iraq had been a terrible mistake and that Afghanistan too was on the road to disaster. Meant to bolster American hegemony, these invasions had in fact weakened it by exposing the limits of American power, while bogging down and nearly exhausting the US military machine in what appeared a "forever war."[97] At the same time, American unilateralism had undermined the UN collective security apparatus that—despite the Bush administration's frustrations with it in 2002—had become since the Cold War a powerful tool for legitimizing American dominance. The arrival of the "Great Recession" in late 2007–08, further eroded American authority, as a financial panic

---

[96]For an account of the critical mistakes made in the early stages of the war see: Thomas Ricks, *Fiasco: The American Military Adventure in Iraq* (New York: Penguin Press, 2006).
[97]Dexter Filkins, *The Forever War* (New York: Vintage Books, 2009).

made possible by neoliberal cutbacks in regulation spread throughout the globalized economy.[98]

Elected in 2008 amidst that downturn on a promise of "hope" and "change we can believe in," Barack Obama would spend much of his eight years in office working to stabilize, rather than transform, American global hegemony. Eschewing any opportunity to remake the global financial system in the wake of the crisis, Obama chose to bolster it instead by bailing out troubled international banking houses with public funds.[99] Not entirely unlike Richard Nixon's strategic retrenchment following the Vietnam War, Obama did not seek to transform or abandon American global primacy, but make it more sustainable in an era of diminished public support and diminished American capabilities. He began to withdraw troops from Iraq at the same time he initiated a new surge in Afghanistan to put down the Taliban insurgency. Meanwhile he also increasingly embraced air power and high-tech drone warfare to strike targets—mostly Islamic terrorists—without the need for deploying large numbers of troops and with little concern for international borders. Indeed, while these drone strikes were often clear violations of sovereignty and international law, the administration leaned into the supposedly humane aspects of this form of targeted warfare. Drones limited civilian casualties while also allowing the US government to kill almost anyone it wished across large swaths of the former colonial world.[100] US troops would redeploy to Iraq in 2014 to fight the rise of a new, more radical Islamic terrorist group—the "Islamic State" or "ISIS"—but this time in much smaller numbers, supported by drones and airstrikes.

At times it appeared that the President had managed to restore something of the old "new world order" feeling of the 1990s, such as when he arranged UN Security Council authorization for European and US intervention in the 2011 Libyan civil war. Subsequent airstrikes so weakened the Gaddafi regime that it soon fell to the rebel opposition. At other times, the strain of war and economic recession showed, as when Obama demurred from launching airstrikes on Syria in 2013 following Syrian President Bashar al-Assad's use of chemical weapons amidst the civil war there. Obama had warned in 2012 that Assad's use of such weapons against anti-regime rebels was a "red line" that, if crossed, would trigger an American military response. Wary of unleashing the sort of chaos that had followed Gaddafi's fall in Libya, and wary of Congressional and public skepticism, Obama instead chose to do

---

[98]Daunton, *Economic Government of the World*, 731–70; Hahnhimäki, *Pax Transatlantica*, 84–91.
[99]On Barack Obama's political shift from a radical campaign to a centrist presidency see: Shenk, *Realigners*, 295–339.
[100]See: Moyn, *Humane*, 267–311.

nothing.[101] Assad's Syrian regime was eventually able to stabilize its rule—surviving in power for another decade by relying on an alliance with Russia and Iran that marked the emergence of a new anti-American block in central Asia.[102]

America's newfound reticence to police the world was again highlighted when Russia seized the Crimean Peninsula from Ukraine in 2014. Though the United States organized international sanctions in response—and began providing some security assistance to the Ukrainians—most came to accept this clear violation of Ukrainian sovereignty as a fait accompli that had to be lived with.[103] Hoping to restore something of the empire he believed had been unfairly snatched away from Russia by the US expansion of NATO at the end of the Cold War, Russian President Vladimir Putin's invasion in many ways marked the end of the era that the Soviet collapse had inaugurated. Where in 1991 Saddam's seizure of Kuwait had allowed the United States to mobilize the international community to pronounce an end to the "law of the jungle," Putin's 2014 invasion of Crimea suggested that "the jungle had grown back"—as the neoconservative intellectual Robert Kagan would put it in 2018.[104] Many around the world, no doubt, would suggest that the United States had never really meant to cut down the jungle, or its hierarchies, in the first place.

---

[101] On Libya and Syria see: Hahnhimäki, *Pax Transatlantica*, 58–60; Haslam, *Hubris*, 179–82; Nolan D. McCaskill, "Obama: Not Bombing Syria 'Required the most Political Courage'," *Politico*, May 15, 2017: https://www.politico.com/story/2017/05/15/obama-justify-not-bombing-syria-238394.

[102] Assad's regime later collapsed in the final months of 2024: Maya Gebeily and Timour Azhari, "Syrian Rebels Topple Assad Who Flees to Russia in Mideast Shakeup," *Reuters*, December 8, 2024, https://www.reuters.com/world/middle-east/syria-rebels-celebrate-captured-homs-set-sights-damascus-2024-12-07/.

[103] Haslam, *Hubris*, 210–17.

[104] Robert Kagan, *The Jungle Grows Back: America and Our Imperiled World* (New York: Alfred A. Knopf, 2018).

Conclusion: Hierarchy in a Flat World

In the opening vignette of his 2005 book *The World Is Flat: A Brief History of the 21st Century*, the *New York Times* columnist Thomas Freidman describes what he called his "own Columbus-like journey of exploration" to Bangalore, India. There, playing golf on a course surrounded by the offices of major American corporations like Microsoft and IBM, and meeting with Indian entrepreneurs erecting call and data centers, he came to what was, for him, a startling conclusion: the world Columbus had traversed by sail five hundred years earlier was no longer round, "it was flat." By flat, he meant that the global economy was a deeply integrated but level playing field, that information and transportation technology, combined with loosened international financial and trade regulations had created a world where Indian firms could compete on an equal footing with those from the United States and Europe. Individuals with verve and a good idea, Friedman seemed to imply, could now compete for wealth in a seamless world of capitalist competition, unburdened by unequal histories. Few were more breathlessly enthusiastic about the flattening world he was describing than Friedman himself, yet all the same he sounded two warnings. One was that "it's not only software writers and computer geeks who get empowered" by a flat world, "it's also Al Qaeda and other terrorist networks" who gained new opportunities. The other was that "America was going to be challenged" to be, Friedman wrote, "our best" by new business competition from around the world. These, though, were the rare dour notes in 400-plus pages of *The World Is Flat*'s major key celebration of the new globalized world.[1]

---

[1] Thomas Freidman, *The World Is Flat: A Brief History of the 21st Century* (New York: Farrar, Straus, and Giroux, 2005), 3–7.

Friedman's enthusiastic story about golfing in Bangalore provides a good place to conclude our consideration of the United States and the ends of empire, as it sits at the convergence of many of the stories we have been following in this book. Much like Friedman, we began with Columbus—both the man himself and his mythologized likeness in *Discovery*, the statue that once stood alongside *The Rescue* outside the US Capitol. It was Columbus the man who set in motion the process of global integration that produced not only the United States but, in the long run, the modern interconnected world that Friedman observed from his Indian tee box. Columbus the symbol, meanwhile, helps explain Friedman's surprise at his conclusion that Indian firms were able to compete on even terms with those from the United States. Disguised as the advance of "civilization," the European invasion of the Americas disappears into a mythologized rendering of Columbus's supposed "discovery" of a "New World," with narratives of "progress" obscuring—as we have seen—a more sordid tale about the violent overthrow of global hierarchies and the establishment of a new world order of imperial violence. In seeing an India that has "caught up," Friedman appears unaware of the degree to which it, like much of the non-European and non-American world, was in fact deliberately "set back" by centuries of imperial world-ordering. Even if we could speak of a Westphalian sovereign equality governing relations between states, the past three centuries have ensured that some states are privileged with being more equal than others.

The myopic view of history Friedman employs, of course, was and remains central to the constellation of ideas that make up "American exceptionalism," allowing Americans to see the subjugation of neighboring peoples and the seizure of their land as part of a heroic victory for humanity (like that depicted in *The Rescue*). That is, to see a vertically ordered, hierarchical world as somehow "flat." The fact that Friedman's fairway was surrounded by American firms, not Indian ones, thus appears a perfectly natural and inevitable result of the processes of history—the triumph of the supposedly superior "West over the rest"—rather than the consequence of an oft-deliberate project of violent, national self-aggrandizement that eventually allowed US companies to force their way into the economic lives of people on the other side of the world.[2] Much the same could be said for the individualist, fossil-fuel powered, high technology, and high consumption world that Friedman finds so stimulating: it too loses its contingency and instead gains totalitarian control over our definitions of what "modern" must look like and, by extension, curtails our ability to imagine what other forms of "the future" might follow it. What the Catawba mapmaker we encountered in Chapter 3 found so alien—the emerging grid of capitalist modernity—now claims a universality that theoretically leaves no corner

---

[2]Niall Ferguson, *Civilization: The West and the Rest* (New York: Penguin Books, 2012).

of the planet with the ability to resist its relentless transformations. As this book has documented, the United States has played an essential role in making this the case, not only in helping to construct and determine the shape of the hierarchically integrated, globalized world we live in, but also in making it appear the inevitable outcome of history.

Since the election to determine Barack Obama's successor as president in 2016, however, questions have emerged about how much longer the United States will be able to play such an outsized role in ordering the world. Whatever comment might be made about *The World Is Flat*'s interpretation of the history of globalization, Friedman's warnings about the risks to American power in the twenty-first century proved prescient, if not perhaps in the way he suggested. Al Qaeda did not in fact take advantage of the flat world to wage a relentless terrorist campaign against the United States, as Friedman feared. Yet, at the time he was writing the terrorist group had already set in motion events that would do significant damage to American power. The September 11th attacks provided the impetus for the United States to engage not only in a semi-colonial nation-building project in Afghanistan, but also, and more significantly, in a "performative war" in Iraq.[3] As Chapter 8 considered, these attempts to demonstrate American dominance of the global hierarchy ironically did much to undermine that position in the long run, drawing a significant chunk of US military might into two, decades long, quagmires while sapping the will of the American public for overseas military deployments. However much Obama's retrenchment may have stabilized the situation in the 2010s, there can be no doubt that the United States emerged from the post-9-11 conflicts weaker than it entered them.

Friedman's second factor—neoliberal trade liberalization—was also part of that story of relative decline, if again for slightly different reasons than *The World Is Flat* suggested. While the United States, in the aggregate, grew wealthier in the neoliberal age, not all Americans shared in that prosperity. Middle- and working-class Americans instead saw a constriction of their economic opportunities, as technological change and reduced regulation made it easier for companies to move jobs overseas, in effect exposing Americans to competition with lower-wage workers in the Global South. Indeed, a carnival mirror version of the transfer of wealth from the developed world that the G-77 had called for did emerge, but it was unevenly structured—only benefiting some in a few countries like India and China— and was very much at the expense of average Americans. Though the United States remained the world's wealthiest society, the declining prospects of those in the middle bands of America's internal hierarchy undermined the stability of the country's political system. The growing discord was already evident during the Obama years, as both the major American political parties

---

[3]Butt, "Why Did the U.S Invade Iraq?"

struggled to cobble together enough votes in Congress to pass significant legislation or find space for functional compromise.

This political semi-paralysis only deepened after Obama's departure, as his two relatively unpopular successors, Donald Trump and Joseph Biden, traded terms governing via executive orders between 2016 and 2024, while confronting the new limits to American power following Russia's 2021 invasion of Ukraine and the growing influence of an economically dynamic China. The accelerating climate crisis, meanwhile, has revealed natural, material limits on economic growth that do much to undermine capitalism's claims on a moral future. No longer able to plausibly suggest that "the living standards of the rich can be extended to the poor, on a global scale, without putting an unbearable burden on the earth's natural resources"—as the historian Christopher Lasch put it in 1991—the narratives of economic progress on which the US vision of world order has long relied appear as exhausted as the American political system itself.[4]

Whether the 2020s mark part of the permanent decline of the United States or merely a 1970s-style dip in fortunes, it seems unlikely either way that Americans will give up the long habit of hierarchy-making we've been tracking in this book. Both Biden and Trump, for example, have demonstrated a commitment to visions of the world that require the United States to sit at the top of a heap. Biden and the Democrats, on the one hand, stuck to the neoliberal hyperpower model introduced in Chapter 8, with the United States positioning itself as the defender of civilization—or the "rules-based order," as the Biden administration preferred to call it—against the jungle. Though this order was ostensibly a multilateral system of global governance defending human rights and liberal political institutions, the close relationship between "the rules" and "what the U.S. wants" was made clear for all to see in the differential treatment of Russia's attacks on civilians in Ukraine and Israel's on Palestinians following its 2023 invasion of Gaza. Trump's "Make America Great Again" vision, meanwhile, suggested that even the limited gestures toward Westphalian equality implied in the "rules-based order" were several gestures too many, preferring an approach to the world closer to the "American system" style of competitive, protectionist imperialism discussed in Chapter 4. Accepting American decline as a fact—rather than denying it, as Biden usually did—Trump promised to reverse that decline through more openly hierarchical uses of American military and economic power.

In this alone, perhaps, the 47th president may be a departure from precedent—not in the imperial uses of American power, of course, but in abandoning any premise that US interests overlap with those of civilization writ large. How long Trump will be able to maintain the pretense that

---

[4]Christopher Lasch, *The True and Only Heaven: Progress and Its Critics* (New York: W.W. Norton and Company, 1991), 532.

his conception of "US interests" coincides at all with those of the average American also remains a question. While his predecessors generally thought it prudent to suggest their actions were good for both most Americans and all of humanity, Trump seems less concerned with such appearances. If, as the German philosopher Walter Benjamin once wrote, "there is no document of civilization which is not at the same time a document of barbarism"—that is, that everything that claims to be civilized is premised on a barbaric act—Trump might just scrape clean the civilizational veneer of much of the American project, fully revealing what lies beneath.[5] For all that we have documented in this book, that lost veneer seems likely to be missed. Regardless, if we accept Friedman's suggestion that a flat world is a more equal world, then clearly Columbus could still set sail today without fear.

---

[5] Walter Benjamin, "Theses on the Philosophy of History," in *Illuminations: Essays and Reflections*, Hannah Arendt ed., Harry Zohn trans. (New York: Schocken Books, 1969), 256.

BIBLIOGRAPHY

Online Sources

Cornell Law School, *Legal Information Institute*, www.cornell.law.edu.
General Assembly of the State of Georgia, "Acts of the General Assembly of the State of Georgia, Passed in Milledgeville, November and December 1827," *HathiTrust*, https://babel.hathitrust.org/cgi/pt?id=nyp.33433001215882&seq=7.
George Washington University, *National Security Archive*, https://nsarchive.gwu.edu.
Kipling, Rudyard, *The Poems of Rudyard Kipling*, The Kipling Society, https://www.kiplingsociety.co.uk/poems.htm.
Library of Congress, "The Inaugural Site," https://www.loc.gov/classroom-materials/inaugurations/an-orderly-transition/the-inaugural-site.
Luxembourg Center for Contemporary and Digital History, https://www.cvce.eu/en.
Public Papers of the Presidents, *The American Presidency Project*, Online by John Woolley and Gerhard Peters, https://www.presidency.ucsb.edu.
United States Department of State, *Foreign Relations of the United States*, Historical Documents, https://history.state.gov/historicaldocuments.
United States National Archives and Records Administration, "Milestone Documents," https://www.archives.gov/milestone-documents/list.
Yale University Law School, *The Avalon Project: Documents in Law, History, and Diplomacy*, https://avalon.law.yale.edu.

Articles

Aber, Samuel L. "Worldmaking at the End of History: The Gulf Crisis of 1990–91 and International Law," *American Journal of International Law* 117, no. 2 (April 2023): 201–50.
Adas, Michael. "Contested Hegemony: The Great War and the Afro-Asian Assault on the Civilizing Mission Ideology," *Journal of World History* 15, no. 1 (March 2004): 31–63.
Adelman, Jeremy. "Empires, Nations, and Revolutions," *Journal of the History of Ideas* 79, no. 1 (January 2018): 73–88.
Beck, Robert J. "The Grenada Invasion, International Law, and the Scoon Invitation: A Thirty Year Retrospective," in *Grenada: Revolution and Invasion*, Patsy Lewis et al., eds. Kingston: The University of the West Indies Press, 2015, 164–79.
Benbow, Mark. "All the Brains I Can Borrow: Woodrow Wilson and Intelligence Gathering in Mexico, 1913–15," *Studies in Intelligence* 51, no. 4 (December 2007): 1–12.

Benjamin, Daniel and Steven Simon. "New 9-11 Evidence Points to Deep Saudi Complicity," *The Atlantic*, May 20, 2024, https://www.theatlantic.com/ideas/archive/2024/05/september-11-attacks-saudi-arabia-lawsuit/678430/.

Bockman, Johanna. "Socialist Globalization against Capitalist Neocolonialism: The Economic Ideas behind the New International Economic Order," *Humanity* (Philadelphia, PA) 6, no. 1 (Spring 2015): 109–28.

Breen, T.H. "Ideology and Nationalism on the Eve of the Revolution: Revisions Once More in Need of Revising," *Journal of American History* 84, no. 1 (June 1997): 13–39.

Butt, Ahsan I. "Why Did the United States Invade Iraq in 2003," *Security Studies* 28, no. 2 (April/May 2019): 250–85.

Byrnen, Rex and Paul Noble. "The Gulf Conflict and the Arab State System: A New Regional Order?" *Arab Studies Quarterly* 13, no. 1/2 (Winter/Spring 1991): 117–40.

Chardell, Daniel. "The Origins of the Iraqi Invasion of Kuwait Reconsidered," *Texas National Security Review* 6, no. 3 (Summer 2023): 52–78.

Fieleke, Norman S. "The Uruguay Round of Trade Negotiations: An Overview," *New England Economic Review* (July/August 1995): 3–14.

Fryd, Vivien Green. "Two Sculptures for the Capitol: Horatio Greenough's 'Rescue' and Luigi Persico's 'Discovery of America'," *The American Art Journal* 19, no. 2 (1987): 16–39.

Gleijeses, Piero. "A Test of Wills: Jimmy Carter, South Africa, and the Independence of Namibia," *Diplomatic History* 23, no. 4 (October 1999): 657–85.

Gleijeses, Piero. "Review of: Our Sister Republics: The United States and the Age of American Revolutions by Caitlin Fitz," *Journal of Latin American Studies* 49, no. 1 (January 2017): 174–6.

Gleijeses, Piero. "The Limits of Sympathy: The United States and the Independence of Spanish America," *Journal of Latin American Studies* 24, no. 3 (October 1992): 481–505.

Hickey, Donald. "The Legacy of 1812: How a Little War Shaped the Transatlantic World," *London Journal of Canadian Studies* 28, no. 1 (2021): 1–14.

Inikori, Joseph E. "Atlantic Slavery and the Rise of the Capitalist Global Economy," *Current Anthropology* 61, no. 22 (2020): S159–S171.

Kagan, Robert and William Kristol. "Toward a Neo-Reaganite Foreign Policy," *Foreign Affairs* 75, no. 4 (June/July 1996): 18–32.

Katz, Friedrich. "Pancho Villa and the Attack on Columbus, New Mexico," *The American Historical Review* 83, no. 1 (February 1978): 101–30.

Kirkpatrick, Jeane. "Dictatorships and Double Standards," *Commentary* 68, no. 5 (November 1979): 34–45.

Knight, Franklin W. "The Haitian Revolution," *American Historical Review* 105, no. 1 (February 2000): 103–15.

Krepp, Stella. "Fighting an Illiberal World Order: The Latin American Road to UNCTAD, 1948–1964," *Humanity* (Philadelphia, PA) 13, no. 1 (Spring 2022): 86–103.

Lamar, Quinton Curtis. "A Diplomatic Disaster: The Mexican Mission of Anthony Butler, 1829–1834," *The Americas* 45, no. 1 (July 1988): 1–17.

Lee, Karis. "'Ground [the Statues] into Dust!'—The Downfall of Two District Memorials," *Boundarystones: WETA's Local History Website*, July 8, 2020, https://boundarystones.weta.org/2020/07/08/ground-statues-dust-downfall-two-district-memorials.

Loureiro, Felipe P. "Making the Alliance for Progress Serve the Few: U.S. Economic Aid to Cold War Brazil (1961–1964)," *Journal of Cold War Studies* 25, no. 1 (Winter 2023): 168–207.

Matthewson, Timothy M. "George Washington's Policy towards the Haitian Revolution," *Diplomatic History* 3, no. 3 (Summer 1979): 321–36.

McCaskill, Nolan D. "Obama: Not Bombing Syria 'Required the Most Political Courage'," *Politico*, May 15, 2017, https://www.politico.com/story/2017/05/15/obama-justify-not-bombing-syria-238394.

Moynihan, Daniel Patrick. "The United States in Opposition," *Commentary* 59, no. 3 (March 1975): 31–44.

O'Rourke, Kevin H. and Jeffrey G. Williamson. "When Did Globalization Begin," Working Paper, *National Bureau of Economic Research*, April 2000, http://www.nber.org/papers/w7632.

Osiander, Andreas. "Sovereignty, International Relations, and the Westphalian Myth," *International Organization* 55, no. 2 (Spring 2001): 251–87.

Pincus, Steve. "Rethinking Mercantilism: Political Economy in the British Empire, and the Atlantic World in the Seventeenth and Eighteenth Centuries," *William and Mary Quarterly* 69, no. 1 (January 2012): 3–34.

Pinhiero, John C. "Religion without Restriction: Anti-Catholicism, All Mexico, and the Treaty of Guadalupe Hidalgo," *Journal of the Early Republic* 23, no. 1 (Spring 2003): 69–96.

Reinstein, Robert J. "Slavery, Executive Power, and International Law: The Haitian Revolution and American Constitutionalism," *The American Journal of Legal History* 53, no. 2 (April 2013): 141–237.

Sareen, T.R. "India and the War," in *The Impact of the Russo- Japanese War*, Rotem Kowner ed. London: Routledge, 2007, 239–51.

Schroeder, Paul W. "Stealing Horses to Great Applause: Austria Hungary's Decision in 1914 in Systemic Perspective," in *An Improbable War: The Outbreak of World War I and European Political Culture before 1914*, Holger Afflerbach and David Stevenson, eds. New York: Berghan Books, 2007, 17–43.

Simeonov, Simeon Andonov. "Consular Recognition, Partial Neutrality, and the Making of Atlantic Diplomacy, 1778–1825," *Diplomatic History* 46, no. 1 (January 2022): 144–72.

Solarz, Marin Woiciech. "Third World: The 60th Anniversary of a Concept That Changed History," *Third World Quarterly* 33, no. 9 (October 2012): 1561–73.

Stagg, J.C.A. "The Madison Administration and Mexico: Reinterpreting the Gutiérrez-Magee Raid of 1812–1813," *The William and Mary Quarterly* 59, no. 2 (April 2002): 449–80.

Stevens, Simon. "From the Viewpoint of a Southern Governor: The Carter Administration and Apartheid, 1977–1981," *Diplomatic History* 36, no. 5 (November 2012): 843–80.

Thronveit, Trygve. "The Fable of the Fourteen Points: Woodrow Wilson and National Self-Determination," *Diplomatic History* 35, no. 3 (June 2011): 445–81.

Tooze, Adam. "Capitalist Peace or Capitalist War: The July Crisis Revisited," in *Cataclysm 1914: The First World War and the Making of Modern World Politics*, Alexander Anievas ed. Boston: Brill, 2015, 66–95.

Tucker, Robert W. "Woodrow Wilson's 'New Diplomacy'," *World Policy Journal* 21, no. 2 (Summer 2004): 92–107.

Tzouvala, Ntina. "Sanctions, Dollar Hegemony, and the Unraveling of Third World Sovereignty," *Yale Journal of International Law*, June 10, 2024, https://yjil.yale.edu/posts/2024-06-10-sanctions-dollar-hegemony-and-the-unraveling-of-third-world-sovereignty.

Vergerio, Claire. "Beyond the Nation State," *Boston Review*, May 27, 2021, https://www.bostonreview.net/articles/beyond-the-nation-state/.

Books

Aboitiz, Nicole CuUnjieng. *Asian Place, Filipino Nation: A Global Intellectual History of the Philippine Revolution*. New York: Columbia University Press, 2020.

Abu-Lughod, Janet. *Before European Hegemony: The World System A.D. 1250–1350*. New York: Oxford University Press, 1989.

Adams, John Quincy. *The Writings of John Quincy Adams, Volume VII: 1820–1823*. Worthington Chauncey Ford ed. New York: Macmillan, 1917.

Adelman, Jeremy. *Sovereignty and Revolution in the Iberian Atlantic*. Princeton: Princeton University Press, 2006.

Akiboh, Alvita. *Imperial Material: National Symbols in the U.S. Colonial Empire*. Chicago: University of Chicago Press, 2023.

Anastacio, Leia Castaneda. *The Foundation of the Modern Philippine State: Imperial Rule and the American Constitutional Tradition, 1898–1935*. New York: Cambridge University Press, 2016.

Anderson, Carol. *Eyes off the Prize: The United Nations and the African American Struggle for Human Rights, 1944–1955*. Cambridge: Cambridge University Press, 2003.

Anderson, Fred. *The Crucible of War: The Seven Years War and the Fate of the British Empire in North America*. New York: Knopf, 2000.

Armitage, David. *The Declaration of Independence: A Global History*. Cambridge, MA: Harvard University Press, 2007.

Asselin, Pierre. *Vietnam's American War: A History*. New York: Cambridge University Press, 2018.

Auden, W.H. *The Complete Works of W.H. Auden: Poems, Volume II*. Princeton: Princeton University Press, 2022.

Aydin, Cemil. *The Politics of Anti-Westernism in Asia: Visions of World Order in Pan-Islamic and Pan-Asian Thought*. New York: Columbia University Press, 2007.

Bacevich, Andrew J. *American Empire: The Realities and Consequences of U.S. Diplomacy*. Cambridge, MA: Harvard University Press, 2002.

Barksdale, Kevin T. *The Lost State of Franklin: America's First Secession*. Lexington: University of Kentucky Press, 2009.

Bartel, Fritz. *The Triumph of Broken Promises: The End of the Cold War and the Rise of Neoliberalism*. Cambridge, MA: Harvard University Press, 2022.

Baylin, Bernard. *Atlantic History: Concept and Contours*. Cambridge, MA: Harvard University Press, 2005.

Baylin, Bernard. *The Ideological Origins of the American Revolution*. Cambridge, MA: Harvard University Press, 1967.
Bayly, C.A. *The Birth of the Modern World, 1780–1940: Global Connections and Comparisons*. Oxford: Blackwell, 2004.
Beckert, Sven. *Empire of Cotton: A Global History*. New York: Alfred A. Knopf, 2015.
Bell, Duncan. *Reordering the World: Essays on Liberalism and Empire*. Princeton: Princeton University Press, 2016.
Benjamin, Walter. *Illuminations: Essays and Reflections*. Hannah Arendt ed., Harry Zohn trans. New York: Schocken Books, 1969.
Bentley, Matthew and John Bloom. *The Imperial Gridiron: Manhood, Civilization, and Football at the Carlisle Indian Industrial School*. Lincoln: University of Nebraska Press, 2022.
Benton, Lauren A. *Law and Colonial Cultures: Legal Regimes in World History, 1400–1900*. Cambridge: Cambridge University Press, 2002.
Bevilacqua, Alexander. *The Republic of Arabic Letters: Islam and the European Enlightenment*. Cambridge, MA: Harvard University Press, 2018.
Blackburn, Robin. *The Making of New World Slavery: From the Baroque to the Modern, 1492–1800*. New York: Verso, 2010.
Blackburn, Robin. *The Overthrow of Colonial Slavery: 1776–1848*. London: Verso, 1988.
Blackhawk, Ned. *The Rediscovery of America: Native Peoples and the Unmaking of U.S. History*. New Haven: Yale University Press, 2023.
Blight, David. *Race and Reunion: The Civil War in American Memory*. Cambridge, MA: Belknap Press, 2001.
Borgwardt, Elizabeth. *The New Deal for the World: America's Vision for Human Rights*. Cambridge, MA: Harvard University Press, 2005.
Borneman, Walter. *Polk: The Man Who Transformed the Presidency and America*. New York: Random House, 2008.
Borstelmann, Thomas. *The Cold War and the Color Line: American Race Relations in the Global Arena*. Cambridge, MA: Harvard University Press, 2001.
Bourdieu, Pierre. *Language and Symbolic Power*. Gino Raymond and Matthew Adamson trans. Cambridge, MA: Harvard University Press, 1991.
Brack, Gene M. *Mexico Views Manifest Destiny, 1821–1846*. Albuquerque: University of New Mexico Press, 1975.
Brands, H.W. *The Specter of Neutralism: The United States and the Emergence of the Third World, 1947–1960*. New York: Columbia University Press, 1989.
Brands, Hal. *From Berlin to Baghdad: America's Search for Purpose in a Post-Cold War World*. Lexington: University of Kentucky Press, 2008.
Brands, Hal. *Making the Unipolar Moment: U.S. Foreign Policy and the Rise of the Post-Cold War Order*. Ithaca: Cornell University Press, 2016.
Brantlinger, Patrick. *Dark Vanishings: Discourse on the Extinction of Primitive Races, 1800–1930*. Ithaca: Cornell University Press, 2003.
Brenes, Michael. *For Might and Right: Cold War Defense Spending and the Remaking of American Democracy*. Amherst: University of Massachusetts Press, 2020.
Brewer, John. *The Sinews of Power: War, Money, and the English State*. Cambridge, MA: Harvard University Press, 1988.

Brucken, Rowland. *A Most Uncertain Crusade: The United States, the United Nations, and Human Rights, 1941–1953*. Dekalb: Northern Illinois University Press, 2014.

Burgin, Angus. *The Great Persuasion: Reinventing Free Markets since the Depression*. Cambridge, MA: Harvard University Press, 2012.

Burke, Kyle. *Revolutionaries for the Right: Anticommunist Internationalism and Paramilitary Warfare in the Cold War*. Chapel Hill: University of North Carolina Press, 2018.

Burke, Roland. *Decolonization and the Evolution of International Human Rights*. Philadelphia: University of Pennsylvania Press, 2010.

Byrnes, Sean T. *Disunited Nations: U.S. Foreign Policy, Anti-Americanism, and the Rise of the New Right*. Baton Rouge: Louisiana State University Press, 2021.

Cain, P.J. and A.G. Hopkins. *British Imperialism: 1688–2015, 3rd Edition*. New York: Routledge, 2016.

Camin, Hector Aguilar and Lorenzo Meyer. *In the Shadow of the Mexican Revolution: Contemporary Mexican History, 1910–1989*. Luis Alberto Fierro trans. Austin: University of Texas Press, 1993.

Capozzola, Christopher. *Bound by War: How the United States and the Philippines Built America's First Pacific Century*. New York: Basic Books, 2020.

Chamberlin, Paul Thomas. *The Cold War's Killing Fields: Rethinking the Long Peace*. New York: HarperCollins, 2019.

Chamberlin, Paul Thomas. *The Global Offensive: The United States, the Palestinian Liberation Organization and the Making of the Post-Cold War Order*. New York: Oxford University Press, 2012.

Chapman, Peter. *Bananas: How the United Fruit Company Shaped the World*. New York: Canongate Books, 2022.

Chibber, Vivek. *Locked in Place: State-Building and Late Industrialization in India*. Princeton: Princeton University Press, 2003.

Chibber, Vivek. *The Class Matrix: Social Theory after the Cultural Turn*. Cambridge, MA: Harvard University Press, 2022.

Chollet, Derek and James Goldgeier. *America between the Wars: From 11/9-9/11*. New York: Public Affairs, 2008.

Clark, Christopher. *The Sleepwalkers: How Europe Went to War in 1914*. New York: Harper Perennial, 2012.

Clymer, Adam. *Drawing the Line at the Big Ditch: The Panama Canal Treaties and the Rise of the Right*. Lawrence: University of Kansas Press, 2008.

Cohen, Lizabeth. *A Consumers Republic: The Politics of Mass Consumption in Postwar America*. New York: Alfred A. Knopf, 2003.

Cohrs, Patrick. *The New Atlantic Order: The Transformation of International Politics, 1860–1933*. Cambridge: Cambridge University Press, 2022.

Coll, Steven. *Ghost Wars: The Secret History of the CIA, Afghanistan, and Bin Laden from the Soviet Invasion to September 10, 2001*. New York: Penguin Books, 2004.

Coll, Steven. *The Achilles Trap: Saddam Hussein, the C.I.A., and the Origins of America's Invasion of Iraq*. New York: Penguin, 2024.

Connelly, Matthew. *A Diplomatic Revolution: Algeria's Fight for Independence and the Origins of the Post-Cold War Era*. New York: Oxford University Press, 2002.

Cooper, Frederick. *Africa since 1940: The Past of the Present*. Cambridge: Cambridge University Press, 2002.

Cooper, Frederick. *Colonialism in Question: Theory, Knowledge, History*. Berkeley: University of California Press, 2005.
Cumfer, Cynthia. *Separate Peoples, One Land: The Minds of Cherokees, Blacks, and Whites on the Tennessee Frontier*. Chapel Hill: University of North Carolina Press, 2007.
Cumings, Bruce. *The Korean War: A History*. New York: Modern Library, 2010.
Daunton, Martin. *The Economic Government of the World, 1933–2023*. New York: Farrar, Straus, and Giroux, 2023.
Davis, David Brion. *Inhuman Bondage: The Rise and Fall of Slavery in the New World*. New York: Oxford University Press, 2006.
Dobbins, James, Seth G. Jones, Benjamin Runkle, and Siddharth Mohandas. *Occupying Iraq: A History of the Coalition Provisional Authority*. Santa Monica: RAND Corporation, 2009.
Dorrien, Gary. *Imperial Designs: Neoconservatism and the New Pax Americana*. New York: Routledge, 2004.
Dosman, Edgar J. *The Life and Times of Raul Prebisch, 1901–1986*. Montreal: McGill University Press, 2008.
Downs, Jacques M. *The Golden Ghetto: The American Commercial Community at Canton and the Shaping of American China Policy, 1784–1844*. Hong Kong: Hong Kong University Press, 2014.
Dubois, Laurent. *Avengers of the New World: The Story of the Haitian Revolution*. Cambridge: Belknap Press, 2004.
Dudziak, Mary. *Cold War Civil Rights: Race and the Image of American Democracy*. Princeton: Princeton University Press, 2000.
Dunn, Richard. *Sugar and Slaves: The Rise of the Planter Class in the English West Indies, 1624–1713*. Chapel Hill: University of North Carolina Press, 1972.
Dusinberre, William. *Slavemaster President: The Double Career of James Polk*. New York: Oxford University Press, 2003.
Echerick, Joseph. *The Origins of the Boxer Uprising*. Berkeley: University of California Press, 1987.
Eichengreen, Barry. *Globalizing Capital: A History of the International Monetary System, 3rd Edition*. Princeton: Princeton University Press, 2019.
Ekbladh, David. *The Great American Mission: Modernization Theory and the Construction of an American World Order*. Princeton: Princeton University Press, 2010.
Elliott, J.H. *Empires of the Atlantic World: Britain and Spain in America*. New Haven: Yale University Press, 2006.
Elliott, J.H. *Imperial Spain: 1469–1716*. London: Edward Arnold, 1963.
Ellsberg, Daniel. *Secrets: A Memoir of Vietnam and the Pentagon Papers*. New York: Penguin Books, 2002.
Eschen, Penny M. Von. *Satchmo Blows Up the World: Jazz Ambassadors Play the Cold War*. Cambridge, MA: Harvard University Press, 2006.
Esdaile, Charles. *The Peninsular War: A New History*. New York: Palgrave Macmillan, 2003.
Ferguson, Niall. *Civilization: The West and the Rest*. New York: Penguin Books, 2012.
Ferrer, Ada. *Cuba: An American History*. New York: Scribner, 2021.
Fichter, James R. *So Great a Proffit: How the East Indies Trade Transformed Anglo-American Capitalism*. Cambridge, MA: Harvard University Press, 2010.

Filkins, Dexter. *The Forever War.* New York: Vintage Books, 2009.
Findlay, Ronald and Kevin H. O'Rourke. *Power and Plenty: Trade, War, and the World Economy in the Second Millenium.* Princeton: Princeton University Press, 2007.
Fitz, Caitlin. *Our Sister Republics: The United States in an Age of American Revolutions.* New York: W.W. Norton, 2016.
Foner, Eric. *Reconstruction: America's Unfinished Revolution, 1863–1877.* New York: Perennial Classics, 1998.
Ford, Lisa. *Settler Sovereignty: Jurisdiction and Indigenous People in America and Australia, 1788–1836.* Cambridge, MA: Harvard University Press, 2010.
Forsyth, David P. *The Politics of Prisoner Abuse: The United States and Enemy Prisoners after 9/11.* New York: Cambridge University Press, 2011.
Fowler, Will. *Independent Mexico: The Pronunciamiento in the Age of Santa Anna, 1821–1858.* Lincoln: University of Nebraska Press, 2016.
Fowler, Will. *Santa Anna of Mexico.* Lincoln: University of Nebraska Press, 2007.
Franczak, Michael. *Global Inequality and American Foreign Policy in the 1970s.* Ithaca: Cornell University Press, 2022.
Freeland, Richard M. *The Truman Doctrine and the Origins of McCarthyism: Foreign Policy, Domestic Politics, and Internal Security.* New York: Alfred A. Knopf, 1972.
Freidman, Thomas. *The World Is Flat: A Brief History of the 21st Century.* New York: Farrar, Straus, and Giroux, 2005.
Frum, David and Richard Perle. *An End to Evil: How to Win the War on Terrorism.* New York: Random House, 2003.
Frymer, Paul. *Building an American Empire: The Era of Territorial and Political Expansion.* Princeton: Princeton University Press, 2017.
Fukuyama, Francis. *The End of History and the Last Man.* New York: The Free Press, 1992.
Garavini, Giuliano. *After Empires: European Integration, Decolonization, and the Challenge from the Global South, 1957–1986.* New York: Oxford University Press, 2012.
Gerstle, Gary. *The Rise and Fall of the Neoliberal Order: America and the World in the Free Market Era.* New York: Oxford University Press, 2022.
Getachew, Adom. *Worldmaking after Empire: The Rise and Fall of Self-Determination.* Princeton: Princeton University Press, 2019.
Gilman, Nils. *Mandarins of the Future: Modernization Theory in Cold War America.* Baltimore: Johns Hopkins University Press, 2003.
Gleijeses, Piero. *Shattered Hope: The Guatemalan Revolution and the United States, 1944–1954.* Princeton: Princeton University Press, 1991.
Go, Julian. *The British and American Empires: 1688–the Present.* New York: Cambridge University Press, 2011.
Goscha, Christopher. *Vietnam: A New History.* New York: Basic Books, 2016.
Green, Michael D. *The Politics of Indian Removal: Creek Government and Society in Crisis.* Lincoln: University of Nebraska Press, 1982.
Greenberg, Amy S. *A Wicked War: Polk, Clay, Lincoln and the 1846 U.S. Invasion of Mexico.* New York: Alfred A. Knopf, 2012.
Greene, Jack P. *Peripheries and Center: Constitutional Development in the Extended Polities of the British Empire and the United States, 1607–1788.* Athens: University of Georgia Press, 1986.

Greene, Jack P. and Philip D. Morgan, eds. *Atlantic History: A Critical Appraisal.* Oxford: Oxford University Press, 2009.
Greenwald, Emily. *Reconfiguring the Reservation: The Nez Perces, Jicarilla Apaches, and the Dawes Act.* Albuquerque: University of New Mexico Press, 2002.
Guardino, Peter. *The Dead March: A History of the Mexican-American War.* Cambridge, MA: Harvard University Press, 2017.
Hahnhimäki, Jussi M. *Pax Transatlantica: America and Europe in the Post Cold War Era.* New York: Oxford University Press, 2021.
Halberstam, David. *War in a Time of Peace: Bush, Clinton and the Generals.* New York: Scribner, 2001.
Hämäläinen, Pekka. *Indigenous Continent: The Epic Contest for North America.* New York: Liveright, 2002.
Hamilton, Alexander, James Madison, and John Jay. *The Federalist Papers.* Nashville: Nelson Books, 2014.
Hamnett, Brian R. *The End of Iberian Rule on the American Continent, 1770–1830.* Cambridge: Cambridge University Press, 2017.
Harbutt, Fraser J. *The Iron Curtain: Churchill, America, and the Origins of the Cold War.* Oxford: Oxford University Press, 1986.
Harbutt, Fraser J. *Yalta 1945: Europe and America at the Crossroads.* Cambridge: Cambridge University Press, 2010.
Haslam, Jonathan. *Hubris: The American Origins of Russia's War against Ukraine.* Cambridge, MA: Harvard University Press, 2025.
Haynes, Sam W. *James K. Polk and the Expansionist Impulse.* New York: Longman, 1997.
Haynes, Sam W. *Unfinished Revolution: The Early American Republic in a British World.* Charlottesville: University of Virginia Press, 2010.
Helleiner, Eric. *The Forgotten Foundations of Bretton Woods: International Development and the Making of the Postwar Order.* Ithaca: Cornell University Press, 2014.
Helleiner, Eric. *The Neomercantilists: An Intellectual History.* Ithaca: Cornell University Press, 2021.
Henderson, Timothy J. *A Glorious Defeat: Mexico and Its War with the United States.* New York: Hill and Wang, 2007.
Herring, George C. *From Colony to Superpower: U.S. Foreign Relations since 1776.* New York: Oxford University Press, 2008.
Hickey, Donald. *The War of 1812: A Forgotten Conflict.* Chicago: University of Illinois Press, 2012.
Hietala, Thomas. *Manifest Design: American Exceptionalism and Empire.* Ithaca: Cornell University Press, 1985.
Hixon, Walter. *The Myth of American Diplomacy: National Identity and U.S. Foreign Policy.* New Haven: Yale University Press, 2008.
Holden, Robert H. and Eric Zolov, eds. *Latin America and the United States: A Documentary History.* New York: Oxford University Press, 2000.
Holton, Woody. *Forced Founders: Indians. Debtors, Slaves, and the Making of the American Revolution in Virginia.* Chapel Hill: University of North Carolina Press, 1999.
Hopkins, A.G. *American Empire: A Global History.* Princeton: Princeton University Press, 2018.

Howe, Daniel Walker. *The Political Culture of American Whigs*. Chicago: University of Chicago Press, 1979.
Howe, Daniel Walker. *What Hath God Wrought: The Transformation of America 1815–1848*. New York: Oxford University Press, 2007.
Hudson, Peter James. *Bankers and Empire: How Wall Street Colonized the Caribbean*. Chicago: University of Chicago Press, 2017.
Hunt, Michael H. *Ideology and U.S. Foreign Policy*. New Haven: Yale University Press, 1987.
Hunt, Michael H. *The American Ascendency: How the United States Gained and Wielded Global Dominance*. Chapel Hill: University of North Carolina Press, 2007.
Huntington, Samuel. *The Third Wave: Democratization in the Late 20th Century*. Norman: University of Oklahoma Press, 1991.
Immerman, Richard H. *Empire for Liberty: A History of American Imperialism from Benjamin Franklin to Paul Wolfowitz*. Princeton: Princeton University Press, 2010.
Immerwahr, Daniel. *How to Hide an Empire: A History of the Greater United States*. New York: Picador, 2019.
Inikori, Joseph E. *Africans and the Industrial Revolution in England: A Study in International Trade and Economic Development*. Cambridge: Cambridge University Press, 2002.
Irwin, Ryan. *Gordian Knot: Apartheid and the Unmaking of the Liberal World Order*. New York: Oxford University Press, 2012.
Jacobson, Matthew Frye. *Barbarian Virtues: The United States Encounters Foreign People at Home and Abroad, 1876–1917*. New York: Hill and Wang, 2000.
James, C.L.R. *The Black Jacobins: Toussaint L'Ouverture and the San Domingo Revolution*. New York: Penguin Classics, 2022.
Jansesn, Jan C. and Jürgen Osterhammel. *Decolonization: A Short History*. Princeton: Princeton University Press, 2013.
Jordan, Winthrop D. *White over Black: American Attitudes toward the Negro, 1550–1812*. New York: W.W. Norton, 1968.
Kagan, Robert. *The Jungle Grows Back: America and Our Imperiled World*. New York: Alfred A. Knopf, 2018.
Karl, Rebecca E. *Staging the World: Chinese Nationalism at the Turn of the Century*. Durham: Duke University Press, 2002.
Karp, Matthew. *This Vast Southern Empire: Slaveholders at the Helm of American Foreign Policy*. New York: Cambridge University Press, 2016.
Katznelson, Ira. *Fear Itself: The New Deal and the Origins of Our Time*. New York: Liveright, 2013.
Keene, Edward. *Beyond the Anarchial Society: Grotius, Colonialism and Order in World Politics*. Cambridge: Cambridge University Press, 2002.
Kennedy, Paul. *The Parliament of Man: The Past Present and Future of the United Nations*. New York: Random House, 2006.
Khalidi, Rashid. *The Hundred Years's War on Palestine: A History of Settler Colonialism and Resistance, 1917–2017*. New York: Henry Holt, 2020.
Kim, Jessica M. *Imperial Metropolis: Los Angeles, Mexico, and the Borderlands of American Empire, 1865–1941*. Chapel Hill: University of North Carolina Press, 2019.

Klooster, Wim. *Revolutions in the Atlantic World: A Comparative History*. New York: New York University Press, 2009.
Kramer, Paul. *Blood of Government: Race, Empire, the United States, and the Philippines*. Chapel Hill: University of North Carolina Press, 2006.
Kupperman, Karen Ordahl. *Indians and English: Facing off in North America*. Ithaca: Cornell University Press, 2000.
Kynaston, David. *Till Times Last Sand: A History of the Bank of England, 1694–2013*. New York: Bloomsbury, 2020.
LaFeber, Walter. *Inevitable Revolutions: The United States in Central America, Expanded Edition*. New York: W.W. Norton, 1984.
LaFeber, Walter. *Michael Jordan and the New Global Capitalism*. New York: W.W. Norton, 2002.
LaFeber, Walter. *The New Empire: An Interpretation of American Expansion, 1860–1898*. Ithaca: Cornell University Press, 1968.
LaFeber, Walter. *The Panama Canal: The Crisis in Historical Perspective*. New York: Oxford University Press, 1978.
Lang, Andrew F. *A Contest of Civilizations: Exposing the Crisis of American Exceptionalism in the Civil War Era*. Chapel Hill: University of North Carolina Press, 2021.
Lasch, Christopher. *The True and Only Heaven: Progress and Its Critics*. New York: W.W. Norton, 1991.
Latham, Michael E. *Modernization as Ideology: American Social Science and "Nation Building" in the Kennedy Era*. Chapel Hill: University of North Carolina Press, 2000.
Latham, Michael E. *The Right Kind of Revolution: Modernization, Development, and U.S. Foreign Policy from the Cold War to the Present*. Ithaca: Cornell University Press, 2011.
Lawrence, Mark Atwood. *The End of Ambition: The United States and the Third World in the Vietnam Era*. Princeton: Princeton University Press, 2021.
Leffler, Melvyn P. *For the Soul of Mankind: The United States, the Soviet Union, and the Cold War*. New York: Hill and Wang, 2007.
Lemon, James T. *The Best Poor Man's Country: Early Southeastern Pennsylvania*. Baltimore: Johns Hopkins University Press, 2002.
Lepore, Jill. *The Name of War: King Phillip's War and the Origins of American Identity*. New York: Vintage Books, 1999.
Levy, Jonathan. *Ages of American Capitalism: A History of the United States*. New York: Random House, 2021.
Lewis, James E. *The American Union and the Problem of Neighborhood, 1783–1829*. Chapel Hill: University of North Carolina Press, 1998.
Lindert, Peter and Jeffery Williamson. *Unequal Gains: American Growth and Inequality since 1700*. Princeton: Princeton University Press, 2016.
Little, Douglas. *American Orientalism: The United States and the Middle East since 1945, 3rd Edition*. Chapel Hill: University of North Carolina Press, 2008.
Logevall, Fredrik. *Choosing War: The Lost Chance for Peace and the Escalation of the War in Vietnam*. Berkeley: University of California Press, 1999.
Logevall, Fredrik. *Embers of War: The Fall of an Empire and the Making of America's Vietnam*. New York: Random House, 2012.
Love, Eric T.L. *Race over Empire: Racism and U.S. Imperialism, 1865–1900*. Chapel Hill: University of North Carolina, 2004.

Lüthi, Lorez M. *Cold Wars: Asia, The Middle East, Europe.* Cambridge: Cambridge University Press, 2020.
Lynch, John. *The Spanish-American Revolutions, 1808–1826.* New York: W.W. Norton, 1973.
MacLachlan, Colin M. *Spain's Empire in the New World: The Role of Ideas in Institutional and Social Change.* Berkeley: University of California Press, 1988.
Malkasian, Carter. *The American War in Afghanistan: A History.* New York: Oxford University Press, 2023.
Manela, Erez. *The Wilsonian Moment: Self Determination and the International Origins of Anticolonial Nationalism.* New York: Oxford University Press, 2007.
Manley, Michael. *The Poverty of Nations: Reflections on Underdevelopment and the World Economy.* London: Pluto Press, 1991.
Marichal, Carlos. *Bankruptcy of Empire: Mexican Silver and the Wars between Spain, Britain, and France 1760–1810.* Cambridge: Cambridge University Press, 2007.
Marr, David G. *Vietnamese Anticolonialism, 1885–1925.* Berkeley: University of California Press, 1971.
Martin, Jamie. *The Meddlers: Sovereignty, Empire, and the Birth of Global Economic Governance.* Cambridge, MA: Harvard University Press, 2022.
Maurer, Noel. *The Empire Trap: The Rise and Fall of U.S. Intervention to Protect Property Overseas, 1893–2013.* Princeton: Princeton University Press, 2013.
May, Robert E. *Manifest Destiny's Underworld: Filibustering in Antebellum America.* Chapel Hill: University of North Carolina Press, 2002.
Mazower, Mark. *No Enchanted Palace: The End of Empire and the Ideological Origins of the United Nations.* Princeton: Princeton University Press, 2013.
McConville, Brendan. *The Kings Three Faces: The Rise and Fall of Royal America, 1688–1776.* Chapel Hill: University of North Carolina Press, 2006.
McCullough, David. *John Adams.* New York: Simon and Schuster, 2001.
McFarlane, Anthony. *War and Independence in Spanish America.* New York: Routledge, 2014.
McKnight Nichols, Christopher and David Milne, eds. *Ideology in U.S. Foreign Relations: New Histories.* New York: Columbia University Press, 2022.
McPherson, James M. *Battle Cry of Freedom: The Civil War Era.* New York: Oxford University Press, 1988.
Mearsheimer, John J. *The Great Delusion: Liberal Dreams and International Realities.* New Haven: Yale University Press, 2018.
Mikaberidze, Alexander. *The Napoleonic Wars: A Global History.* Oxford: Oxford University Press, 2022.
Milanovic, Branko. *Global Inequality: A New Approach for the Age of Globalization.* Cambridge, MA: Harvard University Press, 2016.
Milne, David. *America's Rasputin: Walt Rostow and the Vietnam War.* New York: Hill and Wang, 2008.
Mishra, Pankaj. *From the Ruins of Empire: The Intellectuals Who Remade Asia.* New York: Farrar, Strauss, and Giroux, 2012.
Morgan, Edmund S. *American Slavery, American Freedom: The Ordeal of Colonial Virginia.* New York: Norton, 2003.
Morgan, Michael Cotey. *The Final Act: The Helsinki Accords and the Transformation of the Cold War.* Princeton: Princeton University Press, 2018.
Morrison, Dane A. *True Yankees: The South Seas and the Discovery of American Identity.* Baltimore: Johns Hopkins University Press, 2014.

Moyn, Samuel. *Humane: How the United States Abandoned Peace and Reinvented War*. New York: Farrar, Straus, and Giroux, 2021.
Moyn, Samuel. *Not Enough: Human Rights in an Unequal World*. Cambridge, MA: Harvard University Press, 2018.
Moyn, Samuel. *The Last Utopia: Human Rights in History*. Cambridge, MA: Harvard University Press, 2010.
Nash, Gary. *The Urban Crucible: Social Change, Political Consciousness, and the Origins of the American Revolution*. Cambridge, MA: Harvard University Press, 1979.
Ninkovich, Frank. *The Wilsonian Century: U.S. Foreign Policy since 1900*. Chicago: University of Chicago Press, 1999.
O'Brien, Thomas F. *The Century of U.S. Capitalism in Latin America*. Albuquerque: University of New Mexico Press, 1999.
Onuf, Peter. *Jefferson's Empire: The Language of American Nationhood*. Charlottesville: University of Virginia Press, 2000.
Ormond, David. *The Rise of Commercial Empires: England and the Netherlands in the Age of Mercantilism*. Cambridge: Cambridge University Press, 2003.
Osterhammel, Jürgen. *The Transformation of the World: A Global History of the Nineteenth Century*. Princeton: Princeton University Press, 2014.
Osterhammel, Jürgen and Niels Peterson. *Globalization: A Short History*. Princeton: Princeton University Press, 2005.
Overy, Richard. *Blood and Ruins: The Last Imperial War, 1931–1945*. New York: Viking Press, 2021.
Owsley Jr., Frank Lawrence and Gene A. Smith. *Filibusters and Expansionists: Jeffersonian Manifest Destiny, 1800–1821*. Tuscaloosa: University of Alabama Press, 1997.
Pagden, Anthony. *Lords of All the World: Ideologies of Empire in Spain, Britain, and France c. 1500–1800*. New Haven: Yale University Press, 2005.
Palen, Marc William. *Pax Economica: Left-Wing Visions of a Free Trade World*. Princeton: Princeton University Press, 2024.
Palen, Marc William. *The Conspiracy of Free Trade: The Anglo-American Struggle over Empire and Economic Globalization, 1846–1896*. Cambridge: Cambridge University Press, 2016.
Parker, Jason C. *Hearts, Minds, Voices: U.S. Cold War Public Diplomacy and the Formation of the Third World*. New York: Oxford University Press, 2016.
Patel, Kiran Klaus. *The New Deal: A Global History*. Princeton: Princeton University Press, 2016.
Pérez, Louis A. *Cuba and the United States: Ties of a Singular Intimacy*, 2nd Edition. Athens: University of Georgia Press, 1997.
Pérez, Louis A. *Cuba under the Platt Amendment, 1902–1934*. Pittsburgh: University of Pittsburgh Press, 1986.
Pérez, Louis A. *The War of 1898: The United States and Cuba in History and Historiography*. Chapel Hill: University of North Carolina Press, 1998.
Piketty, Thomas. *Capital in the Twenty-First Century*. Arthur Goldhammer trans. Cambridge: Belknap Press, 2014.
Pletcher, David M. *The Diplomacy of Annexation: Texas, Oregon, and the Mexican War*. Columbia: University of Missouri Press, 1973.
Pletcher, David M. *The Diplomacy of Involvement: American Economic Expansion across the Pacific, 1784–1900*. Columbia: University of Missouri Press, 2001.

Pletcher, David M. *The Diplomacy of Trade and Investment: American Economic Expansion in the Hemisphere, 1865–1900*. Columbia: University of Missouri Press, 1998.
Pomeranz, Kenneth. *The Great Divergence: Europe, China, and the Making of the Modern World Economy*. Princeton: Princeton University Press, 2000.
Power, Samantha. *"A Problem from Hell": America in the Age of Genocide*. New York: Harper Perennial, 2002.
Pratt, Julius W. *America's Colonial Experiment: How the United States Gained, Governed, and in Part Gave Away a Colonial Empire*. New York: Prentice Hall, 1951.
Pratt, Julius W. *Expansionists of 1898: The Acquisition of Hawaii and the Spanish Islands*. Gloucester MA: Peter Smith, 1959.
Preston, Andrew. *Sword of the Spirit, Shield of Faith: Religion in American War and Diplomacy*. New York: Alfred A. Knopf, 2012.
Prucha, Francis Paul. *The Great Father: The United States Government and the American Indians*. Lincoln: University of Nebraska Press, 1984.
Rabe, Stephen G. *The Most Dangerous Area in the World: John F. Kennedy Confronts Communist Revolution in Latin America*. Chapel Hill: University of North Carolina Press, 1999.
Radchenko, Sergey. *To Run the World: The Kremlin's Cold War Bid for Global Power*. Cambridge: Cambridge University Press, 2024.
Rahnema, Ali. *Behind the 1953 Coup in Iran: Thugs, Turncoats, Soldiers, and Spooks*. Cambridge: Cambridge University Press, 2015.
Record, Jeffrey. *Wanting War: Why the Bush Administration Invaded Iraq*. Washington, DC: Potomac Books, 2010.
Regele, Lindsay Schakenbach. *Manufacturing Advantage: War, the State, and the Origins of American Industry, 1776–1848*. Baltimore: Johns Hopkins University Press, 2019.
Renda, Mary A. *Taking Haiti: Military Occupation and the Culture of U.S. Imperialism, 1915–1940*. Chapel Hill: University of North Carolina Press, 2001.
Richter, Daniel K. *Facing East from Indian Country: A Native History of Early America*. Cambridge, MA: Harvard University Press, 2003.
Ricks, Thomas. *Fiasco: The American Military Adventure in Iraq*. New York: Penguin Press, 2006.
Rivage, Justin du. *Revolution against Empire: Taxes, Politics, and the Origins of American Independence*. New Haven: Yale University Press, 2017.
Rodgers, Daniel T. *Age of Fracture*. Cambridge, MA: Harvard University Press, 2011.
Rodriguez O., Jaime E. *The Independence of Spanish America*. Cambridge: Cambridge University Press, 1993.
Roleau, Brian. *With Sails Whitening Every Sea: Mariners and the Making of an American Maritime Empire*. Ithaca: Cornell University Press, 2014.
Rosenberg, Emily S. *Spreading the American Dream: American Economic and Cultural Expansion, 1890–1945*. New York: Hill and Wang, 1982.
Rosenblatt, Helena. *The Lost History of Liberalism: From Ancient Rome to the Twenty-First Century*. Princeton: Princeton University Press, 2018.
Rosenthal, Jill. *From Migrants to Refugees: The Politics of Aid along the Tanzania-Rwanda Border*. Durham: Duke University Press, 2023.
Rostow, W.W. *The Stages of Economic Growth: A Non-Communist Manifesto*. Cambridge: Cambridge University Press, 1960.

Ruppel, Kristin T. *Unearthing Indian Land: Living with the Legacies of Allotment.* Tucson: University of Arizona Press, 2008.
Sargent, Daniel T. *A Superpower Transformed: The Remaking of American Foreign Relations in the 1970s.* New York: Oxford University Press, 2015.
Sarotte, M.E. *Not One Inch: America, Russia, and the Making of the Post-Cold War Stalemate.* New Haven: Yale University Press, 2021.
Saunt, Claudio. *Unworthy Republic: The Dispossession of Native Americans and the Road to Indian Territory.* New York: W.W. Norton, 2020.
Schoultz, Lars. *Beneath the United States: A History of U.S. Policy towards Latin America.* Cambridge, MA: Harvard University Press, 1998.
Schoultz, Lars. *In Their Own Best Interest: A History of the U.S. Effort to Improve Latin Americans.* Cambridge, MA: Harvard University Press, 2018.
Schroeder, Paul W. *Stealing Horses to Great Applause.* New York: Verso, 2025.
Sehat, David. *The Myth of American Religious Freedom.* New York: Oxford University Press, 2010.
Sellers, Charles. *The Market Revolution: Jacksonian America, 1815–1846.* New York: Oxford University Press, 1991.
Sexton, Jay. *The Monroe Doctrine: Empire and Nation in Nineteenth Century America.* New York: Hill and Wang, 2011.
Sharman, J.C. *Empires of the Weak: The Real Story of European Expansion and the Creation of the New World Order.* Princeton: Princeton University Press, 2019.
Shenk, Timothy. *Realigners: Partisan Hacks, Political Visionaries, and the Struggle to Rule American Democracy.* New York: Farrar Straus and Giroux, 2022.
Shephard, Todd. *The Invention of Decolonization: The Algerian War and the Remaking of France.* Ithaca: Cornell University Press, 2006.
Sherry, Michael S. *In the Shadow of War: The United States since the 1930s.* New Haven: Yale University Press, 1995.
Shoemaker, Nancy. *Pursuing Respect in the Cannibal Isles: Americans in Nineteenth Century Fiji.* Ithaca: Cornell University Press, 2019.
Silver, Peter. *Our Savage Neighbors: How Indian War Transformed Early America.* New York: W.W. Norton, 2008.
Simms, Brendan. *Three Victories and a Defeat: The Rise and Fall of the First British Empire.* New York: Basic Books, 2009.
Slobodian, Quinn. *Globalists: The End of Empire and the Birth of Neoliberalism.* Cambridge, MA: Harvard University Press, 2018.
Smith, Robert Freeman. *The United States and Revolutionary Nationalism in Mexico, 1916–1932.* Chicago: University of Chicago Press, 1972.
Sommers, Jeffrey. *Race Reality and Realpolitik: U.S.-Haiti Relations in the Lead Up to the 1915 Occupation.* Lanham: Lexington Books, 2016.
Specter, Matthew. *The Atlantic Realists: Empire and International Political Thought between Germany and the United States.* Stanford: Stanford University Press, 2022.
Stagg, J.C.A. *The War of 1812: Conflict for a Continent.* Cambridge: Cambridge University Press, 2012.
Steib, Joseph. *The Regime Change Consensus: Iraq in American Politics, 1990–2003.* New York: Cambridge University Press, 2021.
Steil, Benn. *The Battle of Bretton Woods: John Maynard Keynes, Harry Dexter White and the Making of a New World Order.* Princeton: Princeton University Press, 2013.

Stein, Stanley J. and Barbara H. Stein. *Apogee of Empire: Spain and New Spain in the Age of Charles III, 1759–1789*. Baltimore: Johns Hopkins University Press, 2003.
Stein, Stanley J. and Barbara H. Stein. *Edge of Crisis: War and Trade in the Spanish Atlantic 1789–1808*. Baltimore: Johns Hopkins University Press, 2009.
Stein, Stanley J. and Barbara H. Stein. *Silver, Trade, and War: Spain and America in the Making of Early Modern Europe*. Baltimore: Johns Hopkins University Press, 2000.
Steinbock-Pratt, Sarah. *Educating the Empire: American Teachers and Contested Colonization in the Pacific*. New York: Cambridge University Press, 2019.
Stephanson, Anders. *Manifest Destiny: American Expansionism and the Empire of Right*. New York: Hill and Wang, 1995.
Stern, Philip J. and Carl Wennderlind, eds. *Mercantilism Reimagined: Political Economy in Early Modern Britain and Its Empire*. New York: Oxford University Press, 2014.
Stromquist, Shelton. *Reinventing the People: The Progressive Movement, the Class Problem, and the Origins of Modern Liberalism*. Urbana: University of Illinois Press, 2002.
Stueck, William. *Rethinking the Korean War: A New Diplomatic and Strategic History*. Princeton: Princeton University Press, 2002.
Sugrue, Thomas J. *Sweet Land of Liberty: The Forgotten Struggle for Civil Rights in the North*. New York: Random House, 2008.
Suri, Jeremi. *Power and Protest: Global Revolution and the Rise of Détente*. Cambridge, MA: Harvard University Press, 2003.
Taylor, Alan. *The Civil War of 1812: American Citizens, British Subjects, Irish Rebels, & Indian Allies*. New York: Alfred A. Knopf, 2010.
Terrel, Ian and Jay Sexton, eds. *Empire's Twin: U.S. Anti-Imperialism from the Founding Era to the Age of Terrorism*. Ithaca: Cornell University Press, 2016.
Thornton, Christy. *Revolution in Development: Mexico and the Governance of the Global Economy*. Berkeley: University of California Press, 2021.
Thornton, Russell. *American Indian Holocaust and Survival: A Population History since 1492*. Norman: University of Oklahoma Press, 1990.
Tocqueville, Alexis de. *Democracy in America*. Henry Reeve trans. New Rochelle: Arlington House, 1965.
Tocqueville, Alexis de. *Democracy in America*. J.P. Mayer and Max Lerner, eds., George Lawrence trans. New York: Harper and Row, 1966.
Tomlins, Christopher. *Freedom Bound: Law, Labor, and Civic Identity in Colonizing English America, 1580–1865*. Cambridge: Cambridge University Press, 2010.
Tooze, Adam. *The Deluge: The Great War, America and the Remaking of the Global Order, 1916–1931*. New York: Penguin Books, 2014.
Tutino, John, ed. *New Countries: Capitalism, Revolutions, and Nations in the Americas, 1750–1870*. Durham: Duke University Press, 2016.
Tzouvala, Ntina. *Capitalism as Civilization: A History of International Law*. New York: Cambridge University Press, 2020.
Vaïsse, Justin. *Neoconservatism: The Biography of a Movement*. Arthur Goldhammer trans. Cambridge, MA: Harvard University Press, 2010.
Verney, Michael A. *A Great and Rising Nation: Naval Exploration and Global Empire in the U.S. Early Republic*. Chicago: University of Chicago Press, 2022.

Virgil. *Aeneid*. Robert Fitzgerald trans. New York: Random House, 1983.
Wallace, Anthony F.C. *Jefferson and the Indians: The Tragic Fate of the First Americans*. Cambridge, MA: Harvard University Press, 1999.
Wallerstein, Immanuel. *The Modern World-System II: Mercantilism and the Consolidation of the European World-Economy, 1600–1750*. Berkeley: University of California Press, 2011.
Wallerstein, Immanuel. *The Modern World-System III: The Second Era of Great Expansion of the Capitalist World Economy, 1730s–1840s*. Berkeley: University of California Press, 2011.
Wallerstein, Immanuel. *World-System's Analysis: An Introduction*. Durham: Duke University Press, 2004.
Weaver, John C. *The Great Land-Rush and the Making of the Modern World, 1650–1900*. Montreal: McGill-Queens University Press, 2003.
Wertheim, Stephen. *Tomorrow the World: The Birth of U.S. Global Supremacy*. Cambridge, MA: Harvard University Press, 2020.
West, Elliott. *Continental Reckoning: The American West in the Age of Expansion*. Lincoln: University of Nebraska Press, 2023.
Westad, Odd Arne. *The Cold War: A World History*. New York: Basic Books, 2017.
Westad, Odd Arne. *The Global Cold War: Third World Interventions and the Making of Our Times*. New York: Cambridge University Press, 2007.
Whitaker, Arthur P. *The United States and the Independence of Latin America, 1800–1830*. New York: W.W. Norton, 1964.
White, Richard. *The Republic for Which It Stands: The United States during Reconstruction and the Gilded Age, 1865–1896*. New York: Oxford University Press, 2017.
Williams, William Appleman. *The Contours of American History*. New York: W.W. Norton, 1988.
Williams, William Appleman. *The Tragedy of American Diplomacy, 50th Anniversary Edition*. New York: W.W. Norton, 2009.
Wood, Gordon. *Empire of Liberty: A History of the Early Republic*. New York: Oxford University Press, 2009.
Woods, Colleen. *Freedom Incorporated: Anticommunism and Philippine Independence in the Age of Decolonization*. Ithaca: Cornell University Press, 2020.
Wright, Lawrence. *The Looming Tower: Al Qaeda and the Road to 9/11*. New York: Vintage Books, 2007.
Yokota, Kariann Akemi. *Unbecoming British: How Revolutionary America Became a Postcolonial Nation*. New York: Oxford University Press, 2011.
Young, Marilyn. *The Vietnam Wars: 1945–1990*. New York: Harper Perennial, 1991.
Zahra, Tara. *Against the World: Anti-Globalism and Mass Politics between the World Wars*. New York: W.W. Norton, 2023.
Zubok, Vladislav. *Collapse: The Fall of the Soviet Union*. New Haven: Yale University Press, 2021.
Zubok, Vladislav. *The World of the Cold War, 1945–1991*. New York: Pelican Books, 2025.

INDEX

Note: *Page numbers in italics refer to figures and tables; page numbers followed by "n" denote footnotes.*

Aber, Samuel L. 250–1
Adams, John Quincy 19, 23, 43, 67, 75, 80, 89, 91, 99–105, 107, 140
Adams, Henry 92
Adelman, Jeremy 96
Afghanistan 8, 21, 248, 249, 267–9, 273, 274, 279
Africa 7, 11, 15, 18, 21, 98, 132, 181, 185, 195, 198–202, 204, 209, 220, 222, 226–8, 234, 235, 256, 263
Afro-Asian Conference, Bandung (1955) 211
Aguinaldo, Emilio 125, 141–2, 146, 147
Algeria 200, 204
Algonquin communities 33, 57–8
Alliance for Progress 210–11, 213, 228
American Revolution 3–4, 19, 20, 23–6, 35, 38–46, 54, 56, 60, 62, 75, 86–8, 93, 111, 127
Amritsar Massacre (1919) 182
Anglo-French wars (eighteenth-nineteenth century) 12, 56, 75, 95, 111, 118
Anglo-Iranian Oil Company 212, 215
Anglo-Saxon race 111, 130–1, 146, 172
anti-American sentiment 113–14, 275
anti-colonial nationalism 174, 184, 236
anti-imperialism 19, 177
Apess, William 24, 25
Arab Cooperation Council 249
Arab-Israeli conflict 225, 226
Arab world 226, 249–51, 271

Arbenz, Jacobo 215–16
Armitage, David 5
Articles of Confederation 47, 51, 69
  government under 47–8, 50
Asia 7, 21, 98, 118–20, 124, 174, 185, 187, 198, 199, 200, 201 n.49, 209, 244, 260, 275
Atlantic Charter (1941) 184, 190
Atlantic World 11–13, 35, 37 n.51, 38, 39, 46, 56, 93
Auden, W.H. 22

Baath Party 249–50
Bamewawagezhikaquay 57
Banque Nationale d'Haïti 160
barbarism 8, 110, 131, 146–7, 281
Bartel, Fritz 243
Batista, Fulgencio 194, 216
Battle of Manila Bay (1898) 141
Battle of San Jacinto (1836) 109
Beckert, Sven 9–11, 9 n.22
Bell Trade Bill 207
Belser, James E. 3
Benjamin, Walter 281
Bennet, James Gordon 110
Bevilacqua, Alexander 17
Biden, Joseph 266, 280
bin Laden, Osama 248, 266–8
Blackburn, Robin 17, 37 n.51
Black Hawk War (1832) 83
Blaine, James G. 132–3, 136
Boarchard, Edwin 162
Bockman, Johanna 224
Bolívar, Simón 24, 96–9, 103, 104
Borgwardt, Elizabeth 190
Boston Manufacturing Company 120

Boxer Uprising, China 156–8, *157*, 175
Brands, H.W. 211
Brands, Hal 255
Brantlinger, Patrick 65
Brazil 93 n.29, 136, 213–14, 229, 244, 254
Breese, Sidney 111
Bretton Woods system 190–1, 221, 224, 230, 238
British East India Company (EIC) 118, 119, 123
British Empire 4, 12–13, 18, 26, 35, 38, 39, 46–8, 54, 61, 75, 80, 84, 188, 195, 197, 230
  asiento (slave trade) 95
  authoritarian reformers, late eighteenth century 40–1, 43
  Caribbean possessions, seventeenth-eighteenth century 35
  Central African Federation, withdrawal from 227
  civil war (with North American colonies) 39
  colonial preferences, eighteenth century view of 42–3
  defeat of, American Revolution 25, 38–40, 43–4, 60
  end of Second World War 184
  hands-off approach, to North American colonies 29–30
  imperial system, hierarchies of 25
  justification, invading North America 31–3
  support for Native Americans, War of 1812 75–6
  wars, eighteenth-century 39–41
  wars, seventeenth century 34–5
Bryan, William Jennings 134–5, 168, 169, 181
Buchanan, James 110–11
Bulletin of the American Art-Union 3
Burgess, John W. 131
Burton, Robert 32
Bush, George H.W. 248
Bush, George W. 5, 249–50, 255, 266, 268, 270–2

Cabot, John 26–7
Calhoun, William H. 139–40

Canada 48, 60, 75, 76, 257
Canning, George 102
capitalism 8, 10 n.23, 19, 169, 178, 186, 190, 199, 202, 206, 208, 231, 238, 241, 245, 247, 254, 257, 277, 280
Caribbean 9, 10, 35, 62, 93, 102, 127, 118, 141, *153*, 158, 160, 164, 166, 169, 170, 192, 194, 216, 244
Carranza, Venustiano 170–1
Carter, Jimmy 239–40, 242, 257
Castro, Fidel 216
Catawba Confederacy 85; *See also* deerskin map, Catawba territory
Central African Federation 227
Central Intelligence Agency (CIA) 215–16, 242, 266, 268
Chardell, Daniel 249
Charter of the Economic Rights and Duties of States (CERDS) 224, 225, 234
Che Guevara 219
Cherokee Nation v. Georgia (1831) 81–2
Cherokees 57, 72, 79–84
Chesapeake colonies 35–6
Chibber, Vivek, *The Class Matrix* 14, 16–17
China/Chinese 15, 120–1, 156, 157–8, 174, 195
  imperial government, nineteenth century 123–4, 123 n.153
Chinese Communist Party (CCP) 259
Christianity 18–19, 31, 33, 111, 130
Churchill, Winston 198
civilization 8, 21, 22, 32–3, 54, 64, 67–74, 82, 107, 110, 121–2, 124, 126, 127, 129–32, 140, 145–7, 152, 156, 158, 164, 166–7, 171, 174, 176, 180, 185, 209, 220, 247, 248, 252, 253, 270, 271, 278, 280, 281
Civil Rights Movement, US 212, 226, 236
Civil War, US (1861–65) 87, 106, 124, 127–8
Clark, Christopher 176
Clark, Joseph G. 122

Clark, William 122
Clay, Henry 99, 103–4, 133
Cleveland, Grover 134–6
Clinton, Bill 248, 255–66
　global leadership 261
　rogue states 265
Coalition Provisional Authority, US (Iraq) 272
Cobden, Richard 196
Cohen, Lizabeth, "consumers republic" 231
Cold War 21, 185, 188, 198–206, 210, 211, 214, 217, 221–3, 226, 238–9, 247, 249, 250, 256, 261, 263, 266, 267, 273
colonies/colonialism, North America 7, 20, 26–38, 40–1
　slavery 36–7, 37 n.51
　violence 30
Columbus, Christopher 3, 9, 31, 93, 277–8
Commentary 235, 237, 241
Common Fund for Commodities 224, 239
communism 21, 198, 199, 201, 204, 205, 208–9, 213, 215, 227, 236, 239, 257
"Conference on Problems of Developing Countries", Cairo (1962) 224
Connelly, John 230
Cooper, Frederick 4–5
cotton cultivation 78, 84, 132
Cuba 125, 138, 143, 148–51, 194
　war for independence 138–41
Custer, George 129

Darwish, Mahmoud 225
Darwin, Charles 130–1, 137
Dávila, Miguel 168
Dawes Severality Act (1887) 154–5
De Bow's Review 118
Declaration of Independence, US 3, 5, 9, 41, 45
"Declaration of the Rights of Man and Citizen" (1789) 88
decolonization 6–7, 21, 37, 46, 67, 75–7, 87, 185, 198–206, 200, 211, 212, 250

Africa 222
　Cuba 125
　of Haiti 88–92
　Mexico 113
　Philippines 125
　Spanish America 92–6, 93 n.28, 93 n.29
deerskin map, Catawba territory 85–6, 86, 278
democracy 45, 77–84, 169, 172, 177, 178, 180, 182, 183, 190, 194, 198, 214, 223, 229, 247, 259, 268, 271
Democratic Alliance (DA), Philippines 207
Democratic Party, US 78–9, 84, 106–7, 115, 133–4, 186, 271, 280
Democratic Review 110
dependency theory 223
Dessalines, Jean-Jacques 89
Dewey, George 141–2
Díaz, Porfirio 159, 171
Dillingham, Albert 164
dispossession, of Indigenous people 31, 32, 34, 36, 45, 64, 65, 73, 77, 129
Dole, Sanford 136
"dollar diplomacy" 166–72, 187
Dominican Republic 136, 152, 162–4, 194
Donne, John 32
Dosman, Edgar J. 219
Downer, Silas 43–4
Drago, Luis M. 162–3, 166
Du Bois, W.E.B. 143, 175
Dulles, John Foster 205, 211
du Rivage, Justin 40, 45

Egypt 211
Eisenhower, Dwight D. 1, 203, 205, 206, 209–12, 214–16, 225
empire; *See also individual entries*
　anticolonialism 15
　expansion 12, 55
　of liberty 20, 46–51
　motifs 4–5
　of trade 85–124
　transitions 87
enforced globalization 9–14

England 11, 13, 18, 25, 27–37, 39, 40, 62, 84
"English liberty" 39, 43
Eurocentric world 'order', before First World War 173–5
Europe/European 4, 8–12, 15, 20, 21, 25, 27, 28, 31, 34, 36, 38, 44, 48, 51, 54, 57–9, 61, 64, 67, 69, 71, 79, 83, 84, 87, 98, 100–5, 109, 118, 119, 122, 124, 129, 131, 132, 136, 140, 144, 145, 152, 154–7, 163, 171–6, 178, 179, 184, 185, 195, 200–6, 212, 216, 222, 258, 274
  agriculture 64, 72, 79
  arrival in North America 58
  Christian antipathy, toward Islamic world 17
  civilization 174, 176
  colonialism 11, 12, 17, 27, 30–1, 34, 36, 105, 119, 145, 175, 176, 203, 205, 212
  powers 8, 12, 15, 17, 63, 69, 102, 105, 123–4, 178, 205
Exploring Expedition, United States (Ex Ex) 122–3

Federalist Party, US 63–4, 69, 72, 73, 77, 81, 82, 84, 88, 91
Ferdinand, Archduke Franz 176
Fichter, James 120
filibusters 107–9
First Sino-Japanese War (1894–95) 156
First World War 21, 158–9, 175–7, 183, 188, 199
Fiske, John 131
Fitz, Caitlin 97–8
Ford, Gerald R. 233–5
formal empire 5–8, 21, 87, 144, 150, 152, 166, 181, 182, 184, 248
Fowler, Will 113
France/French 25, 27, 39, 44, 48, 51, 56, 59, 62, 88–92, 96, 97, 100, 102, 119, 123, 129, 132, 144, 156, 157, 176, 185, 195, 200, 204, 233, 253, 261
  in North America 59
  troops in Haiti 91–2
Franczak, Michael 234, 240

Franklin, Benjamin 65–6
free trade 133, 177, 178, 192, 196, 197, 257
Freidman, Thomas, *The World Is Flat: A Brief History of the 21st Century*, the *New York Times* 277–9
French Revolution (1789) 13, 56, 88
Friendship (ship) 123
frontier colonization, US 67–72
Frymer, Paul 70

Gaines, Edmund P. 108
García, Calixto 141
General Agreement on Trade and Tariffs (GATT) 192, 213, 257
Generalized System of Preferences 224
Geneva Accords (1954) 215
Georgia (US) 73, 79–84
Germany 79, 111, 128, 132, 136, 156, 162, 163, 169, 175, 178, 181–4, 186, 190–3, 205, 230, 233, 257, 261, 272, 281
Getachew, Adom 179, 220
Gleijeses, Piero 97–9
global commodity prices 223, 224, 233
global economy 29, 127, 213, 222–4, 233, 258, 265, 277
global hegemony 228, 234, 255, 266, 274
global hierarchy 7, 21, 87, 107, 112, 117, 124, 127–35, 156–8, 177, 181, 199, 232, 234, 238, 240, 249, 250, 253, 260, 264, 266–9, 278, 279
globalization 173, 177, 185, 255–61
Global North 223, 262
Global South 205, 209, 210, 212, 214, 217, 220, 223–6, 228, 241, 242, 244, 247
"Glorious Revolution" (1688) 39
Goldgeier, James 264
Goulart, João 214
Grant, Ulysses S. 105, 132–3
Gray, Robert 32
Great Depression (1929-) 183–4, 186–8
Great Divergence 117–24
Great Recession (2007–08) 21, 273

Great War 151–82, 186; *See also* First World War
Greene, Jack P. 51
Greenough, Horatio, *The Rescue* 1, 2, 3, 6, 18, 84, 212, 278
Grenville, George 40
Group of Seven states (G-7) 258, 260
Group of 77 states (G-77) 220, 232, 233, 240, 241, 279
    anti-American aspect 225
    global economic system reform 220–3
    rise of 221–7
Gulf War 248–55; *See also* Persian Gulf War

Haiti/Haitian
    political instability 169
    Revolution 88–92
Haklyut, Richard 32
Hämäläinen, Pekka 30, 33, 59
Ham, Clifford 168
Hamilton, Alexander 48–9, 62
Hamnett, Brian 96
Hanna, Mark 135
Harding, Warren G. 171
Harrison, Benjamin 136
Harrison, William Henry 71, 73–4, 76, 77
Hawaii 121, 144–5, 153, 155
    reciprocity treaty, United States 135–6
Hay, John 15
Haynes, Sam W. 6 n.16
Helleiner, Eric 192
Helsinki Accords (1975) 237
Herald 111
de Herrera, José Joaquín 114
Herring, George 62, 112
Heureaux, Ulises 163
Holy Alliance (1815) 102
Honduras 136, 152, 168
Hoover, Hebert 187
Hopkins, A.G. 10, 155
House Committee on Indian Affairs 81
Houston, Sam 110–11
Hudson, Peter 151, 160
Huerta, Victoriana 169–70

Hukbalahap (also, the "Huks") 207, 208
human rights 212, 236, 240
Human Rights Watch 262
Hunt, Michael 15–16, 18
Hussein, Saddam 249–53, 255–6, 270–2

Iberian Peninsula 95
imperialism 21, 133, 145, 148, 164, 173, 176, 223
India 200
    Partition of 200
Indian Boarding Schools 154
Indian Removal Act (1830) 53, 77–9, 81
Indigenous people. *See* Native American communities
industrial development, US 128–30
industrialization 78, 84, 117–24, 197
inequality 42, 159, 169, 186, 191, 207–8, 236, 243
"Insular Cases," US Supreme Court 145
inter-imperial war 12–13
International Bank for Reconstruction and Development 195
international law 4, 112, 158, 162, 252, 265, 268, 272, 274
International Monetary Fund (IMF) 191, 195, 196, 244
International Trade Organization (ITO) 192, 196, 198, 203
Iran-Iraq War (1980–88) 249
Iraq 5, 21, 232, 248–56, 264–75, 273
    invasion of Kuwait (1990) 249
Iraq Liberation Act (1998) 265
Iroquois League 58–9
Irwin, Ryan 221, 227
Israel 225–6, 232, 236, 249, 250, 252–3, 267, 280

Jackson, Andrew 70, 76–81, 83, 84, 104, 105, 109, 122
Japan/Japanese 156, 157, 172–4, 183–8, 190–2, 205, 207, 212, 220, 230, 233, 248
Jarvis, Samuel Miller 151, 152
Jay, John 62

Jay's Treaty (1794) 62
Jefferson, Thomas 9, 23–4, 44–6, 48, 62, 68, 70–2, 74, 83, 90–2
Jim Crow laws 144 n.62, 212, 229
Johnson, Lyndon 216, 227, 229
John, Stonewall 34
John XXIII, Pope 219
Jordan, Winthrop, *White over Black* 17

Kagan, Robert 275
    Foreign Affairs 262
Kennan, George F. 157
Kennedy, John F. 210, 211, 216, 226, 227, 229
"Kennedy Round" of trade negotiations (1964–7) 213
Kim, Jessica M. 117
King, Rufus 51
Kirkpatrick, Jeane 241
Kissinger, Henry 220, 228, 229, 232–6, 239
Knox, Henry A. 67–70
Korea 176, 204, 214
Kramer, Paul 147
Kristol, William, *Foreign Affairs* 262
Kristoni/metal maker 58–9
Kuwait 232, 248–51, 253, 256, 275

LaFeber, Walter, *Inevitable Revolutions* 15
land speculators, US frontier 49–50, 107
Lansdale, Edward 208
Laocoön and His Sons 3
Latham, Michael 206
Latin America 21, 24, 97, 107, 159, 201, 222, 223, 229, 243
    disunity, US interest in 101–5
    loans from US 192–3
    revolutionary era 112
    struggle for independence from Spain 97
Lawrence, Mark Atwood 229
League of Nations 178, 181, 183
Lenin 177, 177 n.98
Lepore, Jill 33
Levy, Jonathan 30, 128
liberalism 19, 44, 86, 93, 130, 238, 271

liberal world order 184, 197, 198, 201, 205, 208, 220, 223, 237–8
Locke, John 44, 64
Lodge Jr., Henry Cabot 205
Louverture, Toussaint 88–9, 91

Madison, James 63, 69, 73, 75–6, 90, 101, 102
Mahan, Alfred Thayer 136–7
Manela, Erez 181
"Manifest Destiny" 87, 110
Manley, Michael 222–3, 244–5
Marshall, John 81
Marshall Plan/European Recovery Program 203, 210, 230
Martí, José 138–40, 196
Martín, Ramón Grau San 194
Massachusetts Bay Company 30
Mather, Increase 33
Maurer, Noel 158, 169, 202
May, Robert E. 108
McCullough, David 24
McKinley, William 135, 136, 139–40, 143, 146, 147, 156, 158, 186
Melville, Herman, *Moby Dick* 122
mercantilism 27–8, 40, 95, 96
Mexico/Mexican 20, 58, 59, 87, 93, 100, 102, 105, 107, 110–16, 127, 158, 159, 160, 167, 169–, 71, 187, 191–3, 196, 243–5, 257
    Anglo-American immigrants, Texas 108–9, 108 n.86
    anti-American sentiment 113
    decolonization 113
    financial issues and political instability, nineteenth century 116–17
    oil contracts 170–1
    US war with 105–6
    world trade, views on 197
Middle East 6, 17, 179, 181, 202, 221, 225, 232, 249–51, 253, 255, 261, 266, 267, 269, 271
Milošević, Slobodan 263
Mitterrand, François 252
modernization/"modernization theory" 128, 137, 148, 154, 206–18, 223, 228, 238, 288
Monroe Doctrine 101–5, 163–5, *165*

Monroe, James 99
Morales, Carlos 164
More, Sir Thomas, *Utopia* 31–2, 45
Morgan, Lewis Henry 66, 68
Moynihan, Daniel Patrick 234–6, 235, 239
Moyn, Samuel 236, 262

Napoleonic Wars, French Revolution and (1792–1815) 13, 46, 101, 120, 131
National City Bank, New York 160
National Endowment for Democracy 5, 271
National Liberation Front (NLF), Vietnam 216, 217
Native American communities 11, 12, 25–7, 30–3, 36, 42, 49, 51, 54–5, 55, 57, 76–84, 87, 93, 98, 110, 115, 120, 121, 127, 129, 144, 145, 154, 155, 217
   European-Americans and relationship with 12, 27, 30, 31, 36, 57–9, 64–7, 69, 83, 84, 154
   European-style government, polities different from 57–8
   Jefferson administration 70–2
   land transfers from 67–74
neocolonialism 149, 150, 158, 171
neoconservatives 255, 262, 263–4, 269
neoliberalism/neoliberals 238, 260
neomercantilism 99–100, 133
neutralism, Cold War 211, 221
New Deal coalition 186–97, 202–3
"New Deal for the World" vision 221
New England 29, 33, 35–6, 99, 121
New International Economic Order (NIEO) 220, 224, 225, 233, 234, 238
   Declaration on the Establishment of a New International Economic Order (NIEO) 220, 224–5, 233–4, 238, 252
"new world order," 1990s 249–55, 265, 274, 278
Nicaragua 133, 136, 152, 168, 169, 187, 194, 241
Nicholson, Francis 85
Ninkovich, Frank 177

Nitze, Paul 204–5
Nixon, Richard M. 227–30, 232–3, 259, 274
North American colonization 13, 28–9, 40, 41, 93
North American Free Trade Agreement (NAFTA) 257
North American Trust Company 151
North Atlantic Treaty Organization (NATO) 198, 205
Northwest Ordinance (1787) 50, 144
Nyerere, Julius 222, 223

Obama, Barack 274–5, 279–80
Obwandiyag ("Pontiac") 42, 49
Onitositah, "Overhill" Cherokees of Tennessee 72
"Open Door Notes"/Open Door policy (1899–1900) 15, 157–8
Operation "Rolling Thunder" 216–17
Opium Wars 123–4
Organization of African Unity 235–6
Organization of the Petroleum Exporting Countries (OPEC) 232, 233
O'Sullivan, John 110
Otis, Harrison Gray 159
Otis Jr., James 43
Ottoman rule, of Greece 12, 98, 176, 179, 180, 181

Pacific Squadron, US 123
Pakistan 200
Palen, Marc William 133
Palestine 204, 225, 226, 250, 252, 280
Panama
   Canal Zone *153*, 161, 239
   Congress (1826), US delegation to 103–5
Pan-Arab nationalism 221–2
Paredes y Arrillaga, Mariano 114
Parsons, Talcott 208–9
Peace Corps 210
Pentagon Papers 230
Perez, Louis A. 139, 140, 149
Permanent Court of Arbitration, The Hague 173
Persian Gulf War 254; *See also* Gulf War

Persico, Luigi, *Discovery of America* 1, 2, 3, 6, 9, 18, 212, 278
Philippines 21, 125, 127, 130, 137, 141–3, 146–7, *148*, 153–4, 172, 206–8
Pickney, Charles 90
Pilgrims, Plymouth Company 29–30
Platt Amendment 150, 152, 187
  Platt, Orville 150
Pletcher, David 134
Poinsett, Joel 99
"Point Four" program 210
Polk, James K. 1, 106–7, 109–15
Portillo, José López 244
postcolonial 6–7, 6 n.16, 20, 21, 60–7, 201
  economies 223
  world 202
poverty 72–3, 164, 169, 205–8, 241, 260, 263
Pratt, Julius W. 137, 145
Pratt, Richard Henry 154
Prebisch, Raul 223, 224
Proclamation of 1763 40, 42, 45
Progressive Movement 154, 167
pronunciamiento 113–14
Protestantism 8, 77, 99, 130
proxy wars, Cold War 202, 256
Putin, Vladimir 275

Al Qaeda 248, 266–70, 277, 279
Quasi War (1798–1800) 91

race/racial/racist/racism 79, 226
  anti-Mexican 110, 111
  citizenship 77
  civilized *vs.* savage 130
  hierarchy 16, 43, 94, 110, 160, 212, 226
  ideology 17–18, 37, 37 n.51
Raleigh, Sir Walter 28, 29
Reagan, Ronald 240–3, 245
Reconstruction Era 144
Red River War (1874–5) 129
"Red Sticks," Muscogee 76
Reid, Thomas 64
Republican Party, US 128, 132, 133–6, 138, 186, 257

Republican National Committee 135
Republic of Texas 109–12
Revolutionary War, American 47, 56, 61–2, 118
Rhodesia 226, 227, 234, 239
Richmond, John 121
Richter, Daniel K. 26, 27
Rockingham, Marquess of 41
Roman Catholicism 39, 99, 111, 154
Roman invasion, of Britain (43 CE) 32
Roosevelt Corollary (1904) 161–2, 164, 187, 215
Roosevelt, Franklin D. 184, 186–8, 190, 193–4, 196, 198, 203, 215
Roosevelt, Theodore 141, 143, 146, 148, 151–3, 158, 161, 163–8, *165*
Rosenberg, Emily 137–8
Rostow, Walt Whitman 208–10
Roxas, Manuel 207
Royal African Company 37
Rumsfeld, Donald 269
Russia 102, 156, 174, 176, 254, 257, 259, 266, 272, 275, 280
Russo-Japanese War (1904–5) 172–3
Rwanda 263

Saint Domingue (Haiti) 87, 88, 91; *See also* Haiti/Haitian
de Santa Anna, Antonio López 109, 114
Santo Domingo (Dominican Republic) 133, 163; *See also* Dominican Republic
Schmidt, Helmut 233
Schoolcraft, Henry 66
Second Creek (Muscogee) War (1836–7) 83
"Second Great Awakening" 77
Second Seminole War (1835–42) 83
Second World War 7, 21, 183–4, 188, 190, 217, 221, 233
self-determination 57, 151–82, 184, 198, 199, 226
September 11th terrorist attacks 266–75, 279
Serbia 263, 264
Seven Years War (1756–63) 12–13, 40–2, 59

Sevier, John 64–5
Sexton, Jay 19
Shafter, William 141
Shenk, Timothy 186
Silver, Peter 42
　anti-Indian sublime 67
slavery/slaves 35–7, 37 n.51, 38, 45, 78, 84, 88–9, 90, 103, 106, 107, 109, 117, 127
Smith, Adam (Smithian growth) 63
Smith, John 28–9
socialist globalization (as alternative to liberal globalization) 224
Somalia 255–61
South Africa 226–7
South Vietnam 215, 225, 230
sovereignty 5, 8, 9, 21, 38, 54, 59, 79, 162, 215
Soviet Union 177, 202, 206, 231, 237, 245, 254, 261, 267
Spanish America 92–6, 93 n.28, 93 n.29, 118
Spanish-American War (1898) 126, *126*, 138–42, 175
Spanish Empire 39
　commercial penetration, US 118
　Cuba 125, 138–41
　Napoleon's invasion of Spain (Peninsular War 1808–14) 96
　Philippines 125, 141–2
　Treaty of Paris (1898) 142–3
stagflation (1970s) 231–2
Stalin 198, 199
Stieb, Joseph 255, 265
Strachey, William 32, 130
"structural adjustment," lending 243–4
Strong, Josiah 130
Sudan 268
Sun Yat-Sen 174

Taft, William Howard 146, 154, 166–7
Tagore, Rabindranath 176
Taliban 267, 268, 273, 274
Tanzania 223–4
Tecumseh's War (1811–13) 74–5
Teller Amendment 143, 149
de Ternant, Jean-Baptiste 90
Texas Revolution 108–9
"third wave" of democratization 248

Third World 201–2, 201 n.50, 206, 208, 213, 221–3, 234–5, 239, 241, 250, 253; *See also* Global South
de Tocqueville, Alexis, *Democracy in America* 53–4, 83–4, 117
Tomlins, Christopher 31
Townsend Acts (1767) 41
Tracy, Benjamin Franklin 137
trade 9–12, 17, 20, 27–8, 31, 33, 41, 42, 47, 56, 59, 62, 70–1, 75, 77, 84, 87, 90–2, 95, 96, 101, 103, 104, 127, 132, 133, 136, 145, 157–60, 173, 177, 178, 184, 187, 191–3, 196, 197, 201, 207, 216, 223, 244, 257–62
　Latin America and Pacific 128
　liberalization 248
　negotiations 257
　open global trading system, potential problems of 197
　trans-Atlantic 78
Treaty of Fort Wayne (1809) 73
Treaty of Ghent (1814) 76–7
Treaty of Paris (1783) 46, *46*, 47, 48, 54, 56, 59–60, 80, 143
Treaty of St. Louis 74
triangle trade 35, 37, 63
Trujillo, Rafael 194
Truman, Harry S. 198, 205
Trump, Donald 280–1
Tsar Alexander I, Russia 102
Tydings-McDuffie Act (1934) 187
Tyler, John 112, 114
Tyrrell, Ian 19

United Fruit Company 159, 212, 216
United Nations (UN) 184, *189*, 190, 195, 201, 232
　General Assembly 21, 195, 220, 222, 224
　General Assembly Resolution 3379 236
　Human Rights Commission 262
　Monetary and Financial Conference 191
　Security Council 195, 221, 226, 227, 250, 253, 272
　Security Council Resolution 660 250

trust territories 184, 195
United Nations Charter (1945) 184
United Nations Conference on Trade and Development (UNCTAD) 219–20, 224, 240
United States (US)
  Airforce 253, *254*
  colonial enterprise 26–38
  Constitution 48, 50–1
  economy 10, 13, 15, 47, 48, 119–20
  empire of liberty 20, 46–51
  European-Americans and relationship with Native Americans 64–7, 156
  exceptionalism 14–20, 236, 239, 240, 278
  expansionism 127, 144, 188
  exports 35, 61–3, 134–7, 158, 163, 193
  foreign policy 5, 15, 16, 126, 187, 193, 214, 226
  foreign markets, securing 136
  foreign trade and investment, late nineteenth and early twentieth century 158, 159
  global hierarchy 127–35
  global leadership 248–9
  imperial competition 131–2
  imperial era, end of 24–5
  independence 4–5, 8
  Indigenous continent, and 56–60
  industrial development 128–30
  Information Agency 210
  interventions, Caribbean basin 62, 87, 93, 102, 141, *153*, 158, 160, 164, 166, 169, 170, 216, 244
  merchants and manufacturers 63, 75, 87, 90, 95–7, 107, 112–23
  Mexican War (1846–48) 105–6
  military primacy, quest for 261, 264
  military support, South Vietnam 225
  new empire (1898), and 142–50
  in opposition, UN General Assembly 228–37
  policymakers 87, 102, 103, 176, 185, 196, 199, 205, 211, 216, 220, 221, 226, 227, 240
  political loyalty to 61–2
  postwar planners, Second World War 185, 221
  progress of humanity, belief in 24–5
  shapes peace, after First World War 178–9
  Spanish America, decolonization of 92–6, 93 n.28, 93 n.29
  support for Israel 225–6
  trade to Asia 118, 119
  world-systems 9–14, 9 n.22, 19, 21
Uruguay 257, 258
US-China Relations Act (2000) 259

de Vattel, Emer, *The Law of Nations* 64
Venezuela 162, 163, 269
Vergerio, Claire 4
Vietnam 8, 204, 214–18, 225, 228, 230, 235, 256, 257
"Vietnam Syndrome" 256, 257
Vietnam War 225, 229, 242, 274
Virgil 3, 8
  The Aeneid 20
Virginia Company 30
Volcker Shock 242–3, 245, 260

Walker, Robert J. 111
Wallace, Anthony 71–2
Wallerstein, Immanuel 9, 9 n.22, 10 n.23
Wall Street Journal 255, 267
War of 1812 (1812–15) 75–8, 97, 101; *See also* "Tecumseh's War" (1811–13)
War of 1898. *See* Spanish-American War (1898)
War on Terror 266–75
"Warsaw Pact" (1955) 198, 201
Washington, George 42, 68–9, 89–91
weapons of mass destruction (WMDs) 264–5
Western Hemisphere 8, 9, 21, 25, 84, 92, *94*, 103, 118, 160, 165, 178, 188, 213
Westphalian sovereignty 4–5, 8, 21, 25, 60, 131, 186, 278, 280

whiteness/white settlers 18, 72, 77–9, 89
Williams, William Appleman 7, 15, 16
Wilson, Harold 183, 232, 233
Wilson, Woodrow 21, 152, 154, 166–82, *180*
Wirt, William 98
Woodbury, Levy 111
Wood, Leonard 149
Worchester, Samuel 82
 Worchester v. Georgia (1832) 82

World Bank 195, 219, 221, 223, 238, 244
world-systems theory 9–14, 9 n.22, 19, 21
World Trade Organization (WTO) 258, 259

Xiaoping, Deng 252

Yokota, Kariann Akemi 6 n.16, 61

Zelaya, José Santos 168
Zionism 236